AUSTRALIAN

DECIMAL BANKNOTES

Paper issues

Second Edition

Michael P. Vort-Ronald

Dedicated to

Ian Trevor Everett
(1942-1996)

For the many hundreds of pages of newspaper research and other material he provided for past and future articles and publications, and for his friendship.

Note Printing Australia, Craigieburn, Victoria.

AUSTRALIAN DECIMAL BANKNOTES

Paper issues

(1966 - 1999)

Second edition

Michael P. Vort-Ronald

Publisher:
Michael P. Vort-Ronald, Banking and Currency Museum,
3 Graves Street, Kadina, South Australia, 5554.
Phone (08) 8821 2906 Fax (08) 8821 2901
A.B.N. 73 975 917 060

First edition published 1985
Second edition June 2000.

National Library of Australia card number and ISBN
ISBN (Hard cover) 0 9587580 8 5
ISBN (Soft cover) 0 9587580 9 3

Front cover: The two main stages of printing a banknote - Simultan (background) printing, Intaglio (main) printing, with the finished note.

Back cover: The 50 different serial letter prefixes of Australian Decimal Star Replacement notes assembled by the author and sold by auction in 1988.

Notes illustrated to a maximum of two thirds linear size to comply with Reserve Bank of Australia preferences.

Wholly produced in South Australia by:
Hyde Park Press, Adelaide. Setting, printing and binding.
Adelaide Art Engravers, Frederick Bergmann,
Reserve Bank of Australia, Michael P. Vort-Ronald. Photography.

PREFACE

The first edition of *Australian Decimal Banknotes* published in July, 1985, revised the decimal section of my first book *Australian Banknotes*, published in 1979.

Four years have elapsed since the polymer $100 note replaced its paper predecessor, and it is now time to finalise the record of the paper decimal notes which served Australia well from 1966 to 1996.

The paper notes began with $1, $2, $10 and $20 issues on 14 February, 1966, as direct replacements of the Ten Shilling, One Pound, Five Pound and Ten Pound notes respectively. A $5 note was issued on 29 May, 1967, $50 (9 October, 1973) and $100 (26 March, 1984). The $1 note was last issued on 11 May, 1984 and the $2 note on 17 June, 1988, to be replaced by coins of equivalent values.

The $1 to $50 notes were designed by Gordon Andrews and the $100 note by Harry Williamson. There were twelve signature combinations from Coombs - Wilson to Fraser - Evans, as well as the major change from "Commonwealth of Australia" to "Australia" commencing with the introduction of the $50 note in 1973. Other minor changes were; variations to metal thread positions, serial numbers, legal tender clauses and signature titles.

The paper $5 note was replaced by a newly-designed polymer note on 7 July, 1992, the $10 on 1 November, 1993, $20 on 31 October, 1994, $50 on 4 October, 1995 and $100 on 15 May, 1996. A Bicentenary polymer $10 was issued in 1988, and a recoloured $5 issued on 24 April, 1995. An overprinted Bi-centenary polymer $10 note was issued at $14 in 1988 for collectors and as souvenirs. It was the first of many specialist issues produced by Note Printing Australia. The first paper specialist note was a $20 with a red overprint and special red serial numbers commemorating the 80th anniversary of the first Commonwealth note. It was first released at the Numismatic Association of Australia Coin Fair in Brisbane in 1993. In late 1999, Note Printing Australia announced that it would cease issuing all special products except for the continuation of the uncut polymer note series. Now that it is unlikely that any further "Official" paper note issues will be produced, it is time to close off the paper record. This edition will also explain the specialist issues which contained paper notes, and provide an introduction to the new polymer notes.

I am grateful for the assistance given by the Reserve Bank of Australia in the way of access to archives and the provision of photographs, and to the many friends and colleagues who assisted me to keep collectors and the public up to date through my writing for the *Australian Coin Review* (since 1975), and my current editorship of that magazine. Frequent cross-referencing to those articles will be given throughout this book to provide further reading.

For detailed information on pre-decimal notes the following two companion volumes are recommended:

> *Banks of Issue in Australia* (1788-1914) published in 1982 and *Australian Banknotes* 2nd edition (1913-1966), published in 1983. See page 415.
> A further book, *Australian Polymer Banknotes,* is planned for 2002.

Banking and Currency Museum,
3 Graves Street Kadina 5554,
South Australia.

Michael P. Vort-Ronald,
Fellow of the Numismatic
Society of South Australia Inc.

ACKNOWLEDGEMENTS

Advertiser Newspapers Ltd., Adelaide: Supply of photograph of David Malangi.

Andrews, Gordon: Information and permission to reproduce text from *A Designer's Life.*

Cable, Professor K.J., Randwick: Information on Greenway's architecture.

City of Sydney, Dr. Shirley Fitzgerald: Information on Greenway's architecture.

Crean, Frank, and **Robinson, Eric**: Information on the change from "Commonwealth of Australia" to "Australia".

C.S.I.R.O., Melbourne: Central Information Service, B. Walby, Peter Robertson, Carla Flores, John Lenaghan, information and photographs.

Department of Agriculture, Sydney: Supply of photograph of William Farrer.

Department of Works, Sydney: Information on Greenway's buildings.

Dixson Galleries, Sydney: Access to collections for study and photographing, information and supplying photographs.

Everett, Ian: Stepney: Newspaper and other research. Ian died 9th October, 1996.

Flint, Alan: Information on note printing and printing errors.

Fyfe, John, Sydney: Loaning of misprinted notes for photographing, and information.

Gartner, John, Mt. Macedon: Past editor and founder of the *Australian Coin Review,* for encouraging me to write about this hobby from 1975, publishing numerous articles and for instigating my first book in 1979. John died 2nd February, 1998.

Geology Department, University of Adelaide: Assistance in locating information and photographs of rock strata formations used on the $100 note.

Grolier Society of Australia Pty. Ltd., Crows Nest: Permission to condense information from *Australian Encyclopaedia.*

Gulgong Historical Society: Diane Campbell, information on Gulgong's buildings.

Herald and Weekly Times Ltd., Melbourne: Permission to reproduce photograph of Sir Charles Kingsford Smith from *The Old Bus.*

Historic Houses Trust N.S.W.: Suzanne Briggs, Gary Crocket, information on Macarthur.

Jacob, Peter G., Adelaide: Supply of photographs of auroras in Antarctica.

ACKNOWLEDGEMENTS - continued

Jeffries, B.C., Adelaide: Department of Agriculture (Sheep & Wool), information on sheep and grasses, and photographs.

Mawson Institute for Antarctic Research, University of Adelaide, the late Dr. F. Jacka: Assistance with Mawson material and photographs; Mark Pharaoh, Mawson Antarctic Collection.

Mitchell Library, Sydney: Access to collections and photographing notes and material.

National Library of Australia, Canberra: Supply of photographs.

Noble, Jim, Sydney: Use of illustrations from Noble Numismatic and Spink auction catalogues.

Pope, John S., Goolwa: Information on Sir Charles Kingsford Smith and *Southern Cross Replica.*

Powerhouse Museum, Haymarket: Ian Debenham, information on Hargrave and his flying machines.

Pratley, Ross and Carol, Sydney: For assistance, information and board during my many research trips to Sydney.

Reserve Bank of Australia, Sydney: Les Coventry, David Emanuel, David Reynolds, Alan Seymour, supply of photographs, access to Archives and records, supplying information and checking data. Note Issue Department, Sydney and Note Printing Australia, Craigieburn, Victoria, Franca Cavaliere.

Robinson, Frank, Lilydale, Vic: Information on plate letters.

Royal Society of South Australia, Adelaide: Permission to use photographs of Sir Douglas Mawson's rock strata.

S.A. Merino Sheepbreeders Assoc.: John Burt, information on Merino embargos.

Shaw, W. Hudson, Sydney: Information and assistance, Lawrence Hargraves' early models.

Smith, James A., Devonport, Tasmania: Information on the ship *Waverley.*

Stewart, Peter, Richmond N.S.W.: Information on John Tebbutt, and assistance.

Sydney Morning Herald, Sydney: Supply of photographs.

State Library of South Australia, Adelaide: Access to newspaper archives.

Teale, Leonard, Sydney: Information on Gulgong and Henry Lawson.

Tebbutt, John Halley, Windsor N.S.W.: Great-grandson of John Tebbutt the astronomer, information and assistance.

ACKNOWLEDGEMENTS - continued

Treasury (Commonwealth), Canberra: Information on note signatories and supply of photographs.

Vort-Ronald, Shaun: Editorial assistance.

Waite Institute, Adelaide: Information on Sir Ian Clunies Ross.

For information and assistance with note issues and varieties, various correspondents, colleagues and collectors including:

Ayres, Kevin
Damon, Harry
Downey, John
Goodwin, Rod
Leverington, Lloyd
McDonald, Greg
Melmeth, Paul
Mumford, Lyall
Patten, Gary
Petterwood, Graeme
Seymour, Frank
Skinner, Dion
Taylor, Frank
Watson, John
Bamford, Graeme
Dawson, Phil
Downie, Ken
Hannaford, Paul
Mathieson, John
McDonald, Ian
Mira, Bill
Noble, Jim
Onyet, Gil
Prince, David
Shaw, Judy
Sparks, Barry
Thompson, Elizabeth
Winsor, Barrie
Cooper, Colin
de Young, Scott
Freehill, Mark
Jewell, Ray
McCarthy, Michael
Meallin, Chris
Morton, Grant
Nugent, Steve
Peake, Harold
Safstrom, Bob
Shepherd, Graham
Tarrant, John
Toyer, Evan
Apologies for any missed.

For general information:

In relation to the Reserve Bank Board of the Reserve Bank of Australia:

"It is the duty of the Board, within the limits of its powers, to ensure that the monetary and banking policy of the Bank is directed to the greatest advantage of the people of Australia and that the powers of the bank under this Act, the Banking Act 1959 and the regulations under that Act are exercised in such a manner as, in the opinion of the Board, will best contribute to the stability of the currency of Australia; the maintenance of full employment in Australia; and the economic prosperity and welfare of the people of Australia."

Reserve Bank Act 1959.

The Reserve Bank of Australia's Head Office is at 65 Martin Place, Sydney, New South Wales, 2000. The Bank opened an Internet site http://www.rba.gov.au/ on 28 November, 1997. It now carries a range of information on the functions and operations of the Bank, and includes: About the RBA; What's New; Speeches; Media Releases; Reports and Statements; Bulletin Articles and Statistics; Other Publications; Polymer currency; Other Sites; Careers and Employment. E-Mail: rbainfo@rba.gov.au

Note Printing Australia, a subsidiary of the Reserve Bank of Australia, is situated alongside the Hume Highway near Craigieburn (25 km north of Melbourne) Victoria. Postal address P.O. Box 21, Craigieburn, VIC. 3064.

GLOSSARY

Bank, the: Reserve Bank of Australia, Sydney, from 1959. Up to 1959 was Commonwealth Bank.

Banknote: From 1910, Australian Government paper money was defined as "notes". Although the term "banknote", when strictly applied, refers only to notes printed for and used by the private banks, "banknote" is the commonly used name for paper money.

Front: The side of the note containing facsimile signatures and legal tender clause. Also called the obverse (or face) of the note. The opposite side is the Back (or Reverse).

Gothic: Abbreviation of "Gothic No. 18" serial numbering. Standard linotype (USA) font, the first style used for numbering Australian decimal notes.

Illustrations of notes: Reduced to approximately two-thirds linear size as preferred by the Reserve Bank of Australia. Other note features reproduced full size or larger by special permission.

Metallic thread: A fine thread of aluminium or metalised plastic embedded vertically in the note during manufacture of the paper, for security reasons. Early decimal notes had this thread near the centre, but it was later moved to the left side of the notes to avoid undue wear and tear caused by the former position being in close proximity to the natural fold area.

Observed: Observed by the writer or by other persons who have communicated with the writer, or recorded in numismatic auction catalogues or literature.

OCR-B: Abbreviation for "OCR-B II" serial numbering. Internationally accepted series of standard type fonts specially devised to facilitate high-speed optical recognition of printed characters. All notes converted to this type except the $1, but specimen notes in the $1 denomination were issued with OCR-B in the "T.A.A." specimen note books.

Prefix: Letter(s) appearing in front of serial number numerals on banknotes.

Printed: Total notes printed in any particular series, calculated by the writer from known serial number ranges, or estimated from information currently available on types and varieties. Totals include star replacement notes inserted to replace faulty notes in early issues. Totals presumed as issued unless stated otherwise.

Serial numbering: Two numbers on the front of paper $1-$50, and the backs of $100 paper notes and all polymer notes, to facilitate recording (the $5 polymer note has only one number).

Specimen note: A complete note overprinted "Specimen" for use as an example of a particular issue. Later notes also had "Specimen No.   " added. They were notes not intended for general circulation and are not considered legal tender.

Star replacement note: Notes issued from 1966 to 1971 with serial numbers commencing with a "Z" and finishing with an asterisk (*). These notes replaced notes spoiled during manufacture.

Watermark: Profile(s) of Captain James Cook, security features not generally visible until the note is held up to light.

CONTENTS

CONTENTS - continued

CONTENTS - continued

Chapter 1: DECIDING TO GO DECIMAL

A report of the Decimal Currency Committee presented to the Commonwealth Government in 1960 stated *Interest in decimal currency is at least as old as Federation....* Decimal currency thinking was, in fact, a lot older.

A Royal Commission in England in 1838 recommended a decimal system, but it was not until 1849 that the minting of the florin was undertaken as the first practical step towards adopting that recommendation. Another nine years were to pass before the matter again came to a head.

By 1858 there was as good deal of interest in the decimal system in England in the House of Commons, as well as among men of science. One of a series of commissions of enquiry was appointed as far back as 1856.

William H.R. Jessop, M.A. arrived in Adelaide from England in 1858 and was elected to the membership of the Adelaide Philosophical Society two months later. In June, 1859, he wrote a letter to the editor of the *South Australian Register* referring to decimal systems in Europe, Canada and the United States of America, and followed it up with two papers which were read to the Adelaide Philosophical Society in August and September of that year. In relation to coins he proposed that:

> *The single unit be the Farthing, 2 farthings = Burra, 5 farthings = Penny, 10 farthings = Mark, 2 Marks = Groat, 5 marks = Shilling, 10 marks = Florin, 2 florins = Crown, 5 florins = Half Sovereign and 10 florins = Sovereign.*

While generally supporting a decimal system, the society (in relation to money) resolved:

> *3. That in the construction of a decimal system of money it is desirable to retain the imperial sovereign as its basis, inasmuch as that coin is one most generally recognised as a standard of value".*

The matter failed to gain much support in Australia and the commissioners enquiring into decimal currency in England presented their final report in 1859 in which the decimal currency idea was described as *"...one of the wildest crotchets which ever entered into a theorising brain..."*

The Decimal Coinage Report, 4 October, 1859, as reported in the *South Australian Register*, concluded with:

> *"...the coinage established among us by a series of happy accidents is about the best which could possibly be selected if we were starting afresh, untrammelled by the habits of centuries under the guidance of abstract science. In short, we have the best coinage in the world, and the Commission deserves abundant gratitude for having placed this very satisfactory circumstance distinctly on record."*

Reference and further reading: *William Jessop and his decimal system,* 1859, by J.H. Love, *South Australiana,* Vol. V, No. 1, March 1966: *South Australian Register,* 7 June 1859, *The Decimal Question*, letter to the editor by Jessop, and *Decimal Currency for Australia?*, August 1959, *Bank of New South Wales Review.*

The first Australian Commonwealth Parliament set up a Select Committee in 1902 to investigate the feasibility of a change to a decimal system. The Adelaide *Advertiser* of April 23, 1902, reported on those findings:

> *PROPHETIC CALL FOR DECIMAL CURRENCY*
>
> *A bold departure from our existing monetary system is recommended by the Select Committee appointed by the Federal House of Representatives to enquire into and report upon the subject.*
>
> *This is nothing less than the adoption by the Commonwealth of a decimal system of coinage. As everyone is aware, the British currency does not lend itself easily to hurried or extensive calculations, and where untrained or sluggish minds are concerned the possibilities of error are very great.*
>
> *The losses and illegitimate gains which accrue every year from business operations conducted in terms of our pounds, shillings, and pence, would probably be found startling if they could only be ascertained. And though our school system does not provide some guarantee against buyers or sellers being victimised in the hasty transactions of the shop or market, not every mind, even when it can claim to be instructed, is so constituted as to be able easily and swiftly to grapple with arithmetical subtleties.*
>
> *In some of the large retail houses in England special experts are employed for the purpose of stating rapidly the product of such a calculation as 19 and one quarter yards at 7 shillings five and three quarter pence per yard, and one firm is said to pay its "calculating department" as much as 1,000 pounds a year...*
>
> *It is true that a certain facility in dealing with the currency problems of daily life may be acquired in our schools, but why should the children's school time and brain power be wasted, and clerks and business people, to say nothing of the general public, be put to unnecessary trouble when, as the Select Committee contend, the use of decimal money would simplify matters so enormously.*
>
> *There is wisdom in the suggestion that as one means of promoting a familiarity therewith the system should be taught in the schools. The introduction of the decimal system would certainly lessen the present burden upon the scholars, who, according to one authority, would be saved 10 months of arithmetical drudgery if our duodecimal coinage gave place to a decimal one.*

The advice was not heeded, and for a number of years after that, Australia tried to influence other countries in what was then the British Empire to consider changing to a decimal system, but without success.

The next important stage was in 1937 when the Royal Commission on Banking included in its recommendation the desirability of a change to decimal currency by dividing the pound into 1,000 parts.

Twenty years later, in 1957, an organisation called the Decimal Currency Council was formed to interest Australians in decimal currency, and to encourage the Commonwealth Government to make the change.

In 1959 a Decimal Currency Committee was formed to investigate the feasibility of Australia changing to a decimal currency. Its Chairman was Walter Scott, Governing Director of W.D.Scott & Co. Pty. Ltd., Management Consultants. The Secretary was Dr. N.W. Davey of the Commonwealth Treasury who later became an official observer in South Africa for that country's changeover to decimal currency in 1961. Other members of the committee were: Sir Kenneth Coles, Alderman Dorothy Edwards, Mr. A.W. Henderson, Mr. D.H. Merry, Mr. Sidney Powell and Mr. F.S. Vine.

The Committee met 23 times, studied written evidence from State Governments and Federal Ministers, received 200 submissions from various groups which had made a special study of currency, and took evidence from 150 individuals. The Committee reported to the Federal Government in August 1960, and recommended that a decimal system should be introduced from the second Monday in February, 1963. Late in 1961 Federal Cabinet confirmed its support in principle for adoption of a decimal currency system, but decided not to introduce it at that time.

The practicalities of a changeover seemed enormous. An article by F.G. Waite in the Commonwealth Bank's magazine *Bank Notes* of February 1961 titled *Watch Those Decimals*, gave a list of the main types of mechanical equipment which the committee estimated would be in use in 1963 and economically worth converting.

Adding machines	105,900
Accounting machines	26,600
Cash registers	73,900
Electric petrol pumps	64,500
Price-computing scales	57,300
Punched card tabulators	1,200
Franking machines	3,700
Cheque writers	900
Taxi meters	8,500
Ticket issuing machines	4,600
	347,100

The Decimal Currency Committee estimated that upon a changeover in 1963 the cost of converting monetary machines (not coin operated machines) would amount to about 30 million pounds ($60 million), even when machines too old for conversion were excluded. The committee also arrived at a figure for savings in the business sector of approximately 6.5 million pounds ($13 million) per year.

On 7 April, 1963, the Treasurer (and later Prime Minister, Harold Holt), announced in Canberra that he would introduce legislation in parliament later that year to set up a statutory authority to plan and administer preparations for a changeover to decimal currency, planned for February, 1966.

The new system was to be based on a major unit equal to the existing ten shillings, with the minor unit to be one hundredth of the major unit. The Government announced that it would pay "reasonable compensation" to owners of a large proportion of monetary machines which required conversion for use under the new system, but compensation would not be available for old sterling machines obtained from overseas after his announcement.

The following day Mr. Holt said that Federal Cabinet was looking for a name for the new currency "with an Australian flavour". Of the names suggested to date, he favoured "Auster".

The Government had for some time been considering the size of the present coins, and even if there had been no decision to adopt decimal currency, some changes were believed necessary to change the threepence, which was too small, and the penny, which was too large.

A few days later Mr. A.D. Fraser (Labor, N.S.W.) announced a competition for new names, and suggested names began to pour into Parliament House. The winner of the competition was to be presented with an engraved scroll and five notes of the basic decimal unit (equal to 50 shillings) "hot off the presses". Some of the early names suggested were: Fisher (after Andrew Fisher, ex Prime Minister who introduced the first Australian Government-designed and printed notes in 1913), Berra, Stral, Victa, Newal, Tasma, Quee, Cook, Smithie, Alp, Brumbie, Anzac, Melba, Magpie, Camber, Regal, Eureka, Monash, Hughes, Billy, Pacific and Noodle.

Letters to the press suggested such names as Koala, Kanga, Ross, Emu and Merino. Suggestions that names of current politicians could be used seemed ludicrous when one attempted to rationalise the equivalent values of the denominations e.g., were five Faddens or ten Holts equal to one Menzies, or how many Calwells was a shilling worth, and so on.

The name "cent" seemed to be universally accepted as appropriate for the minor unit, and naturally "dollar" was an early and widely supported suggestion, even to the point of calling it the "Australian Dollar".

Letters and suggestions to and from the press at first appeared regularly, but slowly abated until 4 June, 1963, when the Federal Government announced that the appointment of the Chairman of the Decimal Currency Board would be Walter Scott, previous chairman of the Decimal Currency Committee. Other members of the board were:

Mr. A.N. Armstrong.	Deputy Chairman. Deputy Managing Director of the Commonwealth Banking Corporation.
Sir Kenneth Coles.	Chairman of G.J.Coles and Co. Ltd. who had been a member of the previous Committee.
Norman Robertson.	Chairman of MacRobertson (Australia) Ltd.
Mr. A.W.B. Coady.	Chairman of the Electricity Commission of New South Wales.
Mr. F.P. O'Grady.	Director-General of Posts and Telegraphs.
Mr. L.B. Brand.	Assistant Secretary, Loans and Investment Branch, Commonwealth Treasury.
Dr. N.W. Davey.	Executive Officer of the Board, who had been Secretary to the previous Decimal Currency Committee.

The Board's Research Officer was Richard Hardman who was quoted as saying :

> *...the fundamental advantage of a decimal currency arises from the fact that the units of monetary measurement are on the same basis as the system of notation. Treating money in the same way as numbers leads to definite advantages, in terms of savings in time and effort, in education and in office and clerical operations - in short, savings accrue in any task which involves monetary calculations. Last, but by no means least, the Board also felt that decimal currency would bring with it a much broader range of cash registers and other 'monetary machines'."*

A Bill providing for the introduction of the new currency system and formally establishing the Decimal Currency Board was brought down in Parliament and became law on October 30, 1963.

The Government intended that the Board should act in an advisory capacity on financial and other issues involved in the change-over. Later it would be required to give effect to the Government's decisions. It would also have the primary responsibility for examining many of the problems likely to arise during the change-over, and for carrying through appropriate action to overcome them. Eventually it would need to draw up and administer a publicity program to ensure that the change-over was carried out with a minimum of disruption to the community.

It was suggested at the time that ministerial opinion was hardening in favour of a name from the "short list" of possible names for the principal unit, namely Royal, Crown, Dollar, Pound or Sovereign.

Almost unanimous support however, had been expressed at the annual conference of the Australian Council of Retailers for the name "Dollar", but speculation was short-lived, and on the following day the Government announced that Federal Cabinet had decided on the names for the new decimal currency.

The major unit would be called the "Royal" - equivalent in value to the existing ten shilling note. The coins would be a 50 cent piece known as a "Crown", a 20 cent piece known as a "Florin", a 10 cent piece known as a "Shilling", and five, two and one cent coins.

"The Government", it was stated, "has made a close and careful examination of possible names for the major currency unit". Hundreds of suggestions were sifted through. Lists of names had been culled from Australian history, geographical features, names of prominent people, flora and fauna, and Aboriginal words. "It became clear that none of the names of typically Australian associations would be fully acceptable to the public", said Mr. Holt. "Every suggested Australian name was lacking in one or more of such desirable attributes as dignity, pleasing sound, ease of pronunciation, brevity and suitability of the initial letter for contraction in writing".

The Government decided that the name "Royal" had a number of features which made it worthy of adoption and it had the advantage of emphasising Australia's link with the Crown, which would continue to be represented on the new coins by the appearance of the effigy of the reigning monarch. Mr. Holt added that "Royal" was a dignified word with a pleasing sound and could easily be expressed in the plural. It was associated historically with coinage, having been used in England in the form "Royal" or "Ryal" in the 15th century and the name "cent" was a natural and inevitable term for the minor unit in a decimal system.

About 1,000 names were considered before the name "Royal" was chosen. The Treasurer issued a list of 998 names which had been suggested. Some of them were: Ausdol, Dauler, Dolaroo, Doolaus, Dollauster, Ducat, Noble, Unite and Wollar. People's names included Barton, Chifley, Churchill, Curtin, Deakin, Dobell, Downer, Fadden, Hovell, Hughes, Hume, Kelly, Menzies (and variations such as Menz, Menza, Menzea, Menzee and Menzten), Monash, Sturt and Tennant. Among slang expressions suggested were Dinkum, Fiddley, Spin and Spondu. Some others were: Reap, Sheaf, Stock, Ewe and Wool, and Anz, Anzs, Anzac, Anzdollar and Anzus.

The winner of Mr Frazer's prize for sending the first letter opened of the 450 letters which suggested the name finally adopted, was retired headmaster Mr. A.A. Briggs, 82 years. By that time however, the prize had seemingly been reduced to three "Royals".

The Leader of the Federal Opposition (Arthur Calwell) later stated that the next Labor Government would certainly not accept "this quaint terminology". He said that the decision of the Government was extraordinary and showed a sign of antiquated thinking. "The names chosen by the Government will be generally unacceptable to the Australian people". The term they wanted was the "Australian Dollar".

Fig. 1. 1963 satirical "funny money" One Royal note

In 1963 a satirical "funny money" note was produced for the University of New South Wales Foundation Day. Uniface and printed in purple, it depicted a hot air balloon "Inflation" on the left and "King Ming" (Prime Minister Menzies) on the right. It bore the printer's imprint "Wentworth Press, Sydney 69 6942". They are now collectors' items.

The Melbourne *Age* of 7 June, 1963, stated *"Those new names are not likely to gain popular currency very easily. Apart from any practical or emotional objections to the royal, there is the point that the Government has made a philological blunder in converting an adjective into a noun. The royal has some sort of history as a coin, and therefore as a noun, but Australians have never used it other than as an adjective. The English (gossip columnists in particular) sometimes refer to the 'royals'. Citizens in the rugged outposts of the Commonwealth, with more respect, call them members of the Royal family. There are, we must admit, a few other instances, all pretty obscure, when royal is used as a noun. A royal is a sail, a small 18th century mortar and that beast so often encountered in our hinterland, a stag with 12 or more points to his antlers".*

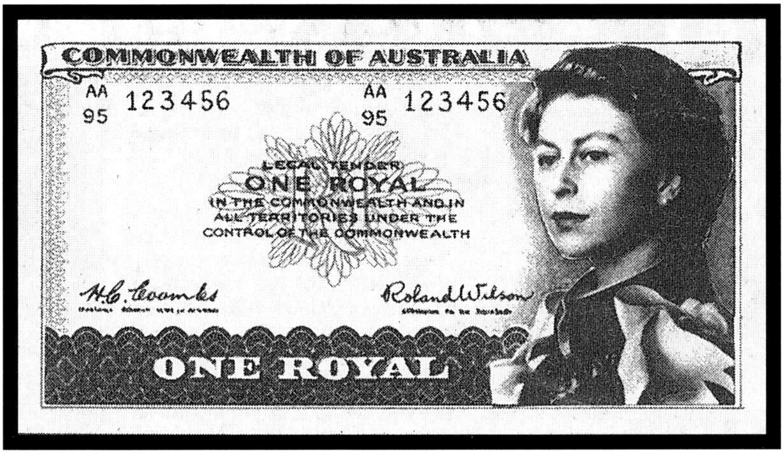

Fig. 2. Artist' essay of a One Royal note.

In 1996 an artist's essay of a One Royal note (illustrated above) surfaced in Sydney through coin dealer Mark Duff and later appeared in various public auctions . The essay featured The Queen and the serial numbers AA over 95 123456. An article in the *Sydney Morning Herald* of April 18, 1996, titled *The right Royal currency coined by Menzies*, by Adam Harvey, quoted Mr. Duff as saying that the note came from the estate of a former high-ranking government official who had been involved in the development of decimal currency.

Some of the early designs for the "Royal" were merely the existing designs with the word "Royal" substituted. The Reserve Bank's Note Printing Branch at Fitzroy (Melbourne) developed a number of design concepts, some of which were adapted further by an Italian design firm.

Preliminary sketches with stylised images were prepared, and some quite intricate drawings were developed to the engraving stage. One design used the existing design and colours of the ten shilling note with "One Royal" substituted for "Ten Shillings". Another One Royal design featured an Aboriginal portrait in brown with stylised emus and kangaroos on one side, and a futuristic art deco design on the back in blue and reddish tones. In the corners of the note were "RI" with a vertical bar through the "R". A 10 Royal design featured Captain James Cook in blue on the front with the title "Commonwealth of Australia" as in the existing ten shilling note, but other denominations were headed "Reserve Bank of Australia". A 5 Royal design featured Lake Eucumbene on the back in blue tones, while a 20 Royal note depicted Queen Elizabeth II on the front in purple and a flock of sheep on the back in purple and brown tones. Colour pictures of some of the designs were reproduced in the *Australian Magazine* of May 16-17, 1998, in a story "Love me tender" by Tim Bowden with photography by Russell Shakespeare (See illustrations next pages). Other note designs were a red and yellow $20 with Henry Parkes designed by Brian Sadgrove and a brown-purple 50 pound note also featuring Parkes. A $50 note design by Bruce Weatherhead featured explorer and scientist Sir Paul Edmund de Strzelecki (1797-1873) on a horse with cockatoos flying past, and on the other side, Lady Jane Franklin (1792-1875), second wife of Sir John Franklin (1786-1847), polar explorer and Governor of Tasmania. Both the $20 and $50 designs were submitted for later polymer notes. The designs formed part of an exhibtion by the Reserve Bank of Australia in Sydney from 18 May, 1998.

Fig. 3. Front, One Royal note design using former 10/- note.

Fig. 4. Back, One Royal note design.

Fig. 5. Back, Five Royals note design, Lake Eucumbene, N.S.W.

Fig. 6. Front, Ten Royals note design, Captain James Cook.

Fig. 7. Front, Twenty Royals note design, Queen Elizabeth II.

Fig. 8. Back, Twenty Royals note design.

Finally, on 19 September, 1963, the Federal Treasurer (Mr. Holt) announced that the new currency unit was to be the Dollar. In adopting the name he said:

> *"....The Government believes it is giving effect to the preference clearly shown by a substantial majority of the Australian people. One reason the Government did not select dollar in the first place was that it would not be a distinctive Australian name. However, now that there is clearly a major body of opinion in favour of dollar, the Government feels the disadvantage it first saw will be more than offset by the advantage of having a currency name which not only has considerable support, but is familiar to Australians generally. It is also a name readily recognised throughout the world, and especially among a number of neighbouring countries, particularly those in the Pacific region..."*

The dollar symbol decided upon was the dollar sign as used in the United States and Canada, and an early announcement by the Treasurer was that there would be at least $1, $10 and $20 notes equivalent to the existing ten shilling, five pound and ten pound notes respectively.

The official dollar symbol is a capital S crossed by two vertical strokes; however, a capital S crossed by one vertical stroke is also acceptable. The Reserve Bank's *Currency* magazine of October 1984 in an article titled *Currency in the Limelight* advised that the Bank's researchers had concluded that there was no definitive theory regarding the origin of the dollar sign, but listed some possibilities:

> *The S in the sign is a broken 8. That figure was used on the old Spanish pieces of eight, meaning 8 reales. The two bars appeared as the Pillars of Hercules on pieces of eight minted in Mexico City as early as 1732.*
>
> *The dollar sign developed from the abbreviation* ***ps****. This abbreviation stood for a coin called the peso, or Spanish dollar, which was common throughout the American colonies. People began to write the s superimposed on the* ***p****, and eventually just an s with two vertical lines through it. After Congress established the American dollar, which had about the same value as the peso, people began to use the peso symbol as a dollar sign. Yet another theory suggests that the sign is derived from a contraction of the Spanish word milhores, meaning thousands, and which would have been written as* ***m*** *over* ***s****.*

Dollar is apparently a corruption of the German word "thaler", a shortened form of Joachimsthaler, named after Joachim's Valley, a silver mining district in Bohemia. The first coin was struck from the valley's silver in 1518 and bore an effigy of St. Joachim. The use of similar large silver coins soon spread over most of Europe. In England, such coins were called crowns.

In a way, Australia, by forsaking the word royal for dollar, repeated history. The Spanish piece-of-eight (or reale, for which royal is the English equivalent) was usually called the dollar.

Australia was not the first country to suggest the name "Royal" for decimal currency. A Royal Commission in England reported on 23 February, 1920, and came out against the adoption of a decimal currency. One Bill before parliament advocated the main unit of decimal currency to be a "Royal" worth 4/2d.. The first country to use decimal currency was the U.S.A. in 1786, followed by France in 1799. Further reading: *Decimal Currency, its History and its Practicability in Australia* by N.E. Renton, *Australasian Insurance & Banking Record,* September 1958.

Chapter 2: DESIGNING THE NOTES

The following information was extracted from letter files in the Reserve Bank of Australia Archives, Sydney, after the 30 year "closed period" to access had expired. File numbers are quoted in brackets.

The first step in the process of selecting the successful designer was a letter written on 29 July, 1963, by the Governor of the Bank (Dr. H C. Coombs) to nine well-known designers inviting them to a meeting at the Note Printing Works at Fitzroy on 13 August, 1963 (N-a-156). Those invited were Hal Missingham, Douglas Annand, Gordon Andrews, Richard Beck, Max Forbes, Strom Gould, Alistair Morrison, George Hamori and Malcolm Warner. The letter advised that a small committee within the Bank had been set up comprised of W.H. Wilcock, General Manager of Note Issue Department; M.W.F. Brown, Works Manager of Note Printing Works and the Secretary of the Bank, A.C. McPherson. Russell Drysdale had also agreed to join the committee as artistic adviser.

It was proposed that a general discussion be held *"on the many problems involved in order particularly to demonstrate the scope available for the employment of the graphic arts and at the same time the limitations imposed by security and production requirements."*

A further page in the letter gave some themes or motifs to be considered in note design -

> *Following is a list of famous persons whose portraits could be considered and opposite their name, if not directly opposite, a motif which might be considered to be associated with them.*

Early seafaring explorers such as Tasman, Dampier, Cook	*Tasman's map, the "Endeavour"*
Early inland explorers - Sturt, Burke and Wills, Leichardt	*Ayers Rock, Alice Springs (landscapes or pastoral scenes such as by Streeton, Namatjira, Nolan) Darwin, etc.*
Early Governors such as Macquarie, Phillip, King, Bourke, Mitchell, Hunter, Darling and Brisbane	*Botany Bay, Port Arthur, a modern capital city.*
National identities such as Kingsford Smith, Ulm, Hargrave, Scott, Mawson, Hargreaves, Kendall, Lawson, Patterson, Flynn, Herbert Murray, Melba, Lalor, Monash, Essington Lewis.	*Many matters suggest themselves here such as aircraft, gold mining scenes, flora and fauna, Flying Doctor Service, steel industry, Snowy Mountains, polar exploration, Barrier Reef, Barossa Valley,*

Three Sisters at Katoomba, Blue Lake, Mt. Gambier, the opera house, cultural centre, Melbourne, Warragamba, Hume, Rum Jungle, Weipa, Mt. Isa.

Portraits of unidentified aborigines | *Aborigine art.*

Previous commitments prevented Gould and Warner from participating, and Morrison, Missingham and Annand from submitting designs. The latter three remained as consultants and Andrews, Beck, Hamori and Forbes agreed to submit designs. The seven men agreed to work as a team; as a united, yet autonomous group.

Each of the four designers agreed to produce designs for both sides of the series of four notes, and all members of the group would act in a critical and advisory capacity. They would all meet regularly to review the work in progress; judging, criticising, assessing, and generally contributing whatever they could towards the success of the project. Each of the designers agreed that, although no one could tell him what to do or how to do it, he would accept and abide by any group decision that some particular aspect or portion of the design could be improved.

A letter (N-a-156) of 16 August, 1963, from Alistair Morrison (Chairman of the Currency Note Design Group) to Russell Drysdale set out the procedures needed to complete the task, from which the following has been extracted or summarised:

At the end of a specified time the designers were to submit for consideration four series of designs from which to make a choice, each series to consist of a set of eight actual-size drawings in colour (four notes - both sides) accompanied by explanatory notes fully clarifying any points which may otherwise have been ambiguous or obscure. These were to be accompanied by a written description of the proposed design of the two remaining notes of the series which were not required immediately. All technicalities were to be planned and worked out in detail - such items as the type of lathework; the pattern, colours and rainbowing of the offset backgrounds; the form, character and disposition of all the complex elements of the design; the watermark and the depth of the intaglio.

After the Bank decided on the preferred designs, those approved designs would then need to be converted, by the designer, into the larger tone working drawings, and any other working drawings, lettering assemblies, photographs or colour work which may be required by the printing processes involved.

The next step was to be the conversion, by technicians and engravers, of the working drawings into line work, and into offset and engraved plates. This would require very close collaboration between the designer and the various technicians and engravers involved. All work, right up to the time of ink mixing, was expected to require the supervision of the designer. The work was expected to take at least six months and was dependent on a name for the currency unit being officially advised beforehand.

The Secretary of the Reserve Bank of Australia replied on 11 September, 1963, and said how grateful the Bank was for the completeness of the proposals, which the Bank broadly agreed with. It was pointed out, however, that it should be made perfectly clear that it was not to be assumed that the design selected, or indeed any of the designs submitted, would ultimately be approved for the new notes. The Bank also accepted the suggestion that a fee for actual designing be 400 guineas for each side of each note to each of the four designers, totalling 12,800 guineas. (A guinea was one pound one shilling - a gold English coin not produced for over a century, the equivalent of $2.10). A basic rate of 5 guineas per hour with a maximum of 25 guineas per day each, plus travelling and accommodation expenses, was also agreed upon (N-a-156).

On the 7th August, 1963, the Governor of the Bank wrote to the Editor of National Biography, Canberra, for suggestions as to names of famous Australians whose portraits might be used, but no fresh suggestions resulted.

The first meeting of the Designers' Panel took place on 17 September, 1963, two days before the announcement by the Treasurer of the Government's decision to rename the main currency unit the "Dollar".

There was much debate and discussion about the proposed note designs. Many drawings were made, discussed, discarded or modified - and modified - and modified. While somewhat lengthy and numerous, the various official letters do show the work which led up to the final designs, and are worthy of inclusion to allow a greater appreciation of the processes involved in creating a new note series.

In October 1963, the first summaries of the designers' proposed themes were drawn up by the Currency Design Group (N-a-156).

(1) GORDON ANDREWS

$1.00 Queen's head + Caroline Chisholm
Background to Caroline Chisholm: Old ships, symbolising immigration.

$2.00 Henry Lawson + Francis Greenway
Abstracted symbols of Snowy River country

$5.00 William Farrer + John Macarthur
Symbols of wheat and wool

$10.00 Henry Parkes + Sir Edward Thomson
Abstracted symbols of building and education

$20.00 Lawrence Hargrave + John Flynn
Abstracted symbols of flight

Watermark: Captain Cook

The heads are to be the main feature, with the slight abstract images to back them up. The main decorations will be lathe-work.

(2) RICHARD BECK

	Theme	*Front*	*Back*
$1.00	*Flora and Fauna*	*The Queen*	*Dampier*
$2.00	*Aboriginal Art*	*Aborigine's head*	*Daisy Bates*
$5.00	*Exploration, Gold*	*Sturt*	*Hargreaves*
$10.00	*Flora & fauna, Barrier Reef*	*Banks*	*Cook*
$20.00	*Flying Doctor Sheep, Cattle*	*Flynn*	*Farrer*

Watermark: Captain Cook.

(3) GEORGE HAMORI

	Front	*Back*
$1.00	*Portrait of Her Majesty Queen Elizabeth II Australian Coat-of-Arms.*	*Anonymous sailor from ship "Endeavour", at wheel of ship.*
$2.00	*Portrait of William Farrer Background illustration: Modern agricultural setting.*	*Anonymous shearer in action.*
$5.00	*Portrait of Sir Douglas Mawson. Background: Ship "Aurora" or "Discovery".*	*Research scientist using microscope in a laboratory.*
$10.00	*Portrait of Colonel Shortland (Newcastle) or Sir John Monash as a civilian. Background: Industrial development.*	*Oil drillers at work.*
$20.00	*Portrait of Sir Charles Kingsford Smith. Illustration: "Southern Cross" aeroplane.*	*Anonymous nurse on duty in the Flying Doctor service.*
$50.00	*Portrait of Dame Nellie Melba or Henry Lawson. Illustration: Sydney Opera House.*	*Typical aborigine engaged in bark painting.*

Watermark: Captain Cook (wearing hat)

P.S. Mr Hamori has told me that he intends using the Coat-of-Arms on the front of ALL notes.

I have told him that I believe that there will be objection to the use of the Opera House as it is so very much a State symbol. (initials AM).

(4) MAX FORBES (submission as provided, dated 24 October 1963)

One Dollar;

Front, *Portrait of The Queen, Australian Coat of Arms, Australian Flowers.*
Back, *Australian Flowers.*

Two Dollars;

Front, *Portrait of John McArthur, Australian Coat of Arms, Merino Sheep.*
Back. *Series of sheep, from earliest to present day breeds.*

Ten Dollars;

Portrait of Charles Sturt, Australian Coat of Arms, Australian Animals.
Back, *Australian Animals, major illustrations to be Kangaroo, Emu, Koala Bear.*

Twenty Dollars;

Front, *Portrait of Sir Charles Kingsford Smith, Australian Coat of Arms, Birds.*
Back, *Australian Birds in flight. Both land and sea birds.*

Five Dollars;

Front, *Portrait of Captain Cook, Australian Coat of Arms, Coral and Shells.*
Back, *Series of Marine Life, Coral, Shells, Fish.*

Fifty Dollars;

Front, *Portraits of Sir Douglas Mawson, Australian Coat of Arms, Minerals.*
Back, *Illustrations of a variety of Australian Minerals.*

At a meeting held on 8 November, 1963, some designs to a fairly advanced stage of the front and back of one note by each of the designers were tabled (S-a-767).

Gordon Andrews	*$20*	*Front:*	*Lawrence Hargrave*
		Back:	*John Flynn*
			Abstract of symbols of flight.

Richard Beck	*$2*	*Front:*	*Aborigine's head*
		Back:	*Daisy Bates* *Aboriginal art.*
Max Forbes	*$2*	*Front:*	*Portrait of Charles Sturt* *Australian Coat-of-Arms* *Australian animals*
		Back:	*Australian animals, major illustrations to be Kangaroo, Emu, Koala Bear.*
George Hamori	*$2*	*Front:*	*Portrait of William Farrer* *Background illustration - modern agricultural setting* *Australian Coat-of-Arms.*
		Back:	*Anonymous shearer in action.*

Provision in each case was made for the watermark with Captain Cook.

The submissions were discussed and refinements suggested. On December 5, 1963, at a further meeting, stage 2 designs (fronts and backs) of the notes presented at the previous meeting in November were tabled, together with stage 1 designs for a second note from each of the designers, as under (S-a-767).

Gordon Andrews

$20 note (stage 2)
Front: *Portrait of Sir Charles Kingsford Smith*
Abstract background depicting flight
Serial numbers - lefthand bottom corner and in a vertical position on right side.
Back: *Portrait of Lawrence Hargrave.*

$10 note (stage 1)
Front: *Portrait of Francis Greenway and scene depicting architecture*
Back: *Portrait of Henry Kendall*

Richard Beck

$2 note (Stage 2)
Front: *Portrait of aboriginal head*
background aboriginal bark painting
Back: *Panel showing aboriginal and other figures*

$10 note (Stage 1)
Front: *Portrait of Sir John Monash*
Back: *Panel depicting mining*

Max Forbes

$2 note (Stage 2)
Front: *Portrait of Captain Cook*
Australian Coat-of-Arms
Serial numbers - bottom lefthand corner and top righthand corners
Back: *Australian animals and the "Endeavour".*

	$10 note (Stage 1) *Front: Portrait of Sir Charles Kingsford Smith.* *Australian Coat-of-Arms.* *Back: Southern Cross Aircraft and birds in flight.*
George Hamori	*$2 note (Stage 2)* *Front: Portrait of William Farrer* *Background depicting modern agriculture.* *Australian Coat-of-Arms.* *Serial numbers bottom lefthand and top righthand corners.* *Back: Scene depicting a shearer in action.*
	$10 note (Stage 1) *Front: Portrait of Sir John Monash* *Australian Coat-of-Arms* *Back: Engineering scene.*

A number of prints and photographs of H.M. The Queen taken by Douglas Glass were tabled and it was agreed that the Bank would obtain as soon as possible four copies of each print for use by the designers. Further submissions were recorded on 30 December, 1963 (N-a-156).

GORDON ANDREWS

20 Dollar

Front: Portrait of Sir Charles Kingsford Smith with symbols of flight
Back: Portrait of Lawrence Hargrave; illustrations of experimental box kites and decorative scroll work symbolising air currents.

10 Dollar

Front: Portrait of Francis Greenway with a composite background of details of his architecture.
Back: Portraits of Henry Lawson surrounded by dream-like composite image of his time and people.

2 Dollar

Front: Portrait of John McArthur with a decorative background using home and sheep in typical country landscape
Back: Portrait of William Farrer with a decorative background of wheat stalks.

1 Dollar

Portrait of Her Majesty with the Australian coat of arms woven into a suitable Australian background (possibly abstract Aboriginal patterns).
Back: Portrait of Dame Nellie Melba with parade of operatic costumes depicting her successes.

RICHARD BECK

20 Dollars

Front: *Banks portrait; background of aboriginal floral motif*
Back: *Fauna and flora motif*

10 Dollars

Front: *Monash portrait; background of tribal bark paintings*
Back: *Saga of figures depicting Australian mining and engineering*

2 Dollars

Front: *Portrait of aboriginal; background of tribal bark paintings*
Back: *Tableau of Australian figures with Daisy Bates*

1 Dollar

Front: *Portrait of the Queen; mechanical screen background with suggestion of flora*
Back: *Captain Cook and figures relating to Australian history*

50 Dollars

Front: *Portrait of Mawson; background of mechanical screen suggesting the elements*
Back: *Saga of figures suggesting history of Australian exploration.*

5 Dollars

Front: *Kingsford Smith portrait; background of aboriginal art (bird motifs)*
Back: *Saga of figures depicting Australian history of flight.*

MAX FORBES

20 Dollars

Front: *Portrait of Dame Nellie Melba, with grouping of musical motifs.*
Back: *Theatre interior with grouping of people in theatre dress of period.*

10 Dollars

Front: *Portrait of Sir Charles Kingsford Smith Australian coat of arms; birds.*
Back: *The Southern Cross; Australian land and sea birds in flight.*

2 Dollars

Front: *Portrait of Captain Cook; Australian coat of arms; undersea flowers; map*
Back: *The "Endeavour", with grouping of Australian flora and fauna.*

1 Dollar

Front: *Portrait of the Queen; Australian coat of arms; Australian flowers.*
Back: *Government House, Sydney; Australian flowers.*

50 Dollars

Front: *Portrait of Sir Douglas Mawson; Australian coat of arms; Antarctic.*
Back: *Mawson's ship, with grouping of people in the Antarctic.*

5 Dollars

Front: *Portrait of John McArthur; Australian coat of arms; merino sheep.*
Back: *McArthur homestead; grouping of sheep from earliest to present breeds.*

GEORGE HAMORI

20 Dollars

Front: *Sir Charles Kingsford Smith*
Back: *Nurse of the Flying Doctor service on duty. In the background is featured a Northern Territory landscape with the first Flying Doctor aircraft, "Victory".*

10 Dollars

Front: *Sir John Monash*
Back: *Snowy Mountains Hydro-Electric Scheme; engineer at work.*

2 Dollars

Front: *William Farrer*
Back: *Australian shearer with farm in background*

1 Dollar

Front: *Her Majesty Queen Elizabeth II*
Back: *Unknown sailor from the first Fleet.*

50 Dollars

Front: *Dame Nellie Melba*
Back: *Aboriginal bark painter*

5 Dollars

Front: *Sir Douglas Mawson*
Back: *Radio telescope, Parkes; scientist at instrument panel*

Fig. 9. Front, Richard Beck's final $1 design.

The front of Richard Beck's final $1 design featured Her Majesty Queen Elizabeth II with a background of wattle leaves and flowers. Queen Elizabeth II was featured on Gordon Andrews' accepted $1 design, see $1 Section, Chapter 7.

Fig. 10. Back, Richard Beck's final $1 design.

The back incorporated figures from Australian history, including soldiers, an Aboriginal, swagman, singer, farmer and pastoralists.

The front of Richard Beck's final $2 design featured an Aborigine with tribal bark paintings while the back had a tableau of Australian figures with Daisy Bates. Daisy Bates (1861-1951) was born Daisy O'Dwyer Hunt in Ballychrine, Tipperary, Ireland in 1861, and migrated to Australia in 1884 where she later married John Bates. She became a social worker among the Australian Aborigines who gave her the name of "Kabbarli" (Grandmother). She was created a C.B.E. in 1934 and died on 18 April, 1951.

Fig. 11. Front, Richard Beck's final $10 design, Sir John Monash.

The front of Richard Beck's final $10 design featured Sir John Monash. See also, pages 42 and 43. Sir John Monash was eventually featured on the back of the Australian polymer $100 note, see Fig. 482.

Sir John Monash also featured on the front of an unadopted Twenty Pound note design from the 1950s. Other people who were featured on the front of Twenty Pound note designs were Captain John Macarthur (who appeared on the $2 design by Gordon Andrews), and Adam Lindsay Gordon.

On the back of Richard Beck's final $10 design were figures depicting Australian mining and engineering.

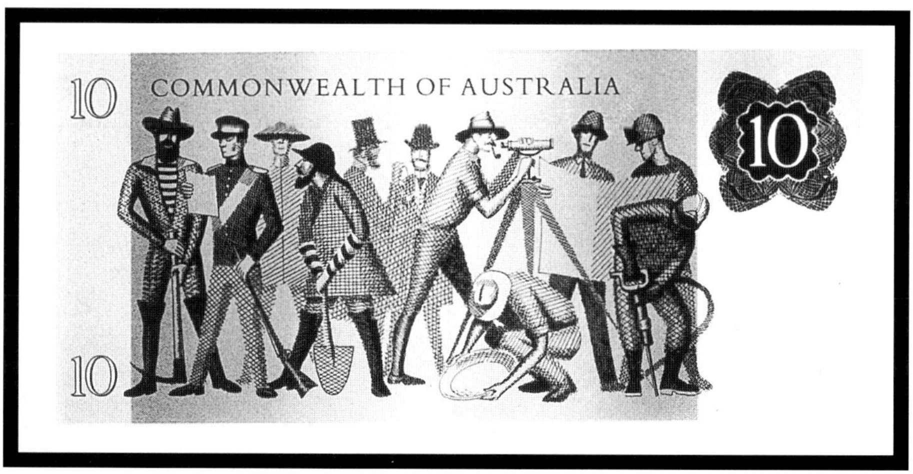

Fig. 12. Back, Richard Beck's final $10 design, Australian Mining and Engineering.

Fig. 13. Front, Richard Beck's final $20 design, Sir Joseph Banks.

Richard Beck's final $20 design featured Sir Joseph Banks on the front with a shadow-like floral motif in the background. The left side floral motif on the back appears to have originated from Plate 80 of *Illustrations of Botany of Captain Cook's Voyage in HMS Endeavour 1768-71*, by Joseph Banks and Dr. David Solander, British Museum, 1900. It is named *Castanospermum Australe.*

The centre illustration appears to be *Xylomelum*, a family of five species which are remarkable for their thick, woody, pear-shaped capsules, (possibly Woody Pear). The right side illustrations appear to be *Banksia* at top, and *Pittosporum* (Native Apricot) at the bottom. Sir Joseph Banks and Australian flora also featured on Gordon Andrews' $5 design which was introduced from 29 May, 1967. See Page 181.

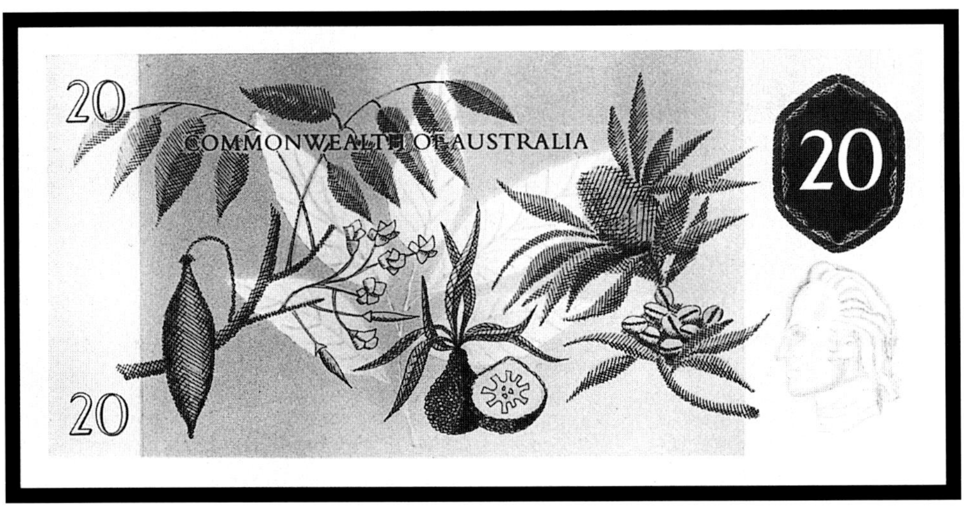

Fig. 14. Back, Richard Beck's final $20 design.

Fig. 15. Front, Max Forbes' final $1 design, Queen Elizabeth II.

Max Forbes' final $1 design featured Her Majesty Queen Elizabeth II on the front with the Australian coat-of-arms and Australian Wattle leaves and flowers. The coat-of-arms (which was used on the fronts of all his designs) depicted an Emu facing away from the shield.

Fig. 16. Back, Max Forbes' final $1 design.

On the back was Australian flora, including Sturt's Desert Pea, Banksia (Bottle Brush), Telopia (Waratah) and Wattle. Above the Sturt's Desert Pea flowers was a Cockatoo (possibly a Major Mitchell), and to the left of the Waratah, a Kookaburra.

Fig. 17. Front, Max Forbes' final $2 design, Captain James Cook.

The front of Max Forbes' final $2 design featured Captain James Cook with the Australian coat-of-arms, a landing party in a long-boat and a ship in sail (presumably the *Endeavour*) in the background. Captain James Cook's profile was later featured on all decimal paper notes as a watermark, and as an Optically Variable Device (OVD "hologram") on the Bicentenary polymer $10 note. See Watermarks, page 109, and page 382.

Fig. 18. Back, Max Forbes' final $2 design, *Endeavour.*

On the back was Cook's ship the *Endeavour*, with Australian flora and fauna which included a Koala, Frill necked lizard, a male Kangaroo and a female Kangaroo with joey, Emu and Dingo. The space at bottom right was reserved for the Captain Cook watermark.

Fig. 19. Front, Max Forbes' final $10 design, Sir Charles Kingsford Smith.

Max Forbes' final $10 design featured Sir Charles Kingsford Smith on the front with his aeroplane the *Southern Cross* and the Australian coat-of-arms. Sir Charles Kingsford Smith was featured on the accepted $20 design by Gordon Andrews. See $20 Section in Chapter 7.

Fig. 20. Back, Max Forbes' final $10 design.

On the back were Australian birds including a black Swan with a cygnet, a White Faced Heron, a Noisy Friarbird, Wedge Tailed Eagle, Kookaburra and Magpie.

Fig. 21. Front, Max Forbes' final $20 design, Dame Nellie Melba.

The front of Max Forbes' final $20 note featured Dame Nellie Melba, the Australian coat-of-arms and a lyrebird. Dame Nellie Melba was born Helen Porter Mitchell at Richmond, Victoria, on 19 May, 1861. In 1882 she married Charles Nisbett Frederick Armstrong from whom she separated after the birth of her son. She became a world famous soprano singer and adopted the name Melba. Dame Melba died in Sydney on 23 February, 1931, and was buried at Lilydale, near Melbourne.

From 15 May, 1996, Dame Melba appeared on the front of the Australian polymer $100 note, see Fig. 481. Further reading: *Melodies and Memories*, Nellie Melba, Thomas Nelson Australia, 1980.

On the back of Max Forbes' final $20 design were depicted people from the goldfields. In the centre background was a group of people standing under a flag.

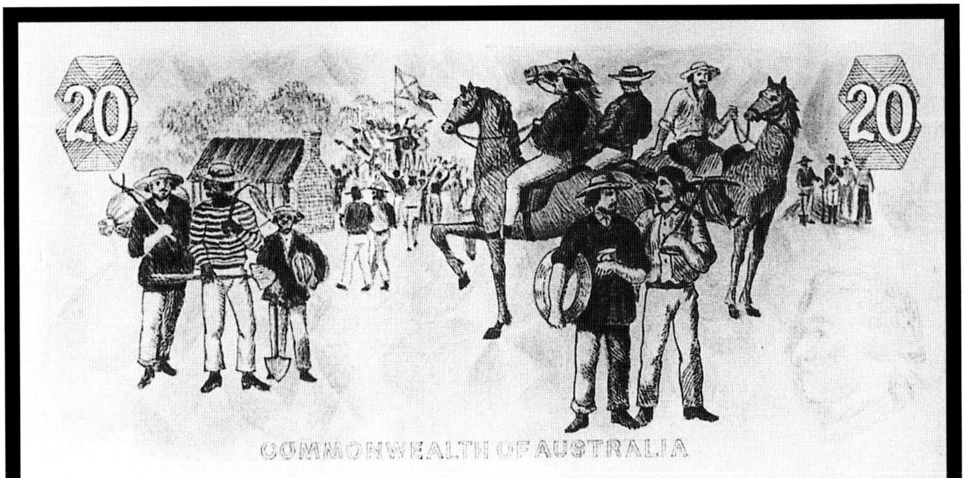

Fig. 22. Back, Max Forbes' final $20 design.

Fig. 23. Front, George Hamori's final $1 design.

George Hamori's final $1 design featured Queen Elizabeth II on the front with the Australian coat-of-arms. On the back was an unknown sailor at the wheel of a ship from the First Fleet. The First Fleet consisted of two King's ships, six convict transports and three storeships, carrying a total of 1,487 persons. After a journey of eight months and one day they arrived at Sydney Cove in January, 1788. The Fleet's vessels consisted of the King's ships H.M.S. *Sirius*, 520 tons (commanded by Arthur Phillip), and *Supply* (170 tons). The transports were; *Alexander* (452 tons), *Lady Penrhyn* (333 tons), *Charlotte* (335 tons), *Scarborough* (430 tons), *Friendship* (274 tons), and *Prince of Wales* (350 tons). The storeships were; *Fishburn* (378 tons), *Golden Grove* (375 tons) and *Borrowdale* (275 tons). By comparison, the largest ship *Sirius* was smaller than the smaller Sydney ferry boats with a tonnage less than that of the larger Manly ferry steamers. The Supply was later depicted on the Bicentenary polymer $10 note, see Fig. 469. Further reading, *Australian Encyclopaedia,* The Grolier Society, Sydney, 1964.

Fig. 24. Back, George Hamori's final $1 design.

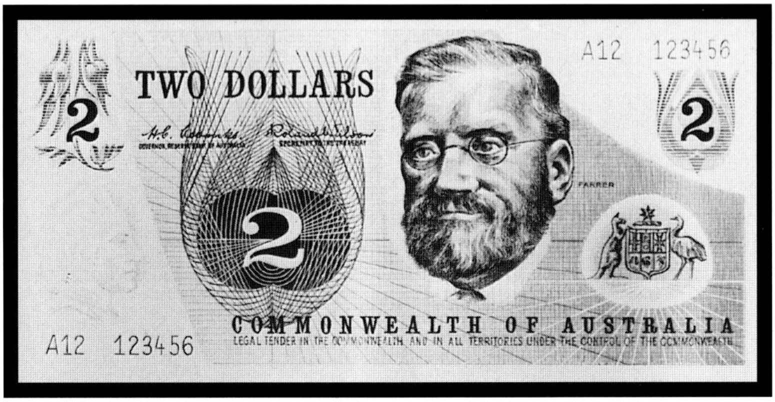

Fig. 25. Front, George Hamori's final $2 design.

George Hamori's final $2 design featured William Farrer on the front with the same coat-of-arms as that depicted on the other denominations. For information on Farrer, see $2 notes, Chapter 7, (Farrer was used on the back of the $2 note designed by Gordon Andrews). On the back was featured a shearer shearing a sheep with a typical Australian homestead and a windmill in the background. The only time a windmill has been featured on an issued Australian note was upon the introduction of the polymer $10 note first released in 1993, where it appeared in the clear window as a security feature.

Fig. 26. Back, George Hamori's final $2 design.

George Hamori's final $10 design featured Sir John Monash on the front dressed as a civilian. John Monash finally appeared on issued Australian notes from 15 May, 1996, on the back of the New Note Series polymer $100 notes. Sir John was born in West Melbourne on 27 June, 1865. He studied arts, engineering and law at the University of Melbourne. He later formed a private engineering practice and his involvement in military matters saw him appointed as Commander of the 4th Infantry Brigade after the outbreak of the First World War. In 1918 he was knighted and later appointed Commander of the Australian Corps and promoted to lieutenant-general. After the war he was Director-General of Repatriation and Demobilisation, and was general manager (and later chairman) of the State Electricity Commission of Victoria for over ten years, He died on 8 October, 1931. See also, page 34.

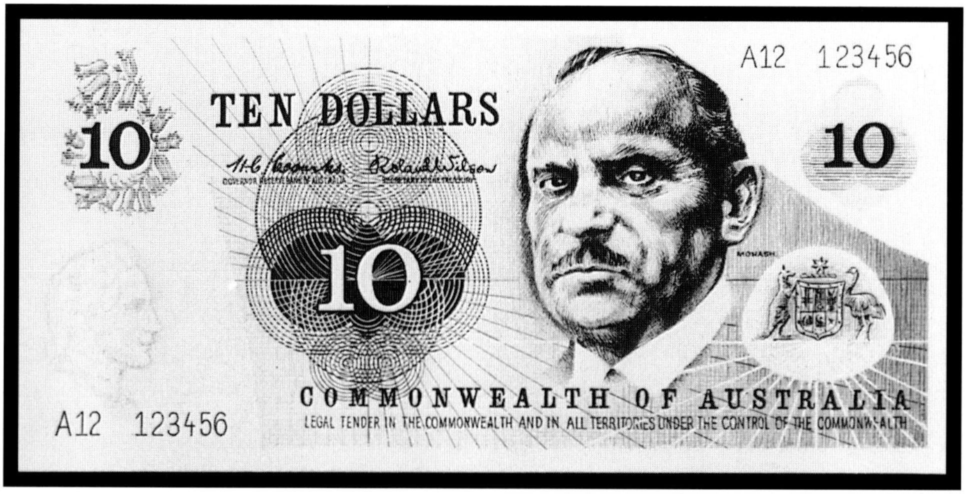

Fig. 27. Front, George Hamori's final $10 design, Sir John Monash.

Fig. 28. Back, George Hamori's final $10 design, Snowy Mountains Hydro-electric Scheme.

The back of George Hamori's final $10 design featured a workman at the Snowy Mountains Hydro-Electric Scheme. The scheme was a combined irrigation and hydro-electric project which provided for the waters of the Snowy River and other rivers in south-eastern New South Wales to be diverted by 145 km of tunnels and 80 kilometres of aqueducts through the mountains to the Murray and Murrumbidgee Rivers. On the way, the steep descent through the tunnels generates large quantities of power via turbines in seven power stations.

The scheme's main storage is Lake Eucumbene with a water capacity equal in volume to nine times that of Sydney Harbour, with its 116 metre high earth and rock fill dam wall, one of the highest of its type in the world (see Fig. 5). It is just one of sixteen dams included in the scheme which was commenced after July, 1949, and completed in 1972, at a total cost of around $800,000,000.

Fig. 29. Front, George Hamori's final $20 design, Sir Charles Kingsford Smith.

The front of George Hamori's final $20 design featured Sir Charles Kingsford Smith who appeared on the front of the accepted $20 design by Gordon Andrews. See $20 notes, Chapter 7.

On the back was a nurse of the Royal Flying Doctor Service (R.F.D.S.) with a Northern Territory landscape and the first Flying Doctor aircraft, "Victory". The R.F.D.S. was originated in 1928 by the Australian Inland Mission of the Presbyterian Church of Australia.

The Reverend John Flynn (who later appeared on the back of the Australian polymer $20 note from 1995) developed a scheme utilising aeroplanes, wireless and medicines to provide services for the people of the outback. Rev. Flynn was born on 25 November, 1880 and died on 5 May, 1951.

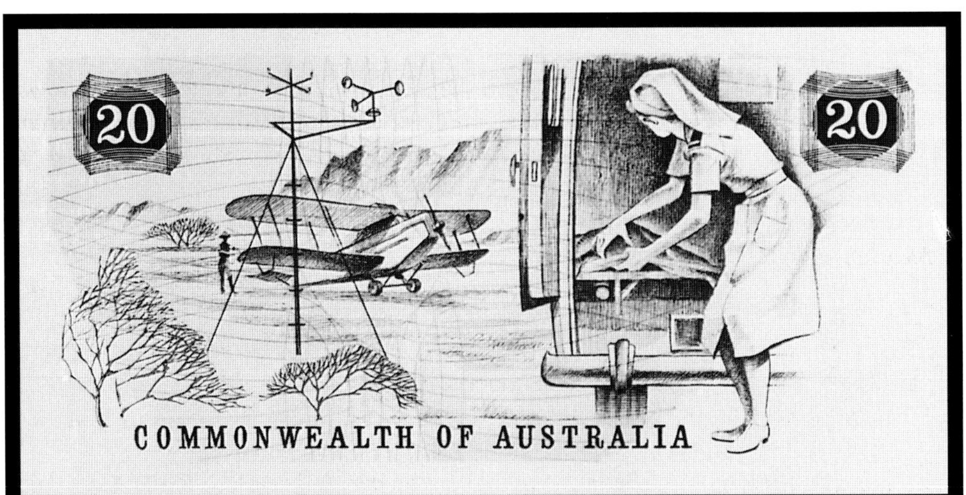

Fig. 30. Back, George Hamori's final $20 design, Royal Flying Doctor Service.

Today, no one is more than two hours away from medical help, and the Flying Doctor is there 24 hours a day, 365 days a year.

The service is divided into sections. The Central Section operates from four locations; Adelaide, Alice Springs, Port Augusta and Ayres Rock (Uluru), serving the whole of South Australia and the southern part of the Northern Territory, a total of 2.3 million square kilometres. In the 1998/99 financial year the Central Section's service flew over 3.3 million kilometres to help 38,000 people including 6,828 patients who were flown for emergency or specialist care. The section then employed 116 people and cost over $13 million annually to run.

At the next meeting held on 31 January, 1964, each designer presented designs for three notes together with first stage designs for a fourth note. The following points of interest emerged from discussion of the designs (N-a-156).

Gordon Andrews

All notes - Serial numbers have been repositioned at the bottom right and lefthand corners of the designs

$1 note (First stage)

Front: *Portrait of Her Majesty the Queen in conjunction with Australian Coat-of-Arms. Certain changes to the Coat-of-Arms are proposed to make it more heraldic in appearance.*

Back: *The proposed portrait of Dame Nellie Melba has been abandoned and the back depicted an aboriginal scene with a reproduction of a bark painting of a number of fish. As a result of panel discussions, the back is to be re-designed to include an aboriginal kangaroo hunt in place of the fish scene.*

Richard Beck

$1 note (First stage)

Front: *Portrait of Her Majesty the Queen and Australian Coat-of-Arms. Certain modifications of the Coat-of-Arms are proposed.*

Back: *Mr. Beck has decided to dispense with the portrait of Captain Cook to achieve continuity of appearance in the backs of all notes. $1 will now show figures relating to Australian history.*

Max Forbes

$20 note (First stage)

Front: *Portrait of Dame Nellie Melba with group of musical motifs.*

Back: *The proposed theatre scene has been replaced with a representation of the goldfields era.*

$1 note

Back: *It is now proposed to include with the Australian flowers a colonial era home in place of Government House, Sydney.*

George Hamori *All notes*

the one colour appearance of the $10 and $20 notes was commented upon and Mr. Hamori will endeavour to bring out the second colour more prominently.

Size and style of numerals to be used for the serial numbers was discussed, and a new and improved watermark of Captain Cook produced by Portals Ltd. was very favourably received and approved.

Mr. Morrison described the way Australia's new notes were born in the *Sydney Morning Herald* of 11 January, 1966; *"It started with all of us - the design and advisory panels - getting together for a general briefing and discussion. Then the designers went off to start. Over the months they all submitted hundreds and hundreds of drawings and plans. Everybody commented, criticised and discussed everybody else's work, then went away to work on a design with the discussion in mind. In the end, everybody submitted their finished designs for the notes to the advisory panel. The advisory panel unanimously decided on Mr. Andrews' designs."*

On 6 April, 1964, Alistair Morrison wrote to the Secretary of the Bank (S-a-768) and recommended the acceptance of Gordon Andrews' designs.

> *...The designs submitted by Gordon Andrews are outstanding. They are fresh and forward-looking; they are contemporary and yet timeless - they will not "date"; they are Australian in feeling, yet subtly so: they represent a completely new conception in currency note design, and yet, - and this is most important - they would be universally acceptable to and comprehensible by the average person; they are most original but not outre; they are neither gimmicky nor contrived. We believe the Andrews series of notes would not only increase Australia's prestige internationally but also that the Australian people would be proud of their currency, in much the same way as Sydney people are proud of their Opera House - because it, too, is unique...'*

The recommendation was heeded and Morrison confirmed by letter to Gordon Andrews on 18 April, 1964, that his designs had been accepted and approved, subject to certain minor modifications. Andrews was also asked to complete the project, that is, briefly, to prepare all the necessary final drawings and assemblies, and to supervise the work of production through all remaining stages. He was also informed that it would be necessary for him to leave for Europe within weeks, with other representatives of the Bank.

The Secretary of the Bank also asked Morrison to impress on Andrews *the extreme importance of continued secrecy about all matters connected with the project - about who was designing the notes, about the designs themselves, about the whole deal. Any indiscretion - any leakage - could lead to abandonment of the project.*

Two days later Andrews discussed further design points with Brown, Beck, Morriss and Bruce Stewart, which Brown listed in a letter to the General Manager, Note Issue Department on 24 April, 1964. (S-a-768).

(a) *All the portraits with the exception of the $1 dollar note require to be drawn up to seven times the required size and be in continuous tone. Some of the copy available of the subjects is unsuitable as they stand, and will require interpretation by the artist undertaking this work to present them in suitable form for engraving and detail.*

These original drawings can then be used as copy for interpretation into line drawings ready for engraving.

These portraits will require some adjustment in the present designs, as no allowance has been given for the tolerance required between the intaglio background printings. This is not a serious matter and will not demand any major alteration to designs.

(b) *Mr. G. Andrews requires to redraw the main titles as he is not satisfied with the existing lettering.*

All the titles are reductions in various sizes from the original drawing and will only require one master drawing to be made for the wording "Commonwealth of Australia".

Other details of various changes that are required by the Artist himself or for technical reasons are as follows:-

<u>$1 Front</u>

Fig. 31. Front, final Gordon Andrews' $1 design.

The values on the front and back require to be filled in with white line guilloche work. Mr. Andrews is to prepare a design of the line work he thinks applicable for these numerals. The front design will be different to the back.

The Coat of Arms is intended to be treated in a heraldic manner and Mr. Andrews requires to both check the details and refine the unit. The position of this unit provides a strict registration between intaglio and background printings and requires a tolerance to be provided. This will be undertaken when the unit is redrawn. For aesthetic reasons Mr. Andrews also wishes to redraw the wavy lines in the intaglio printing of this design.

Fig. 32. Back, final Gordon Andrews' $1 design.

<u>*$1 Back*</u>

The aboriginal bark paintings are a composite design and have been photographed from original pieces of art, the figures on the right hand side have been added by Mr. Andrews. He wishes to check both the accuracy and the photographic work and also the details of his own art work. It is then his intention to provide us with a completed drawing four times enlarged.

<u>*Background Tints*</u>

Mr. Andrews envisages these patterns to be obtained from mechanical rulings and I do not think this will create any problems to Organisation Giori. It will be the intention to introduce variable thicknesses to the actual lines and to discuss with Organisation Giori the possibility of these patterns being planned in both juxtaposition and superimposition.

<u>*$2 Front*</u>

The patterns of white line work to be incorporated in the values for both front and back are to be provided by Mr. Andrews.

The bands surrounding the sheep are to be redrawn for aesthetic reasons. Their position in relation to the background tint will also be taken into account to prevent the present tight register between intaglio and background tint printings.

The curls in the sheep do not meet Mr. Andrews' approval and he intends to redraw this part of the design. The portrait on this value will need particular attention and modification around the collar in order to save an unsightly edge of the background tints. Other areas of the portrait need to be shaded off in order to loose the edges of the background tints.

Fig. 33. Front, final Gordon Andrews' $2 design.

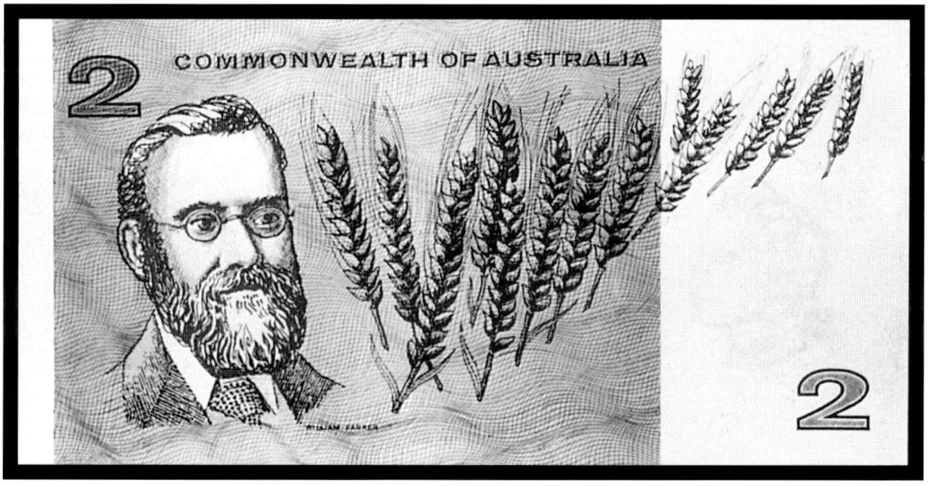

Fig. 34. Back, final Gordon Andrews' $2 design.

<u>*$2 Back*</u>

Very little alteration is required to this design and it is thought that the original drawing of the wheat by Mr. Andrews will be sufficient for our engraving needs. Shading to the portrait is required in which to loose the edges of the background tints.

<u>*Background Tints*</u>

It is thought that both front and back tints can be obtained from mechanical rulings and their composition will be determined after experiments with Organisation Giori.

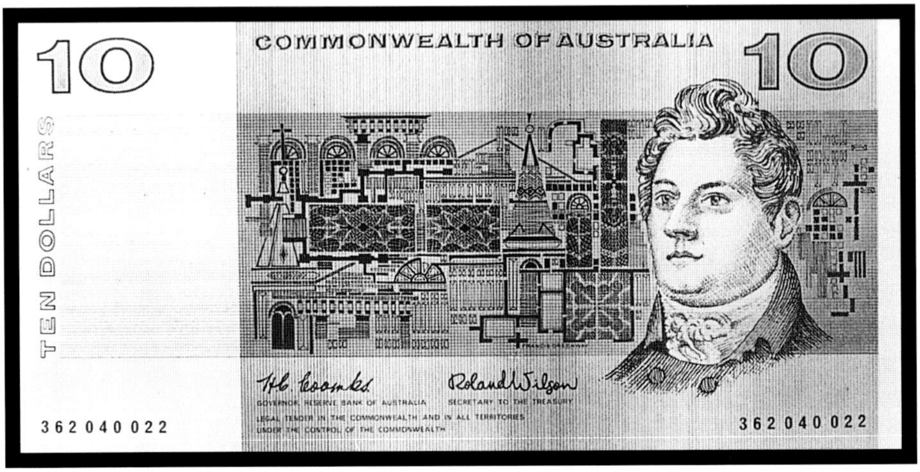

Fig. 35. Front, final Gordon Andrews' $10 design.

<u>*$10 Front*</u>

The details for both front and back values figures in white line work are to be provided by Mr. Andrews.

The register of the intaglio vignette to the background tints requires adjustment to give greater tolerance between printings. The white line panels in this design are not to Mr. Andrews' liking and he would prefer to change them. He has been supplied with sample pieces of guilloche work to bring about these changes. When this work is being undertaken, consideration should be given to the portrait for some means of either shading or other engraving to hide the edge of the background tints where they break off before entering the actual portrait area.

Fig. 36. Back, final Gordon Andrews' $10 design.

$10 Back

Shading of the portrait for the edge of the background tints is required. The remainder of this design can be engraved from the existing enlarged drawing by Mr. Andrews.

Background Tints

The front tints can be obtained by mechanical ruling.

The wave pattern on the back has special meaning to the design and Mr. Andrews would prefer to supply a line drawing for this particular wavy line pattern. Care will have to be taken to ensure that a correct step and repeat join is allowed for in the design and also that both edges of the tints can be joined satisfactorily when the printing plate is made.

Fig. 37. Front, final Gordon Andrews' $20 design.

$20 Front

The white line patterns for the values of both front and back are to be provided.

The portrait has to be shaded to allow the edge of the background tints to be lost.

The various shapes denoting wings on this design cannot, to my knowledge, be obtained via any geometric lathe. The original shapes have, I think, been obtained via some form of pendulum machine and which in all probability could never repeat these shapes correctly even if it was available to us. The white line pieces have been obtained by reversing photographs of the original patterns and could not have been produced by the original pendulum machine in this form.

The particular shapes are most appropriate to this design and appeal much more to Mr. Andrews than any form of geometric design we have so far produced on our lathe. As we cannot hope to achieve anything appropriate in this direction we shall attempt to redraw and either pantograph or cut these shapes by hand engraving. Mr. Andrews is to attempt to locate this special machine thought to be with the C.S.I.R.O., but I am of the opinion that knowledge of the plant used to create these designs could only be of interest rather than practical help at this stage.

Experimental work with these pieces is already in hand.

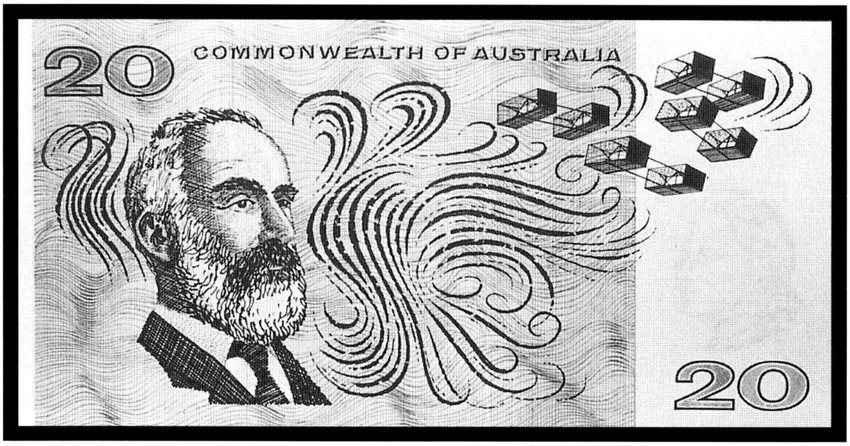

Fig. 38. Back, final Gordon Andrews' $20 design.

$20 Back

The portrait requires shading for the background tints to run under.

I understand that the box kites in the design are to be changed at the instigation of the Prime Minister.

The intaglio lines denoting air currents can be engraved from the original drawings prepared by Mr. Andrews.

Background Tints

The front tints are to be mechanically ruled and should not be a problem.

The back wavy line tint is similar to the back of the $10 note and will require to be drawn up by Mr. Andrews in order to obtain the effects he wishes to illustrate. The same conditions required for the $10 back wavy line tint will apply to this drawing.

Mr. Andrews stated that he would prefer to have all the portraits prepared and executed under his direct supervision rather than possibly undertaken by Organisation Giori staff, and where he thinks that the Continental approach might not be in keeping with the rest of the designs. I think this is desirable and preferable.

All the above points were discussed at length with Mr. Andrews on 20th April, and no real difficulties were expressed that would prevent the technical requirements being carried out to both his and our satisfaction.....

....In order to get the engraving under way in the shortest possible time there would be an advantage in completing the $1 back design just followed by the front design and then follow through in order of values.....

The trip to visit Organisation Giori (Simultan press manufacturers) in Milan was deemed a success. There Andrews met and discussed technicalities with the Giori artist Masino, and was satisfied that Masino understood his techniques and that his designs would not suffer in interpretation through "banknoteising". Masino's artwork was to be presented to Note Printing in a manner which would allow the engraving of the portraits to be commenced by their staff. The art work would also show in complete detail the patterns to be used in the background tints. The patterns would later be made up by Giori for the Simultan plates. It was expected that the first design ($2) would be completed in about four to six weeks, followed by the $1, $10 and $20 at corresponding intervals. Andrews also requested that the full stop after the Governor's signature currently on the pre-decimal notes, be omitted from the decimal notes, and the concession was duly granted by the Governor (N-a-156).

Gordon Andrews later stated in his autobiography *(A Designer's Life)*:

...Monty Brown was a constant source of knowledge. He introduced us to Bruce Stewart and Peter Morriss, two of the Bank's top engravers and artists who provided unstinted co-operation. In fact, the trust and support given to me from Dr Coombs down was outstanding in my experience. Once I had been commissioned to take my designs through to the finished product I was allowed absolute freedom to develop ideas without interference.

In June, 1964, the work remaining could be broken down into two stages (S-a-768).

A *The preparation of all finished drawings and the issuing of detailed instructions; and, concurrently, the inspection, supervision and correction of work being carried out by others.*

B *The second stage would be after the completion of all finished drawings. The work would then consist of inspection, supervision and correction.*

It was expected that the first stage would last at least another six months, during which time Andrews would be working very long hours, including many week-ends, and on this project alone. During the final stage the work was likely to be intermittent and spasmodic, but would continue until October 1965. (Later correspondence requested that it be only four and a half months to keep to the program.)

Andrews' work included detailed inspection, supervision and correction of all production through each process, comprising intaglio, offset backgrounds, letterpress numbering etc., and through each stage of the processes in such a way as to ensure that all instructions were faithfully and accurately carried out.

After negotiation, the Bank agreed to pay Gordon Andrews 800 guineas per side for 8 sides for all work anywhere directly or indirectly involved in the program up to on or about 30th October, 1964, and 40 guineas for each day required by the Bank or considered necessary by Mr. Andrews for all work after completion of the program. Expenses for necessary interstate and overseas travel would also be reimbursed, (N-a-156).

Gordon Andrews had experienced difficulty in obtaining portraits suitable for engraving, and he did not draw any of the heads, although he was responsible for their incorporation in the overall plan. The original drawings of the portraits used on the decimal notes were six times the finished size on the notes and they contained all the detail required for the engraver. Some time into the finished design stage Gordon Andrews suffered a mild coronary, but after medication and a lot of walking, he made a complete recovery.

Sydney artist Guy Warren was commissioned to produce portraits for use in connection with the new designs, namely those of John Macarthur, William Farrer, Francis Greenway and Sir Charles Kingsford Smith. (In 1985 he received the Archibald Prize for his painting "Flugelman with Wingman").

Another artist, Alfred Cook of Sutton Forrest, New South Wales, was engaged to do portraits of Henry Lawson and also of Macarthur. Later he did portraits of Sir Joseph Banks and Caroline Chisholm for the $5 note.

Neither Warren or Cook did any design work, but their task was to produce full-tone renderings to assist the engravers. The portrait of Macarthur used as a reference an early chalk drawing, whilst photographs were used as references for the other portraits. Free use was made of any photographic material available to enable the engravers to pick out more faithfully the salient points of the portraits, i.e. beards, eyes, forehead, etc. to enable them to more closely approach the perfection of design for which Gordon Andrews strove.

Peter Morriss was appointed Senior Artist/Engraver in 1964 and was put in charge of the team responsible for turning Gordon Andrew's note designs into security engravings and printing plates. He had joined the Bank in 1950 as a trainee and had worked mainly on designing and/or engraving postage stamps. He later became Administration Manager at Note Printing Australia (NPA), then Assistant Manager, General Manager (Works) and Assistant General Manager, in which role he established a team of specialists (and much of the equipment) required for the development and later production of polymer notes. In 1985 he moved to the Melbourne branch of the Reserve Bank of Australia and became Deputy Manager for Victoria, and retired in 1989. In 1996 he received the Order of Australia (OAM) medal (general division) for his work in the design and engraving of postage stamps and the engraving and development of currency notes.

The Mitchell Library in Sydney supplied the Bank with early portraits by unknown artists of Farrer, Greenway, Lawson and Hargrave, and a photograph by Dr. Julian Smith of Charles Kingsford Smith. In addition, the library supplied photographs of Lawson's manuscripts, and photographs from the Holtermann Collection of the Mudgee and Gulgong districts of New South Wales for the $10 note. Qantas supplied an early portrait of Lawrence Hargrave by an unknown photographer for the $20 note.

The first coloured pictures of the new notes were published by the *Australian Women's Weekly*. See also, Chapter 12.

Fig. 39. Front cover, *The Australian Women's Weekly*, January 26, 1966.
Reproduced by courtesy of *The Australian Women's Weekly*.

● Here are the backs of the dollar notes. The faces are on the cover.

The notes show: One dollar, the Queen (front) and aboriginal motifs (back). Two dollars, John Macarthur, pioneer grazier (front), and William James Farrer, pioneer of scientific wheat breeding. Ten dollars, architect Francis Greenway (front) and writer Henry Lawson. Twenty dollars, airman Sir Charles Kingsford Smith (front) and aeronautical pioneer Lawrence Hargrave.

Permission to photograph the notes in color (never previously allowed) was given with the stipulation that they be reproduced at least five percent bigger or smaller. Ours are smaller.

The actual size of the one dollar note is 140 millimetres by 70 millimetres (about 5½in. by 2¾in.) The others are proportionately bigger. All the notes are half as wide as they are long. Later there will probably be a five-dollar note, midway in size between the two and the ten.

Designer of the notes, Mr. Gordon Andrews, said his main aim was to make them timeless, not fashionable.

"Basically they are in the design and color of today," he said, "but they should last 20 years. One can't do an expressionist painting on a banknote."

Fig. 40. Page 3, *The Australian Women's Weekly,* January 26, 1966.
Reproduced by courtesy of *The Australian Women's Weekly.*

The Danmark's National Bank loaned Harold J. Bard for the engraving of the portraits of Sir Charles Kingsford Smith and Lawrence Hargrave on the $20 note. In his autobiography, *A Designer's Life,* Andrews said of the $20 note:

> *A well known British engraver was brought to Australia to do the portraits of Kingsford Smith and Lawrence Hargrave. While the Bank's engravers were enthusiastic supporters of my concept of capturing the spirit of a strong Australian character, the Englishman chose to ignore such an unconventional approach. He rejected the idea of gutsy engraving and cut his work exactly as he had always done. The result is a pair of bland, uninteresting portraits which we could do nothing with.*

The following persons or organisations were also acknowledged for contributions towards the preparation of designs for the $1, $2, $10 and $20.

> David Malangi was the Aboriginal artist of a bark painting on which part of the design of the $1 note was based.
> Mr. Karel Kupka for the loan of negatives of photographs of Aboriginal bark paintings for the $1 note.
> Mr. J.L. Stephen Mansfield for advice on the Coat-of-Arms and heraldry for the $1 note.
> Library of the Art Gallery of New South Wales for access to the book *Art Myth and Symbolism* (of Arnhem Land) by C.P. Mountford.
> Mr. D.L. Jackson, Faculty of Agriculture, University of Sydney, for supply of wheat specimens for the $2 note.
> Mr. David Moore for photographs of architectural details of Francis Greenway buildings for the $10 note and photographs on which engravings of air currents were based for the $20 note.
> Commonwealth Scientific and Industrial Research Organisation (CSIRO) for supply of material on which the illustrations of pendulum movements were based for the $20 note.
> Professor A.D. Trendall, Deputy Vice-Chancellor of the Australian National University for assistance in early deliberations on designs.

It is now history that the $1, $2, $10 and $20 notes were completed and issued on time, on the 14th February, 1966. The $5 followed in 1967 and the $50 in 1973. Thus ended Gordon Andrews' designs, although he later acted as a consultant for the design of the $100 note by Harry Williamson.

He was also engaged by the Bank to advise on design aspects of substituting plastic for paper in Australian notes and submitted many designs aimed at incorporating a clear area. Two such designs are illustrated in his book *A Designers Life*, which also illustrates some of the designs that he submitted in response to a decimal coin design competition (later won by Stuart Devlin).

THE $5 NOTE

Early discussions on a design for the $5 note took place in June, 1965, and the necessary stages of implementation were outlined in a letter from Morrison to the Secretary of the Bank on 1st July, 1965, (N-a-159). The letter proposed that Mr. Andrews should receive the same fees as for the individual notes of the first series ($1, $2, $10, $20). For the designs: 400 guineas for each side; for Stage 2, including portraits: 800 guineas per side and for Stage 3, 40 guineas for each day required by the Bank or considered necessary by Mr. Andrews.

On the 16th February, 1966, two days after the launch of Australia's decimal notes, a meeting took place in the Board Room of the Reserve Bank in Sydney. Present were the Governor and Deputy Governor of the Bank, and Messrs. Wilcock, McPherson, Knight, Wilson, Morrison, Andrews, Missingham and Annand. The main purpose of the meeting was to discuss preliminary matters associated with the design of a $5 note. Consideration was given to the portraits which might be used for the note and following discussion it was agreed that the initial designs should incorporate portraits of Joseph Banks on the front and Caroline Chisholm on the back. Purple or mauve was suggested as its colour (N-a-159). A $50 was also discussed, see following.

For the $5 note the Mitchell Library, Sydney, allowed access to portraits of Joseph Banks and Caroline Chisholm, and to a water-colour painting of the *"Waverley"*. In addition, access was supplied to Joseph Fowles' Sydney in 1848 which provided illustrations of elevations of Sydney streets, and photocopies of a title page of the *Shipping Gazette*, as well as a handbill of a meeting of the Family Colonisation Society. The Royal Botanic Gardens and National Herbarium gave advice, research, and supplied illustrations of Australian flora.

THE $50 NOTE

At the meeting of 16th February, 1966, it was also agreed that Mr. Andrews should submit preliminary designs for a possible $50 note with "Industry" as its theme. It was tentatively agreed that portraits of Sir John Monash and Essington Lewis should be used for the design, using a gold tone for the colouring of the note (N-a-159).

The eventual note featured Lord Howard Florey on the front, and Sir Ian Clunies Ross on the back and was issued on 9 October, 1973, the first note to bear "AUSTRALIA" instead of "COMMONWEALTH OF AUSTRALIA". Early designs of this note bore the latter title.

In his autobiography, *A Designer's Life*, Gordon Andrews describes the technique used to produce the "Medallioning" in the background design of the front of the note (see Fig. 297).

> *One of the useful and beautiful techniques available in the mechanical department is called medallioning. It is produced by a machine which converts a three dimensional model to a two dimensional line pattern. A model is placed on a bed, a stylus is passed across the surface and by moving up and down, transfers the action through a series of linkages to a diamond pointed stylus which cuts through an emulsion on the surface of a glass plate. The resulting effect is then used as a negative to produce a positive line pattern.*

The $50 note was originally designed as a $100 note which is illustrated in Andrews' book. Florey appears on the note which includes "Commonwealth of Australia" and Phillip-Randall signatures. Plates had already been cut for $100 and had to be modified to $50 because it was felt that the issue of a $100 first, would suggest inflation.

The following were acknowledged as assisting with this denomination.

> Sir Macfarlane Burnet, Professor Sir Rutherford Robertson and the CSIRO for research assistance in assembling material on which the design for the $50 note was based. The Queen's College and the Sir William Dunn School of Pathology at Oxford University for allowing a wide range of photographs to be taken by Christopher Ridley for use in the preparation of the design on the front of the $50 note.

Fig. 41. Gordon Andrews, designer of Australia's first decimal notes.

Gordon Andrews

Gordon Andrews was born in Sydney, New South Wales, on 10 January, 1915, the son of E.G. Andrews, Mechanical Engineer, designer and inventor. Gordon was aged 51 years at the time he designed the notes, and believed that designing skills were in the family genes. He began his career by studying Mechanical Engineering, and later, design at Sydney Technical College. His work has ranged from designs for better chairs and saucepans, showrooms and exhibitions for Olivetti in the United Kingdom, the format and illustrations for a set of Italian pre-University students' encyclopaedias, a studio building with a parabolic arched roof designed for pre-fabrication basically from giant plywood laminated arches and steel connectors, to the concept, design and production of the Australian exhibition at the National Fair in 1960 at Lausanne, Switzerland. He was elected Fellow of the Society of Industrial Artists and Designers in 1953. Later commissions included graphics and signage for Cameron Offices and the National Athletics Stadium in Canberra and the Reserve Bank of Australia Note Printing building at Craigieburn, Victoria. In 1985 he was awarded a gold medal by the Design Institute of Australia and in 1988, elected to the Faculty of Royal Designers for Industry (England) as an honorary member.

Gordon Andrews wrote a pictorial autobiography *A Designer's Life* which was originally published by New South Wales University Press in 1993 to co-incide with an exhibition of his work at Sydney's Powerhouse Museum. It is now available from Andrews Designs, 408 Glenrock Parade, Tuscott,

N.S.W. 2250, RRP $40.00 plus $7 post. It has large format, 192 pages and 205 colour plates. Further reading: *The man who had designs on our money,* by Joe Rollo *The Age* newspaper, 25 April, 1995; *Some Thoughts on the New Australian Bank Notes* by the designer, Gordon Andrews in ART and Australia, March 1966 and *A Designer's Life* in the R.B.A. magazine *Currency*, November 1993.

In his autobiography Andrews revealed that after an initial briefing by the Bank's Works Manager, Monty Brown, and meeting technicians, he:

> *theorised that by contriving a pattern of lines varying in thickness, juxtaposed and superimposed, a ratio of more ink to paper would be achieved, in effect, giving white lines on colour and making it difficult for a photographer to find the right exposure. If exposed for thick lines, the fine lines disappear; expose for the thin ones and the thick lines burn in or flare, closing the thin white lines in between."*

His book also revealed that designing the variations of his wave patterns was slow and painstaking without the use of modern computer graphics:

> *I had to cut a number of templates and generate arrangements on the drawing board by tiresome trial and error. Once satisfied with a result , I would take it to the Fitzroy Printing Works where the basic wave line was drawn accurately, a negative was made and set up in the step-and-repeat camera, which was programmed to produced the "swelled" waves and repeated to give the pattern I wanted....I went back to the drawing board many, many times...".*

At that time he shared working space in an old terrace house at Walker Street, North Sydney with the photographer David Moore and his colleague Harry Williamson (who later designed the $100 note).

By 1999, then 85 years of age, he had turned to producing highly acclaimed whimsical sculptures assembled from timber offcuts and found metal parts. His house at Lovett Bay was destroyed by bushfire and he rebuilt. After some time he moved to Avalon Beach for easier mobility. In an interview with Malcolm Andrews published in the *Newcastle Herald* of 10 April, 1999, he revealed that he had been persecuted as a child by his teacher at Public School for his inability to master the three Rs. He was humiliated in front of the class by the teacher who announced that Gordon was "so stupid he'll never find a job better than night soil collection." He went home and unsuccessfully tried to hang himself. So much for the teacher's opinion - Gordon's art was later gladly carried in the pockets of all Australians for thirty years.

THE $100 NOTE

An internal report of the Reserve Bank of Australia in 1975 suggested the development of a higher value note and by 1976 it had established a steering panel which included Gordon Andrews and Philip Cox (an architect with acknowledged design skills) as outside consultants. The panel briefed three designers - Les Mason, Max Robinson and Harry Williamson - to develop possible lines of approach. The theme "discovery" was adopted. On 31 August, 1976, the designs were submitted with written support material. Assessments of the designs were made which reached different conclusions and further development work continued on the designs for the next three years.

Fig. 42. Front, Les Mason's first $100 design.

Fig. 43. Back, Les Mason's first $100 design.

Les Mason's first design (illustrated above) depicted Captains Matthew Flinders, William Dampier and James Cook on the front and on the back was depicted a ship, the *Batavia*, with marine life and flora and Seal Island in King George's Sound. Captain Matthew Flinders (1774-1847), Navy captain, hydrographer and discoverer was featured on the last ten shilling note prior to decimal currency, see One Royal design, Fig. 3. William Dampier (1651-1715), circumnavigator and adventurer, was the first Englishman to give a firsthand account of Australia. Captain James Cook, see Watermarks, Chapter 4.

The *Batavia* was a Dutch merchant ship commanded by Francois Pelsaert which was wrecked in 1629 off the coast of Western Australia. Of the surviving crew and passengers, 125 people were murdered by other crew members who were in turn later tried and hanged on Seal Island, the first white persons to be executed on Australian soil.

Fig. 44. Front, Les Mason's third and final $100 design.

Fig. 45. Back, Les Mason's third and final $100 design.

Les Mason's final (third) design (illustrated above) was changed on both the front and the back, but the dominant features remained the same, large "100" figures and the title of "Australia" in cursive on the back, (a concept not previously used, which eventually did appear on the polymer notes).

On the back the ship was moved to the top and the handwritten text (believed to be from Flinders' journal now located in the Mitchell Library, Sydney), relocated at the bottom. A different flower and other modifications were also shown. The botanical specimens were probably based on drawings made by the First Fleet artists.

Max Robinson's designs (illustrated next page) featured John Hunter (1737-1821), Captain of the First Fleet *Sirius* and second Governor of N.S.W. (1793-1800) on the front, with a Frill necked lizard, cockatoo, wombat and kangaroo with joey. Robinson's first design for the back included a whale, and his final (third) design in 1978 depicted a koala, emu, kookaburra and pelican.

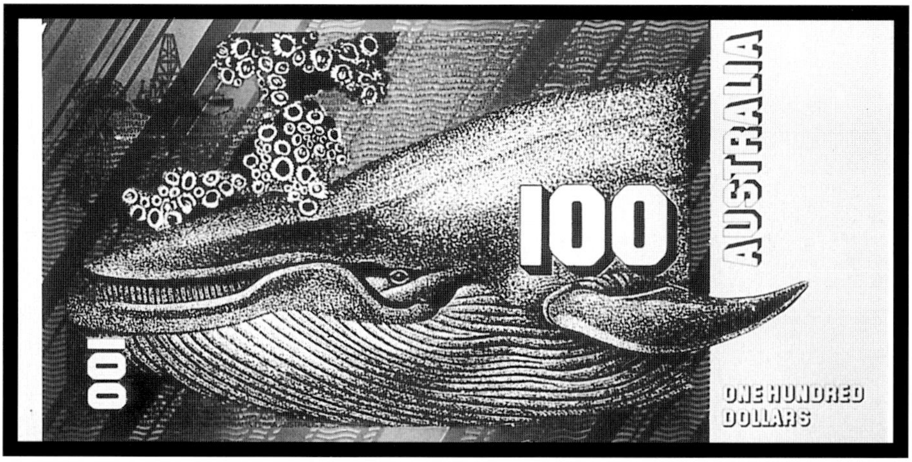

Fig. 46. Back, Max Robinson's first $100 design.

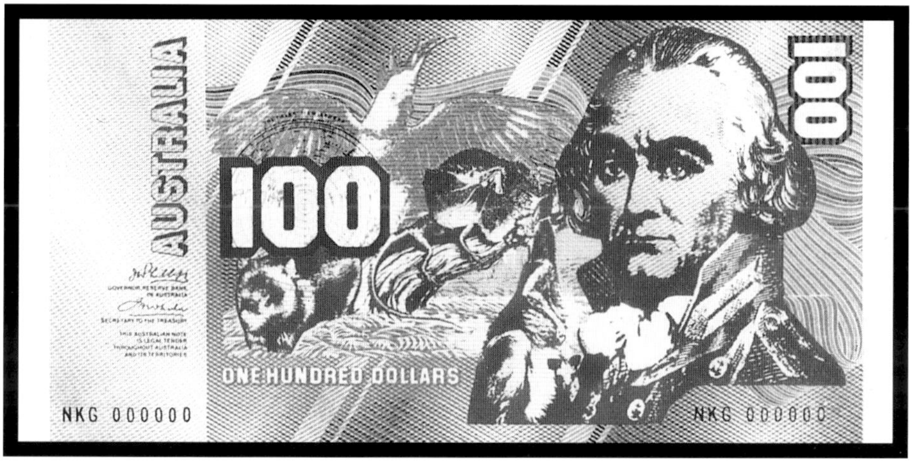

Fig. 47. Front, Max Robinson's third and final $100 design, Captain John Hunter.

Fig. 48. Back, Max Robinson's third and final $100 design.

Fig. 49. Front, Harry Williamson's second and third (1980) $100 designs.

Fig. 50. Back, Harry Williamson's second $100 design.

Fig. 51. Back, Harry Williamson's third and final $100 design, 1980.

Harry Williamson's first design featured Abel Tasman on the front, but this was changed to Phillip Parker King for the second and third designs. Phillip Parker King (1791-1856), Rear-admiral and explorer, was the first Australian to obtain the rank of Admiral in the British Navy. Williamson's second design, and third design (1980) depicted John Tebbutt. See illustrations on previous page.

The Note Printing Branch developed a design which included a portrait of Sir Douglas Mawson, and in April 1980 it was agreed that the Williamson design, incorporating the Note Printing Branch (N.P.B.) Mawson front, offered "rich design possibilities".

The first N.P.B. design incorporated Knight-Wheeler signatures and the second and third designs Knight-Stone signatures. The first front design bore a larger portrait of Sir Douglas Mawson than the second and third designs. All three designs also featured the Aurora, the South Pole and ice-caps with later modifications to the background designs. See illustrations this and next page.

Fig. 52. Front, Note Printing Branch's first $100 design.

Fig. 53. Front, Note Printing Branch's second $100 design.

Fig. 54. Front, Note Printing Branch's third and final $100 design.

Fig. 55. Note Printing Branch's third and final $100 design.

The back of N.P.B.s third and final $100 design (illustrated above) featured Cook, Dampier, Tasman and Megellan. Abel Janszoon Tasman (1604-1659) was the Dutch discoverer of Tasmania and New Zealand. Ferdinand Magellan (1480-1521) was the first navigator to cross the Pacific from east to west and initiator and leader of the first expedition to circumnavigate the world. He was Portuguese.

Much of the original research on Mawson was done by Bruce Stewart when the Note Printing Branch design was first developed. He received a lot of assistance from Dr. F. Jacka, Director of the Mawson Institute for Antarctic Research, University of Adelaide. Bruce Stewart was responsible for the initial drawings of the portraits and a lot of the engraving. John Mackie and Lyell Dolan did the majority of the engraving and hand-proofing and Lyell Dolan did a lot of important work into all areas of the original work, including the design in Fig. 55. Another N.P.A. staff design featured Burke & Wills.

The Advisory Committee included Don Sanders, Don Parr, Peter Morriss, Gordon Andrews and Philip Cox. Also active on the committee from time to time were Marc Diamond, Jim Mallyon, Kevin Thompson and George Gettens. Assisting the designer were Geoff Sceats, Don Addison, Ian Whittaker, John Cardamone and the designer's partner, Terri Williamson.

The process of production began around the end of 1983 and the note was first issued on 26 March, 1984. See also, end of Chapter 3, Informing the Public.

References: *The Bank's Baby* by Ron Stuart, and *My Designs on Money* by Harry Williamson, *Currency* (R.B.A.), April 1984. The illustration below, courtesy of *The Australian*, shows the designer holding $1 million in $100 notes.

Fig. 56. Harry Williamson holding $1,000,000 in new $100 notes

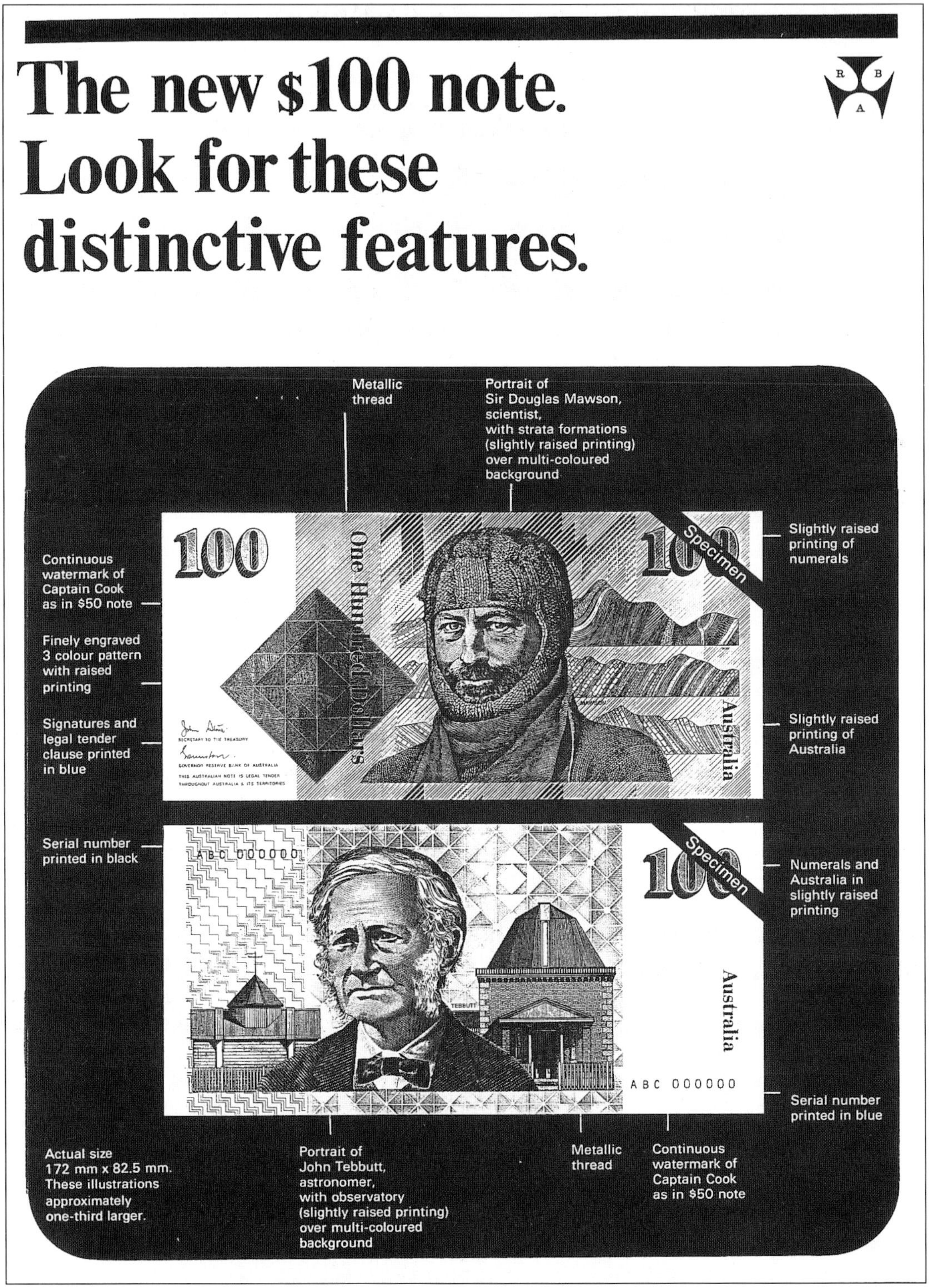

Fig. 57. Reserve Bank of Australia $100 information poster.

Chapter 3: INFORMING AND EDUCATING THE PUBLIC

Fig. 58. Dollar Bill

An advisory panel of media experts in co-operation with the Decimal Currency Board's public relations division developed a cartoon character called *Dollar Bill.*

The Board used *Dollar Bill* in its publications to help get the message across. After December 7, 1964, *Dollar Bill* appeared in animated and semi-animated cartoon form for brief film and television appearances. He also appeared in comic strips that explained decimal currency and factors involved in the two-currency period. Newspapers co-operated by running columns about decimal currency, and the *Sydney Morning Herald* ran a daily column from 15 January headed "Today is C-30" etc., counting down to "C day". Conversion problems were explained and information simplified.

Crosswords and puzzles helped the public in mental conversion of pre-decimal amounts and other aspects of the changeover. Dollar Bill was also used in brochures and posters for schools, education programs and general displays. Newspaper editorial columns were directed at special sections of the community such as business, women, children and country people. The Board also engaged in daily radio advertising and a Dollar Bill jingle to the tune of "Click go the shears"

In come the dollars and in come the cents
to replace the pounds, the shillings and the pence
be prepared, folks, when the coins begin to mix
on the 14th February 1966

Clink go the cents folks clink, clink, clink,
changeover day is closer than you think
Learn the value of the coins and the way that they appear
and things will be much smoother when the decimal point appears.

On the 10th January, 1966, the Reserve Bank of Australia released pictures of the designs of the new notes for the first time.

On the 17th January, 1966, the Decimal Currency Board began the major phase of its public education program in readiness for the conversion to decimal currency. It was announced that every Australian home would receive in the mail two booklets explaining the new currency and how it worked. They were delivered from 17 January to 21 January to about 4,000,000 letterboxes in envelopes addressed to *The Householder from the Decimal Currency Board.*

The 16 page booklet called *Dollars and Cents and You* contained basic information needed for the change of currency on Monday, 14 February. One such question and answer in the booklet was:

> *What happens when you don't have the exact amount in dollars and cents to pay for something priced in shillings and pence?*
>
> *Exactly what occurs most of the time when you shop now - offer a higher amount and receive change. This applies whether the price is in pounds shillings and pence or dollars and cents. As long as you offer an amount which is a multiple of 6d or 5c, it can be regarded as a dollar amount or a pounds shillings or pence amount. The shop assistant will give you correct change in pounds shillings and pence if the shop is selling in pounds shillings or pence, or in dollars and cents if the prices are in that money.*

£ s.d. to dollars and cents

A guide for you when you go shopping after 14th February.

PENCE TO ROUND CENTS

1d. ... 1 cent	7d. ... 6c
2d. ... 2c	8d. ... 7c
3d. ... 2c	9d. ... 8c
4d. ... 3c	10d. ... 8c
5d. ... 4c	11d. ... 9c
6d. = 5c exactly	1/- = 10c exactly

SHILLINGS TO CENTS

1/- = 10 cents exactly	6/- = 60 cents
2/- = 20c	7/- = 70c
3/- = 30c	8/- = 80c
4/- = 40c	9/- = 90c
5/- = 50c	10/- = 100 cents = $1

POUNDS TO DOLLARS

£1 = $2 £5 = $10 £10 = $20

Remember this rhyme to convert pence to cents

One and two remain the same,
The only difference is the name,
Three to nine lose one it's true,
And for the rest you take off two.

Produced by the Decimal Currency Board

SHOPPING IN DOLLARS AND CENTS

Keep this card with you when you go shopping

Fig. 59. Decimal Currency Board conversion shopping card, outside cover.
(Commonwealth of Australia copyright reproduced with permission).

The second publication shown in the previous illustration was a fold-over card setting out what to do when shopping with the old and new currencies, or both. Similar, but less complete material was released through newspapers, television and radio in the five weeks following the distribution of the envelopes.

Decimal currency telephone enquiry bureaus opened in State capitals from Monday, 24 January, 1966, to March 1 where "Dollar Jills" answered any enquiries. The Board employed 29 "Dollar Jills", seven each in Sydney and Melbourne, five in Brisbane, four each in Adelaide and Perth, and two in Hobart.

Fig. 60. Consolation prize, PIX / Bank of N.S.W. competition.

A series of articles publicising the currency changeover, together with a PIX/Bank of New South promotion, appeared in PIX magazine from 18 December 1965. The articles, in the form of a competition, offered as first prize a South Pacific cruise, with $500 cash and $250 in traveller's cheques, and a movie camera and projector. Consolation prizes (1,000) were in the form of newly issued one dollar notes on souvenir cards as illustrated above. Brymay *Redheads* matches also featured as collectors' items, a series of 48 matchbox labels with "Dollar Bill", as per the next illustration.

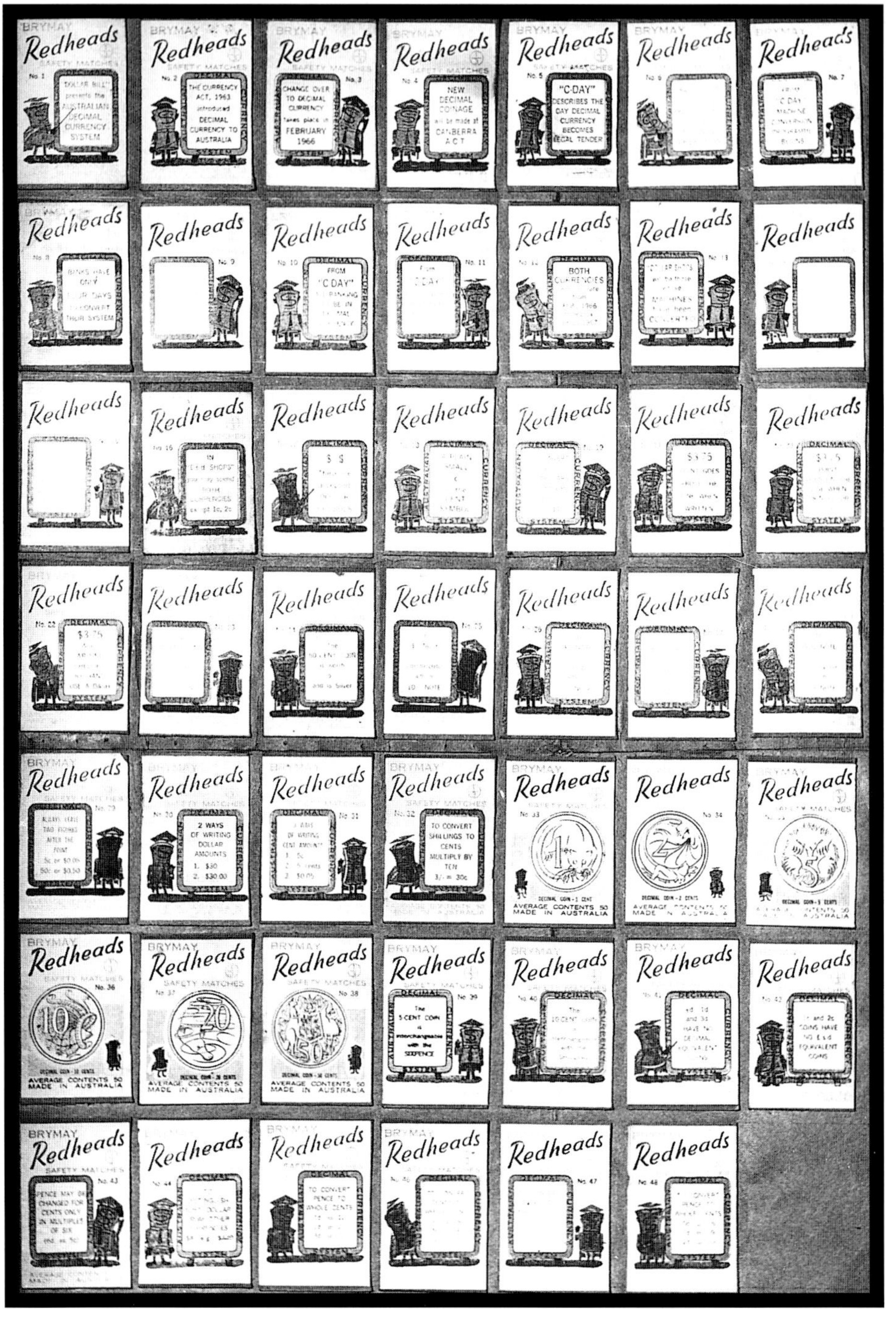

Fig. 61. Redheads Matchbox labels, 1966, for decimal conversion.

On 10 January, 1966, The Reserve Bank of Australia issued the following press statement:

AUSTRALIAN DECIMAL CURRENCY NOTES

On 23 December 1965, the Rt. Hon. the Treasurer of the Commonwealth, Mr. Harold Holt, announced that supplies of $1, $2, $10 and $20 notes of the new design would be available on 14 February 1966, at banks throughout Australia and that further details, including full descriptions and photographs of the new notes, would be released by the Governor of the Reserve Bank on 10 January.

Today, Dr. H.C. Coombs said that the decision to change over to decimal currency had presented an unusual and challenging opportunity to produce completely new currency notes for Australia. It was most gratifying to both the Bank and the Government that in two and a half years the new notes had been designed and taken right through to the production stage, so that approximately 160 million pieces are now issueable, against the actual issue of existing notes of approximately 158 million.

It was an undertaking involving many people, including designers, artists, photographers, engravers, machinery experts and production workers, both in Australia and overseas, and both from within and outside the service of the bank.

An early decision was made to issue initially notes in denominations of $1, $2, $10 and $20, and similar in basic colour to the notes they are replacing. It was also decided that the size of the new notes would be as follows.

$1	*140 mm x 70 mm*	*(10/-*	*136.5 mm x 76.2mm)*
$2	*145 mm x 72.5 mm*	*(One pound*	*155.6 mm x 80.9 mm)*
$10	*155 mm x 77.5 mm*	*(Five pounds*	*166.7 mm x 79.4 mm)*
$20	*160 mm x 80 mm*	*(Ten pounds*	*181 mm x 79.4 mm)*

It will be seen that each note is smaller than the one it replaces and that both dimensions increase with the value of the note. The new sizes are considered to have a number of advantages and are consistent with modern currency note trends.

(Information given about the designer and the designing of the notes has been extracted and included in Chapter 2, "Designing the notes".

The Queen's Portrait

The design panel expressed the hope that it might be possible to have a new portrait of Her Majesty for the $1 note. Because of their knowledge of his work generally, and more particularly, of his appreciation of the engraver's art, they expressed a preference for Mr. Douglas Glass of London as the photographer. Her Majesty graciously consented and Mr. Glass took a large number of photographs at Buckingham Palace. From those approved for use, a final selection was made (see Fig. 150).

Security features

In guarding against the acceptance of forgeries the public should look for high quality and clarity in printing and attention is drawn especially to the following security considerations in the new notes:

- *(a)* *the main features of the notes have been printed by the recess process from hand engraved original dies resulting in a raised ink film giving a slightly embossed feel.*
- *(b)* *Particular attention has been paid to the design of the background tints, which have been reproduced in clearly defined patterns of thick and thin lines printed with great clarity.*
- *(c)* *A portrait of Her Majesty appears on the front of the $1 note. On all other denominations there are portraits both front and back. These portraits are important security features of the notes.*
- *(d)* *As for previous issues, the new notes are printed on special paper obtained from Portals Ltd. of England. This paper has a characteristic feel and special crispness. The paper also has a metallic thread embedded in it and running down near the centre of each note. Each note contains a newly designed watermark portrait of Captain James Cook.*

The Press Release then went on to give details of the persons whose portraits appeared on the notes.

$10 forgeries were discovered in December, 1966, which prompted calls for a change of design. The *Australian Coin Review* in February 1967 said, among other things:

> *...But it has taken us just 12 months to announce our belief that the entire range of Australian decimal notes, from one dollar to twenty dollars, is just about the easiest to forge range of notes of value in the entire world. This is not news to printers throughout Australia. Ask any printer and he will agree...It is a pity that, by adding several colours to the Decimal notes to make them attractive (and there is no doubt about them being very pleasing to the eye), the notes themselves have been made far easier to copy than the old engraved notes of pre-1966...And at least one printer has found the temptation too strong. Already Australian police have $140,000 worth of forged ten dollar notes...*

For further information, see FORGERIES, Chapter 12.

The supply of the new coins to banks throughout Australia involved 70 Commonwealth Police, 75 Reserve Bank Officers, 50 Department of Supply drivers, and State police, "some armed with sub-machine guns". The secret delivery of 350,000,000 coins ($25 million) from the Australian and London mints to over 5,000 bank branches began on 29 November, 1965, and was completed on 3 February 1966. It was called "Operation Fastbuck". Those involved later received a set of uncirculated 1966 coins in a black plastic wallet with gold coloured embossing on the inside cover *Presented by the Reserve Bank of Australia to .... as a memento of his participation in "Operation Fastbuck" Nov. 1965 - Feb. 1966.* Two weeks after "C" day another operation called "Operation Roscoe" collected the withdrawn pre-decimal coinage.

Everyone connected with the operation received a special identification card with their photograph. Escort vehicles accompanied delivery convoys. The coins were kept in special stores in State capitals up to fourteen months before deliveries to banks began. Special precautions were taken in the storing of the high denomination coins. They were stored secretly, often in the Department of Supply's ammunition and explosives factories where special alarms had been installed.

The longest coin delivery run finished on 3 February after covering 2,700 miles, taking exactly one month. It covered 25 towns and 183 bank branches in western New South Wales.

Some five cent coins got into circulation before they were officially released. The release of the new one and two cent pieces to business people commenced on 7 February in minimum lots of $5.

Prior to the introduction of decimal notes the Commonwealth Bank of Australia issued training vouchers to staff to familiarise them with the handling of the new-sized and coloured notes. Brown coloured plastic blank discs were also used to represent one and two cent pieces. The vouchers were different sizes and colours with a denomination figure on the left and right sides and the words "Training voucher only" at the bottom. Only one side was printed.

"1"	Fawn,	14 x 7 cm.	"10"	Blue,	15.5 x 7.8 cm.
"2"	Green,	14.5 x 7.3 cm.	"20"	Pink,	16 x 8 cm.

Fig. 62. The first published picture of $1,000,000 - 14 January 1966.

The new decimal notes were shown to the public for the first time on January 10 at a press, radio and television conference at the Reserve Bank's Head Office in Sydney, with officials of the Reserve Bank of Australia and the Decimal Currency Board present.

To facilitate the changeover to decimal currency, all banks were closed to the public from 3.00 pm. on Wednesday 9 February and re-opened the following Monday 14 February, 1966, at 10.00 am. Because of its geographical position, Norfolk Island was the first Australian Territory to switch to decimal currency, since it was 90 minutes ahead of Eastern Standard Time in Australia. To mark the occasion, the Norfolk Island Lions Club arranged a ceremony at one minute past midnight on "C-day". The president of the Lions Club, Holder Christian, the great-great-great-great grandson of Fletcher Christian of *Bounty* fame, presented \$100 in notes to open an appeal for comforts for the Norfolk Island Hospital and it thus became the first legal decimal currency transaction in the Commonwealth and the Territories.

The day after "C-day" brought forth about 1,000 calls for help in handling decimal currency to the Decimal Currency Board's Advice Centre. Many people believed that they had been overcharged. Most complaints were about food prices.

Some bank branches in Sydney ran out of one and two cent coins and \$1 notes, and fresh supplies were brought from head offices by taxi-cab while the customers waited. To meet the requirements of an enormous volume of business caused by the demands for the new currency, the Reserve Bank of Australia released a further \$185,000,000, bringing the total of dollars and cents in circulation to \$1,028,000,000.

The day after "C-day" notes were found with small tears at the top near the centre, probably the result of people curious to inspect the metallic security strip.

A long publicity drive was undertaken to inform owners of various vending machines and cash registers of arrangements regarding some compensation for loss incurred in changing over to decimal currency. Numerous problems were encountered with the new coins either not working in, or alternatively, jamming vending machines.

Huge volumes of old coins were cashed in. In a five-hour trading day on 17 February, 1966, the Bank of New South Wales in Sydney was left with 48 tons (nearly 49 tonnes) of pennies, some \$50,000 worth, bringing the total of pennies since "C-day" to \$250,000.

FIVE DOLLARS

The introduction of a \$5 note was provided for and anticipated at the time of the changeover to decimal currency, but it was not issued at the same time as the \$1, \$2, \$10 and \$20 because it had no pre-decimal equivalent and may have confused or complicated the changeover. It was issued from 29 May, 1967. A Press Release from the Reserve Bank of Australia on 15 May stated, in part:

> *AUSTRALIAN FIVE DOLLAR NOTE*
>
> *On 4 May 1967, the Treasurer, the Right Honourable William McMahon, M.P., announced that \$5 notes would go on issue at banks throughout Australia and the Territory of Papua and New Guinea on 29 May, and that further details would be released by the Governor of the Reserve Bank on 15 May.....*

The $5 note, which measures 150 mm x 75 mm, is basically mauve in colour with the main features being overprinted in black. The new note incorporates the highest standards of security printing and attention is especially drawn to the following security features which should be looked for in guarding against the acceptance of counterfeits.

(a) *The main features have been printed by a special printing process from engraved original dies resulting in a raised ink film giving an embossed feel. This is particularly evident on the front of the note where the main black printing can easily be felt by running the fingers across the note.*

(b) *The background printing on the note has been produced in clearly defined patterns of thick and thin lines printed with great clarity.*

(c) *The notes are printed on special paper which has a characteristic feel and special crispness. The paper contains a watermark portrait of Captain Cook and an embedded metal thread running down near the centre.*

FIFTY DOLLARS

The intention to introduce a $50 note was announced on 15 December 1972. A Press Release by the Reserve Bank of Australia on 12 September 1973, gave details (in part):

AUSTRALIAN $50 NOTE

The Governor of the Reserve Bank of Australia, Sir John Phillips, announced today that the Australian $50 note would be available from banks on 9 October 1973. Sir John said that the intention to issue the new note had been announced on 15 December 1972.

The $50 note was designed by Mr. Gordon Andrews, the designer of the notes of the other denominations already in circulation; he received considerable research assistance in assembling material on which the design was based from, in particular, Sir Macfarlane Burnet, Professor Sir Rutherford Robertson and the Commonwealth Scientific & Industrial Research Organisation....

The $50 note, measuring 165 millimetres by 82.5 millimetres, is 5 millimetres longer and 2.5 millimetres wider than the $20 note, thus conforming to the progressive sizes of the current issues. It bears on both front and back the heading 'Australia' instead of 'Commonwealth of Australia' which currently appears on other denominations; corresponding changes have been made in the legal tender clause on the note. It is intended to incorporate these changes progressively in all Australian notes.

The new note is predominantly gold in colour with the main features overprinted in blue-black, brown and green..(similar security details to $5 then)*...a watermark consisting of multiple portraits of Captain Cook appearing on the left-hand side when looking at the front.*

SPECIAL AUTHORITY FOR PRESS AND TELEVISION STATIONS

Authority under the Reserve Bank Act 1959-1966 is given to press and television stations to publish black and white photographs of the front and back of the Australian $50 note, subject to their not forming part of an advertisement and, in the case of press reproduction, the *dimensions not exceeding 130 millimetres x 65 millimetres. The authority does not extend to the separate sale or issue of photographs of the note. This authority expires on 11 October 1973 after which all negatives, prints, blocks and other relevant material must be destroyed.*

Official records of the final preparations for designing and producing the $50 and $100 notes were still within the 30 years closed period (at the time of writing) and thus not available for public perusal and study until at least the years 2004 and 2015 respectively.

Decimal Currency Conversion Table

BANKING AND ACCOUNTING TABLE

Conversion of Amounts of £ s. d. to Dollars and Whole Cents

Pence	Cents	Shillings	Cents	£ s. d.	$
1	1	1	10	10 0	1.00
2	2	2	20	11 0	1.10
3	2	3	30	12 0	1.20
4	3	4	40	13 0	1.30
5	4	5	50	14 0	1.40
6	5	6	60	15 0	1.50
7	6	7	70	16 0	1.60
8	7	8	80	17 0	1.70
9	8	9	90	18 0	1.80
10	8	10	100	19 0	1.90
11	9			1 0 0	2.00
12	10				

The Banking and Accounting Table converts £ s. d. amounts expressed in whole pence to decimal currency amounts expressed in whole cents. (It is consistent with section 10 of the *Currency Act*, 1963.)

To convert an amount of £ s. d. to dollars and cents:

* Multiply the pounds by two—to give dollars
* Add the equivalent of the shillings and pence

e.g., £23 17s. 10d.

£23 (× 2)	$46.00	
17s. 10d.	1.78	(from table)
£23 17s. 10d.	$47.78	

A Decimal Currency Board Publication

Fig. 63. Decimal Currency Board Decimal Currency Conversion Table.
(Commonwealth of Australia copyright reproduced by permission).

ONE HUNDRED DOLLARS

The intention to introduce a $100 note was announced on 8 July 1983. A Press Release by the Reserve Bank of Australia dated 20 March 1984, gave details (in part):

> *AUSTRALIAN $100 NOTE*
>
> *Details of the design of the new Australian $100 note which will be available from banks on 26 March 1984 were released by the Reserve Bank today.*
>
> *The note was designed by Mr. Harry Williamson, a graphic designer of Sydney, New South Wales. Staff of the Reserve Bank's Note Printing Branch advised on special aspects of security printing and translated the design to the printing plates in consultation with Mr. Williamson. Gordon Andrews, designer of the notes already in circulation, and Mr. Philip Cox acted as consultants. The theme of the note is scientific discovery...*
>
> *...The new note measures 172 x 82.5 mm. It is 7 mm longer than and the same height as the $50 note. The differential in length was adopted after consultation about features which could help the blind and visually impaired to distinguish the note.*
>
> *The $100 note has a multicoloured background but is predominantly blue/grey. The serial numbers are printed on diagonally opposite corners of the back of the note. The number in the upper left corner is printed in black and that in the lower right corner is printed in blue. The numbering system continues that used for the existing series of notes; the prefix letters ZAA-ZZZ have been allocated to the $100 note and the numbers will comprise six digits. The signatures and legal tender clause are printed in blue on the front of the note:* (Similar security features to the $50 note were listed)....
>
> *Attached are further notes about Mawson and Tebbutt and outline drawings of the note detailing particular items depicted in the design...*

To present the new note to the public a 30 second and a 60 second "Commercial" and a short documentary were prepared by the Reserve Bank for screening on television. James Dibble was the presenter of the commercials. The note was shown to the public for the first time on 20 March, 1984.

Despite the criticisms and the $10 forgeries of 1966-67, the new notes survived and became accepted - so much so, that many people still preferred them to the new polymer notes which began to replace them from 1992. By 1996, after the introduction of the polymer $100, paper notes all but disappeared from circulation.

A proclamation under the Currency Act 1965 appeared in the Commonwealth Gazette of 8 June 1967 which signalled the end of Australia's dual currency period which had operated from 14 February, 1966. As from 1 August, 1967, Dollars and Cents became Australia's sole legal currency and all financial transactions were to be solely in $ & c. Further reading: *Australian Coin Review*, July 1967.

Chapter 4: PRINTING THE NOTES

This chapter is set out in three parts: (A), Fitzroy; (B), Craigieburn and (C), Note paper and security features.

Part A - FITZROY

Fig. 64. South-western corner, Note Printing Branch, Fitzroy, 1981.

The printing of Australian notes was first carried out in the King's Warehouse (now Queen's Warehouse) situated in an area bound by Blyth Street, Wharf Road and Footscray Road, West Melbourne. Those premises are discussed in detail in *Australian Banknotes*, Second Edition.

In 1924, new premises were occupied at 115 Victoria Parade, Fitzroy (Melbourne). These premises were expanded and enlarged over the years and ended up occupying an entire block. There the designing and printing of pre-decimal and decimal notes and stamps took place, as well as cheques, bonds, securities and other similar material issued or used by the Australian Government.

The Note Issue Department of the Commonwealth Bank of Australia was originally in Collins Street, Melbourne. On moving to Fitzroy in 1933 to share the premises with Note Printing Branch it was renamed Note Issue Branch. The two branches lost their separate identities in 1963 to operate as the Note Issue Department of the Reserve Bank of Australia. See also, Fig. 454.

From 1982, Note Printing activities were transferred to Craigieburn. The Fitzroy premises was originally intended to be retained for use in printing stamps and other material, but it remained vacant, during which time several tele-movies were filmed there. In 1986 a building development company purchased the property. The garages and laundry were demolished and erected in their place were two, five half-storey car parks. The rest of the building was completely gutted, renovated and leased as modern office space, and restaurants were planned. For further information on Craigieburn, see Part B, following.

The production of Australian notes involved many different processes and craftsmen from the design stages to the improvement and maintenance of equipment. Some were: Artists and Engravers for engraving and/or repairing printing plates; Chemists for assaying burnt notes claims, or colour-matching ink samples; Carpenters, Engineers, Machinists, Maintenance Engineers, Electricians, Cleaners; Painters and Drivers, are but a few of the classifications.

Some of the processes or machinery purchased included: Mechanical engraving on geometric lathes; Plastic moulding of note images; Electrotyping and composing; Photographic and platemaking; Gravure cylinder making; Drying facilities for printed sheets of notes; Ink mill for mixing and producing ink; Laundry for cleaning wiper cloth; Drilling machines for cancelling spoils; Guillotines for cutting notes; Machines for intaglio printing, background printing or numbering; "Vacuumatic" machines for sheet counting and for note counting and tissue-laying machines for inserting tissue between notes after printing. In addition, there were departments involved in security, purchasing, staff development, production, research and management.

Fig. 65. Geometric lathe used for designing the background print of notes.

An article prepared by the Note Issue Department of the Reserve Bank of Australia in the Bank of Adelaide Staff Magazine, *The Money Makers - banknote production in Australia,* circa 1970, included:

> *The printing plates for this process are prepared from an original hand engraved steel die, using a system of duplication by impression and electro-deposition. Some of the specialist equipment used in these processes has been hand designed and developed by Note Issue Department technicians.*
>
> *The process requires a duplicate of the original die to be made and to be fitted to what is virtually a heating and cooling box. This unit is then used to impress the number of images required into a sheet of plastic, which is held flat by vacuum during the process. The face side of the plastic sheet then receives a fine coating of silver, after which electro-deposition methods are used to produce a metal master plate from which metal altos (negative plates) can in turn be grown. By similar electro-deposition methods the metal altos are used to provide the actual printing plates.*

Portraits were drawn for the engravers from old photographs, chalk drawings and paintings. It took two to three months to engrave a portrait. An engraver borrowed from the United Kingdom to assist with the initial preparations for changeover produced the two portraits on the $20 note, and to the professional eye, the difference in style can be seen.

Fig. 66. Artist putting the finishing touches on a drawing to be used in note production.

Once the master plate had been made, duplicates of it could be prepared and used as printing plates. Three printing plates were fitted to the cylinders in the intaglio presses. A fairly substantial quantity of nickel is used in the manufacture of the printing plates.

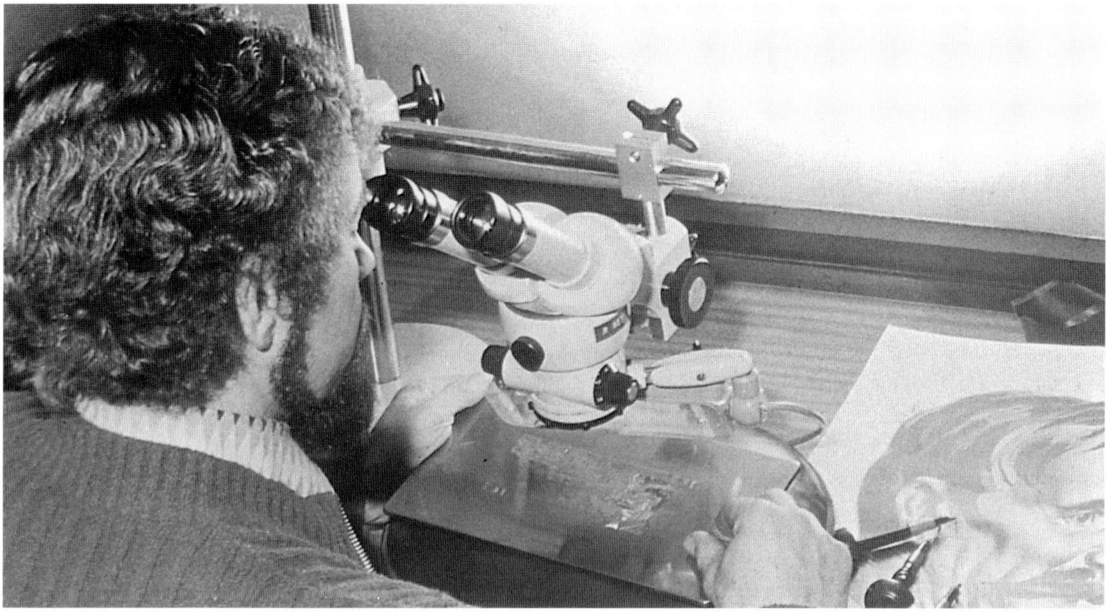

Fig. 67. Hand engraving original die.

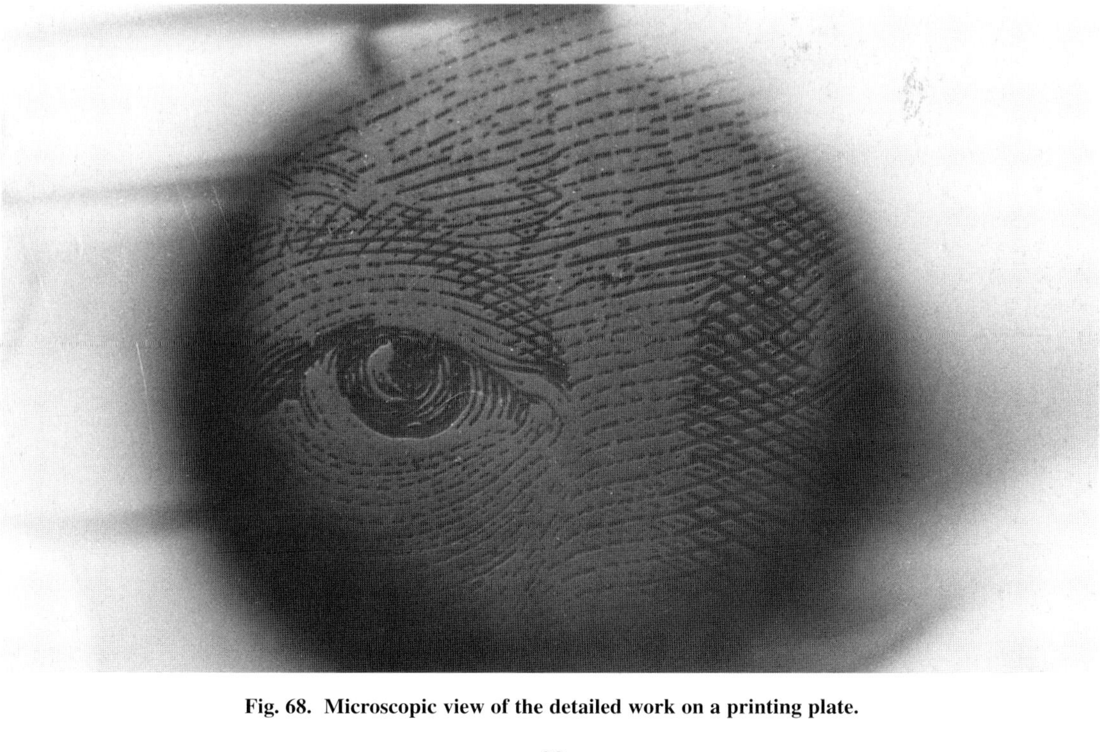

Fig. 68. Microscopic view of the detailed work on a printing plate.

Fig. 69. Plate separation.

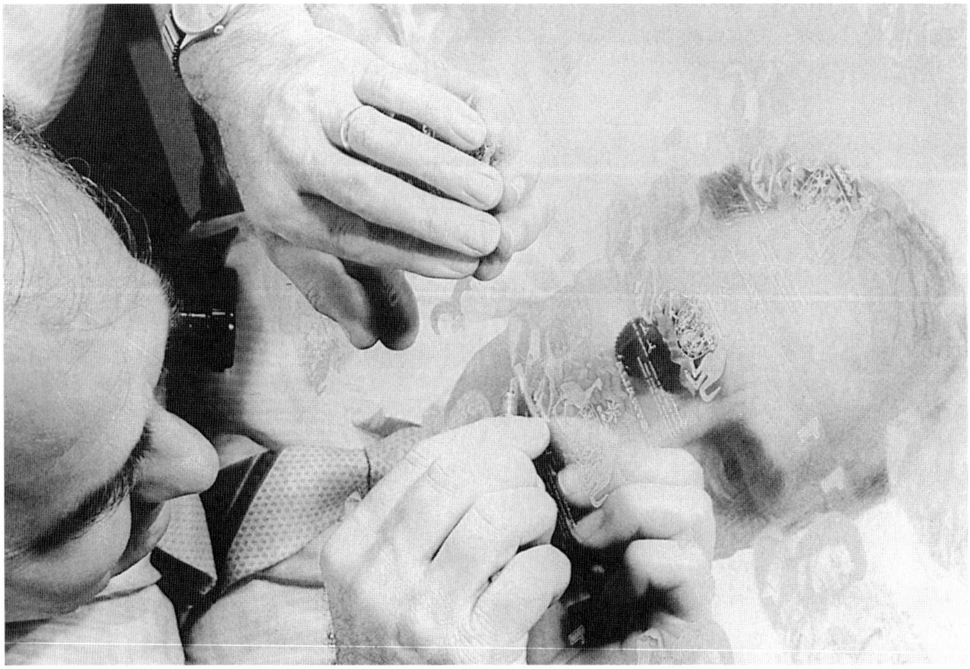

Fig. 70. Repairing a damaged printing plate.

Fig. 71. Measuring a quantity of pigment for a batch of ink.

The ink used for note printing is prepared in-house. One of the N.P.A. (Craigieburn) displays explained the various processes used in ink production in the following terms: "Pigments" are the solids or colouring matter in the ink obtained from either of two groups - inorganic material derived from minerals and organic material synthesised from complex organic intermediates. "Vehicles" are the resins of various types blended with selected vegetable oils, the composition of which determines its printability. "Driers" are metal catalysts needed to accelerate the oxidation drying process of an ink, with "additives" including compounds and reducers to control the characteristics of ink flow. Other additives such as anti-oxidation and slip compounds are used to impart the required properties.

Fig. 72. Final dispersion and milling the ink before use.

Perfecting the background design and colours on notes called for programming with a geometric lathe, a long intricate process of building up the background tints onto glass negatives. The lines produced by such a lathe ironed out the crude quality of the originals which were hand drawn. The master lines produced are stepped and repeated to the overall pattern. The patterns are eventually separated into their particular colours and separate plates are produced for each colour. See Fig. 65.

Original work on background designs was carried out at Organisation Giori in Milan, Italy, necessitating visits to Italy by the designer and managerial and technical staff. Thus the background printing plates for the denominations were originally produced in Milan, but the original set of five printing plates for the $20 notes was produced at Note Printing Branch. Now all such plates are produced in Australia.

Fig. 73. Simultan (background design) printing machine.

The Note Printing Branch of the Reserve Bank of Australia had considered for some time, upgrading and purchasing of additional equipment. The decision to "go decimal" gave them the opportunity to do that. Two "Simultan" indirect letterpress machines made by Koenig and Bauer A.G. of West Germany were purchased in association with Organisation Giori, a firm specialising in security printing installation.

The Simultan is an intricate machine employing the dry offset (or indirect letterpress) process which was used for the multi-coloured backgrounds of the notes. It is capable of printing three designs on one side and two on the other simultaneously as the sheet passes through the machine - hence the name "Simultan". It can also introduce different colours into each design. The first printing process of the decimal notes is the run through the simultan machine to print the background design.

In considering the purchase of new machines, comparisons were made between machines, their costs and the costs of incidentals, and between Organisation Giori and Thomas De La Rue.

Incidentals including plate making, various capabilities as to production, and ability to stick to the strict timetable, were important factors. In the end there was some doubt that De La Rue's had enough experience either of their prototype machine or of the techniques required in that field, and the General Manager of Note Issue Department (W.H. Wilcock) in a letter to the Governor of the Bank on 5 September, 1963, asked that authority be given to proceed with the purchase of two Giori five colour dry offset machines, at a cost of approximately 185,000 Australian pounds, with ancillary equipment estimated to cost approximately 30,000 pounds. A decision on the purchase of a numbering machine was deferred (Reserve Bank Archives file N-a-156).

A letter for the General Manager, Note Printing Branch, to the Governor, Sydney, on 16 September, 1964, advised the new machinery ordered (N-a-414).

> *MACHINERY - GIORI SIMULTAN DRY OFFSET PRESSES*
>
> *We refer to our letter of 19th September, 1963, and now advise for record purposes that the undermentioned four orders for equipment, for the two Giori Simultan Dry Offset Presses mentioned in the above letter, have been placed with:-*
>
> 1. *Security Printing Machinery and Equipment Ltd., Weinbergstrazze 3, Zurich 1, Switzerland - for one Security Printing Multinex Machine and Accessories at a cost of U.S. $21,954 C.I.F. Melbourne.*
> 2. *Ormag S.R.L., Nevegro Di Segrate (Milano), Via F. Baracca 26, Italy, for one Mercury Vapour Printing Down Installation at a cost of U.S. $5,962 C.I.F. Melbourne.*
> 3. *Rotary Fotogravur, Einrichtungen G.M.G.H., 52 Siegburg Bez. Koln, Alfred Strasse 32-34, West Germany - for Photographic Machinery and Materials at a cost of 83883 Deutschemarks C.I.F. Melbourne.*
> 4. *Klimsch & Co., Schmittstrasse 12, Frankfurt (Main), West Germany - for two Vacuum Printing Frames, Plate Whirler and Security Printing Materials at a cost of 26872.5 Deutschemarks C.I.F. Melbourne.*

With the exchange rates as at 18 September, 1963, the following costs of the items above in Australian pounds was 9,899-17-10, 2,688-9-10, 9,557-2-9, and 3,061-13-11 respectively.

Despite the very best preparations using the best available equipment, one incident regarding the printing of the notes in preparation for decimal currency occurred which is worthy of special comment. At a most crucial stage of the production program, one of the two Simultan machines printing the background designs for the one dollar notes suffered an accidental major breakdown. This necessitated no less than three tons of machine parts being flown out from Germany, together with German engineers to effect speedy repairs, whilst the remaining machine was kept in operation twenty-four hours a day for six weeks (N-a-159).

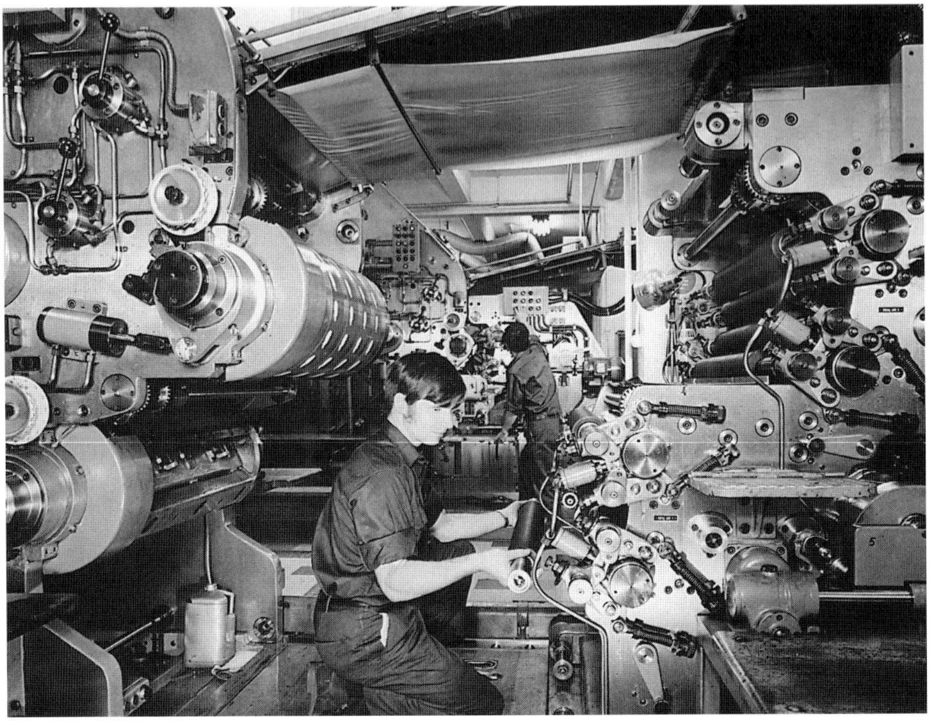

Fig. 74. Checking a Simultan machine.

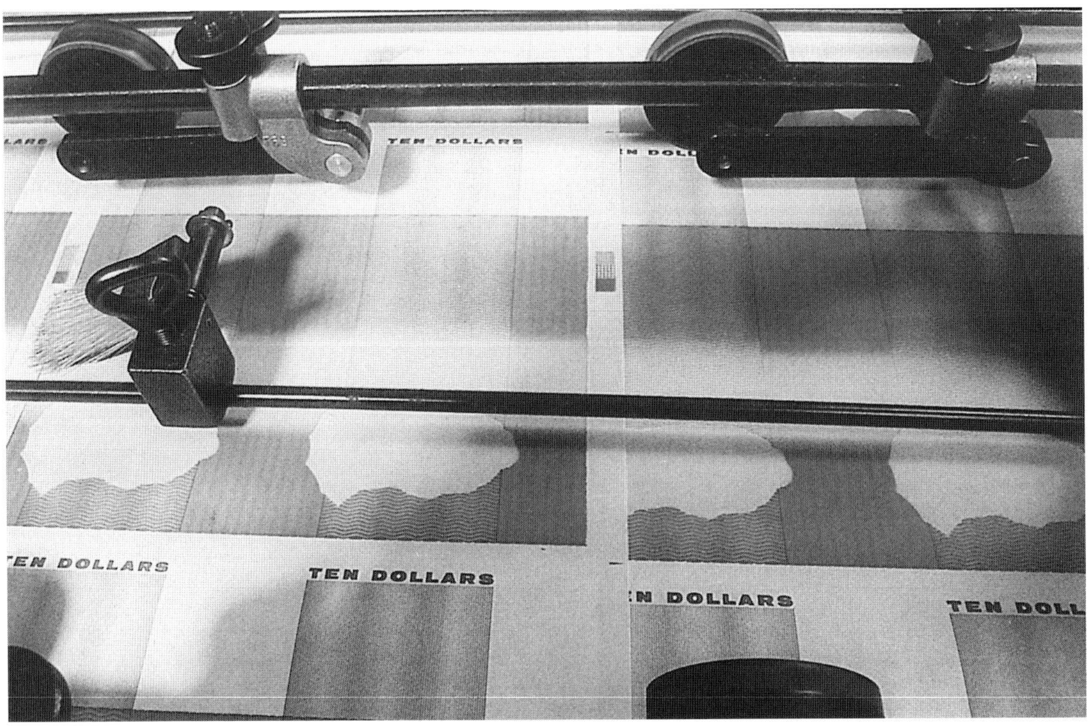

Fig. 75. Simultan printing.

$1 notes were printed 35 to a sheet and all other denominations 24 to a sheet. Later, $2 notes were printed 45 to a sheet, $5, $10 and $20 notes 40 to a sheet, and $50 and $100 notes 32 to a sheet.

Decimal designs were in reverse to the "white line" principle used in the pre-decimal notes. Fine white lines on the paper reading between solid lines of ink made it possible to get some strength and character into the colour. This enabled the superimposing of a hairline in one colour down the centre of another colour in perfect register from one corner of the sheet to another. This took advantage of the Simultan's capability of printing five patterns in one revolution of the machine. The machine is about 11 metres long, uses 19 electric motors to drive various parts, and weighs approximately 29 tonnes.

The background design on the notes has a rainbow effect in that the colours gradually change near the centre. Although standard ink ducts were fitted to the presses, the introduction of a specialised variable control of the oscillation of the inking rollers, even during an ink run, made the presses particularly adaptable to "rainbow" or "iris" printing. Each plate cylinder is served by its own separate inking unit, which in turn, can virtually be turned into a two-colour unit by ink separators in the duct. Using each duct in this manner, it becomes possible to apply six colours in three different designs on one side of a sheet and four colours in two different designs on the other. This method of printing therefore allows ten different colours to be applied to a sheet in one single pass through the press.

The actual printing is carried out from very lightly etched magnesium printing plates transferring their ink film to their appropriate sets of blanket cylinders. In each case the blankets receive the ink transference from the first print cylinders in each bank, and as the blanket cylinders revolve they accept the ink film from each of the printing plates in turn. In timing with this operation, sheets of paper are fed into the press by swing-grippers and pass between the two inked-up offset blanket cylinders under pressure in order to receive their impression.

Two of these machines were initially used, each with a capacity of 6,000 sheets per hour, and a practical speed of 5,000. Infinite care had to be applied in setting up these presses. Special calibrating equipment was used to determine variations in the thickness of blankets and plates before any fitting to the press was undertaken. The make-ready included the use of imported condensor paper .015 mm thick. The benefit obtained from this system of printing lies in the fact that when the press was eventually set up, it allowed sheets to be continuously printed with the five designs in correct register, despite any vagaries of the paper due to stretching or shrinkage.

The Super Simultan II is capable of printing up to four designs on each side at up to 8,000 sheets per hour. The Standard Simultan machines were older, smaller and slower and could print two designs on one side of a sheet and three designs on the other at up to 6,000 sheets per hour.

The main features of the notes were printed by the recess process from hand engraved original dies, resulting in a raised ink film. Steel plates, hand engraved, took at least five months to perfect each side. Once the die was completed, a complicated system of duplication of the original die was undertaken by impressions and electro-deposition in order to obtain a master plate. Only one original die could ever be used, as apart from the length of time needed to produce another, it would be impossible for any one engraver, no matter how skilled, to produce two dies that were identical in all dimensions involved in engraving.

The second stage of note printing is the intaglio process. Three machines of Australian design were purchased from R.W. Crabtree and Sons (Australasia) Pty. Ltd. for the printing of the intaglio design of the notes. These were to supplement the ten intaglio machines of English manufacture already in use in the Note Printing Branch. A rate of 1,250 sheets printed an hour per machine produced the most desired result.

The main security feature obtained by the intaglio printing is in the varying ink film thickness that can be deposited onto the paper, which ranges from the finest dots almost invisible to the naked eye, to the heaviest lines where the thickness of the ink can readily be felt by the fingers. In other parts of the world this type of printing is referred to as taille douce, direct plate, steel plate engraving, or copper plate.

Super Intagliocolour machines are designed to print from an engraved surface on one side only and are capable of printing up to three colours from each plate at up to 8,000 sheets per hour. Intagliocolour 6s machines were older, smaller and slower and could print up to 6,000 sheets per hour.

Fig. 76. Printing the main (Intaglio) design.

Fig. 77. Printing $20 notes on the Hoe Press - Intaglio.

Fig. 78. The more advanced Intagliocolour machine later superseded by the Super Intagliocolour machine.

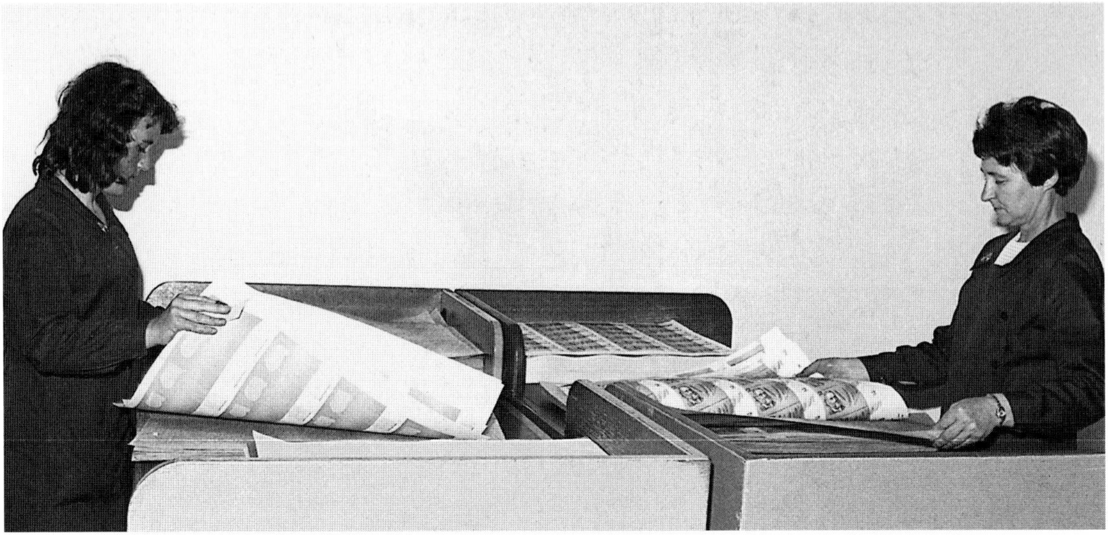

Fig. 79. Sheets of notes being "de-tissued".

Only one side at a time is printed on a sheet. Initially this was because the intaglio ink remained wet for a long time. To prevent "set off" or "wet ink transfer" from one sheet to another, paper referred to as "tissue" was inserted between the sheets of notes. The development of quick-drying inks later, meant that this practice was no longer required. Printing error notes with set off often show a diagonal straight line in the set off which is where the interleaving tissue had folded over and thus failed to prevent the fault. Usually the backs were printed first, then later the fronts. The reason for this was to allow for any changes of signature which might occur from time to time on the fronts.

The raised ink film gives a slightly embossed feel which is considered a security feature. A test to indicate the embossed effect of the intaglio ink can be carried out by placing thin "silver paper" on top of the printing and rubbing firmly to obtain an impression of the design.

The sheets of notes are inspected for printing errors by specially trained staff, and any found with errors or not of the required standard are marked on the front with a special marking pen, similar to a felt pen. In early decimal issues this mark was a large inverted purple tick, and in later issues, a vertical orange line. See Figs. 373 and 374. Sheets which had more than a certain number of cancelled notes were extracted completely and not forwarded for the printing of serial numbers.

The final process was the serial numbering. This was done separately by letterpress machine. A sheet of notes has the same serial numerals on each note, but the serial lettering changes from e.g. AAA, AAB, AAC etc. Sheets are printed and numbered in reams (500). During 1966 to 1971 the practice of issuing star replacement notes (see Chapter 8) kept a section of 100 notes in numerical order (except for any star notes). From 1972, notes were electronically counted and, depending on how many marked error notes were ejected, the chronological sequence could be broken several times, and start e.g. 407 and end 512. Because of the way in which reams are guillotined, it was possible to get sections of notes from banks with identical serial numerals, but different prefix letters. Where one ream ended and another began, a break in serial number prefixes could occur in sections of new notes.

Fig. 80. Printing serial numbers on notes with the Heidelberg letterpress machine.

Fig. 81. Printing serial numbers on notes with a Super Numerota numbering machine.

Fig. 82. Super Numerota numbering machine

Fig. 83. Placing cut notes in order after guillotining, before further processing.

Super Numerota II machines were capable of numbering notes at speeds of up to 8,000 sheets per hour. Super Numerota I machines had the same capabilities, but fewer electronic controls.

The serial letters I, O, M, W and Z were not used in serial lettering in general circulating paper notes from 1966 to 1971 except the Z in star replacement notes from ZAA ($1) to ZXA ($20). After the discontinuation of star notes the Z was introduced into the ordinary issues in the signature combination of Phillips-Wheeler (Australia) . The serial letter combinations first using the Z for other than star notes were BSZ, HGZ, NLZ, TBZ and XJZ for the $1 to $20 notes respectively.

Up to 1971, a serial number sequence started at 000001 and concluded at 1000000. With the discontinuation of star replacement notes it was decided it was no longer necessary to use the number 1000000. Its use was never practical because the letterpress machine which numbered the notes only had 6 digit numbering boxes. To use 1000000 a seventh digit was required which meant printing the number 1000000 on a special hand press. This involved time waste and interruption to the rate of production. Consequently the serial number 1000000 was last used on the following notes in the Phillips-Randall series on the dates shown.

$1	BAL 1000000	13 December 1971
$2	GLR 1000000	25 November 1971
$5	NFT 1000000	1 December 1971
$10	SRP 1000000	3 November 1971
$20	XER 1000000	8 March 1971

Fig. 84. Front, $10 note with 1000000 serial number.

Of the decimal notes printed from 1966 to 1971 with the serial number of 1000000, only fourteen survivors were known as at April 2000. They were:

$1 Coombs-Wilson (AFE); Phillips-Randall (ANC, AVK, AXB): Knight-Wheeler (DBP).
$2 Coombs-Wilson (FBS); Phillips-Randall (GBX, GJK, GJL, GKQ).
$10 Coombs-Wilson (SAY); Coombs-Randall (SEV illustrated); Phillips-Randall (SQU).
$20 Coombs-Wilson (XAU).

There were also 52 pre-decimal 1000000 notes known to have survived. Further reading: *The Oldest Surviving Million Note*, Michael Vort-Ronald, *Australian Coin Review*, April, 2000.

Fig. 85. Guillotining a ream into individual notes.

A ream of sheets is guillotined into bundles of 500 notes and sealed. At all times during the printing processes extensive security is maintained. Each time a stack of sheets is handled, the notes are machine counted and a record card with the notes is signed by the two handlers.

During the first years of decimal currency, following inspection in sheet form and guillotining, the decimal notes in sections of 100 were hand fanned to find any notes with the inverted tick marking. Those marked were removed and star replacement notes (from a special section) were inserted by hand, (see Fig. 86). The serial numbers of the star notes bore no relationship to the serial numbers of the notes being replaced.

All notes now pass through an electronic counting machine which incorporates a Crosfield or scanning head device. The machine counts and wraps the notes in "Sections" of 100 and at the same time, any notes with the felt pen mark are detected by the scanning head and separated into another part of the machine. As this occurs the serial numbers of the error notes are recorded on a printout. Eventually those notes are counted and bundled prior to destruction and their totals balanced off against the printed record and the bulk notes intended for circulation. See Printing Errors, Chapter 9, for examples of error markings.

Initially, each Section was bound with a paper wrapper (see Fig. 341) which was later replaced by a plain transparent plastic wrapper. The Sections are bound into a "bundle" (e.g. 10 Sections of 100 notes equals 1,000 notes). On top of each bundle was placed a cardboard label. The bundle label at Fig. 90 is a machine counted label showing that it was done in 1975 (0275 means $2 1975).

Fig. 86. Note checkers hand-fanning to extract faulty notes and replace them with star notes.

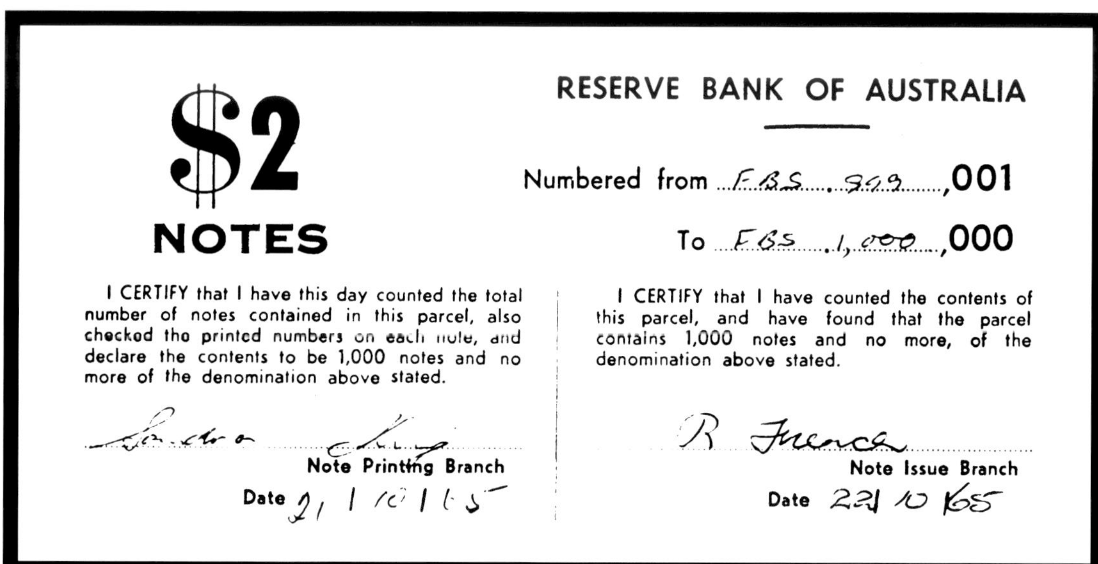

$2 NOTES

RESERVE BANK OF AUSTRALIA

Numbered from F.B.S. 999,001

To FBS 1,000,000

I CERTIFY that I have this day counted the total number of notes contained in this parcel, also checked the printed numbers on each note, and declare the contents to be 1,000 notes and no more of the denomination above stated.

Note Printing Branch

Date 21/10/65

I CERTIFY that I have counted the contents of this parcel, and have found that the parcel contains 1,000 notes and no more, of the denomination above stated.

R. French

Note Issue Branch

Date 22/10/65

Fig. 87. $2 bundle label, hand counted, October 1965 in readiness for changeover, 14 February, 1966.

Fig. 88. Recording $1 exchange numbers.

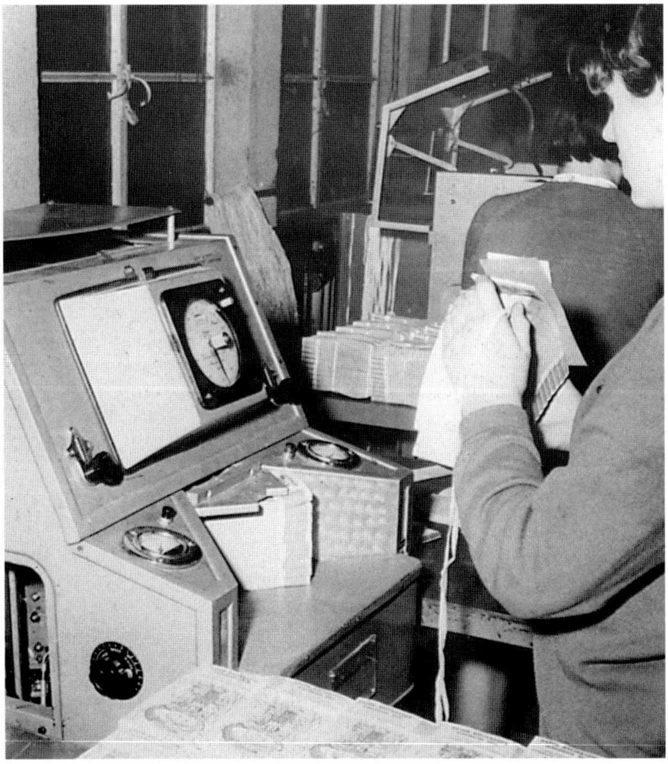

Fig. 89. Vacuumatic note counting machine.

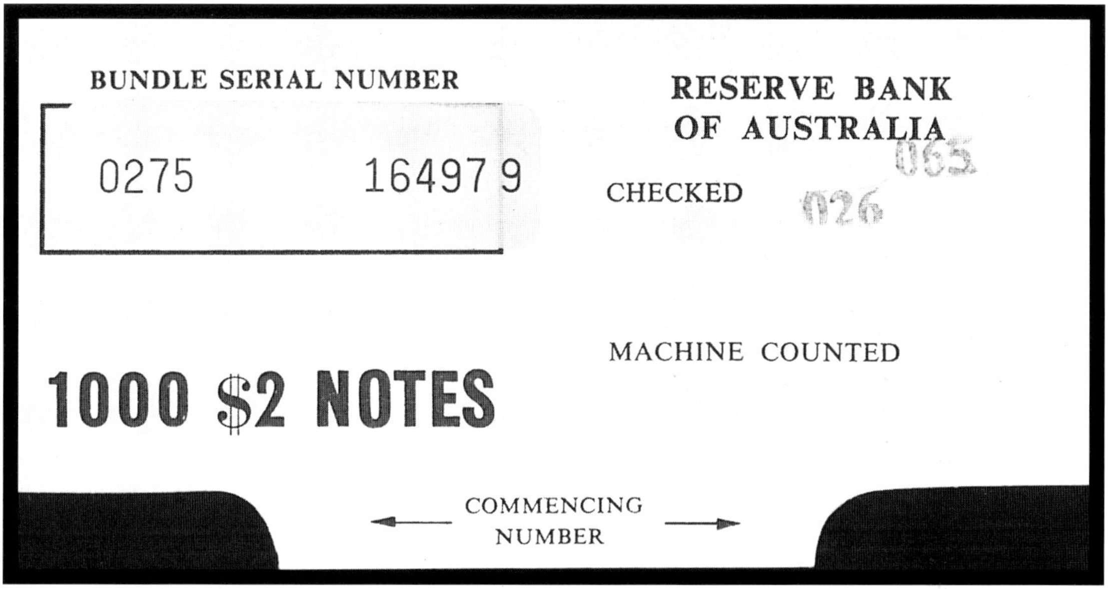

Fig. 90. $2 bundle label, machine counted 1975.

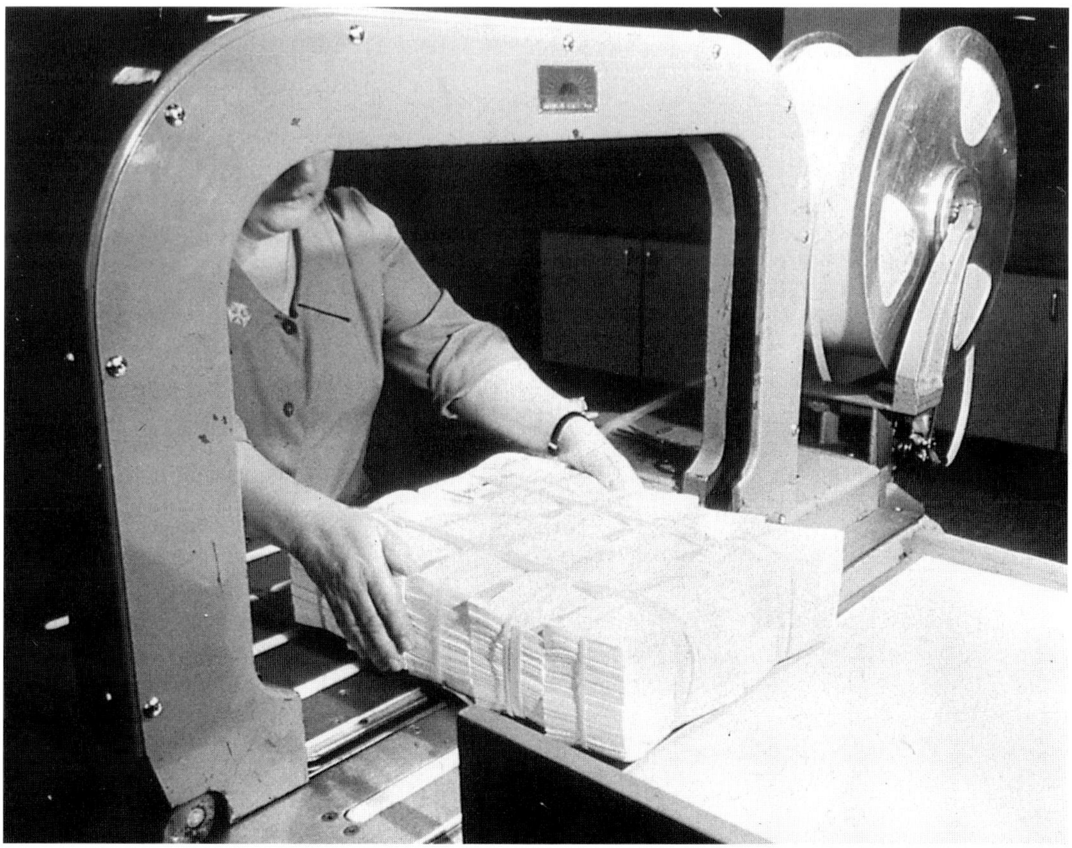

Fig. 91. Bundles of notes being tied, Craigieburn.

Fig. 92. Sub (Shrink) Pack label, 1977.

Ten bundles were machine tied and put into a "Shrink Pack" which then contained 10,000 notes and each shrink pack was labelled accordingly, as illustrated. The shrink pack was then sealed in plastic and containerised with other shrink packs onto wooden pallets for distribution throughout Australia.

In the event of unavoidable delays with the introduction of the first decimal notes, provision was made to use the previous design with dollars printed on them instead of pounds. However, despite enormous difficulties, schedule and quantity was maintained and it was not found necessary to make up printing plates for that purpose, or to obtain additional paper.

Printing of the $1 note commenced in April 1965 at the Note Printing Branch, Fitzroy. By 20 December, 1965, the 150th million note was delivered to Note Issue Branch, consisting of: $1, fifty million, $2, sixty million, $10, thirty million and $20, ten million. By the end of 1965 the total stock of notes in all denominations was 152,860,000, and by the changeover to decimal currency, 160 million.

The pride in a job well done was best expressed in a letter from W.H. Wilcock to the Secretary of the Reserve Bank of Australia on 25 January, 1966, quoting a letter he had received from Russell (Tass) Drysdale, a little less than three weeks before conversion (N-a-148).

> *Yesterday I received a letter from Nugget in the morning, and a visit from Mr. Longmuir in the evening with a copy of the album with the notes so nicely arranged. It was tremendously exciting; and Longmuir, my wife and I sat about the table like children, passing it to one another and reached that mood when we all felt very much that we were, without saying it, intensively Australian.*
> *How pleased and proud you chaps must be. The notes are splendid. The notes are the very fine end product of what was a magnificent operation. Right from the top down through the ranks to the man who oils the machines. I think your boys in the Branch did a marvellous job, so good that it seems almost impertinent to ask you to give them my most sincere congratulations. I feel absurdly proud to know that in a small way I was associated with them. I only wish I could be home for D-Day.*
> *Please give Brownie my best wishes indeed, all who worked so hard to make this great success.*
> *Last night we drank a toast to you all in Melbourne.*

Part B: - CRAIGIEBURN

In 1969, a working committee was set up to make recommendations about the future life of the Fitzroy site. Early the following year that committee recommended that planning commence for a note printing works located on a new and much larger site. Planning and working committees were then set up. The Commonwealth Department of Housing and Construction was then commissioned as architects and engineers for the project. In March, 1971, PA Australia was appointed to advise in the general area of production management. Later that year, representatives of all major parties concerned in the project visited note printing establishments in the United Kingdom, America, Europe, Mexico and Thailand to familiarise themselves with the latest developments. In 1972 the Craigieburn site consisting of 26 hectares of land was purchased, having been chosen after inspection of a total of 21 sites.

The Bank accepted a tender of $1,874,000 from Lewis Construction Co. Pty. Ltd. for the first stage of the construction including site preparation and excavation for the production and service buildings, foundations of the production building including service tunnels, internal road system and carpark, stormwater, water supply and sewerage systems and the outer perimeter security fence. The contractor was given possession of the site on 3 November, 1976, and work commenced at the site on 8 November. The contract provided for completion by 3 August, 1977, and the initial site works were completed on 6 February, 1978.

The Bank accepted a tender of $27,868,684 from the same construction company for Contract 2, the major construction phase of the new note printing works, and work commenced immediately. The contract included construction of the production building, services building, flammable liquids store, trade waste treatment plant and general services.

In 1978 a planning group was set up at Note Issue Department, Fitzroy, to oversee the move from Fitzroy to Craigieburn. The printing hall (the largest of the buildings) was handed over to the Bank in June 1980 and the Bank took over the whole complex on 4 May, 1981.

On that date the Note Printing Branch of the Reserve Bank of Australia prepared to move to its new premises alongside the Hume Highway near Craigieburn, Victoria, about 25 km north of Melbourne. The relocation represented a move from the crowded inner industrial area of Melbourne to an open semi-rural environment zoned for industrial and residential development. The main move of staff was planned for 20 July, 1981, but took place in October, and the last of the existing plant was uplifted from Fitzroy in March 1982.

The key requirement was for minimum interruption to production of notes during the move, and involved the installation and commissioning of new production equipment at Craigieburn before transferring the existing Fitzroy machines. The last day on which notes were printed at Fitzroy was 13 November, 1981, and Craigieburn went solo from 19 October, 1981.

Note printing equipment at the old works consisted mainly of three dry-offset presses, two water-wipe intaglio presses, thirteen old-style calico-wipe intaglio machines, one modern numbering press, four old-style flat-bed letterpress machines used for numbering, five electronic note sorting units and a range of guillotines and other equipment for finishing operations.

Fig. 93. Note Printing Branch, Craigieburn, under construction, 1980.

The aerial photograph (illustrated above) was taken by David Gray for, and reproduced by courtesy of, the Shire of Bulla, Sunbury, Victoria. See also, Frontispiece.

Fig. 94. Note Printing Australia, Craigieburn, Victoria.

In the move to Craigieburn most of the old-style equipment was discarded and new machines purchased to complement relocated plant. Only one of the old "Hoe" machines was transferred. Some additional equipment purchased included:

(a) One "Super Simultan" (background) dry/wet offset press.
(b) Three "Super Intagliocolour" presses, and
(c) One "Super Numerota MK II" numbering press.

All new machines were of larger sheet size capacity and incorporated the latest technological ancillaries. Despite the fact that new machines were being used, note printing procedures generally followed along similar lines to those which were conducted in the former premises at Fitzroy.

Three buildings comprised the new complex - Production building, Staff Centre and Service building situated within a 26 hectare site surrounded by open, windswept and largely featureless landscape. A number of designers submitted proposals for the landscaping of the actual site and Robert Boyle and Associates was selected to develop a plan for the site and co-ordinate construction. As a special feature Robert Boyle established a collection of the flora illustrated on the $5 note. The plants, permanently labelled, are situated in the garden areas between the Production building and the Staff Centre. The Production building is about 100 metres square and rises some 20 metres above the surrounding site. It houses all the production processes related to the manufacture of Australian notes, as well as other specialised security printing.

Fig. 95. Note Printing Australia, Craigieburn Printing Hall, floor layout.

Fig. 96. A sheet of $10 notes before guillotining.

On 14 January, 1984, an article appeared in *The Herald* by Keith Moor and photographer Ian Baker which described operations at the Note Printing Works. The above illustration and Fig. 68 are from that article, courtesy of *The Herald.*

At Craigieburn the Staff Centre provides meals and recreation facilities for all employees on site. The Service Building houses boilers, refrigeration and ancillary power generation plant and related equipment, along with facilities for the destruction of soiled notes and process wastes. A new feature not previously available in the old works was the provision for a fully enclosed public tour and exhibition area.

The responsibility of making and guarding Australia's paper money is taken extremely seriously and security is at least equal to that of any note printing facility in the world. Other such institutions were inspected during the design stages at Craigieburn and the best features incorporated into the design of the new works. More than 50 armed guards patrol and man doors inside the electronically operated steel-barred doors of the complex. The guards have a firing range within the grounds and are required to have regular target practice.

More than 50 closed-circuit television cameras scan the Production building and surrounding area at all times. Other armed guards work inside a control room which monitors signals through a series of television cameras capable of revolving and zooming at the flick of a switch, and unauthorised entry into the grounds can be detected by any one of the many ultra-sensitive micro-wave devices placed in between the two perimeter fences surrounding the buildings.

Organised tours of the note printing works were approved in July 1984 and by the end of 1987 in excess of 14,000 visitors, mostly children and retired people, had visited the complex. The exhibition and display gallery at Craigieburn, aptly named "Our World of Money", was opened in 1988 on the Level 2 Mezzanine Floor and conducted as a "self discovery tour". Admission by the public was free by appointment from 9 am to 2.30 pm Monday to Friday. The Northern Gallery exhibited an antique Albion Press, an explanation of the role and function of the Reserve Bank of Australia, and a short history of Australia's former note printing establishments. Various bays were provided for public viewing onto the production floor below. The main attraction for the visitor was the huge printing hall, which measured 81.5 metres long, 38.5 metres wide and 10.4 metres high, viewed as below:

- Bay 1 - Guillotining and quality control.
- Bay 2 - Notes finishing, computer recording and packaging.
- Bay 3 - Simultan (offset) printing process.
- Bay 4 - Intaglio (recessed) printing process.
- Bay 5 - Notes numbering (letterpress), other security printing equipment and the Hoe intaglio machines.
- Bay 6 - Other security products and notes examination.
- Bay 7 - Notes examination.

Other displays depicted how a banknote is made, and substrates, watermarks and security threads. The Southern Gallery showed artists and their designs, design elements of issued and unissued Australian notes, Geometric lathe and a diorama of an engraver's (Frank Manley) workshop in the 1920s. It also explained and displayed printing methods, the technology of Simultan and Intaglio printing, security printing inks, wartime printings, bonds and other securities, and the printing of Australia's first distinctive banknote, the Ten Shilling note of 1913.

The Eastern Gallery had amenities and a shop, a "did you know" section, and displays of old ancillary machinery, the world's largest banknote?, awards won by NPB, ancient currency, the main exhibit - "200 years of Currency in Australia", a banknote display, gold, coins (including the rare 1930 penny), counterfeits, travellers' cheques and other temporary exhibits. Another display depicted the 1988 commemorative $10 polymer note.

Later, Stage 2 was developed and further interpretive displays were added. These included the Security Control Room, the meaning of "Craigieburn" and what was on the site of the printing works originally, and a recorded tape of "Bill Comerford" who handled the first ten shilling notes to be completed. Other displays included full sheets of notes printed for Australia and for overseas countries, "everyday" products made from recycled polymer notes, mutilated notes, notes issued by other countries and a Video Theatre where various shows could be seen, as had appeared on commercial television such as "Burke's Backyard". For the first time, visitors could inspect an intaglio printing plate at close range. Of special interest was a number of "hands on" exhibits which showed ink making and geometric drawings in operation.

Unfortunately this first-class facility, largely the concept of N.P.A.s Alan Flint with contributions from many of N.P.A.s tradesmen, was eventually closed to the public on 29 August, 1997, partly due to the lack of public transport to the works, and the decline from over 20,000 visitors a year in its hey-day, to 2,000. It is still shown to visiting V.I.Ps and prospective customers from overseas.

Part of the facility was the Gallery Shop which sold souvenirs and numismatic items. N.P.A. also regularly attended coin fairs with a stand to sell special products, as illustrated below.

Fig. 97. Note Printing Australia's stand selling uncut $100 notes at a coin fair.

A banknote's life began when it was printed, checked (replaced if faulty) then batched. The notes in bundles of 10,000 pieces were wrapped and bound into a shrink pack which was then numbered and "stored". Shrink packs were then distributed to Reserve Bank branches where they were held in secure storage until opened and "became money". Therefore, 10 bundles of 1,000 notes were then available for issue to banks as required.

Fig. 98. Examining sheets of $20 for faulty notes.

After the notes were received by various banks they were issued into circulation and moved within society during normal trading. In the course of business the notes re-entered the banking system and were either reissued to the public or the notes forwarded to the Reserve Bank branch in that State which accepted and checked them. If they were in acceptable condition for public use they were reissued to bank branches which, in turn, returned them back to the public sector. If found unacceptable they were cancelled and later returned to the Bank's Note Printing Branch for destruction.

In later years CVCS machines at Reserve Bank branches checked the condition of notes during counting and either repackaged them into sections of 100, or destroyed them by shredding or granulating. See Chapter 11.

On 12 February, 1990, the Reserve Bank announced that its note printing activities would be carried out by an entirely separate division trading under the name of Note Printing Australia (N.P.A.). On 1 July, 1998, the Bank further announced that it had converted its existing division, Note Printing Australia, into a separately incorporated wholly-owned subsidiary of the Bank, to be known as Note Printing Australia Limited. To differentiate between the old and the new, Campbell Fallaw in N.P.A.s Art and Design Department, designed a new logo.

Part C: NOTE PAPER, WATERMARKS AND OTHER FEATURES

The paper used for notes prior to decimal currency was a fine quality mixture of cotton and linen. The ingredients used for the paper were primarily specially selected new cotton and linen cuttings which were first cleaned mechanically to remove dust and foreign matter, and then boiled in a large rotary boiler with lime under steam pressure for several hours. The lime removed impurities and colours and the rags were then transferred to a machine which reduced them to individual fibres. To the fibrous material was then added resin or glue, colouring matter, and fillers to produce a consistent finished product.

The paper for decimal (and pre-decimal) notes was manufactured by Portals Ltd. of London. The decimal paper was said to be the same as that used prior to decimalisation, except that the watermarks were changed and a metallic security thread was embedded in the paper during manufacture. Melamine resin was also added to the paper to give it greater wearing properties. When the $100 note was issued in 1984 it had the appearance of thinner paper, as a section of 100 notes was not as thick as a section of $50 notes. The paper used however, was standard Australian note paper with standard inclusions. It is likely that the difference in thickness from other notes may have been due to the amount of raised intaglio ink in the design which varied from denomination to denomination.

In December, 1981, the *Canberra Times* reported that the Reserve Bank was experimenting with a number of techniques and processes to make notes harder to forge. While the Bank would not concede that plastic-based currency was being considered, it was admitted to be a possibility.

The first circulating polymer note in Australia was a commemorative $10 for the Bi-centenary of Australia in 1988. As it was issued at the same time as paper $10 notes it will be briefly included in Chapter 13, and discussed more fully in *Australian Polymer Banknotes* to be published after 2001. The $5 paper note was replaced by a polymer note in 1992 and each year thereafter a further higher denomination was replaced by polymer, concluding in 1996 with the $100. These are also shown briefly in Chapter 13, but will be dealt with in much more detail in *Australian Polymer Banknotes.*

Watermarks

Watermarks are designs or distinguishing marks inserted into the paper at the time of manufacture to guard against counterfieting. They are produced as a raised pattern in which fewer fibres appear in the thinned bulk, or by a depressed pattern in which there is a heavy fibre concentration causing shading. Light and shade watermarks were first devised in 1845, although the art of watermarking has been known since the late 13th century. The design is etched in a thin sheet of wax from which a die is cast in relief. It is then applied to a dandy-roll, a cylinder covered with wire cloth which rides on a wet web of paper during manufacture. The result is that the paper is either thinned or thickened in a specific area to form a pattern or design.

All paper notes from $1 to $20 had a watermark of the profile of Captain James Cook on the left side of the front, which was slightly different to that used on the pre-decimal notes. The watermark was a mixture of light and dark watermark measuring approximately 32 mm x 24 mm. The $50 and $100 notes had Cook watermarks comprised of two complete profiles in the centre of the left side of the front, one in dark watermark and the other in light watermark. Above and below the two complete profiles is a half profile, with the half and full profiles in vertical line and alternating in dark and light watermark. See also, page 154, *Elimination of watermark proposal.*

Fig. 99. Captain James Cook multiple watermarks in the $50 note.

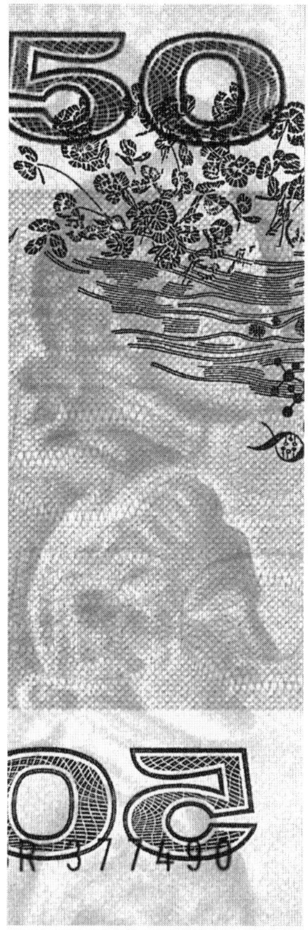

Fig. 100. Captain James Cook

Fig. 101. Cook watermark, $20 note.

The most comprehensive and best-illustrated book observed on Cook is *The Voyages of Captain Cook* by Rex and Thea Rienets, Hamlyn Publishing Group, 1968, England, from which the illustration above was reproduced, courtesy of Reed Educational and Professional Publishing. Cook was persuaded by Joseph Banks to sit for this portrait by Nathaniel Dance in 1776, before he left England on his final voyage. The original painting is in the National Maritime Museum, Greenwich, England.

Captain James Cook

James Cook was born in Yorkshire, England, on 27 October, 1728. As a boy he worked as a farmhand, stable boy and grocer's apprentice. At the age of 18 years he signed indentures for three years with Walker Brothers, Whitby coal shippers. After his apprenticeship he was appointed to the *Mary*, and later, at the age of 24 years, he was appointed mate on the *Friendship*. In 1755 he left the *Friendship* and volunteered for service in the Royal Navy. On July 30, 1757, after service on the *Eagle,* he joined *H.M.S. Solebay* as master, and later, *H.M.S. Pembroke*. From 1758 to 1764 he commanded various ships engaged in survey work.

On 29 March, 1768, the Navy Board purchased a cat-built barque for a voyage to observe the transit of Venus across the Sun's face which was due on 3 June, 1769. On 26 May, 1768, Cook's commission as Lieutenant was signed and the following day he joined the *Endeavour*. The transit observations in Tahiti were successfully carried out and he then sailed to the eastern side of the North Island of New Zealand where he spent the following six months charting the whole coastline.

He then made a running survey of the eastern coast of New Holland (Australia) to its northern extremity. The *Endeavour* fell in with the coast at Point Hicks (named after Zachary Hicks, the First Lieutenant who first sighted it) on 20 April, 1770. From Point Hicks he worked northward, landing at Botany Bay on 29 April, 1770, where he spent a week before proceeding up the coast to Torres Strait. In August, at Possession Island near Cape York, he annexed under the name ***New South Wales***, the coastline he had charted for the first time. In August, 1771, after arriving back in England, he was presented to King George III and was handed his commission of the rank of Commander.

Cook then made plans to completely circumnavigate the world in high southern latitudes. He left England in 1772 and returned on 30 July 1775, completing one of the longest and most dangerous voyages ever undertaken. In February, 1776, he was elected a Fellow of the Royal Society, to which organisation he elaborated his methods for the prevention of scurvy, a task that no-one had previously achieved.

In 1776 a reward of 20,000 pounds was offered for the discovery of a north-west passage from Hudson Bay to the Pacific. Cook left on 12 July 1776 in the *Resolution* to sail to New Zealand via the Cape, then Tahiti, and to work along the North American coast. On 18 January, 1778, he discovered what are now known as the Hawaiian Islands. After exploring other areas he returned to the Hawaiian Islands, but was killed by natives there on 14 February, 1779. As a circumnavigator Cook stands unequalled for the magnitude and accuracy of his work, which was achieved in a relatively short time.

Reference: *Australian Encyclopaedia,* 3rd edition, 1977, Sydney, The Grolier Society of Australia.
Further reading: *The Voyages of Captain Cook*, Rex and Thea Rienits, Paul Hamlyn, England, 1970.

In 1987, the Australian National Maritime Museum endorsed the idea of a full-scale and authentic museum replica of HM Bark *Endeavour* to be built for the people of Australia as a Bicentennial gift funded by the Bond Corporation. Work began in Fremantle, Western Australia, in January, 1988, but ran into financial difficulties, was saved, and is now owned and operated by a non-profit organisation. The ship was launched on 9 December, 1983, and commissioned on 16 April, 1994.

The replica is 33 metres long with a beam of 8.89 metres and displaces 550 tonnes. It carries a crew of 15 full-time professionals with a voyage crew of 30.

Reference and further reading: *A Model Project,* RBA Currency magazine, April 1995; *Endeavour - the Ship that Helped Discover Australia* Mick Vort-Ronald, *Australian Coin Review*, December 1999 - January 2000.

Metallic security thread.

The metallic security thread in decimal banknote paper commenced as an aluminium strip enclosed in plastic about half a millimetre wide, which was embedded in the paper during manufacture. When decimal notes were first introduced, this thread was positioned approximately 65 mm from the left edge of the front of the notes for the $1, and 70 mm from the left in all other denominations.

In July 1976, all paper despatched from the Note Printing Branch's suppliers (Portals in England) had this thread positioned in an area about 55 mm from the left edge of the front in all notes. This was to avoid the natural fold area which, because of the close proximity of the thread, caused undue wear and tearing.

A metallized plastic thread was later used for the same purpose, the position of which could vary up to 5 mm either way of the 55 mm to assist in stacking of new notes. If the thread was placed in the same position on all notes, the extra thickness in the area of the thread would have caused each section to be uneven.

In January 1980, it was proposed in Parliament that additional metal threads should be inserted in future notes to make them more identifiable by the visually impaired. The Treasurer promised to consider the scheme as part of an overall study of new banknote designs by the Reserve Bank. The proposal was that the threads could be inserted in the left side of the notes - the more threads, the higher the denomination. In December that year the matter was again raised with further proposals that braille could be added, but it was argued that this would not have been of any great assistance because only one in ten blind people are estimated to be able to read braille. It was the practice of many blind people to use a special gauge which measured the width of notes, as each note was wider as the value of the denomination increased. However, the $100 note was issued in 1984 with the same width as the $50, but 7 mm longer.

In June, 1981, the Treasurer gave a further assurance that the Reserve Bank was exploring the technical aspects of putting identifying marks on notes. Newspaper reports of March 1984 quoted a Treasury spokesman as saying that the Reserve Bank would mark the notes so that blind people could distinguish their value, and that the scheme would begin as soon as possible, but nothing occurred.

Articles in the *Age* newspaper by Peter Roberts on 14 September, 1983, revealed that an International patent application lodged in March by the CSIRO and the Reserve Bank of Australia described how plastic notes could be made to change colour in response to the warmth of the human hand or how parts of the notes could be given an unforgeable pattern of changing colour similar to that of moire silk. The first plastic notes were produced on machinery at the CSIRO Division of Applied Organic Chemistry at Fishermen's Bend in the mid 1970s. They were at first printed in $7 denominations, and up to 17 scientists had been working on the notes since 1972.

Plate identification letters.

Plate identification letters were very small letters placed within the designs on paper notes to indicate which printing plate printed which note. This enabled the intaglio plate to be located in the event of notes being printed with faults caused by an imperfection on any particular plate. The following information is summarised from an exhaustive study on the subject by Frank Robinson.

One Dollar.

The Plate Identification Letter (PIL) occurred on the front of the note below the Queen's portrait, to the right of the circular regalia, 5 mm above and to the right of the word "Treasury." The addition of the PIL commenced in the Phillips-Wheeler (Australia) series at serial letters BLH and continued until the end of the $1 notes in the signature combination Johnston-Stone, at DPS.

There were 35 notes per sheet (5 across by 7 down) and plate letters ranged from A to 1K (illustrated next page). A sheet layout was as below, the single letter or numeral-letter being the PIL and the three letters the serial number prefixes. PILs ran left to right and down omitting the letter "I". Serial numbering was down, then left to right, omitting letters "I, M, O, W and Z." DBP (test notes) were numbered separately. The serial letter prefix "Z" was used from BSZ onwards. See Fig. 151.

A BLH	B BLR	C BNA	D BNH	E BNR
F BLJ	G BLS	H BNB	J BNJ	K BNS
L BLK	M BLT	N BNC	O BNK	P BNT
Q BLL	R BLU	S BND	T BNL	U BNU
V BLN	W BLV	X BNE	Y BNN	Z BNV
1A BLP	1B BLX	1C BNF	1D BNP	1E BNX
1F BLQ	1G BLY	1H BNG	1J BNQ	1K BNY

Two Dollars.

The PIL on the $2 note was located on the front in the bottom right corner of the sheep's fleece. $2 notes were at first printed 24 to a sheet (4 across by 6 down). PILs A to Z (omitting I and W) were used from left to right and down, while serial letter prefixes ran down then left to right, omitting I, M, O, W and Z. The earliest PIL notes observed were in the Phillips-Wheeler (Australia) issues, commencing at HBR and continuing through to KVY in the Johnston-Fraser issues. The serial letter prefix "Z" was used from HGZ onwards. See Figs. 182 and 192.

Fig. 102. Plate letter position, $1 notes.

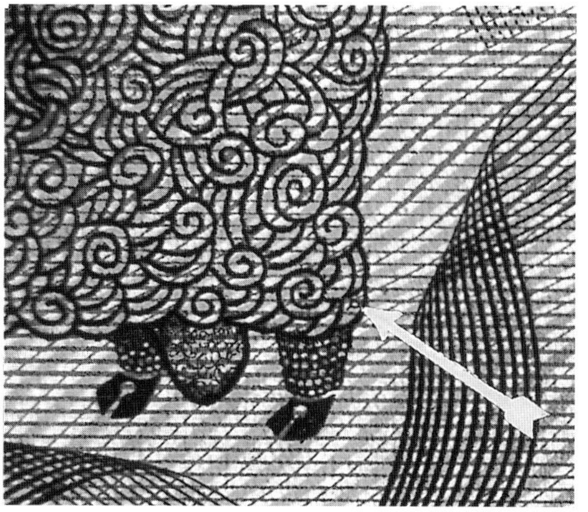

Fig. 103. Plate letter position, $2 notes.

The $2 notes were then printed 45 to a sheet, (5 across by 9 down). These were all Johnston-Fraser issues ranging from KVZ to LQG and with PIL lettering ranging from A to 1V (illustrated above).

Fig. 104. First plate letter position, $5 notes.

Fig. 105. Second plate letter position, $5 notes.

Five Dollars.

The PIL on the front of the $5 note was first located in the Phillips-Wheeler (Australia) notes in the bottom left gumnut on the stalk to the left of the chin of Banks. From the Knight-Wheeler issues it was relocated 19 mm immediately below the "ST" of "AUSTRALIA" (see illustrations above).

The notes were initially printed 24 to a sheet, (4 across by 6 down - see Fig. 223). PILs and serial letter numbering were in the same sequence and letters omitted as mentioned previously, with PILs from A to Z. PILs were first used in the Phillips-Wheeler (Australia) notes from serial letters NKH to QBJ in the Johnston-Fraser notes (omitting NLL). Serial letter prefix "Z" was used from NLZ onwards.

The $5 notes were then printed 40 to a sheet (5 across by 8 down - see Fig. 224) commencing at Johnston-Fraser QBK through to the last serial letters of Fraser-Cole, QPG.

PILs occurred in Knight-Wheeler with Gothic serial numbering up to NVC, and Johnston-Fraser PXB-QFA. OCR-B serial numbering PILs occurred from Knight-Wheeler NVD to Johnston-Fraser PYC and Fraser-Higgins QDF to Fraser-Cole QPG. See Figs. 213 and 214 for serial number types.

Fig. 106. First plate letter position, $10 notes.

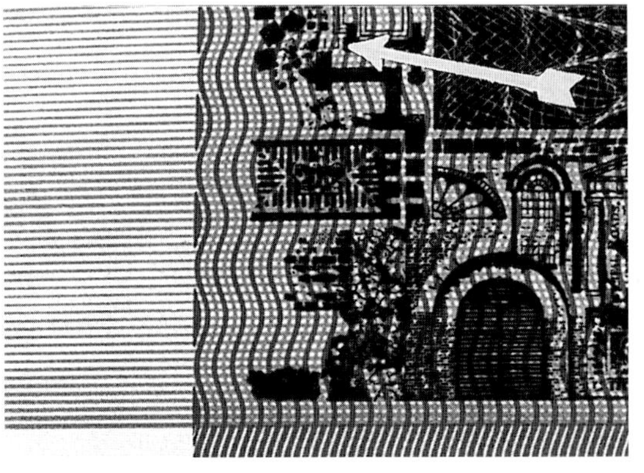

Fig. 107. Second plate letter position, $10 notes.

Ten Dollars.

PILs on the $10 notes were firstly positioned in the top right honeycomb hexagon to the left of the bottom of the portrait of Greenway in issues from Phillips-Wheeler (Australia) to Johnston-Stone. From Johnston-Fraser issues they were repositioned 29 mm vertically below the right hand leg of the first "A" in "AUSTRALIA". See illustrations above.

$10 notes were originally printed in sheets of 24 (4 across by 6 down). PILs were first used in Phillips-Wheeler (Australia) notes from TBF and continued through to UCC in Johnston-Stone. From Johnston-Fraser notes the sheet content was 40 (5 across by 8 down), with PILs commencing at UCD and finishing in Fraser-Cole notes at MRR. Prefixes with "Z" were included in all PIL notes, and the last plate/sheet (MPX-MRR) occurred with or without PILs. See Figs. 96 and 245.

Twenty Dollars.

PILs on the $20 notes were located above the tip of the "wing" to the left of Kingsford Smith's collar. $20 notes were first printed in sheets of 24 notes (4 across by 6 down) in Phillips-Wheeler (Australia) notes from XHB to Johnston-Fraser (OCR-B) VVX. Serial letters EHV to EKZ were used for both OCR-B and Gothic numbering while ELA to ENB was confined to Gothic serial numbering. EHV to ENB were also in sheets of 24. Serial letter prefixes with "Z" were used from XJZ onwards.

Notes were then printed in sheets of 40 (5 across by 8 down Fig. 279) from Johnston-Fraser OCR-B with serial letters VVY to VZZ and EAA to EHU and then from ENC onwards. Johnston-Fraser and Phillips-Fraser issues shared EVJ to EYD and PILs then continued from Fraser-Higgins issues right through the various signature combinations to ADK in the Fraser-Evans notes (illustrated below left).

Fig. 108. Plate letter position, $20 notes.

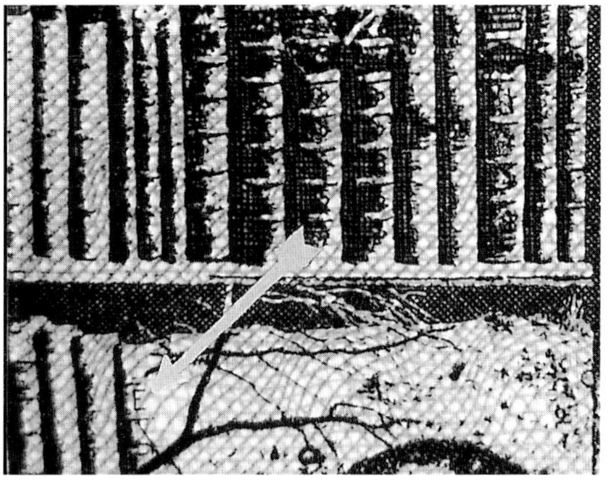

Fig. 109. Plate letter position, $50 notes.

Fifty Dollars.

PILs on the $50 notes were located to the right of the last book on the bottom shelf of books in the centre of the note. Notes were first printed in sheets of 24 (4 across by 6 down). PILs from A to Z were used from Phillips-Wheeler (Australia) YAA to YXH in Johnston-Fraser. See Fig. 315.

From Phillips-Fraser YXJ the notes were printed in sheets of 32 (4 across by 8 down) and PILs continued from A to 1H until somewhere in Fraser-Higgins or Fraser-Cole issues.

Only 18 serial letter prefixes (YAA-YAU) were used for Phillips-Wheeler, and these occur with PILs. The system of numbering was different to that used on other denominations using PILs and may have been similar to that used for the $1 DBP notes, or possibly a continuation of the system still being used on other denominations prior to the introduction of PILs. Normal use of PILs commenced with Knight-Wheeler issues at YAV, (illustrated above right).

One Hundred Dollars.

PILs on the $100 notes were located to the right of Mawson's head near the top of the centre mountain range. Notes were first printed in sheets of 24 (4 across by 6 down Fig. 338) from Johnston-Stone ZAA to Johnston-Fraser ZEH, and PILs from A to Z in the same reverse order as the polymer Bicentenary $10 note. This was because the serial numbers and PILs were on opposite sides of the notes. From Johnston-Fraser ZEJ to Fraser-Cole ZLD the notes were printed in sheets of 32 (4 across by 8 down) with PILs from A to 1E, (illustrated next page).

Fig. 110. Plate letter position, $100 notes.

Fig. 111. Plate letter position, Bicentenary $10 notes.

Ten Dollars (Bicentenary).

D AA00	C AA06	B AA12	A AA18
H AA01	G AA07	F AA13	E AA19
M AA02	L AA08	K AA14	J AA20
Q AAO3	P AA09	O AA15	N AA21
U AA04	T AA10	S AA16	R AA22
Z AA05	Y AA11	X AA17	V AA23

The PILs were located in the foliage under the top of the third tree from the left on the front of the notes. Notes were printed in sheets of 24 (4 across by 6 down). The PILs were used on all issues in Johnston-Fraser from the (dated) series AA 00 to AA 23, to the general circulating AB series, AB 10 to AB 57. As the notes were numbered on the back, the relationship of the PIL lettering to the serial number prefixes was the reverse to that used in paper notes (position as shown above).

Fluorescence

The quickest way to locate a forged $10 note released in 1966/67 (with Coombs-Wilson signatures) was to place notes under ultraviolet (black) light. The forgeries came up white, the genuine notes remained a dark purple (the colour of the light). The same test was effective with later paper forgeries. The UV lights used were the same as the lights used by banks for "invisible signatures" in passbooks, and the same as the purple light used on dance floors.

While all NNS (New Note Series) Australian polymer notes display obvious fluorescence features under long wave ultraviolet (black) light, fluorescence in Australian paper decimal notes seems to have been largely experimental. In most cases, not all notes in any particular signature combination displayed fluorescence. The fluorescence observed in paper notes appears to have been added to various inks prior to printing.

A request to Note Printing Branch, Craigieburn, for information about fluorescence in paper notes in 1988 was answered by *We confirm that in common with other banknote security printers we use fluorescence and for security reasons, prefer not to disclose references to fluorescent inks to the general public.* The following information therefore, is the result of examination of notes in circulation.

One Dollar

The last signature combination of Johnston-Stone in the one dollar denomination contained strong solid yellow fluorescence in the vertical centre of the front from approximately DHB to the final prefix DPS.

Ten Dollars

Johnston-Stone notes from UBH to UCC with numbers below 306800 have been observed with strong orange fluorescence on the backs in the form of alternating vertical wavy lines within the orange banding, which is about 3 cm wide. Johnston-Fraser notes from UCZ to UNC, in a wide range of numbers, displayed the same fluorescence.

Twenty Dollars

The most commonly located fluorescent notes were in this denomination. Some were quite striking. Some Knight - Stone notes (VDR and VDU) displayed strong fluorescent yellow alternating horizontal wavy lines on the backs (see Fig. 112) and strong diagonal fluorescent striping in the vertical centre of the fronts. Other notes (VEE, VEL and VFR) exhibited pale solid fluorescence as a vertical band about 3 cm. wide in the centre on the front and 4 cm. in the centre on the back.

There were several variations in the Johnston-Stone series. One note (VHF) displayed fluorescent yellow alternating diagonal lines in the vertical centre while three others (VKS, VKX and VQF) displayed strong solid yellow fluorescence as a vertical band about 4 cm. wide in the centre of the front, and on the back, alternating horizontal pairs of wavy lines in the vertical centre about 6 cm wide. Other notes (from VNG to VNT) had similar properties while another note (VPE) displayed weak fluorescence on the front, but still exhibited the strongly fluorescent wavy lines within the Simultan design on the back. Johnston-Fraser notes VQT and VRH also displayed strong fluorescence on the back as above, but on the front the vertical fluorescence was narrower and not as strong.

Fifty Dollars

This denomination generally did not exhibit fluorescence, but Knight-Wheeler (side thread) notes have been observed with fluorescent light yellow wavy horizontal lines on the back.

One Hundred Dollars

Fluorescent light yellow wavy lines have been observed at top left on the backs of Johnston-Stone notes with serial letters ZAR and ZAS. These are slightly stronger in some Johnstone-Fraser and Fraser-Higgins notes.

Other minor fluorescent features were noted in various notes as well as fluorescent serial numbers and overprints in the red inks used on Collector Issues.

Further reading: *Fluorescence on Australian Notes,* Michael Vort-Ronald, *Australian Coin Review,* February, 1996.

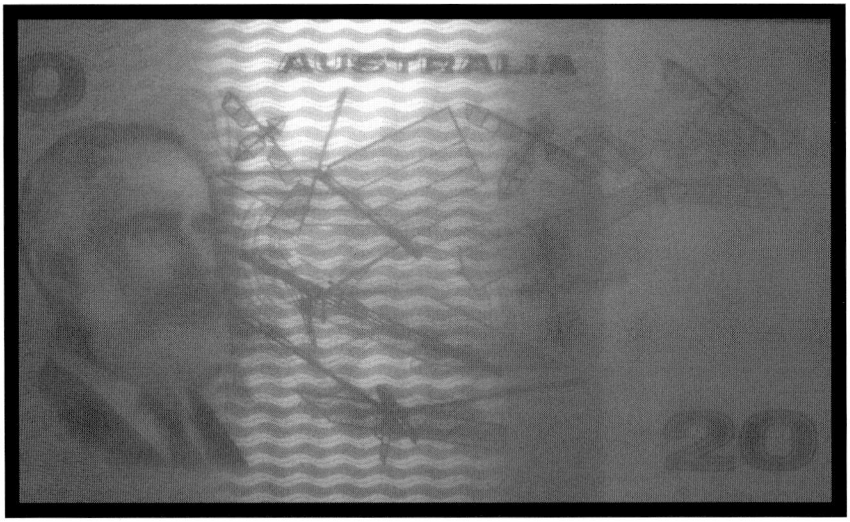

Fig. 112. Back, $20 exhibiting fluorescence.

Chapter 5: NOTE SIGNATORIES AND GENERAL MANAGERS, NOTE PRINTING BRANCH AND NOTE PRINTING AUSTRALIA

Signatories, Reserve Bank of Australia

Fig. 113. H.C. Coombs & signature.

H.C. Coombs

Dr. Herbert Cole Coombs, M.A., Ph.D. (London), Honorary Fellow - London School of Economics, Hon. LL.D (Melbourne), Hon. D. Litt, (W.A.), was born on 24 February, 1906, at Kalamunda, Western Australia. He joined the staff of the Commonwealth Bank on 16 August, 1935. At the outbreak of war in 1939 the Bank, at the request of the Government, made his services available to the Commonwealth Treasury as Assistant Economist. In October 1942, Dr. Coombs resigned from the Commonwealth Bank to become eligible for appointment as a member of the Bank Board. In 1943 he was appointed Director-General of the Department of Post-war Reconstruction. Dr. Herbert "Nugget" Coombs was Governor of the Commonwealth Bank of Australia from 1 January, 1949, to 13 January, 1960, and then Governor of the Reserve Bank of Australia from 14 January, 1960, to 22 July, 1968.

He received an inaugural Companion of the Order of Australia in 1975, but resigned from the order when the ranks of knight and dame were created in 1976. He died in Sydney on 29 October, 1997, aged 91 years. Further reading: Obituary *"Disciple of Keynes was promoter of causes", The Australian,* 30 October, 1997.

At various times he was Chairman of the following: Australian Council of Aboriginal Affairs, Australian Council for the Arts, Australian Elizabethan Theatre Trust and a Chancellor of the Australian National University. On 11 September, 1964, a 365-roomed building at the A.N.U. was opened and named after him, and occupied by the Research Schools of Social Sciences and Pacific Studies.

Fig. 114. J.G. Phillips & signature.

Fig. 115. H.M. Knight & signature.

J. G. Phillips

Sir John Grant Phillips, K.B.E. (1972), C.B.E. (1968), B. Econ. (Sydney), was born on 13 March, 1911, in Sydney, New South Wales. He was an economist with the Economy Department of the Commonwealth Bank from 1937 to 1951 and Investment Adviser to the Bank from 1954 to 1960. From 1960 to 1968 he was Deputy Governor of the Reserve Bank of Australia and Governor from 23 July, 1968 to 22 July, 1975. He was also a member of the Council of Macquarie University and of the Australian Atomic Energy Advisory Committee. He died in October, 1986.

H. M. Knight

Harold Murray Knight, D.S.C., M.Com. (Melbourne), was born on 13 August, 1919, at Melbourne, Victoria. He was employed by the Commonwealth Bank from 1936 to 1940 then served in the Australian Imperial Forces from 1940 to 1943, and the Royal Australian Naval Volunteer Reserve from 1943 to 1945. He rejoined the Bank in 1946 and in 1955 commenced a four year term with the International Monetary Fund in Washington. In 1957 he was appointed Assistant Chief in the Statistics Division within the Research and Statistics Department of the Fund. In 1959 he was appointed Research Economist in the Research Department of the Reserve Bank of Australia. He was Assistant Manager, Investment Department from 1962, Deputy Manager in 1964 and then Manager. He was Governor of the Reserve Bank from 23 July, 1975 to 13 August, 1982.

Fig. 116. R.A. Johnston & signature.

Fig. 117. M.J. Phillips & signature.

R. A. Johnston

Robert Alan Johnston was born at Moonee Ponds, Victoria on 19 July, 1924. In 1940 he joined the Commonwealth Bank. Apart from service in the R.A.A.F. from 1943 to 1946, he remained in the Bank until 1960 and then joined the Reserve Bank of Australia. From 1964 to 1970 he was Deputy Manager, then Manager, Investment Department. In 1970 he was appointed Chief Manager, International Department, where he remained until 1976. In 1973 he was appointed Adviser to the Governor of the Bank. In 1976 and 1977 he was Chief Representative of the Bank in London, and from 1977 to 1979, Executive Director, World Bank Group, Washington. In 1980 he was appointed Secretary to the Reserve Bank. He was Governor of the Bank from 14 August, 1982 to 18 July, 1989, and in 1986 was appointed a Companion in the General Division of the Order of Australia.

M. J. Phillips

Mervyn John Phillips was the only Deputy Governor of the Reserve Bank of Australia to have his facsimile signature on Australian notes. This occurred because of the retirement of the former Governor, H.M. Knight and the appointment of the then Secretary to the Treasury B.W. Fraser, as Governor of the Bank. Mr. Fraser was unable to take up his appointment as Governor immediately, and John Phillips signed in his place as Deputy Governor, with B.W. Fraser signing as Secretary to the Treasury. This occurred on $20 and $50 notes only.

M.J. (John) Phillips, B. Econ. (Sydney), was born 1 April, 1930. He joined the Commonwealth Bank in 1946. In July, 1957, he was promoted to Research Graduate, Economic Department. In 1960 he became Senior Research Officer, Research Department and in May, 1961, was seconded as Research Economist, Port Moresby. In 1962 he was promoted to Manager for the Territory of Papua & New Guinea. In 1970, Assistant Secretary (Board) Secretary's Department, 1973 Deputy Manager, International Department, Manager 1975 and Chief Manager 1976. On 11 March, 1987, he was appointed Deputy Governor and in February, 1990, Chairman of the Board of Note Printing Australia. He retired on 10 April, 1992.

Fig. 118. B.W. Fraser & signature.

Fig. 119. I. Macfarlane & signature.

B.W. Fraser

Bernie William Fraser, B.A., was born on 26 February, 1941, at Junee, New South Wales. He was Secretary to the Treasury from 17 September, 1984, to 17 September 1989. For his personal details up to then, see his entry in "Secretaries to the Treasury", following. Mr. Fraser was Governor of the Reserve Bank from 18 September, 1989, to 17 September, 1996. In 2000 he was Chairman of the Investment Committee for a private company, Australian Retirement Fund.

As an indication of the importance of the position of Governor of the Reserve Bank, the *Sunday Mail* (Adelaide) of 9 July, 1989, reported that the Government had approved an annual salary package for the new Governor of $250,000. This compared with an annual salary of $162,191 for the then Prime Minister Bob Hawke and $121,000+ for the Treasurer, Paul Keating.

I. Macfarlane

Ian John Macfarlane was born in Sydney on 22 June,1946, and was educated at Monash University, Melbourne, where he obtained a Master of Economics degree in 1969 and taught for a short time. From 1970 he worked in the Projects Section of Research Department with the Reserve Bank of Australia for 18 months before spending some time at the Institute for Economics and Statistics at Oxford University. He joined the OECD in Paris, working there for six years mainly on economic forecasts and surveys of member countries. In 1979 he returned to the Reserve Bank and held a number of positions including Deputy Chief Manager, Securities Markets Department; Chief Manager, Financial Markets Group; Head of Research Department and in 1990; Assistant Governor (Economic). He was appointed Deputy Governor on 11 April, 1992, and Governor from 18 September, 1996. While he did not sign any paper notes, he was Governor at the time when some paper Collector Issues were produced bearing previous signature combinations.

Secretaries to the Treasury signatories

Fig. 120. Roland Wilson & signature.

Fig. 121. R.J. Randall & signature.

Roland Wilson

Sir Roland Wilson, K.B.E. (1965), Kt. (1955), C.B.E. (1941), B.Comm. (Tasmania) (1926), Dip. Econ. and Political Science, Dip. Philosophy (Oxford) (1929), Ph. D. (Chicago), was born 7 April, 1904, at Ulverstone, Tasmania. He was a Rhodes Scholar in Tasmania in 1925. In 1933 he was an economist in the Statistician's Branch of the Commonwealth Treasury and was appointed Commonwealth Statistician and Economic Adviser to the Treasury from 1936 to 1940, and again from 1946 to 1951. He was Secretary to the Treasury from 1 April, 1951, to 27 October, 1966. He died in Canberra on 25 October, 1996, aged 92 years.

R.J. Randall

Sir Richard John Randall, Kt. (1964), B.Econ., A.C.I.S., was born on 13 October, 1906, at Birkdale, Queensland. He worked as a woolclasser from 1924 to 1932. He received the Carnegie Research Scholarship at Sydney University in 1937, and was Research Officer for the Premier's Office, Sydney, from 1937 to 1939. He joined the Commonwealth Treasury in 1940 and in 1946 was appointed to the permanent position of Principal Research Officer. From 1957 to 1966 he was Deputy Secretary to the Treasury, and Secretary to the Treasury from 28 October, 1966, to 31 October, 1971. Sir Richard died in Canberra on 15 November, 1982, aged 76 years.

F.H. Wheeler

Sir Frederick Henry Wheeler, Kt. (1967), C.B.E. (1962), B.Comm., was born on 9 January, 1914, in Melbourne, Victoria. He was employed by the State Savings Bank of Victoria from 1929 to 1939. He then became Treasury Research Officer in 1939 and Economist in 1944. He was appointed Assistant

Fig. 122. F.H. Wheeler & signature

Fig. 123. John Stone & signature.

Secretary to the Treasury in 1946. In 1952 he was Treasurer of the International Labour Office in Geneva. He was Secretary to the Treasury from 12 November, 1971, to 8 January, 1979, and died at Woden Valley, Canberra in 1994, aged 80 years.

John Stone

John Owen Stone was born in Perth, Western Australia, on 31 January, 1929. He attended the University of Western Australia where he received First Class Honours (Mathematical Physics) to his Bachelor of Science degree. He was awarded the Rhodes Scholarship for W.A. in 1951, the James Webb Medley Scholarship for Economics at Oxford University in 1953 and First Class Honours in Politics, Philosophy and Economics in 1954. That year he joined the Commonwealth Treasury, serving in London and Canberra. He returned to London as Senior Treasury Representative late in 1957, remaining there until early 1961. Early in 1967 he became Executive Director for Australia, New Zealand and South Africa on the Board of the International Monetary Fund in Washington, D.C., U.S.A., and Executive Director for those countries, and he was also on the Board of the International Bank for Reconstruction and Development, both positions being held until the end of 1970. In November, 1971, he was promoted to the position of Deputy Secretary (Economic) within the Treasury, and later, in 1976 when the Department of Finance was created out of the Department of the Treasury, remained in Treasury to become Deputy Secretary. He is also a Fellow of the Australian Academy of the Social Sciences.

He was Secretary to the Treasury from 8 January, 1979. On 15 August, 1984, he announced his resignation, his last day in office being 14 September, 1984.

Fig. 124. B.W. Fraser & signature.

Fig. 125. C.I. Higgins & signature.

B. W. Fraser

Bernie William Fraser, B.A., was born on 26 February, 1941, at Junee, New South Wales. He attended the University of New England where he gained his Bachelor of Arts, majoring in Economics. He joined the Department of National Development in 1961 and moved to the Treasury in 1963. From 1970 to 1972 he was Treasury Representative in London. When the Treasury was split in 1976 he transferred to Finance and was promoted First Assistant Secretary, General Expenditure Division. He transferred back to Treasury in 1979 as First Assistant Secretary, Resource Allocation Division, and later moved to the General Financial and Economic Policy Division. In 1981, he was appointed Director, National Energy Office and re-designated Deputy Secretary, Department of Resources and Energy. In January, 1984, he transferred back to Treasury as Deputy Secretary, Development and Taxation, holding responsibility for the divisions of Taxation and Industry; Prices, Incomes and Development; and Foreign Investment. He was Secretary to the Treasury from 19 September, 1984 to 18 September, 1989, and then Governor of the Reserve Bank from 19 September, 1989 to 17 September, 1996. See also, signatories, Reserve Bank of Australia.

C.I. Higgins

Dr. Christopher Ian Higgins, B.Ec. (Hons 1), Ph.D., F.A.S.S.A., was born at Murwillumbah, New South Wales, on 3 April, 1943. He graduated with first class honours in economics from the Australian National University in 1963, and then completed a doctorate in applied econometrics at the University of Pennsylvania. He returned to the ABS in 1968 and moved to Treasury in 1970. In the mid 70s he spent another 18 months at the University of Pennsylvania as a Senior Fullbright Hays Scholar and at British Columbia as a Visiting Associate Professor. In September, 1987, he was elected a Fellow of the Academy of Social Sciences in Australia. From 1981 to June 1984, he served as Director, General

Economics Branch of the Economic and Statistics Department of the OECD (Organisation for Economic Cooperation and Development) in Paris. On his return to Canberra he worked briefly as First Assistant Secretary, Financial Institutions Division, before becoming Deputy Secretary (Economics) in 1984 and Secretary to the Treasury from 19 September, 1989. On 6 December, 1990, he collapsed and died after completing a veterans' 3000 metre race at the Australian Institute of Sport athletic field, Canberra.

Fig. 126. A.S. Cole & signature

A. S. Cole

Anthony Stuart Cole, BEc (Syd), was born 17 March, 1947, at Macksville, New South Wales. He began his career in the Federal Treasury in 1968 where he worked in financial areas until he transferred to the Department of Finance in 1977 for two years, before being appointed as Alternate Executive Director of the World Bank in Washington. Later he became First Senior Private Secretary to the then Treasurer, Paul Keating. He then worked at the Australian High Commission in London as "Minister (Economic)" in 1985 and upon his return to Australia worked in the Department of the Prime Minister and Cabinet. He was appointed Chairman of what was then the Industries Assistance Commission. On 14 February, 1991, he was appointed as Secretary to the Treasury following the sudden death of Dr. Chris Higgins. On 23 March, 1993, he was removed from office by the Prime Minister, Mr. Keating. Newspapers speculated that the reason for the removal was "irreconcilable differences" with the Treasurer, Mr. Dawkins.

In 1993 he was appointed as Secretary, Department of Health, Housing, Local Government and Community Services.

Fig. 127. E.A. Evans and signature.

E.A. Evans

Edward Alfred Evans, AC 1999, B. Econ (Hons) (Qld), was born 4 March, 1941 at Ipswich, Queensland. For about ten years he worked in telecommunications in the Postmaster General's Department before graduating from the University of Queensland in 1969 with Honours in Economics, and joined the Australian Treasury. From 1969 to 1975 he was involved in a variety of research and policy areas advising on domestic economic matters, primarily on macroeconomics. For three years from 1976 he was a member of the Australian Permanent Delegation to the OECD in Paris, returning to Australia in 1979. He was promoted within the Treasury to the Senior Executive Service in 1980 as head of the Fiscal and Monetary Policy Branch and, in 1982, to head the General Financial and Economic Policy Division. From 1984 to 1989 he held the position of Deputy Secretary to the Treasury and was heavily involved in taxation and micro-economic reform. He joined the Board of the International Monetary Fund in 1989 as Executive Director representing Australia and a number of other countries, mainly in the Asia Pacific region.

He was appointed Secretary to the Treasury on 24 March, 1993, and took up duty on 10 May, 1993.

GENERAL MANAGERS, NOTE ISSUE DEPARTMENT: FROM 1966 TO 1990, NOTE PRINTING AUSTRALIA, 1990 TO 1998: AND CHIEF EXECUTIVE OFFICER OF NOTE PRINTING AUSTRALIA LIMITED FROM 1998.

Note production was originally carried out by two separate branches of the Reserve bank of Australia - Note Printing Branch and Note Issue Branch, with the major part of the general administration being carried out at Head Office. In 1963, the position of General Manager, Note Issue Department, was created and the two branches were brought together under its control.

In 1969, the Department was reorganised into four divisions and the stamp production and printing activities were carried out by the Printing Division of the Note Issue Department. Besides the General Manager there was also an Assistant General Manager (who directed the Planning and Research function) and a manager for each of the other three divisions, Administrative, Printing and Issuing.

On 12 February, 1990, the Reserve Bank announced that its note printing activities would trade under the name Note Printing Australia and this was further changed from 1 July, 1998, when it became Note Printing Australia Limited, with its head designated as Chief Executive Officer.

Fig. 128. W.H. Wilcock.

W.H. Wilcock

William Howard Wilcock, C.B.E., was born in Ballarat, Victoria, on 21 December, 1904. He joined the Commonwealth Bank at Ballarat on 1 March, 1921. In 1926 he transferred to the Administration, and then Staff Department in 1930. He was closely identified with the arrangements for the amalgamation of the Government Savings Bank of New South Wales and the Commonwealth Bank, and later the amalgamation with the State Savings Bank of Western Australia. In March, 1940, he was attached to the Secretary's Department where he remained throughout the war years. In July 1945, he was appointed sub-inspector and in July, 1946, Senior Sub-inspector.

On 14 January, 1958, he was seconded as Banking Adviser to the Government of the Federation of Malaya and on 24 January, 1959, became Governor and Chairman of the Bank of Negara Tanah Melayu (now the Central Bank of Malaysia). He was later honoured by the award of Knight of the Most Distinguished Order of the Defender of the Realm for his services to Malaysia. He returned to Australia in August 1962 as Adviser to the Governor of the Reserve Bank of Australia and General Manager of the Note Issue Department, succeeding W.C.G. McCracken. Mr. Wilcock retired on 14 November, 1969, and died 11 September, 1999.

At the time of the changeover to decimal currency the Works Manager was M.F.W. (Monty) Brown, (born in England 24 July, 1916) who was closely associated with the production of the new decimal notes. He was formerly Manager of the Bank Note Factory of Waterlow & Sons Limited (U.K). He joined the Reserve Bank on 6 August, 1961, as Production Supervisor, Note Printing Branch and retired on 31 October, 1978, as Chief Manager, Research and Development. He died in Melbourne on 9 June, 1980.

Fig. 129. H.R. Longmuir

H.R. Longmuir

Hervey Rae Longmuir was born at Barham, New South Wales, on 30 August, 1911. He joined the Commonwealth Bank on 15 December, 1931. From 1954 to 1960 he was Assistant Investment Adviser, during which time he spent two years as Secretary of the Note Issue Department. In 1960 he was appointed Manager, Banking Department. From 1965 to 1969 he was Manager, London Office.

He was General Manager, Note Issue Department, from 10 October, 1969, to December, 1971. At the time of his retirement on 1 March, 1973, there were 751 men and women employed in the planning, designing and printing of Australian notes.

Fig. 130. R.A.S. Bywater.

Fig. 131. G.M.E. Sceats.

R.A.S. Bywater

Richard Arthur Samuel Bywater, G.C., G.M., was born in Birmingham, England, on 3 November, 1913. He graduated Master of Science from Birmingham University and joined the British Ministry of Supply after the start of the war in 1939. He was awarded the George Cross and the George Medal for separate acts of bravery, the only civilian to have been awarded both medals. For further reading, see *Man of Millions is a shy hero* by John Hamilton, *Australian Coin Review,* February, 1973, and *The Herald*, Melbourne, 14 December, 1972.

In 1954 he migrated to Australia and was later employed at the Government Explosives Factory at Mulwala, New South Wales, where he became Head of Laboratories. On 30 September, 1957, he joined the Commonwealth Bank as Research Chemist and five years later he became Manager, Planning and Research. In 1965 he was Assistant General Manager, and finally Manager, Note Issue Department, from 7 January, 1972, until his retirement on 11 July, 1976.

G.M.E. Sceats

Geoffrey Mark Edward Sceats was born at Ashfield, New South Wales, on 19 May, 1916. He joined the Commonwealth Bank on 13 October, 1931, and worked at various suburban and country branches. He served approximately four years in the Army and then returned to the Bank. In 1948 he worked in the Staff Department, and in 1957 the Investment Department, which later became attached to the Reserve Bank of Australia. In 1962 he became Assistant Manager for Queensland, and four years later, Deputy Manager for Victoria. In 1970 he was promoted to Manager, Personnel Department, Sydney. He was General Manager, Note Issue Department, from 12 July, 1976, until his retirement on 13 March, 1981.

Fig. 132. D.R. Parr.

Fig. 133. D.B. Addison.

D.R. Parr

Donald Robert Parr, B.Ec., A.A.S.A., A.B.I.A., was born in Sydney, New South Wales, on 28 December, 1925. He joined the Commonwealth Bank on 12 January, 1943. In early 1944 he enlisted in the R.A.A.F. and was discharged at the end of 1945, returning to the Bank. After a series of moves within the Bank he was promoted to Senior Research Officer, Credit Policy, Banking Department in 1958. Upon the formation of the Reserve Bank of Australia in 1959, he became Board Secretary and later Superintendent, Capital Market Section, Investment Department. In 1966 he became Senior Administration Officer in the Research Department, and the following year, Deputy Manager, Banking Department - later Banking and Finance Department. He was then Manager, and later Chief Manager, Securities Markets. On 2 March, 1981, he was appointed General Manager, Note Printing Branch. He concluded his responsibilities at the Note Printing Branch on 2 November, 1983, and transferred to the London Office appointment of Chief Representative in Europe for the Reserve Bank, January, 1984, and retired in July 1989.

D.B. Addison

Donald Bowman Addison was born at Orroroo, South Australia, on 15 May, 1930. He was educated in Adelaide and held positions in metal manufacturing businesses in Canada, Australia and the United States. On 5 September, 1983, he joined the Reserve Bank of Australia and was appointed General Manager, Note Printing Branch, from 3 November, 1983, to 25 August, 1989.

Fig. 134. R.L. Larkin.

Fig. 135. J. Leckenby

R. L. Larkin

Robert Lee Larkin was born on 30 October, 1935, at St. Louis, Missouri, U.S.A. He attained a Batchelor of Science Degree at the United States Naval Academy in 1959 and served for eight years in the United States Navy before immigrating to Australia in 1963. He was employed as an Engineer and Manager in various positions with Australian Paper Manufacturers Ltd., including nine years as Resident District Manager, Petrie Mill in Queensland. Following his attendance at the Harvard University Advanced Management Program in Boston, U.S.A. he was appointed as General Manager of the Note Printing Branch of the Reserve Bank of Australia from 22 November, 1989.

In 1990 N.P.B. functionally separated from the R.B.A. and became Note Printing Australia (N.P.A.). He was appointed Managing Director of the N.P.A. Board in February, 1996, and retired on 30 June, 1998. Board Member Mark Bethwaite was then temporarily in charge until the appointment of Mr. Leckenby.

Mr. Larkin played a key role throughout most of the 1990s in the introduction and commercialisation of polymer-based banknotes, not only within Australia, but also to overseas countries. N.P.A.s Belgium supplier of polymer materials (UCB Films) formed a joint venture company (Securency Pty Ltd) with the Reserve Bank to market polymer substrate to the international banknote printing industry.

In June, 1997, N.P.A. employed 267 staff, compared with 552 staff ten years previously. By the end of 1997, the number of staff had reduced to around 200. On 1 July, 1998, N.P.A. was corporatised and became a wholly owned subsidiary of the Reserve Bank of Australia.

J. Leckenby

John Leckenby was born in England on 28 September, 1944. From 1968 to 1981 he was involved in sales and marketing and General Manager roles with C.I.G. in Perth and Melbourne. He was General Manager of H.K.O. in Hong Kong from 1981 to 1984. From 1984 to 1993 he was Melbourne-based General Manager of C.I.G. Ltd., Cigweld, Email York and Ogden Industries Ltd. He was Group Manager of Email Building Products (Security and Plumbing Hardware) from 1993 to 1998. Mr. Leckenby holds a B.A. (Hons) Geography from King's College, London/L.S.E. and M.B.A. from Monash University. On 17 August, 1998, he was appointed Chief Executive Officer of Note Printing Australia Ltd.

Chapter 6: SPECIMEN NOTES

It is usual practice for note printing institutions to reserve notes from a print run and overprint them as specimens for record or presentation purposes. In the first two types of specimens the overprinted notes bore the first prefix letters of the denominations, AAA, FAA, NAA, SAA, and XAA with the serial numerals 000000. There was a further limited issue of Type two with Phillips - Wheeler (Commonwealth) signatures and different prefixes. Type three first occurred on $50 Phillips-Wheeler (Australia) notes with YAA prefixes, with a further issue of Type three known as "T.A.A." specimens.

Later issues of the Second type, and the Third type, bore serial numbers at or near the commencement of the signature combinations. In 1999 and 2000, $2 notes were offered for sale on the internet which were similar to those in Type three, but with Johnston-Fraser signatures and the absence of "NO VALUE" and "SPECIMEN No." overprinting. At the time of writing they had not been verified as official issues.

The Fourth type of specimen note has only been observed in the $100 denomination. Variations are:

First type	"SPECIMEN" printed in a small oval on each side, Figs. 136, 140.
Second type	"SPECIMEN" printed diagonally 8 times on each side, Figs. 141, 142.
Third type	"SPECIMEN" printed diagonally in large hollow block letters twice on each side, "NO VALUE" and individually numbered with "SPECIMEN No. (4 digit number)" Figs. 143, 144.
Fourth type	"SPECIMEN" printed horizontally under denomination figures twice on the front and once on the back under denomination with specimen number as in Type three, ($100 notes only, Figs. 147, 148).

Fig. 136. Front, $20 specimen. First type.

FIRST TYPE SPECIMEN NOTES

Most of the following information has been extracted from correspondence files in Reserve Bank of Australia Archives released after the 30 year official closed period. File numbers quoted will appear in brackets e.g. (N-a-691).

To mark the occasion of Australia's new decimal currency notes, the Bank prepared a special album "Australian Notes 1966". It contained specimens of the new notes and told the story of their design and production. The text was written and the project handled by Note Printing Branch with Mr. Alistair Morrison in charge of the design.

Seventeen special albums, inscribed by the Governor, were presented to the Queen, Prince Philip, the Governor-General and Lady Casey, the Prime Minister, the Treasurer and other distinguished persons in Australia and abroad. A further 235 albums were made for distribution to those directly involved in the currency notes exercise; Australian and overseas banks, libraries and museums and Australian Government representatives abroad, with 191 being actually distributed. (S-a-777 and N-a-690).

The book contained 12 printed leaves and was covered in a beige coloured linen. It measured approximately 22 cm x 27 cm. On the cover in gold coloured lettering on a brown panel was the Bank's emblem and AUSTRALIAN NOTES 1966. The book told the story of how the notes were produced. The rear portion consisted of pages describing the front and back of each note, with a page opposite printed in brown with two white panels. On each panel mounted with glue were decimal notes to show the front and the back. Two notes of each denomination were included, with a strip of paper at the rear to add the $5 note after its release. All notes were the Oval (First type) specimen.

A $50 note was produced in 1973, but in the Third type specimen, and it too, was sent to the original recipients of the books.

John Sands & Co. of Sydney printed the book for the Reserve Bank of Australia. (N-a-691). A memorandum (N-a-691) dated 24 September, 1965, included:

> *Past practice has been to make specimen notes freely available to central banks and official institutions such as museums, libraries, etc., while, in addition, specimens have been presented to a very restricted list of prominent persons. As indicated in the attached memorandum, an extension to our present list of recipients of specimen notes would be warranted in the light of the changeover to decimal currency and the following preliminary estimates of requirements for presentation albums have been made on this basis:-....*

The special albums were inscribed:

"Presented to
(Governor to write name)
With the compliments of
Reserve Bank of Australia
(Governor to sign)
Governor"

Seventeen special albums were presented to - (N-a-690)

The Queen
The Duke of Edinburgh
The Governor General, Lord Casey
His wife, Lady Casey
The Prime Minister, Sir Robert Menzies
The Federal Treasurer, Harold Holt
Secretary to the Treasury, Sir Roland Wilson
The Federal Treasurer (1/2/66), William McMahon
President of the Senate, Sir Alister McMullin
Speaker in the House of Representatives, Sir John McLeay
Leader of the Opposition, Arthur Calwell
Bank of England, Lord Cromer
Reserve Bank of New Zealand, Gilbert Wilson
Artist Alistair Morrison
Artist Gordon Andrews
Artist Russell Drysdale
Lord Cobbold

The standard albums included:

"With the compliments of
Reserve Bank of Australia"

Otherwise they were identical (N-a-690).

A total of 191 standard albums were issued to -

Totals supplied.	
03	Governor, Deputy Governor and Sir Roland Wilson
07	Reserve Bank Board members
06	Members of the design panel
06	People who assisted with photographs
23	Major Trading, Savings, State and foreign banks.
11	Commonwealth Central banks
35	Other Central banks
33	Libraries and other institutions in Australia and overseas
01	High Commissioner, London
22	On the General Manager's list (mostly printers, and overseas banks)
40	Reserve Bank of Australia - Advisers, Investment Department, Note Printing staff, Managers of Departments and branches
01	Reserve Bank Archivist
02	Retired Treasury officials
01	Mr. E. Kingsford Smith.

Fig. 137. Books for Type One and Type Three specimen notes.

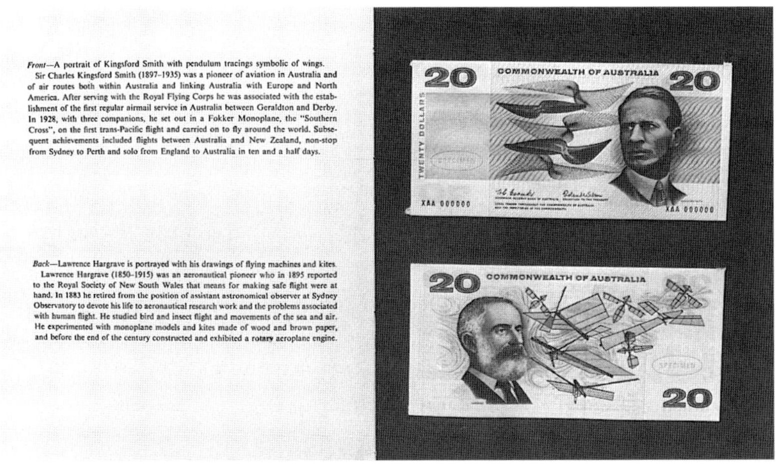

Fig. 138. $20 pages of Type One specimen note book

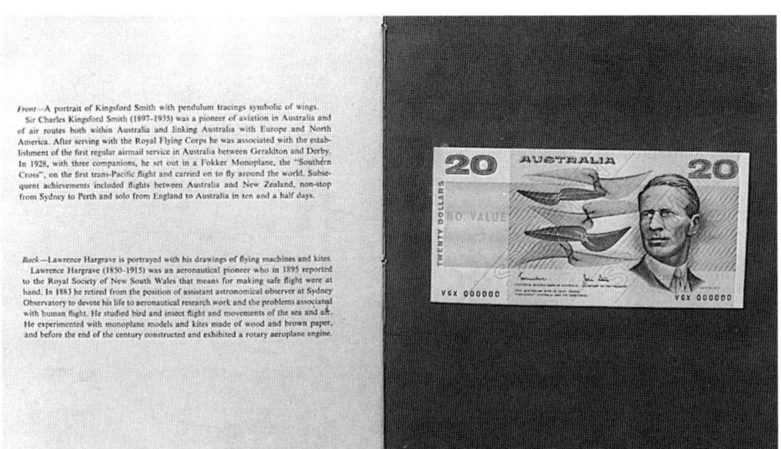

Fig. 139. $20 pages of Type Three specimen note book.

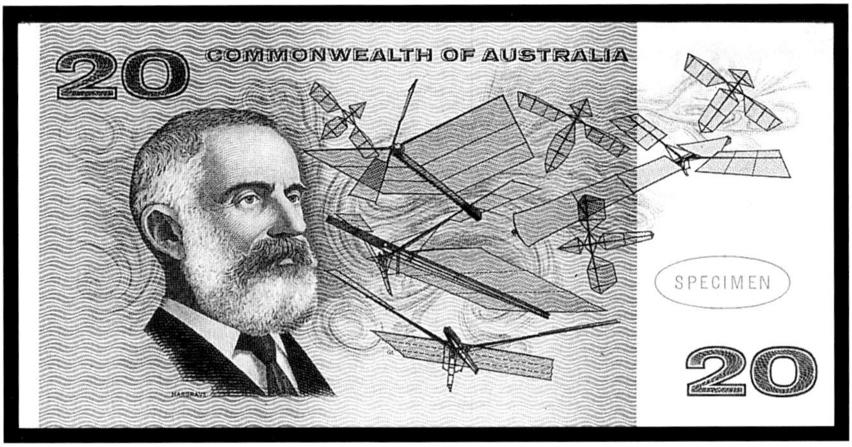

Fig. 140. Back, $20 specimen. First type.

SECOND TYPE SPECIMEN NOTES

The Second type specimen was produced in the $1, $2, $10 and $20 denominations, with the $5 added later. The notes all bore the word "SPECIMEN" eight times on each side. The words were printed diagonally in two horizontal rows of four. The actual words "SPECIMEN" are 23 mm long and 3 mm high. The colour of the words "SPECIMEN" in the Coombs-Wilson notes ($1, 2, 10, 20) was crimson. The same ink was apparently not available at the time of the overprinting of the $5 specimens and these were overprinted in scarlet with the lettering being slightly thinner. Only two full sets and two single notes have been observed with Phillips-Wheeler (Commonwealth) signatures.

Fig. 141. Front, $20 specimen. Second type.

The Second type specimens were sent from the Head Office of the Reserve Bank to other Central banks. Some sets were given to overseas embassies as display pieces for the benefit of intending migrants, and some museums and an Art Gallery also received this type. Only a limited number were produced and issued. Many of the surviving notes in private hands exhibit pin holes from being pinned up on notice boards.

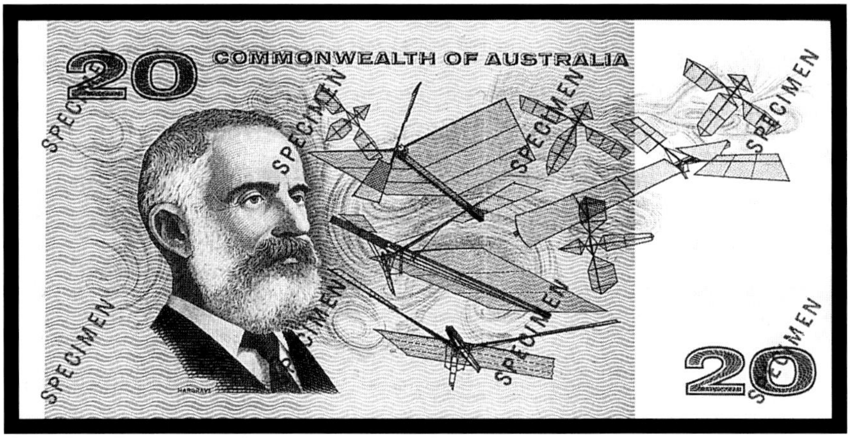

Fig. 142. Back, $20 specimen, Second type.

The following notes of the Second type specimen notes have been observed.

$1 Coombs-Wilson AAA 000000
$2 Coombs-Wilson FAA 000000
$10 Coombs-Wilson SAA 000000
$20 Coombs-Wilson XAA 000000
$5 Coombs-Randall NAA 000000
$1 Phillips-Wheeler (Commonwealth of Australia) BBF 000000
$2 Phillips-Wheeler (Commonwealth of Australia) GRG 000000
$5 Phillips-Wheeler (Commonwealth of Australia) NGT 000000
$10 Phillips-Wheeler (Commonwealth of Australia) STG 000000
$20 Phillips-Wheeler (Commonwealth of Australia) XEV 000000

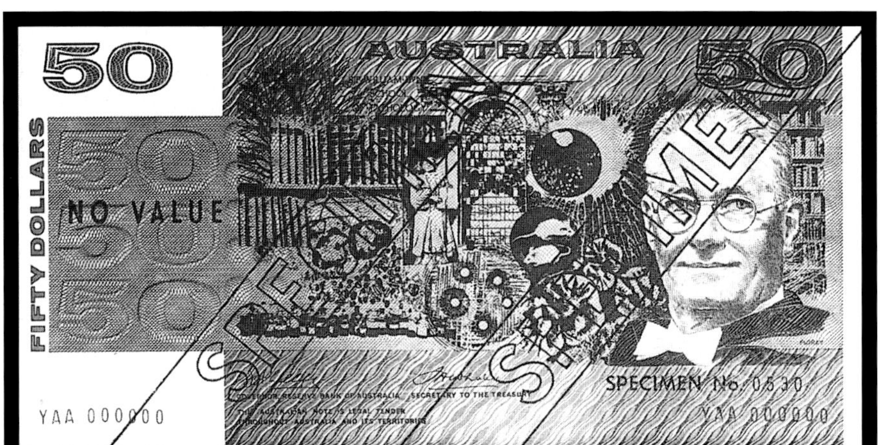

Fig. 143. Front, $50 specimen, Third type.

THIRD TYPE SPECIMEN NOTES

The Third type of decimal specimen note was overprinted in an entirely different manner from the previous types. In the first two types, once issued, there was no way of identifying the individual notes, or one set from another, unless the book containing them was inscribed to a particular recipient. The Third type not only changed the style of overprinting, but added an individual specimen number. Then any note located in possible unauthorised circumstances, could be traced back to the original recipient.

There were two large hollow block words "SPECIMEN" diagonally across the front and the back of Type three specimens. In addition, "NO VALUE" was printed on the left side of the front and the right side of the back, and on the front bottom right was "SPECIMEN No. (and a four digit number)."

Because specimen notes were produced primarily for use by, and within, the Reserve Bank of Australia and for distribution to other central (overseas) banks, the Reserve Bank will not release details of serial number spans or quantities produced. The following details have been compiled mainly from notes recorded in catalogues of public auctions up to June, 2000.

Phillips-Wheeler (Australia) all ending with 000000.

Denomination	Prefix	Lowest number	Highest number	Totals in auctions
$1	BLG	0014	0097	6
$2	HBQ	0014	0097	6
$5	NKG	0014	0066	5
$10	TBC	0014	0097	7
$20	XGY	0014	0097	4
$50	YAA	0001-97, 0195-225, 0530-534		16

Fig. 144. Back, $50 specimen, Third type.

On 21 September, 1982, several men hid themselves in wooden boxes in the same hold of an aircraft carrying consignments of Australian notes, with the intention of stealing the notes during the flight. An employee of T.A.A. noticed the movement of a person inside a box on board the aircraft which had just landed at Rockhampton, Queensland, and alerted others. He then chased and apprehended the man.

Other T.A.A. employees realised that this incident might not have been an isolated one, and their prompt actions led to accomplices being arrested at Townsville, Mt. Isa and Brisbane. On 21 October, 1983, the Governor of the Reserve Bank Mr. R.A. Johnston, presented awards to ten T.A.A. employees. The main cash reward was made to the employee from Rochkampton. Each man received a set of Orrefors glassware and a personally inscribed volume containing specimen Australian notes. The books were modified versions of the books for the Type one notes in 1966, and contained one specimen note of each denomination from $1 to $50 bearing the facsimile signatures of Johnston-Stone, with Type three overprinting.

All notes in the T.A.A. books had "OCR-B" serial numbering. It was of particular significance because "OCR-B" serial numbering was not used on circulating $50 notes of that signature combination, and never used on circulating $1 notes.

Up until June, 2000, the following notes had been observed from the T.A.A. presentations with Johnston-Stone signatures, all notes ending 000000. Sets numbered 13 - 24.

Denomination	Prefix	Lowest number	Highest number	Totals in auctions.
$1	DHY	0013	0025	5
$2	KBL	0013	0042	5
$5	PFY	0013	0042	6
$10	TYV	0013	0042	6
$20	VGX	0013	0043	6
$50	YJK	0013	0042	6

Highest Specimen numbers quoted are in the R.B.A. Collection.

Fig. 145. Front, $1 (TAA) Specimen note with OCR-B serial numbering.

The following single notes have also been observed;

Denomination	Prefix	Number	Totals in auctions
$10	TBC	0097	1
$20	XGY	0097	1

$2 notes similar to this type, but with the signature combination of Johnston-Fraser, and without the words "NO VALUE" or individual specimen numbers, were offered for sale on the internet in December 1999 and January 2000. No official record had been located by January, 2000, to verify them as having been officially issued. Such notes bore the serial letter prefixes KYA and different serial numbers at and around 667500.

Fig. 146. Front, 000000 note from the end of a normal print run.

Almost all specimen notes have serial number numerals 000000, but not all 000000 notes are specimen notes. During a normal print run the sheets of notes are numbered from 999999 in descending order and finish at 000000, exactly 1,000,000 sheets. The last sheet numbered with 000000 was then removed, not issued, and later destroyed. This left the notes, once guillotined, in proper numerical order. The note illustrated above was found in circulation, indicating that the top 000000 sheet had not been removed. A similar $20 note may also have been found in circulation.

The first 000000 sheet in each of the new polymer note issues was donated by the Reserve Bank of Australia from 1992 and auctioned for charity. They were later privately cut up and sold separately.

FOURTH TYPE SPECIMEN NOTES

A fourth type was issued with the introduction of the $100 note. See next page. Card folders autographed by the designer Harry Williamson, contained one or two of the $100 specimen notes and these were presented by the Reserve Bank to people connected with its production. A pair with specimen numbers 0050 and 0550 was sold in a Reserve Bank card folder with a letter to the recipient by Downies Australian Coin Auctions in September, 1994, with the statement "Records indicate that only approximately 66 such pairs were presented, this being just the second that we have offered".

Fig. 147. Front, $100 Specimen, Fourth type.

This type of overprinting obviously took into account the need to render the note not negotiable, but without obscuring or spoiling the design.

On the front of the note the word “SPECIMEN” appears in red under the denomination figures. The word, 26 x 3 mm, is situated 21 mm from the left edge and 7 mm from the right edge. On the back a similar word appears under the denomination figure, under which is a separate specimen number e.g. “SPECIMEN No. (four digit number)”.

All Type four specimen notes were of the $100 denomination with the facsimile signatures of Johnston-Stone and the serial numbers ZAA 000000. Two separate printings may have taken place as there have been nine different notes observed in auctions up to January, 2000, with specimen numbers ranging from 0020 to 0073 and 0520 to 0563. Some recipients received “pairs” with specimen numbers 500 apart, e.g. Dr. Coombs - 0020 and 0520. Further reading: *Nugget Coombs' Specimen Notes,* Michael Vort-Ronald, *Australian Coin Review,* August, 1998.

Fig. 148. Back, $100 Specimen, Fourth type.

Chapter 7: CIRCULATED PAPER NOTE ISSUES

V.	Type	Year	Signatures	Variations
One Dollar				
65	1	1966	Coombs-Wilson	
66		1968	Coombs-Randall	
67		1969	Phillips -Randall	
68		1972	Phillips-Wheeler	"Commonwealth of Australia"
69	2	1974	Phillips-Wheeler	"Australia"
70a		1976	Knight-Wheeler	Centre thread
70b		1977	Knight-Wheeler	Centre thread, DBP prefix
70c		1976	Knight-Wheeler	Side thread
71		1979	Knight-Stone	
72		1983	Johnston-Stone	Replaced by $1 coin 1984.
Two Dollars				
85	1	1966	Coombs-Wilson	
86		1967	Coombs-Randall	
87		1968	Phillips-Randall	
88		1972	Phillips-Wheeler	"Commonwealth of Australia"
89	2	1974	Phillips-Wheeler	"Australia"
90a		1976	Knight-Wheeler	"Gothic" serial numbering
90b		1976	Knight-Wheeler	"OCR-B" centre thread
90c		1976	Knight-Wheeler	"OCR-B" side thread
91		1979	Knight-Stone	
92		1983	Johnston-Stone	
93		1985	Johnston-Fraser	Replaced by $2 coin 1988.
Five Dollars				
105	1	1967	Coombs-Randall	
106		1969	Phillips-Randall	
107		1972	Phillips-Wheeler	"Commonwealth of Australia"
108	2	1974	Phillips-Wheeler	"Australia"
109a		1976	Knight-Wheeler	"Gothic" centre thread
109b		1977	Knight-Wheeler	"Gothic" side thread
109c		1978	Knight-Wheeler	"OCR-B" serial numbering
110		1979	Knight-Stone	
111		1983	Johnston-Stone	
112a		1985	Johnston-Fraser	"OCR-B" serial numbering
112b		1988	Johnston-Fraser	"Gothic" serial numbering
113		1990	Fraser-Higgins	
114		1991	Fraser-Cole	Replaced by polymer note 1992.

Ten Dollars

125	1	1966	Coombs-Wilson	
126		1967	Coombs-Randall	
127		1968	Phillips-Randall	
128		1972	Phillips-Wheeler	"Commonwealth of Australia"
129	2	1974	Phillips-Wheeler	"Australia"
130a		1976	Knight-Wheeler	Centre thread
130b		1976	Knight-Wheeler	Side thread
131a		1979	Knight-Stone	"Gothic" serial numbering
131b		1981	Knight-Stone	"OCR-B" serial numbering
132		1983	Johnston-Stone	
133		1985	Johnston-Fraser	(134 - 1988 polymer commemorative)
135		1989	Fraser-Higgins	
136		1991	Fraser-Cole	Replaced by polymer note 1993.

Twenty Dollars

145	1	1966	Coombs-Wilson	
146		1968	Coombs-Randall	
147		1968	Phillips-Randall	
148		1972	Phillips-Wheeler	"Commonwealth of Australia"
149	2	1974	Phillips-Wheeler	"Australia"
150a		1975	Knight-Wheeler	Centre thread
150b		1976	Knight-Wheeler	Side thread
151a		1979	Knight-Stone	"Gothic" serial numbering
151b		1982	Knight-Stone	"OCR-B" serial numbering
152		1983	Johnston-Stone	
153a		1985	Johnston-Fraser	"OCR-B" serial numbering
153b		1988	Johnston-Fraser	"Gothic" serial numbering
154		1989	Phillips-Fraser	
155		1989	Fraser-Higgins	
156		1991	Fraser-Cole	
157		1993	Fraser-Evans	Replaced by polymer note 1994.

Fifty Dollars

165	1	1973	Phillips-Wheeler	(Australia)
166a		1975	Knight-Wheeler	Centre thread
166b		1976	Knight-Wheeler	Side thread
167		1979	Knight-Stone	
168		1984	Johnston-Stone	
169a		1985	Johnston-Fraser	"Gothic" serial numbering
169b		1988	Johnston-Fraser	"OCR-B" 0.3 serial numbering
170		1989	Phillips-Fraser	
171		1990	Fraser-Higgins	
172		1991	Fraser-Cole	
173		1993	Fraser-Evans	Replaced by polymer note 1995.

One Hundred Dollars

185	1	1984	Johnston-Stone	
186		1985	Johnston-Fraser	
187		1990	Fraser-Higgins	
188		1992	Fraser-Cole	Replaced by polymer note 1996.

SERIAL NUMBER PREFIXES OF AUSTRALIAN DECIMAL PAPER NOTES

A	$20	Gold or red numbers in uncut pairs
A	$50	Red or black numbers in uncut blocks of four
A	$100	Red or black numbers in uncut blocks of four
B	$20	Gold or red numbers in uncut pairs
B	$50	Red or black numbers in uncut blocks of four
B	$100	Red or black numbers in uncut blocks of four
C	$20	Gold or red numbers in uncut blocks of four
C	$50	Red or black numbers in uncut blocks of four
C	$100	Red or black numbers in uncut blocks of four
D	$20	Gold or red numbers in uncut blocks of four
D	$50	Red or black numbers in uncut blocks of four
D	$100	Red or black numbers in uncut blocks of four
E	$20	Gold or red numbers in uncut blocks of four
E	$50	Red or black numbers in uncut pairs
E	$100	Red or black numbers in uncut pairs
F	$20	Gold or red numbers in uncut blocks of four
F	$50	Red or black numbers in uncut pairs
F	$100	Red or black numbers in uncut pairs
M	$20	Red numbers from 80th Anniversary of first Commonwealth note folder
HF	$50	Red or black numbers from Florey portfolio
AA93	$10	Red number from Last and First portfolio
AA94	$20	Red number from Last and First portfolio
AA95	$50	Red number from Last and First portfolio
AA96	$100	Red number from Last and First portfolio
AAA - ADK	$20	General circulation note
AAA - DPS	$1	General circulation note
EAA - EZZ	$20	General circulation note
FAA - FAB	$50	General circulation note
FAA - LQG	$2	General circulation note
MAA - MRR	$10	General circulation note
NAA - QPG	$5	General circulation note
RAA - RZZ	$20	General circulation note
SAA - UZZ	$10	General circulation note
VAA - VZZ	$20	General circulation note
XAA - XZZ	$20	General circulation note
XXV	$5	Uncut vertical and horizontal pairs and blocks of four
YAA - YZZ	$50	General circulation note
ZAA - ZAQ	$1	Star note omitting ZAI, ZAO, ZAM.
ZAA - ZLD	$100	General circulation note
ZFA - ZFS	$2	Star note omitting ZFI, ZFO, ZFM.
ZNA - ZND	$5	Star note
ZSA - ZSJ	$10	Star note omitting ZSI
ZXA	$20	Star note

$10, SAA - UZZ then MAA - MRR. then RAA - RZZ then AAA - ADK.

$20, XAA - XZZ then VAA - VZZ then EAA - EZZ

$50, YAA - YZZ then FAA - FAB.

V.65-68 $1	**ONE DOLLAR**
Type	First. "COMMONWEALTH OF AUSTRALIA".
Issued	14 February, 1966, to June, 1974.
Size	140 mm x 770 mm.
Watermark	The profile of Captain James Cook appears on the left side of the front, facing right. See Fig. 101. A metallic security thread runs vertically through the note approximately 65 mm from the left edge of the front.
Signatures	Coombs - Wilson, Coombs - Randall, Phillips - Randall, Phillips - Wheeler.
Serial numbers	AAA 000001 to BLG 770000. ZAA 00001* to ZAQ 100000*.
Total printed	657,770,000.

Fig. 149. Front, $1 note. First type (V.65).

FRONT

Main print: Dark brown intaglio. 128 mm x 62 mm.
The main features on the front of the note are the exemplification of the Australian Coat-of-Arms drawn by Gordon Andrews in conformity with the Royal Warrant dated 19 September, 1912, and a portrait of Her Majesty Queen Elizabeth II. The original Coat-of-Arms was granted by His Majesty King George V. Near the bottom appears the facsimile signatures of the Governor of the Reserve Bank of Australia and the Secretary to the Treasury. Under the signature titles appears "Legal tender throughout the Commonwealth of Australia and in the Territories of the Commonwealth".

Background print: Dry offset using four colours. 133 mm x 70 mm.
Across the horizontal centre are 78 straight lines close together. The lines in the centre are thinner resulting in the impression of a "glow". The background around the portrait of the Queen and behind the Coat-of-Arms consists of a series of khaki coloured vertical lines between which are two vertical orange lines and a wavy khaki line. The vertical centre of the background rainbows yellow. Vertical orange lines give colouring to the face of the Queen. "ONE DOLLAR" appears on the left in orange framed in khaki.

Fig. 150. Photograph of Her Majesty The Queen as supplied for the design of the $1 note.

The illustration above of Her Majesty the Queen was reproduced from the original photograph supplied to the Reserve Bank of Australia for the specific and only purpose of incorporation into the design of the $1 note. It was one of a large selection taken by Douglas Glass of London, and depicts Her Majesty in the Regalia of the Order of the Garter.

Alistair Morrison, Chairman of the Currency Note Design Group, in a letter to Russell Drysdale on 22 August, 1963, made recommendations in relation to photographs to be taken of the Queen by Douglas Glass (Reserve Bank of Australia Archives file N-a-156):

> *(1) Full range of tone from light highlights to deep shadows; not flat; not merely hard contrast of light and dark, but full tonal range.*
>
> *(2) Simple, clear, sharp outline so that head and shoulders may, if required, be used in silhouette against a light background. This would suggest profile or three-quarters views, but full frontal shots also wanted as these may possibly be required.*
>
> *(3) Also wanted: As above but against graduated tone background, for use if required not in silhouette. Simple clear outline would still be required.*

(4) Some photos wearing crown, some coronet, some tiara, presumably with bare shoulders of formal evening wear. Some in uniform of some kind which would lend itself to rich details of engraving, (folds of heavy cloth, epaulettes, etc.) If bare-headed, remember that hair styles quickly become unfashionable.

(5) General effect to be regal, rather than "domestic". .."

The assignment by Mr. Glass took up a week in many arrangements and a fully qualified Photographer was engaged as an assistant in order that the assignment would be covered should anything happen to him. His fee was 250 pounds (N-a-156).

Her Majesty Queen Elizabeth II

Queen Elizabeth II was born Elizabeth Alexandra Mary, the elder daughter of the Duke of York (later King George VI), in London on 21 April, 1926. The Queen (then Princess Elizabeth) appeared in public on formal Royal business for the first time in 1944. On 20 November, 1947, she married Lieut. Philip Mountbatten, R.N., formerly Prince Philip of Greece and Denmark, the only son of Prince Andrew of Greece. In 1947, King George VI conferred on his son-in-law the titles of Royal Highness and Duke of Edinburgh.

King George VI died on 6 February, 1952, and his daughter Princess Elizabeth then ascended the throne. The coronation of Queen Elizabeth II took place at Westminster Abbey on 2 June, 1953. Her accession was accompanied by a constitutional innovation. She was proclaimed in each of the self-governing countries of what used to be called the British Empire, as Queen of that particular country. The formal abandonment of the principle of indivisibility of the Crown was confirmed by statute in 1953 and a new description, "Head of the Commonwealth" was inserted amongst the Royal titles to allow for the inclusion of republics like India and Pakistan. In 1957 the Queen conferred on her husband the style and titular dignity of a Prince of the United Kingdom.

The *Royal Style and Titles Act 1973* was assented to on 19 October, 1973, at Government House, Canberra. This Act adopted the following title for Her Majesty to be used in relation to Australia and its Territories: *Elizabeth the Second, by the Grace of God Queen of Australia and Her Other Realms and Territories, Head of the Commonwealth.*

There are four children of the marriage: Prince Charles, born 14 November, 1948; Princess Anne, born 15 August, 1950; Prince Andrew, born 19 February, 1960 and Prince Edward, born 10 March, 1964.

On 9 April, 1952, The Queen officially announced that she and her children would be styled and known as the House and Family of Windsor and that their descendants, other than female descendants who marry and their descendants, would bear the name of Windsor. On 8 February, 1960, The Queen further declared that *her descendants, other than the descendants enjoying the style, title or attribute or HRH and titular dignity of prince or princess, and females who marry and their descendants, shall bear the name of Mountbatten-Windsor.*

Coat of Arms

In his book *A Designer's Life*, the designer Gordon Andrews said of his stylised Coat of Arms:

> *....An emu is the last animal in the world I would choose to stylise and although our kangaroo is quite beautiful when seen in full flight through the bush, when standing still and holding the corner of a shield with its forepaws, its long powerful tail sticks out stiffly, refusing to allow the whole assembly to balance. I stuck my neck out when designing the $1 note by turning the tail upwards, thus managing to get the arrangement into a compact space. There was no objection to my solution, only approval from Stephen Mansfield, an authority on heraldry.....*

Mr. J.L. Stephen Mansfield replied on 31 July, 1964 (Reserve Bank Archives file N-a-156):

> *....Having examined Mr. Gordon Andrews' drawing of the Australian coat of arms I am confident in stating that it may be described as "heraldically correct" and entirely in accordance with the blazon, as set forth in the Royal Warrant dated 19th September, 1912.*
>
> *I am greatly impressed with his exemplification of the Arms - the technical term used for particular representation in drawing, carving, etc. of a coat, influenced by the material and technique used, size, position, purpose, current fashion and above all by the style of the artist.....With regard to Mr. Andrews' drawing, I particularly admire the manner in which he has drawn the supporters. Both kangaroo and emu are blazoned "proper" - a term primarily meaning "in natural colours" and not "depicted with photographic realism". With black and white or monotone the representation of "proper" presents a difficulty, which Mr. Andrews has overcome most successfully.....*

Fig. 151. Back, sheet of 35 "Commonwealth of Australia" $1 notes.

Fig. 152. Back, $1 note. First type (V.65).

Fig. 153. Back, $1 note main print (Intaglio) only (error note V.68).

BACK

Main Print: Dark brown intaglio. 136 mm x 58 mm.

Across the top is "COMMONWEALTH OF AUSTRALIA" and a large "1" is at top left and bottom right. The whole main feature is a line interpretation of an Aboriginal bark painting by David Malangi, and of Aboriginal bark paintings and carvings. The initials of Gordon Andrews appear to the bottom left of the tree. See illustration above for example of Intaglio printing.

Background Print: Dry offset in three colours. 84 mm x 70 mm.

The background design consists of a series of horizontal wavy lines alternating in orange and khaki, rainbowed yellow in the vertical centre.

Gordon Andrews described the back of the note as an adaption of Aboriginal paintings and carvings, preserving authenticity and without souvenir trade connotations. The colours were an earthy brown and orange-brown combined with a subdued green.

Fig. 154. David Malangi, 1982.

The above illustration of David Malangi is from a photograph taken in 1982 when he was 55 years of age, and is reproduced by courtesy of *The Advertiser.*

David Malangi

The South Pacific Post of 11 February, 1966, featured an article about David Malangi after an interview with Mr. Karel Kupka, who was in charge of the Australian Aboriginal Research Section of the Paris Museum of the Arts of Africa and Oceana, Paris, France. David was then a 39 year-old Australian Aborigine who lived on Milingimbi, one of the Crocodile Islands off the Arnhem Land coast. One of a number of his paintings collected by Mr. Kupka was a bark painting. Photographs were taken by Max Dupain of the Karal Kupka collection of bark paintings, and negatives were lent to the Reserve Bank of Australia, and later partly reproduced on the back of the $1 note. David then described his painting to Mr. Kupka in the following terms:

> *It is a funeral feast celebrating the eternal renewal of nature and the human species. The figure standing beside the snake is a spirit. The other three figures - all squatting or sitting - are human beings.*
> *The spirit's name is Gurmirringu. The three human figures are musicians, two of whom are beating sticks to accompany singing.*
> *The snake is a second version of the spirit. In the snake form the spirit is called Marramal.*

Other interpretations of the meaning of the design have appeared in newspapers following later interviews with David Malangi. *The Sunday Telegraph* of 11 May, 1969 :

> *...the design representing the mourning rites of the Manurrnu tribe, performed immediately after death. Mortuary rites were later performed to guide the spirit to its final resting place. The mourning ceremony depicted on the one dollar note tells the story of a great hunter, the original guardian spirit of the tribe. He is the central figure on the design. At the end of a day's hunting he has rested by the waterhole to eat his evening meal. Around him on the ground is the food that he has killed or gathered. Although the story is always the same, the layout is often different.*

The Advertiser of 5 March, 1982, interviewed David Malangi at the Adelaide Festival of Arts where he was displaying his work, and the following interpretation was then given:

> *The hunter's wife made him promise not to kill birds or animals at the billabong because it was so beautiful, so he had to go a long way to get his tucker. One day he returned with a dead kangaroo, but he was so tired he rested at the billabong. An evil spirit living in a tree told a big snake to come out and kill the hunter, and when the wife came down to the billabong she found her husband was dead. She took the dead kangaroo back to camp where the people cut it up and cooked it. The picture on the note shows this ceremony...*

The Bank made a payment of $1,000 to David in 1966 through the Department of Welfare in the Northern Territory in recognition of the use of some of his work in the design of the $1 note. On 7 August, 1967, Dr. H.C. Coombs presented him with a medallion attached to a chain by two lugs near the top and housed in a white-lined velvet case. It was inscribed on one side with *Presented to Malangi by Dr. H.C. Coombs, Governor of the Reserve Bank of Australia, 7th August 1967,* and on the other side *To commemorate his contribution to the design of the Australian $1.00 note.* He was also given a fully-equipped fishing box.

The payment is credited with accelerating the promotion of copyright and respect for individual Aboriginal artists. The 1970s were believed to have been David's most productive years, during which he occupied several artist-in-residence positions, including a position at Sydney University. His work was chosen for the 1983 *Perspecta Show* and a set of paintings was commissioned by the State Bank of New South Wales in 1986.

The Royal Australian Mint specially commissioned a bark painting by Malangi for the packaging of the 1990 coin sets. It was named *Yathalamarra Waterhole* and was then valued at $3,000. The painting depicted a Dreamtime story from David's *Ramingining* tribal homeland.

David was born in 1927 at the Glyde River Mouth, Central Arnhem Land, Northern Territory. He became a man who possessed a great sense of humour, wit, physical charm and generosity. He died on 19 June, 1999, at Yathalamarra, Northern Territory. In his obituary he was described as *One of the most important indigenous visual arts figures in the post-war period, an experimenter and innovator to the end - always looking for ways to express and explain his love of his country, the environment and his family...* Aboriginal custom directs that his tribal name of David Daymirringu be used after his death. Reference and further reading: *Dollar note won artist increased respect - Time and Tide* - Obituary by Djon Mundine, *The Australian,* 1 July, 1999.

$1 "COMMONWEALTH OF AUSTRALIA" NOTES

Serial numbering "Gothic" type, as in Fig. 187.

V.65

Signatures

H.C. Coombs Governor, Reserve Bank of Australia.
Roland Wilson Secretary to the Treasury.

Fig 155. Signatures and titles, Coombs-Wilson $1 (V.65).

Issued	14 February, 1966.		
Serial numbers	AAA 000001 - AGE 210000.	Printed	130,210,000.
Star notes	ZAA 00001* - ZAF 35000*.	Printed	535,000.

V.66

Signatures

H.C. Coombs Governor, Reserve Bank of Australia.
R.J. Randall Secretary to the Treasury.

Fig. 156. Signatures and titles, Coombs-Randall $1 (V.66).

Issued	February, 1968.		
Serial numbers	AGE 210001 - AHY 900000.	Printed	37,690,000.
Star notes	ZAF 45001* - ZAH 17000*.	Printed	172,000.

116

V.67

Signatures

J.G. Phillips Governor, Reserve Bank of Australia.
R.J. Randall Secretary to the Treasury.

Fig. 157. Signatures and titles, Phillips-Randall $1 (V.67).

Serial numbers	AHY 900001 - BBE 999999.	Printed	299,100,000.
Star notes	ZAH 17001* - ZAQ 100000*. ZAI, ZAO, ZAM excluded.	Printed	683,000.

V.68

Signatures **J.G. Phillips** Governor, Reserve Bank of Australia.
F.H. Wheeler Secretary to the Treasury.

Fig. 158. Signatures, titles, legal tender clause, Phillips-Wheeler (Commonwealth) $1 (V.68).

Issued May, 1972.

Serial numbers BBF 000001 - BLG 770000. Printed 190,770,000.

No star notes were issued from this signature combination onwards.

From 11 June, 1974, notes with "AUSTRALIA" were issued, slowly replacing notes with "COMMONWEALTH OF AUSTRALIA". See Second type, following.

The change took place following a directive of the then Prime Minister, the Right Honourable E.G. Whitlam (Labor Party). The direction was that whenever possible and as soon as possible, references to "COMMONWEALTH OF AUSTRALIA" should be changed to "AUSTRALIA" in official descriptions generally. It was the Prime Minister's belief that the term "COMMONWEALTH", however relevant it may have been in 1901 upon Federation, no longer carried the same sort of connotations in the 1970s, in particular because of its association with "British Commonwealth" and "Commonwealth of Nations" etc.

These changes did not require any Constitutional authority or an amendment of the Reserve Bank Act. Where possible this was done, including the change on Australian notes.

Early in 1977, the wording on Australian notes was reviewed by the Government (Liberal Party) in the context of the use of the terms "Commonwealth of Australia" and "Australia". Because of the costs involved, and for other reasons, the Government decided not to request the Reserve Bank to change the present wording on Australian notes. One of the other factors was that there was consistency in the use of the expression "Australia" on both notes and coins. See also, $50 notes.

Elimination of watermark proposal

In 1957, consideration was given to the elimination of the watermark from the ten shilling note, but no decision was made, and from then until 1960, nothing much happened to influence any further decisions one way or the other. Correspondence preserved in Reserve Bank of Australia Archives - (File N-a-162) contains discussions on the matter. The conclusions reached in a letter dated 23 September, 1960, were that there was a need to improve the resistance of the 10/- note to the hard usage which it was subjected to in circulation, and it seemed that the use of a non-watermarked paper with coloured fibres in lieu of the present 10/- paper might offer some prospects of success in that regard. The proposed change-over to decimal currency and the need to make what might have been regarded as an interim issue of the new notes, would have provided a good opportunity to test out the superiority of the new type of paper, which was considered to be stronger. Modifications to the designs of the existing 10/- notes were suggested to accommodate any such changes. The idea was approved, but both the old and new notes still used the watermark.

V.69-72 **$1** **ONE DOLLAR.**

Type Second. "AUSTRALIA".

Issued 11 June, 1974 to 11 May, 1984.

Signatures Phillips - Wheeler, Knight - Wheeler, Knight - Stone, Johnston - Stone. Other details as in the First type.

Serial numbers BLG 770001 to DPS 999956.

Printed 1,015,229,901.

Fig. 159. Front, $1 note. Second type (V.69).

FRONT AND BACK

All main design details and features are the same as in the First type, with the following exceptions. "AUSTRALIA" replaced "COMMONWEALTH OF AUSTRALIA" at the top in larger lettering than previously and the legal tender clause was changed to read "This Australian note is legal tender throughout Australia and its Territories". Background design and details remained the same as those in the First type. Some later issues of the "AUSTRALIA" series had a darker khaki appearance.

Fig. 160. Back, $1 note. Second type (V.69).

$1 "AUSTRALIA" NOTES. "Gothic" serial numbering

V.69

Signatures — **J.G. Phillips** Governor, Reserve Bank of Australia.
F.H. Wheeler Secretary to the Treasury.

Fig. 161. Signatures, titles, legal tender clause, Phillips-Wheeler (Australia) $1 (V.69).

Issued — 11 June, 1974.

Serial numbers — BLG 770001 - BYB 999999. Printed 210,230,000.

Sheet content 35 — BLG uncertain, then BLH-BNY, BPA-BQQ, BQR-BSG, BSH-BTX, BTY-BVL, BVN-BYB.

V.70.

Signatures — **H.M. Knight** Governor, Reserve Bank of Australia.
F.H. Wheeler Secretary to the Treasury.

Fig. 162. Signatures and titles, Knight-Wheeler $1 (V.70).

First issued — March, 1976.

Serial numbers — BYC 000001 - CPJ 999945. Printed 314,999,945.
DBP 000001 - DBP 999999. Possibly printed 1,000,000.

Varieties (a) "Centre thread". Metallic security thread approximately 65 mm from the left edge of the front.

Sheet content 35 — BYC-BZR, BZS-CBF, CBG-CCV, CCX-CEK, CEL-CGA.
With variety (c), CGB-CHQ, CHR-CKE.

(b) "Centre thread" DBP serial prefixes (see next page).

(c) "Side thread". Metallic security thread approximately 55 mm from the left edge of the front.

Sheet content 35 — With (a), CGB-CHQ, CHR-CKE, then CKF-CLU, CLV-CPJ.

A letter to the editor of the *Australian Coin Review,* December 1988, from a former employee in Note Issue Administration gave an explanation for the DBP issue.

> *...The cost of printing the $1 note was of concern to the bank given that some 80 million $1 notes were on issue at any one time and their life span was a mere seven months. As early as 1976 the Note Issue was considering options to cut the cost of printing some 100 millions plus $1 notes each year. One consideration was the issue of a more durable note. Alternatively, consideration was being given to withdrawing the note and replacing it with a $1 coin.*
> *The exercise involving the issue of a more durable note called for Portals, who at that time supplied all of the bank's printing paper, to provide a more durable paper. The paper currently in use was referred to as "single fold" paper while the "new" test paper was referred to as a "double fold" paper. The "double fold" paper was of course a more costly paper. One million notes with the DBP prefix were specially printed for the exercise with the first 500,000 being printed on the "double fold" paper and the remainder i.e. from DBP 500001 to DBP 999999 being printed on the "single fold" paper.*
> *Western Australia was chosen for the test area and stocks of both "double fold" and "single fold" notes were despatched to the Reserve Bank, Perth for issue to private banks in the area. As private banks requisitioned $1 notes, a mix of both "double fold" and "single fold" notes were supplied. In due course, as $1 notes filtered back into the Reserve Bank, the DBP notes were outsorted, appropriately tagged and returned to the Note Printing Branch at Fitzroy for wear analysis.*
> *Sadly the tests were to show that the durability of the "double fold" paper was only marginally better than the "single fold" paper and did not justify the additional expenditure arising from the use of the more costly paper. No further notes were printed on "double fold" paper......Notes numbered DBP 000001 to DBP 500000 were printed on the special "double fold" paper.*

Of the DBP notes, 400,000 were sent to Brisbane and to Perth (hence DBP) and later, some to Hobart. High numbered DBP notes have been observed to become semi-transparent in water while low numbers do not, as per other signature combinations. It may be that the test notes were from 500001 to 1000000, bearing in mind that notes were usually numbered backwards, from 999999 to 000001. A DBP note with the serial number 1000000 has also appeared in auction. It is the only known decimal 1000000 printed after the discontinuance of printing 1000000 numbers in 1971.

Frank Robinson's study of plate letters indicates that the DBP notes were numbered in the following batches, 35 notes per sheet:

DBP 000051 - 350050	10,000 sheets = 350,000 notes.
DBP 350051 - 490050	4,000 sheets = 140,000 notes.
DBP 490051 - 500025	285 sheets = 9,975 notes.
DBP 500026 - 850025	None observed, may not have been issued, but could represent 10,000 sheets = 350,000 notes.
DBP 850026 - 990025	4,000 sheets = 140,000 notes.
DBP 990026 - 1000000	285 sheets = 9,975 notes.

From July, 1976, all paper despatched by the Note Printing Branch's suppliers had the security thread positioned in an area approximately 55 mm from the left edge of the front. The change was made to avoid the natural fold area, which, because of its proximity to the metallic thread, caused undue wear and tearing. No records are available as to where the "centre thread" positions ceased and the "side thread" notes commenced, but note BYX 780889 has been seen with side thread and 780890, 1 and 2 with centre thread. However, Frank Robinson's exhaustive study on Plate Identification Letters has enabled sheet contents and prefix ranges to be calculated and these are included in "AUSTRALIA" note references throughout these listings.

V.71

Signatures — **H.M. Knight** Governor, Reserve Bank of Australia.
John Stone Secretary to the Treasury.

Fig. 163. Signatures and titles, Knight-Stone $1 (V.71).

Issued — First despatched from Note Issue Department, May 1979.

Serial numbers — CPK 000001 - DGH 999999. Printed 350,000,000.
DBP omitted and included in V.70.

Sheet content 35 — CPK-CQZ, CRA-CSP, CSQ-CUD, CUE-CVT, CVU-CYH, CYJ-CZY, CZZ-DBN, DBQ-DDD, DDE-DET, DEU-DGH.

V72

Signatures — **R.A. Johnston** Governor, Reserve Bank of Australia.
John Stone Secretary to the Treasury.

Fig. 164. Signatures and titles, Johnston-Stone $1 (V.72).

Issued — February 1983 to 11 May, 1984.

Serial numbers — DGJ 000001 - DPS 999956. Printed 139,999,956.
Notes with OCR-B serial numbering were used on some specimen notes only - see Specimen Notes. The Reserve Bank of Australia declined to disclose how many new notes were destroyed after the issue of this denomination ceased.

Sheet content 35 — DGJ-DHY, DHZ-DKN, DKP-DNC, DND-DPS.

V73-84 — Reference numbers not used.

On 29 April, 1981, the Treasurer (John Howard) issued a press release to announce that the Government had under consideration the possible issue into general circulation of a $1 coin. Because of the short life of low denomination notes, substantial savings in the cost of maintaining the currency would result from the introduction of such a coin. Before reaching any conclusions the Government invited public comment on the proposal. Major users such as banks, vending machine manufacturers, public authorities and others were invited to submit their views.

On 8 July, 1983, the Treasurer (Paul Keating) announced that the Government had agreed to the introduction into general circulation of a $1 coin and a $100 note. A further announcement on 4 August, 1983, gave a detailed description of the new coin, designed by Stuart Devlin (who also designed the lower denomination coins). The $1 note was last officially issued on Friday 11 May, 1984. On Monday 14 May, the $1 coins were issued and from that day onwards the $1 notes began to be withdrawn from circulation. "Legal tender" for $1 coins is an amount not exceeding $10. "Legal tender" is a maximum amount of a particular currency that cannot be refused in payment of a debt.

Fig. 165a. Examining sheets of $2 notes.

V.85-88 **$2** **TWO DOLLARS**

Type	First. "COMMONWEALTH OF AUSTRALIA".
Issued	14 February, 1966 to June, 1974.
Size	145 mm x 72.5 mm.
Watermark	The profile of Captain James Cook is on the left front, facing right. See Fig. 101. A metallic security thread runs vertically through the note approximately 70 mm from the left edge of the front.
Signatures	Coombs - Wilson, Coombs - Randall, Phillips - Randall, Phillips - Wheeler.
Serial numbers	FAA 000001 to HBQ 528000. ZFA 00001* to ZFS 96107*.
Total printed	916,528,000.

Fig. 165b. Front, $2 note. First type (V.85).

FRONT

Main print: Green-black intaglio. 132 mm x 65 mm.
The main features of the front are the portrait of John Macarthur on the right and a stylised ram in the centre with ornamental ribbons. At the top of the note is "COMMONWEALTH OF AUSTRALIA" and a figure "2" in each top corner. At the bottom, the facsimile signatures of the Governor, Reserve Bank of Australia, and the Secretary to the Treasury, appear above those titles, under which is the legal tender clause, "Legal tender throughout the Commonwealth of Australia and the Territories of the Commonwealth." See fig. 166 illustrating an Intaglio printing phase.

Background print: Dry offset using four colours. 138 mm x 72.5 mm.
In the horizontal centre are 80 fine turquoise coloured straight lines which vary in thickness on the left side resulting in three "glows". The remaining pattern around Macarthur and behind the sheep is a continual series of diagonal wavy lines between which are turquoise coloured lines. The bottom and top sections consist of green lines only. All lines fluctuate in thickness, similar to ribbons. In the vertical centre the colours rainbow to yellow, and on the left written vertically is "TWO DOLLARS" in green, lined in turquoise. See Fig. 167 illustrating a Simultan printing phase.

Fig. 166. Front, $2 note, main print (Intaglio) only (error note).

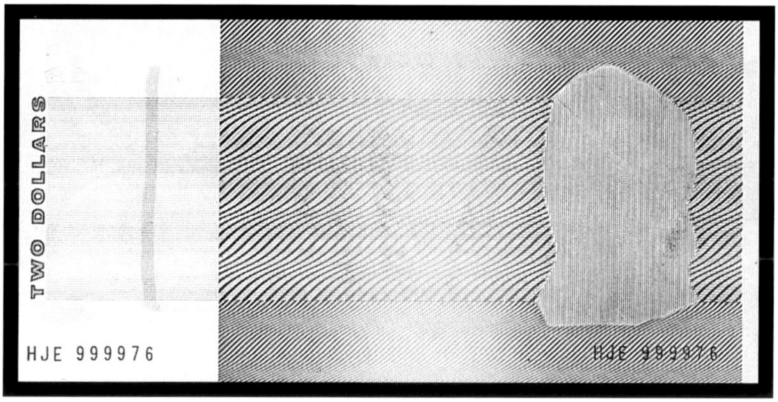

Fig. 167. Front $2 note, background print (Simultan) only (error note).

The two error notes illustrated above show the two main printing stages of the $2 note.

Gordon Andrews was quoted in an interview in the *Sydney Morning Herald* of 11 January, 1966, as saying of the $2 note ...*The two greens are very much brighter, a very blue green and an Australian gum-leaf green, and this combines to become an exciting piece of "op art"* (sic.). He then added, *I don't think I should have said that?* He also stated, according to the newspaper, that he had not used the conventional dollar sign....*a vulgar piece of graphic.*

Fig. 168 is a portion of an unsigned oil painting in, and reproduced by courtesy of, the Dixson Galleries, Sydney. The portrait on the note is very similar to that featured in an oval water-colour which appears as the frontispiece in *John Macarthur*, by M.H. Ellis, Angus and Robertson, 1973. A portion of the frontispiece is reproduced as Fig. 169, by courtesy of the publishers, and Quentin Macarthur Stanham, who possesses the original painting.

Fig. 168. John Macarthur.

Fig. 169. John Macarthur.

John Macarthur

John Macarthur was born in Devonshire, England, and was Christened on 3 September, 1767. At the age of 15 years he joined Fish's Corps, but it was disbanded in 1783, and he retired on half pay to a farm in Devon where he remained for five years. In April 1788, he returned to full pay as ensign, and married Elizabeth Veale in October, 1788. On 5 June, 1789, he attained the rank of Lieutenant by transferring to the New South Wales Corps, being enlisted for duty at Botany Bay. He was "incorrigibly haughty" and invariably quarrelled with almost everyone with whom he came into contact. He left England by ship with his family, bound for Australia.

At the Cape of Good Hope he contracted a critical illness from which (although he made an unexpected recovery) symptoms recurred throughout his life. The family arrived at Port Jackson on 28 June, 1790, and it was not long after, that Macarthur fell out with Governor Phillip. In 1792, he became Regimental Paymaster and by 1793, he was also unpaid Inspector of Public Works. This position gave him extensive and crucial control of the colony's resources. A grant of 100 acres (40 hectares) of land and gifts of stock from his commanding officer, helped to establish Elizabeth Farm at Parramatta in 1793. With unrestricted access to convict labour, he became the first in the colony to clear and cultivate 50 acres (20 hectares) of virgin land, earning him another 100 acre grant. He soon became one of the foremost landholders in the colony, selling produce to the Government. On 6 May, 1795, he was promoted to Captain. He fell out with successive Governors Hunter and King, and was arrested and sent back to England in December, 1802, to stand trial. He carried with him to England, specimens of fleeces from his own flocks, which subsequently were declared *of a very superior quality, equal to the best which comes from Spain.* He energetically canvassed support for an optimistic scheme of colonial wool production to be developed under his personal supervision. His influence enabled him to resign from the Army and return to New South Wales to develop its wool industry. Official approval for his scheme resulted in a 5,000 acre (2,024 hectare) grant of the best land in the colony, to be increased by another 5,000 acres if tangible results were forthcoming. Macarthur obtained rare Spanish sheep from the Royal Flocks for this purpose. He returned to Sydney on 8 June, 1805, and succeeded in obtaining 34 convict labourers to work his combined 8,500 acres (3,440 hectares).

Undisguised hostility took place between Macarthur and Governor William Bligh, and he was arrested and committed for trial on a charge relating to his part ownership of a schooner, the *Parramatta.* In January, 1808, Bligh refused him bail. The commander of the New South Wales Corps ordered Macarthur's release, deposed Bligh, and assumed control of the colony.

Macarthur dabbled in many different enterprises and later went to England to help in the defence of the commander who had released him (Major George Johnston). While in England he learnt that if he returned to Australia he would be arrested for his part in the deposing of Bligh, and he set about exerting his influence in England to remove this possibility. After much negotiation he received permission to return to Australia on the condition that he would in no way involve himself in public affairs. He returned and carried on with his wool production. In 1822, the Society of Arts in London presented him with two gold medals, one for importing 150,000 lbs. (68 tonnes) of fine wool from New South Wales, and the other for the quality of the wool.

Also in 1822, he received his additional grant of 5,000 acres, and in 1824 a further medal for importing the largest quantity of wool into England. Macarthur's son John, in England, secured the incorporation by charter of the Australian Agricultural Company with a capital of one million pounds, to be established on a one million acre (404,700 hectare) grant at Port Stephens, with harbour rights at Newcastle. The company prospered, and within 4 years Macarthur had asserted control of it in New South Wales. He was appointed to the reformed Legislative Council in 1829, but by 1832, he was removed by Governor Bourke on the grounds that he had been *Pronounced a lunatic with little hope of restoration.* He died on 11 April, 1834, and was buried in the vault at Camden Park Estate. A brilliant publicist and organiser, his great service was to focus and promote English interest in colonial potential (albeit for his own benefit). John Macarthur undoubtedly exercised more influence than any other private person in shaping the history of New South Wales from 1796 to 1809. If he did not actually found the wool industry, his services, together with those of his wife and sons, in developing, publicising, and improving the quality of early Australian fleeces, were decisive and crucial points in Australia's history.

Although an excellent father and husband, his temper and temperament (certainly influenced by bouts of illness, which increased in frequency following his return in 1817, and which ended in madness) were such to involve him in almost continual conflict with officials and others with whom he came into contact. Further reading: *Australian Encyclopaedia, 3rd Edition,* 1977, Sydney, The Grolier Society of Australia.

A contrary view of Macarthur is given in *Merinos, Myths and Macarthurs* which expresses the opinion that John Macarthur was unscrupulous, understood nothing about agriculture and contributed nothing of substance to the Australian wool industry. In addition, his wife Elizabeth bore the burden of working the family farms while he spent 12 years out of the colony between 1801 and 1817. Further reading: *Merinos, Myths and Macarthurs,* John Garran and Leslie White, Australian National

University Press, 1985; *Rum Rebellion,* H,V. Evatt, Lloyd O'Neill P/L, Hawthorn, Vic., 1971 and *The Macarthurs of Camden,* S.M. Onslow, Rigby, 1973.

Whatever may be said or thought about the man John Macarthur however, he was one of the pioneers who helped put the Australian wool industry onto a sound footing. His important contribution to the later success of the Australian Merino should therefore be acknowledged.

Elizabeth Farm was built for John and Elizabeth Macarthur from 1793. As fortunes grew the house evolved, with major renovations in 1824, and again in 1835, a year after the death of John Macarthur. This building, named after his wife Elizabeth, is the oldest surviving European-style building in Australia. Since restoration was completed in 1984, Elizabeth Farm has operated as an historic house museum. Situated 20 km from the centre of Sydney at 70 Alice Street, Parramatta, the house and gardens, maintained by the Historic Houses Trust of New South Wales, are open for public inspection from 10 am. to 5 pm. daily.

While the drawing of the merino stud ram on the note is accurate, having been taken from numerous photographic references, no specific sheep was used as a model, and the design is partly stylised.

Fig. 170. Horned Merino ram.

Fig. 171. Poll Merino ram.

The above illustrations, supplied by the South Australian Department of Agriculture, show a horned Merino ram at "Collinsville" which sold for $17,000, and a Poll Merino ram "Pollville", a champion strong-wool Poll Merino at the Royal Show in Adelaide.

MERINO SHEEP IN AUSTRALIA

Governor Arthur Phillip acquired sheep at the Cape of Good Hope in 1787, but they barely survived. The real beginning of Australia's wool industry dates from the introduction of Merino sheep. The first importation is accredited to two naval officers, Henry Waterhouse and William Kent, who had been despatched by Governor John Hunter to the Cape of Good Hope in 1796, to buy cattle and sheep for the government herds. They bought 26 sheep of Spanish Merino blood from the widow of

Colonel Gordon. Waterhouse, master of the *Reliance*, and Kent, master of the *Supply*, bought equal lots at about 4 pounds per head, and transported one group in each ship. It is thought that all the Merinos in the *Supply* died enroute to Sydney, but more than half of the sheep in the *Reliance* are known to have landed safely in June, 1797. Governor Hunter refused to buy them for the government flocks and they were later sold to various colonists, including John Macarthur, who foresaw an industry firmly based on fine-wool production, and his selective breeding methods were entirely directed to that end.

While some sheep breeders remained steadfast in their support of Spanish Merinos, others imported their basic stock from famous Silesian and Saxon studs. By 1826, farmers were paying 20 to 34 pounds each for imported Merino rams, and 70 pounds upwards for Saxon rams. John Macarthur's Saxon Merino ewes were cutting 2-3 lbs of wool in 1840. George Hawker bought a draft of Macarthur Saxons and increased production to 4 lbs by 1860.

Between 1870 and 1900 Hawker introduced Rambouillet Merinos from America and increased size and wool cuts from 4 lbs.to 12 lbs. Judicious use of available genetic material, including some introduction of English longwools, led to the establishment of the large-framed, plain-bodied, strong-wool Bungaree Merinos so well adapted to hot dry pastoral conditions. Merino sheep from Bungaree Stud, near Clare, South Australia (owned by the Hawker family), were featured on the back of the Australian Fifty Pound note from 1914 to 1945 (illustrated below) and One Thousand Pound note from 1914. See *Australian Banknotes,* 2nd edition, Michael P. Vort-Ronald, 1983.

Fig. 172. Back, Australian Fifty Pound note, 1914-1945.

In the 1890s, sheep totals In Australia exceeded 100 million for the first time. In 1895, there were about 40 stations in New South Wales each shearing more than 100,000 sheep annually. Many runs were overstocked, and a series of poor seasons, culminating in the 1902 drought, resulted in heavy losses, reducing numbers to less than 54 million.

An embargo on live Merino exports was gazetted on 28 November, 1929, because some woolgrowers feared that countries which had similar environmental conditions to Australia might break Australia's domination of the world's fine-wool supply. The embargo was lifted for one year in 1968 to allow up to 300 Merino rams to be exported, and was again lifted on 5 July, 1978, for up to a similar number, but in that year and the next, less than the quota was exported. The quota was filled in 1980, but interest from overseas buyers was small in 1981. The Merino embargo was reviewed in 1982 with a visit by Union and Sheep Industry officials to five of the main sheep producing countries which had imported Australian Merino rams. As a result of that trip, the Embargo was continued, but in a modified form. No Merino ewes, or embryos, or ram semen could be exported, but only up to 300 Merino rams selling at more than $1,000 at public auctions could, and any number of rams selling for less than $1,000 at the same approved public ram auctions.

This partially-lifted embargo was reviewed again in June, 1985, to consider the limits on numbers of rams permitted to be sold for export in one year, and the position in relation to possible export of frozen semen which would save the enormous freight costs on rams. There is a genuine rethinking of traditional values and practices among many stud Merino sheep breeders. Those refusing to change are tending to go out of production, while those who skilfully assess and utilise the best of modern technology (both genetic principles with indices based on relative breeding values; and use of techniques such as ultrasound pregnancy diagnosing machines to identify twin-bearing ewes); freezing of ram semen; use of artificial insemination with semen from proven, progeny-tested flock improvers; super-ovulation and embryo transfer; and the use of computers to handle the data collected in objective measurement of flocks to ensure that the quality of the wools produced is acceptable to processors.

In June, 1990, the annual quota limit was set at 900 Merino rams which could be purchased or have semen collected for export at the designated export auction sales. In March, 1997, provision was made for the inclusion of 100 Merino rams on a National Register of Merino Semen Export Donors without having been sold at auction. All semen donors, whether sold at auction or nominated directly to the Register would be part of the annual export quota, with no ram offering semen being physically exported from Australia.

Fig. 173. Back, $2 note. First type (V.85).

Fig. 174. Back $2 note, main print (intaglio) only (error note).

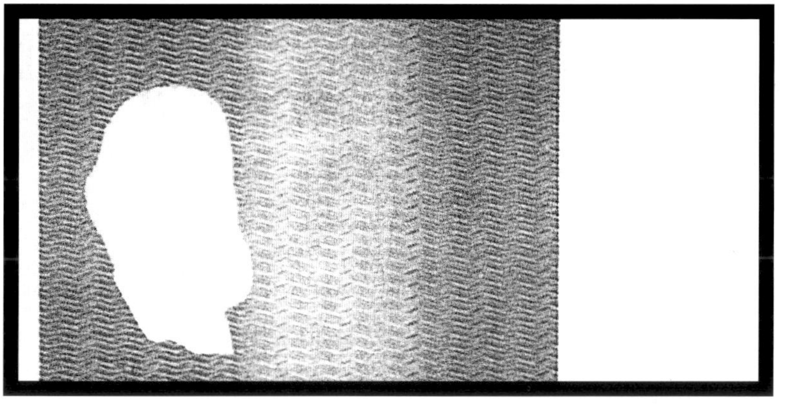

Fig. 175. Back $2 note, background print (Simultan) only (error note).

BACK

Main print: Green-black intaglio. 131 mm x 61 mm.
On the left of the note is a portrait of William James Farrer, reversed from the original. A figure "2" is at top left and bottom right, and the initials of Gordon Andrews appear near the bottom of the third head of wheat. "COMMONWEALTH OF AUSTRALIA" is across the top. See Fig. 174 for example of this printing stage. Across the note are eleven heads of wheat of today, supplied to the designer Gordon Andrews by Mr. D.L. Jackson, Faculty of Agriculture, University of Sydney.

Background print: Dry offset using six colours. 100 mm x 72.5 mm.
The background consists of continual horizontal wavy lines alternating in colour through three shades of green, and turquoise. The background colours rainbow to yellow and orange near the vertical centre and colouring of the face of Farrer are fine vertical green lines. See Fig. 175.

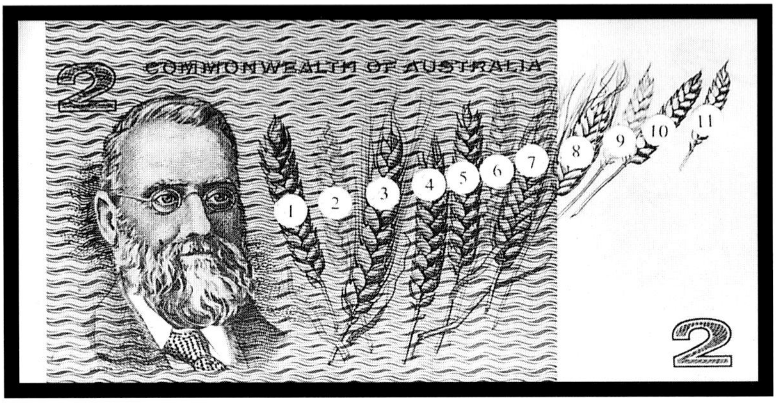

Fig. 176. Back, $2 note, depicting wheat ears.

The wheat heads supplied were believed to have come from the north-western districts of New South Wales which the New South Wales Department of Agriculture identified as follows:

The relatively bald ears numbered 1,2,4,5,6,9,10 and 11 are of the Bencubbin type. This type was one of a series of wheats developed to resist Flag Smut, which by the 1930s, had become so prevalent in many areas that it threatened the future of wheat growing in Australia, reducing the yield of some crops by 50%. The bearded ear, number 3, is probably Spica, one of a number of early-maturing wheats which became important in Queensland from the 1930s, and which is still grown in large areas of that State. The two heavily bearded ears numbered 7 and 8 are of a Duram (Macaroni) variety - probably Dural, a wheat combining high yield and high baking quality, which is particularly popular in the more northern parts of the wheatbelt.

William James Farrer

William James Farrer was born in Westmorland, England, on 3 April, 1845. He studied in England and obtained his Bachelor of Arts degree in 1868. He then studied for the medical profession, but abandoned his studies because of ill-health. On migrating to Australia in 1870, he worked as a tutor and then as a surveyor. His observations during those years doubtless impressed him with the necessity for improving the quality and disease resistance of Australian wheats.

In 1882 he married Nina de Salis, whose father was a State Parliamentarian and land owner. Farrer lived on his father-in-law's Station until his resignation from the Lands Department in 1886, when he settled on his own place adjacent to his father-in-law's property. A small annuity from England enabled him to live modestly and devote his entire energies to the task of wheat improvement. He built a small laboratory and established his wheat breeding plot of less than 3 acres (1.2 hectares) of land, on the banks of the Murrumbidgee River which flowed through his property.

At the time Farrer began his experiments, the Australian wheat industry was in a serious condition. Production was more or less confined to the higher rainfall tableland areas where stem rust disease often drastically reduced the yields of the late-maturing varieties then grown. He knew that earlier-maturing varieties often escaped rust and that others had a degree of resistance to it. It was mainly on his property that he worked for 20 years with great pains and prodigious energy, making from 200 to 400 crosses annually. He kept records of his work and carried on extensive correspondence with co-workers in many parts of the world.

The year 1890 was a calamitous one for the wheat industry. Losses from rust alone exceeded two million pounds ($4 million), and millers were reduced to importing wheat from abroad.

In 1898, Farrer was made Wheat Experimentalist to the New South Wales Department of Agriculture, which enlarged the scope of his work. He was not conspicuously successful in evolving commercially important rust-resistant wheats, and he altered his objectives to the release of an early maturing, more drought-resistant wheat. One of his first experiments was to introduce early-maturing wheats from India, where there was a similar climate, to replace the late-maturing varieties grown by the early Australian colonists.

He introduced from Canada the *Fife* wheats to improve the gluten content and strength of flour in Australian wheats to make a better loaf of bread. He first crossed *Fife* wheats with the Indian wheats, but later realised that he would have to use a variety known as *Purple Straw* to introduce productivity into his new variety. A remarkable result of experiments with this combination produced the variety *Federation* in 1901. Established in 1902, this new wheat expanded into drier areas where rust was less of a problem. By 1903, it was the most popular wheat variety in Australia, and by 1925, it was still the leading wheat.

He successfully bred wheat for resistance to bunt, or stinking smut, 15 years before any other researcher. His variety *Florence,* which was moderately bunt-resistant, has been widely used as a parent in many parts of the world. Farrer used in his breeding programs early-maturing drought-resistant South African wheats. By this means he developed early-maturing varieties which further assisted in extending the wheat belt into drier districts. He died on 16 April, 1906, of heart disease, and was buried on top of a hill behind his homestead. His widow died in 1929, and was buried beside him.

Farrer produced a large number of climatic wheats of commanding commercial and parental value, and enormously extended the wheat belt. He created varieties of much greater value to millers than any previously grown in Australia. In effect, Farrer pioneered scientific wheat breeding in Australia. He was a man of wide culture and reading, sensitive and somewhat reserved in disposition, but generous and sympathetic. In the field of tracing the inheritability of disease resistance and baking quality, he undisputedly took the lead.

Further reading: *Wheat Breeding and Varieties in Australia,* S.L. Macindoe and C. Walkden Brown, 3rd edition, 1968. Division of Plant Industry, N.S.W. Department of Agriculture. *Australian Encyclopaedia, 3rd edition* 1977, Sydney. The Grolier Society of Australia.

Fig. 177. William James Farrer.

The portrait of William Farrer on the $2 note appears to have been based on the photograph reproduced above, provided courtesy of the Department of Agriculture, New South Wales.

$2 "COMMONWEALTH OF AUSTRALIA" NOTES

Serial numbering "Gothic" type, as in Fig. 187.

V.85

Signatures

H.C. Coombs Governor, Reserve Bank of Australia.
Roland Wilson Secretary to the Treasury.

Fig. 178. Signatures and titles, Coombs-Wilson $2 (V.85).

Issued 14 February, 1966.

Serial numbers FAA 000001 - FKD 096000. Printed 192,096,000.

Star notes ZFA 00001* - ZFH 18299*. Printed 718,299.
(ZFH 15600-16000*, 16600-17000*, 17400-18000*, not issued).

V.86

Signatures

H.C. Coombs Governor, Reserve Bank of Australia.
R.J. Randall Secretary to the Treasury.

Fig. 179. Signatures and titles, Coombs-Randall $2 (V.86)

Issued November, 1967.

Serial numbers FKD 096001 - FPS 1000000. Printed 75,904,000.

Star notes ZFH 19001* - ZFK 89000*. Printed 270,000.
(Excluding ZFI).

V.87

Signatures

J.G. Phillips Governor, Reserve Bank of Australia.
R.J. Randall Secretary to the Treasury.

Fig. 180. Signatures and titles, Phillips-Randall $2 (V.87).

Issued October, 1968.

Serial numbers FPT 000001 - GRF 999999. Printed 473,000,000.

Star notes ZFK 89001* - ZFS 96107*. Printed 607,107.
(Excluding ZFM and ZFO).

V.88

Signatures **J.G. Phillips** Governor, Reserve Bank of Australia.
F.H. Wheeler Secretary to the Treasury.

Fig. 181. Signatures, titles, legal tender clause, Phillips-Wheeler (Commonwealth) $2 (V.88).

Issued October, 1972.

Serial numbers GRG 000001 - HBQ 528000. Printed 175,528,000.
No star notes were issued from this signature combination onwards.

From 19 June, 1974, notes with "AUSTRALIA" replacing "COMMONWEALTH OF AUSTRALIA" were issued. See Second type, following.

Fig. 182. Front, sheet of 45 $2 un-numbered Johnston-Fraser notes.

V.89-92 $2 TWO DOLLARS.

Type	Second. "AUSTRALIA".
Issued	19 June, 1974 to 17 June, 1988.
Signatures	Phillips - Wheeler, Knight - Wheeler, Knight - Stone, Johnston - Stone, Johnston-Fraser. Other details as in the First type.
Serial numbers	HBQ 528001 to LQG 999999.
Printed	1,634,578,903.

Fig. 183. Front, $2 note. Second type (V.89).

FRONT AND BACK

All main design details and features are the same as in the First type, with the following exceptions. "AUSTRALIA" replaced "COMMONWEALTH OF AUSTRALIA" at the top in larger lettering than previously and the legal tender clause was changed to read "This Australian note is legal tender throughout Australia and its Territories". Background design and details remained the same as those in the First type.

Fig. 184. Back, $2 note. Second type (V.89).

V.91

Signatures | **H.M. Knight** Governor, Reserve Bank of Australia.
John Stone Secretary to the Treasury.

Issued First despatched from Note Issue Department, May, 1979.

Fig. 189. Signatures and titles, Knight-Stone $2 (V.91).

Serial numbers JDX to JEY, numbers 035002 to 999999 only.
JEZ 000001 - JZG 999999.
JZH to KAJ, numbers 000001 to 266500 only. Printed 383,159,952.
"OCR-B" numbering, "Side thread".

Sheet content 24 JDX-JEY, JEZ-JGA, JGB-JHC, JHD-JJE, JJF-JKG, JKH-JLJ, JLK-JNL, JNN-JPP, JPQ-JQR, JQS-JRT, JRU-JSV, JSX-JTY, JTZ-JVA, JVB-JXC, JXD-JYE, JYF-JZG. With V.92, JZH-KAJ.

V.92

Signatures **R.A. Johnston** Governor, Reserve Bank of Australia.
John Stone Secretary to the Treasury.

Fig. 190. Signatures and titles, Johnston-Stone $2 (V.92).

Issued May, 1983.

Serial numbers JZH to KAJ, numbers 266501 to 999999 only.
KAK 000001 - KRP 999951. Printed 299,999,951.
"OCR-B" serial numbering. "Side thread".

Sheet content 24 With V.91, JZH-KAJ, then KAK-KBL, KBN-KCP, KCQ-KDR, KDS-KET, KEU-KFV, KFX-KGY, KGZ-KJA, KJB-KKC, KKD-KLE, KLF-KNG, KNH-KPJ, KPK-KQL, KQN-KRP.

V.93

Signatures **R.A. Johnston** Governor, Reserve Bank of Australia.
B.W. Fraser Secretary to the Treasury.

Fig. 191. Signatures and titles, Johnston-Fraser $2 (V.93).

Issued July, 1985 to 17 June, 1988.

Serial numbers KRQ 000001 - LNF 999999.
LNG to LQG, numbers 734501 to 999999 only. Printed 422,947,000.
"OCR-B" serial numbering. "Side thread".

Sheet content 24 KRQ-KSR, KSS-KTT, KTU-KUV, KUX-KVY.

Sheet content 45 KVZ-KYZ, KZA-LBA, LBB-LDB, LDC-LFC, LFD-LHD, LHE-LKE, LKF-LNF, LNG-LQG.

V.94-104 Reference numbers not used.

Total of $2 "AUSTRALIA" notes printed, approximately 1,634,578,903. Total of all $2 notes printed, approximately 2,551,106,903. The $2 note was last officially issued on 17 June, 1988, and was replaced by a $2 coin designed by Horst Hahne, Chief Engraver of the Royal Australian Mint.

The design of the coin featured an Aboriginal known locally as "One Pound Jimmy". The 1988 and 1989 coins bear the designer's initials "HH", which did not appear on 1990 coins onwards. The initials were omitted following a Court action for a breach of The Copyright Act for allegedly using a drawing from one of Ainslie Roberts' books without his consent. The drawing was made in the 1950s at Central Mt. Wedge Station, 300 km from Alice Springs. Further reading: *The News,* 30 August, 1989, *Mint fined for use of artwork.*

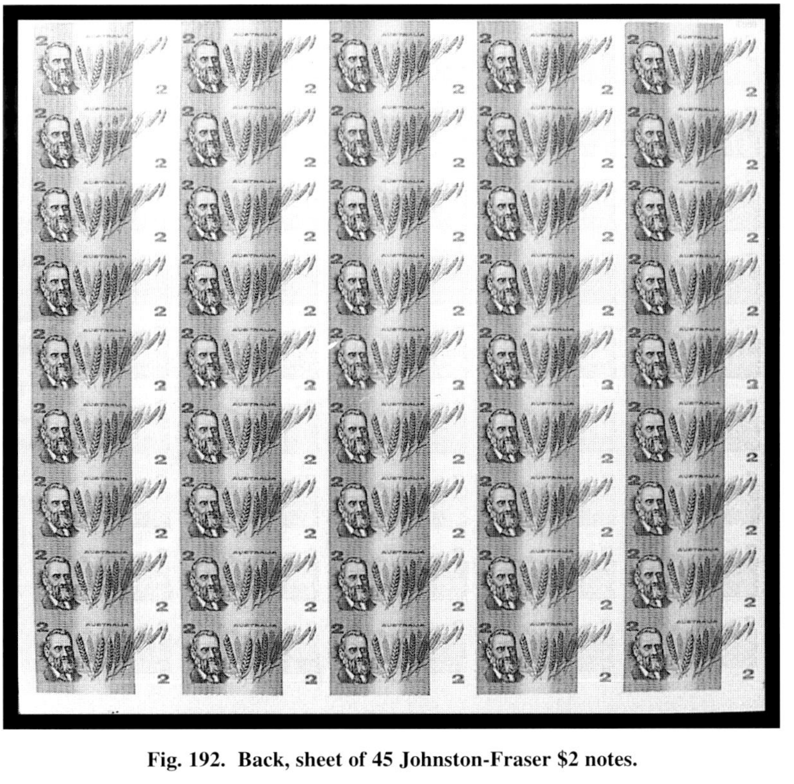

Fig. 192. Back, sheet of 45 Johnston-Fraser $2 notes.

V. 105-107 $5 FIVE DOLLARS

Type	First. "COMMONWEALTH OF AUSTRALIA".
Issued	29 May, 1967 to September, 1974.
Size	150 mm x 76 mm.
Watermark	The profile of Captain James Cook is on the left side of the front, facing right. See Fig. 101. A metallic security thread runs vertically through the note about 70 mm from the left edge of the front.
Signatures	Coombs - Randall, Phillips - Randall, Phillips - Wheeler.
Serial numbers	NAA 000001 to NKG 504000. Printed 197,504,000. ZNA 00001* to ZND 05619*.

Fig. 193. Front, $5 note. First type (V.105).

FRONT

Main print: Purple-black intaglio, (See fig. 194). 138 mm x 67 mm.
The main feature is a portrait of Sir Joseph Banks on the right. The remainder of the design depicts Australian flora. On the top of the note is "COMMONWEALTH OF AUSTRALIA" and a "5" is in each top corner. Under the signature titles at the bottom is the legal tender clause "Legal tender throughout the Commonwealth of Australia and the Territories of the Commonwealth".

Background print: Dry offset using five colours, (See Fig. 195). 142 mm x 75 mm.
Horizontally across the centre of the note are 85 mauve lines. These vary in thickness, and in three places on the left, produce "glows". The background behind the flora and around the portrait of Banks has a pattern of mauve diagonal wavy lines. In between these are maroon coloured wavy lines and "pods". Above and below the centre, the pattern changes to thin white diagonally wavy lines, in between which are maroon wavy lines and mauve "pods". In the vertical centre the background rainbows to khaki and orange and behind the face of Banks are vertical mauve lines. Notes which have a green and purple colour have been affected by chemicals e.g. washing powders.

Fig. 194. Front, $5 note, main print (intaglio) only (error note).

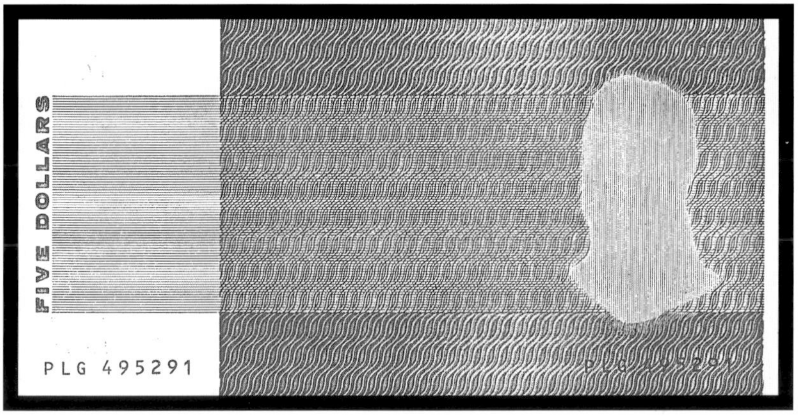

Fig. 195. Front, $5 note, background print (Simultan) only (error note).

Sir Joseph Banks

Joseph Banks was born in London on 13 February, 1743 and attended various universities. In 1761 his father died, leaving him the family home and fortune. In December, 1763, he left Oxford with an Honorary Master of Arts degree, and in 1766, because of his enthusiasm and devotion to botanical studies, was elected a Fellow of the Royal Society. That year he investigated the flora of Newfoundland. The Transit of Venus, due in 1769, was to be observed by an expedition led by Captain James Cook in the Pacific Ocean. Banks obtained permission to join Cook, and, at a personal cost of 10,000 pounds, equipped the expedition with material and personnel for making collections in every aspect of natural science. He took with him Dr. Solander, two draughtsmen - Mr. Buchan for landscape, Sydney Parkinson for objects of natural history, and two attendants. He was with Cook at the landing at Botany Bay in 1770, and returned to England with a somewhat unfavourable impression of Australia.

In 1779 he married Dorothea Weston-Hugessen, who survived him. He was created a Baronet in 1781. Between 1779 and 1785 he supported proposals for the establishment of a penal colony at Botany Bay. In 1786, it was decided to send a batch of convicts as an experiment, and thereafter the colony grew. Once established, Banks played a very influential and prominent part in the administration of the colony, though preferring to stay in England and not be directly involved.

Fig. 196. Sir Joseph Banks.

On 30 November, 1788, Banks was elected President of the Royal Society. By then he was a man of influence. He was invested with the order of the Bath on 1 July, 1795, and sworn to the Privvy Council on 29 March, 1797. He had a hand in the appointment of various Governors and supplied gardeners and explorers for the colony. By middle-age, he had achieved a reputation as an authority on such matters as hydraulics, tanning, coinage, earthquakes, crop diseases and his pet subject - botany. He actively promoted exploration in China, Brazil, Sumatra, Egypt and the Congo Valley. He was the first to bring India-rubber to notice and he advocated the growing of tea in India.

For at least 14 years before his death he lost the use of his legs, but continued to preside over the Royal Society. He died on 19 June, 1820. As directed in his will, his body was interred in the simplest manner, with no monument to his memory.

The illustration of Joseph Banks is a portion of an oil painting (55" x 43") by Thomas Phillips to the order of Don Jose di Mendoza Rios, a Spanish scholar and friend of Banks. The painting, c. 1808-9, is in, and reproduced by courtesy of, the Dixson Galleries, Sydney. The painting from which the portrait on the note was probably based is an oil, 27" x 35", also by Phillips, in 1814. That painting is in the Guildhall Museum, Boston, Lincolnshire, England, the property of the Corporation of Boston.

A great deal of valuable manuscript material was left by Banks and it is now distributed in many countries. Banks Strait, a passage about 21 kilometres wide between the North-East corner of Tasmania and Clarke Island in the Furneaux Group, and Banksia, genus of the family of about 50 species of shrubs and small trees (Proteaceae) were named after him.

Further reading: *Australian Encyclopaedia 3rd edition,* 1977, Sydney, Grolier Society of Australia. *The Endeavour Journal of Joseph Banks,* edited by J.C. Beaglehole, Sydney, Public Library of New South Wales Trustees, Angus and Robertson, 1962. *National Dictionary of Biography,* (U.K.), and various editions of the *Gentlemens Magazine,* c. October, 1820.

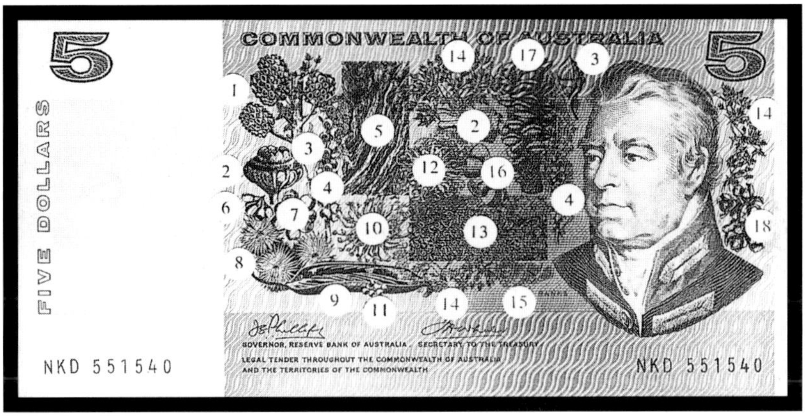

Fig. 197. Flora on the $5 note.

The front of the $5 note features an assemblage of Australian flora. The flora includes a selection of fruit, buds, blossoms and cones of various well-known (and some not so familiar) Australian trees and shrubs. They have been identified on the above illustration as follows:

(1) Cluster of fruit from "Casuarina littoralis" or Black She-Oak. Casuarina is an isolated family of wind-pollinated trees and shrubs, the majority of which occur in Western Australia. The Black She-Oak, however, is found in all States except W.A., and its heavy timber has made it ideal for use as shingles and tool handles.

(2)(3) Large fruit and a bud of "Eucalyptus pyriformis" known as either Pear-fruited or Large-fruited Mallee. This small shrub occurs with long weak straggling stems from one to four metresin height. It has light brown bark with pale brown timber and occurs in western and southern Australia. The large flowers it produces are very attractive, yielding an abundance of pollen and nectar and flowering from April to November. Eucalypts (or gum trees as they are more commonly, though incorrectly, known) are found in some 500 recognised species of which only seven occur naturally outside of Australia. The trees dominate large areas of Australia and provide by far the largest portion of its forest produce. There are vast differences in the sizes and shapes of their fruit and they can be globular, conical, cylindrical or urn-shaped, and may vary from pin-head size up to 10 cm in diameter.

The timber can vary from dark-red, dense, heavy and exceedingly strong Jarrah, to the pale fissile woods of the Ash Group which are excellent for indoor work and for paper pulping. The powerful aroma of eucalypt leaves is due to the secretion of an oily mixture of aldehydes, ketones, terpenes, higher alcohols and esters. Their leaves produce eucalyptus oil used for medicinal purposes, and their flowering attracts bees, thus producing large quantities of honey, each species yielding distinctly coloured and flavoured honey. Systematic plantings of trees abroad really began with the arrival of Ferdinand von Mueller in Victoria in 1852, after which seeds were sent all over the world. Results in California and Brazil have been spectacular,whilst large areas of forests have been planted in a very wide range of countries. "Mallee" or "The Mallee", is a term applied to scrub, and in particular, certain eucalypts. Its distribution is very widespread in the southern half of Australia.

(4) Long slender clusters of the fruit of "Callistemon citrinis" (Red Bottle Brush). Callistemon is a genus of small trees and shrubs native to Australia, commonly known as bottle brushes, a term no doubt derived from the appearance of their flowers. The species shown on the note is the Common Crimson Bottle Brush found in eastern Victoria, Queensland, and in New South Wales. Under cultivation it displays great variation in habit, height, foliage and shade of red, often continuing to bloom for several months.

(5) Weathered wood grain.

(6) Fruit of "Eucalyptus comitae-vallis" (Comet Vale Marlock), a tall erect shrub or small tree in Western Australia which produces long slender poles useful for mine props, and fuel.

(7) Cluster of fruit from "Eucalyptus fraxinoides" (White Ash), a rapid growing slender tree which can reach a height of up to 36 metres and produces pale, very light, but strong, timber. Although able to withstand a fair amount of wind and snow, it is easily killed by bushfires. It flowers freely in December and January.

(8) Magnified scales of "Phebalium squarmulusom". Phebalium is a genus of more than 40 species of shrubs and the foliage is often clothed with scurfy scales. Species are represented in all States.

(9) Large seed pod of "Telopea speciosissima" (Waratah). The Waratah is one of the most attractive flowering shrubs in Australia. Its fruit is a leathery folicle up to 10 cm long, and the flat seeds are winged. The most widely known and spectacular species is that depicted on the note, the brilliant crimson flowers of which are collected in a large globular head surrounded by bracts of the same colour. The shrub can grow up to a height of three to four metres and cultivated plants in suitable soil will often bear up to 50 of these flower-heads simultaneously. It is generally, though unofficially, accepted as the floral emblem of New South Wales.

(10) Blossom of the Fire-wheel tree, the popular name for "Stenocarpus sinuatus", a handsome tree sometimes growing to a height of some 30 metres. It occurs mainly in New South Wales and Queensland, displaying brilliant red waxy flowers. Ten to fourteen individual blossoms are borne in flattened wheel-like clusters, hence the name.

(11) Small cluster of fruit from "Eucalyptus stelluate" (Black Sally), a tree of spreading habit which grows to a height of between six and fifteen metres. Its timber is pale-coloured and because it is not durable, it is used mainly for fuel.

(12) Blossom of "Stenocarpus salignus" commonly known as Beefwood, a name applied to several quite unconnected Australian trees resembling each other by the red colour of their timbers.

(13) Blossom of "Xylomelum pyriforme" known as Woody Pear. It is one of five species of the genus which are known for their exceedingly thick, woody, pear-shaped capsules. It is found in Queensland and New South Wales where it occurs frequently on Hawkesbury sandstone formations. A small tree, it is characterised by its deeply-furrowed corky bark, young shoots covered with reddish-brown hair, and numerous small flowers in dense spikes.

(14) "Cladium procerum" (Sedge). Sedge is a name generally applied to grassy or bush-like plants chiefly in damp situations, on the margins of streams, lakes and swamps. Some 36 genera and about 530 species are represented in Australia.

(15) Leaf skeleton.

(16) Cluster of fruit of Yellow-top Ash known as either "Eucalyptus Virgata" or "Eucalyptus luehmanniana", a mallee-like shrub which grows from one to six metres in height. It has a very hard pale timber and prefers the cold damp Hawkesbury sandstone in N.S.W.

(17) Cluster of fruit from "Banksia integrifolia" or Coast Banksia. Banksias perpetuate the name of Sir Joseph Banks who collected the first specimens in 1770. This species is one of the main-occurring trees of the eastern States. It can attain a height of sixteen metres, often forming groves on exposed dunes and ranging from western Victoria, to Queensland. Its bark is a source of tannin.

(18) Cones of "Callitris rhomboidea". The timber of Callitris is very aromatic, pale chocolate-brown, durable, resistant to termite attacks, and useful for cabinet work.

The design to the right of Banks on the note consists of Sedge at the top, and "Callitris rhomboidia" cones (Port Jackson Cypress Pine) at the bottom. Note Printing Australia at Craigieburn has a garden consisting of many of the trees and shrubs featured on the $5 note.

Fig. 198. Back, $5 note First type (V.105).

Fig. 199. Back, $5 note, main print (Intaglio) only (error note).

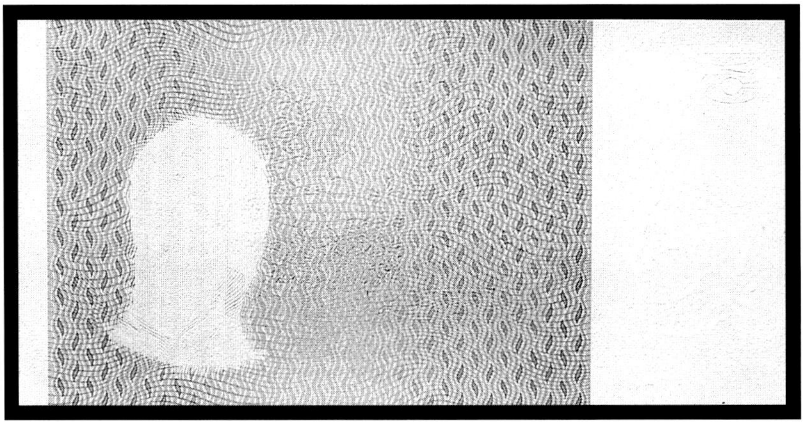

Fig. 200. Back, $5 note, background print (Simultan) only (error note).

BACK

Main print: Purple-black intaglio. (See Fig. 199). 136 mm x 63 mm.

On the left is a portrait of Caroline Chisholm against a background composed of illustrations of women and children of her time and Sydney streets and ships of the period. Along the top of the note is "COMMONWEALTH OF AUSTRALIA" and at top left and bottom right a figure "5". The initials of Gordon Andrews are 14 mm to the right of the point of Caroline Chisholm's chin.

Background print: Dry offset in six colours. 105 mm x 75 mm.

The main background design consists of vertical wavy mauve lines in between which are white lines and maroon "pods". Near the centre of the vertical background the colours rainbow to orange and khaki. In addition there are fluctuating horizontal wavy lines across the background design and colouring the face of Chisholm are fine orange and maroon vertical lines. See Fig. 200.

Gordon Andrews originally submitted a similar design for the back of the $1 note, with the Queen on the front, in October 1963. By December the back had changed to Nellie Melba, and in January, 1964, Melba had been abandoned in favour of an Aboriginal scene. There having been six men on the remaining three notes, the argument for a woman to be included on the $5 could not be ignored, and Caroline Chisholm at last appeared on Australian notes.

The next illustration was probably the one from which the portrait on the note was based. It is from a lithograph in the possession of Sarah Wordsworth, Perth, which originated from a painting by Angelo Collen Hayter, who exhibited five works (including the Caroline Chisholm painting) at the Royal Academy between 1850 and 1852. The picture was also reproduced in the 1990 National Australia Bank calendar.

Fig. 201. Caroline Chisholm from a lithograph in the collection of Sarah Wordsworth, Perth.

Caroline Chisholm

Caroline Chisholm was born Caroline Jones in 1808, near Northampton, England. In 1830 she married Archibald Chisholm, an officer in the forces of the East India Company. They moved to India, and in 1832, she began her benevolent work among the daughters of European settlers. In 1838 they visited South Australia (two years after it was first settled), then Hobart and finally Sydney.

In the early 1830s the bounty system of emigration applied. Agents were paid two pounds per head for every person shipped to Australia, provided that person landed in Australia alive. Large numbers of friendless young girls were conveyed to Sydney where, if they were unable to find immediate placement, they slept in caves and bushes of the Domain, rather than risk the contamination of the streets.

In 1841, after her husband had returned to India for Service, Caroline approached the Bishop for help in assisting the girls, but he told her she was suffering from delusions. Governor Gipps at first said he could not spare a penny to help her. She sent circulars to squatters and families asking them what type of women servants they required. She then collected girls from the streets and recorded their capabilities. Some people began to realise the worth of her work and assisted with funds and in the first two months of operation she found situations for 700 young women, 200 of whom were sent to the country. She obtained the use of a rat-infested barracks and established an immigrant's home for girls arriving from England, where they could stay until they found employment.

She took legal action against the Captain of a ship and the Ship's Doctor for ill-treatment of a woman passenger and won, after the Governor refused to prosecute, resulting in more humane treatment of immigrants on ships between England and Australia.

She accompanied parties of women travelling around the country seeking employment, and was later instrumental in placing men and their families on the land. Captain Bobby Towns lent her 1,000 acres near Shell Harbour, and there she settled 240 families. In one year alone 2,000 people were settled on the soil in New South Wales as a result of her work.

In 1845 she returned to England to make arrangements for children who had been left in Great Britain to be sent to Australia. She succeeded in having the British Government grant free passages for wives and families of convicts sent out in earlier years and was instrumental in establishing the Family Colonisation Loan Society. That society encouraged saving by intending migrants and arranged their passage with the balance of the loan payable after arrival in Australia. The *Slain Castle*, a chartered ship, left England in September, 1850, with 250 emigrating families, and other ships then followed regularly. Eventually the ship *Caroline Chisholm* was built for the Society and in September, 1853, it carried 144 emigrants to Melbourne.

The *Illustrated London News,* page 337, reported her departure for Australia in 1854:

We can turn to pictures of those group meetings where, without parade, without extravagant advertising or placarding, hundreds, nay thousands, assembled to listen to Caroline Chisholm, explaining, with earnest, simple, unadorned eloquence, the common sense view of colonization; and also of those exciting scenes when at the docks, and on shipboard, a band of emigrants, whom her system has enabled to seek in Australia a better reward for their labour than this country could afford, listened with affectionate reverence to her parting words of comfort and advice. But a change has come over the prospects of England and her colonies. It is no longer necessary to stimulate emigration here - the working classes can help themselves without gifts or loans. In Australia the great want is not the raw material of labour, but the re-union of wives and families in comparative poverty here with their successful husbands in that colony. To help in this good work - to lay the prime foundation of a civilised state, by giving gold-diggers wives and little children - this is the next work of Caroline Chisholm. War which has disturbed the plans of bankers, merchants, shipowners, and politicians, has not spared her. The ships promised to be fitted out on Mrs. Chisholm's improved plans of space and ventilation, have been tendered to, and accepted by, Government to carry soldiers and cavalry horses; and Mrs. Chisholm and her numerous wards have been handed over to the Ballarat, a fine fast ship, but with little room, and that room purchased at a very high rate...

In 1854, after her return to Australia, she was involved in other local endeavours. As a result of her lobbying, shelter-sheds were erected on the road to Castlemaine for the benefit of people travelling to the goldfields, and she tried to improve the conditions of women and children living on the goldfields. In 1857 she developed kidney disease and in 1859, she began lecturing on various subjects, mainly political. She discussed the secret ballot, free selection before survey, early closing of shops, and home life.

In 1866 she returned to England as a result of ill-health, and the following year was granted a civil list pension of 100 pounds a year. She died penniless in London on 25 March, 1877, aged 67 years, and was buried in Northamptonshire. Her contemporaries admired her greatly. The French historian Michelet wrote of her *The fifth part of the world, Australia, has up to now but one saint, one legend. The saint is an Englishwoman.* Florence Nightingale declared that she was *Mrs. Chisholm's "friend and pupil"* and London Punch called her *a second Moses, in bonnet and shawl.* Further reading: Australian Encyclopaedia, 3rd edition, 1977, Sydney, The Grolier Society of Australia. *Caroline Chisholm the Immigrant's Friend,* by Margaret Swan, 1936.

The *Waverley* featured on the $5 note is the clipper brig *Waverley* owned by L.J. Castle, copied from a watercolour (14" x 19") painted by Frederick Garling. It is owned and reproduced by courtesy of the Mitchell Library, Sydney. See next illustration.

Waverley

At the top right hand corner of the back of the $5 note is a ship named *Waverley*, as indicated on the flag at the top of the second mast. The question of the identity of the ship was first raised in the Senate on 19 September, 1973 (six years after the issue of the note) and the answer recorded in *Hansard* on 11 October, 1973, page 1185.

The Reserve Bank of Australia, which is responsible under the Reserve bank Act for the Australian note issue, has advised that the vessel depicted on the top right hand corner on the reverse of the Australian $5 note is the Waverley, a barque of 436 tons, built at Whitby in 1838. As the vessel transported many settlers from Dublin to Australia between 1838 and 1847, its inclusion in the design is in keeping with the note's dominant theme - the role played by Mrs. Caroline Chisholm in the establishment and welfare of newcomers to this country. The Reserve Bank has added that records at the Mitchell Library in Sydney disclose that another vessel named Waverley, built in 1863, was wrecked near the Don River in 1880.

Fig. 202. The "Waverley" entering Sydney Heads, owner L.J. Castle.

Following further questions in the Senate, another statement was made regarding the vessel, and it appeared in *Hansard* on 11 April 1978, at page 1155.

> *Following the further question by Senator Devitt on 12 October 1977, the Reserve Bank investigated further the identity of the ship on the note. As a result of additional search of the records of the State Library of New South Wales the Bank has now informed me that it appears there were a number of ships named Waverley in existence at the time. This contributed to some confusion regarding the ship incorporated in the design of the note. The Bank now believes that the ship depicted is the clipper brig Waverley and not the barque Waverley. The brig is understood to have been a tea clipper which it seems was eventually wrecked on the northern coast of Tasmania. Although there is no evidence of an association with Mrs. Chisholm, the brig Waverley was a ship of the period and its incorporation in the design of the $5 note is not considered by the Bank to be inappropriate in the context of showing Mrs. Chisholm against a background of women and children of her time and ships and Sydney streets of the period. In these circumstances and in view of the costs involved, I have not requested the Reserve Bank to change the design of the note. The Bank regrets the error in supplying incorrect information in response to Senator Devitt's earlier questions. The Government is grateful to him and others who have helped clarify this matter.*

An article about the brig *Waverley*, written by Jack Millar, appeared in the Tasmanian *Weekender* of 5 August, 1972, from which the following was extracted.

The 215-ton brig was launched at Yarmouth, England, in 1863. Early in her career the brig was owned and registered in the Port of Sydney, trading from there around the Pacific and to far off China. As was the custom of the day she carried an armoury which included two brass cannon. Her owner, Captain Louis Castle, was a well-known resident in the suburb of Waverley. Beautiful to look at, the brig was copper sheathed to the waterline as a protection against marine growth.

On 9 July, 1880, she sailed in ballast from the River Don, Tasmania, for Melbourne. The Captain declared he did not need a pilot, and would take the brig to sea himself. When it reached the River Don Heads the tricky current touched the ship and swung it broadside to, firmly wedging it and completely blocking the passage. The seas pounded her until she began to break up and she was later moved a short distance to clear the passage, and was eventually sold where she lay for scrap. Her remains are buried on Scotties Island at the mouth of the Don River. On 4 August, 1881, a marine enquiry at Torquay (now Devonport, Tasmania) held that the loss of the *Waverley* was due to negligence on the part of the Captain and his certificate was suspended for three months, and he was ordered to pay the costs of the enquiry.

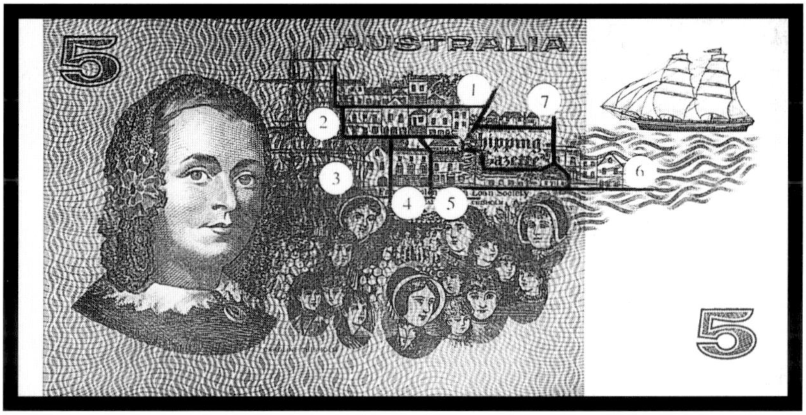

Fig. 203. The buildings on the back of the $5 note.

SYDNEY IN 1848

The buildings depicted on the back of the note are almost exact reproductions of those which existed in Harrington and Pitt Streets, Sydney, in 1848. Not one of those buildings has survived to the present day. At that time Sydney boasted some 7,300 houses, and its suburbs about 2,000. The population of Sydney was nearly 42,000, and its suburbs about 7,500. There were only four banks of issue (issued their own bank notes). The Bank of New South Wales, and the Commercial Banking Company of Sydney were Colonial, and the Union Bank of Australia and the Bank of Australasia were Anglo-Australian.

Harrington Street is in "The Rocks" tourist district of Sydney near the Harbour Bridge, where the original settlement began. It runs north-south and parallel to (and west of) the northern end of George Street. Most of the area was demolished in 1901 because it was the worst affected area in Sydney during a bubonic plague outbreak which claimed the lives of 113 people. When new buildings began to appear, the street was renumbered from the opposite end.

At the northern end of Harrington Street is Playfair Street containing the Westpac (Bank) Museum, and nearby in George Street is the Museum of Contemporary Art.

Pitt Street is a main thoroughfare which commences near Circular Quay at Sydney Cove. It runs north-south and parallel to (and east of) George Street.

Joseph Fowles of 5 Harrington Street, Sydney, was an artist (described as a marine painter) who produced paintings of vessels in oils which he sold for between five and ten guineas each. He arrived in Sydney in 1838. On 14 July, 1848, he published the first of a series *Sydney in 1848* which he advertised as intending to contain about forty issues, but which eventuated as twenty parts. His message to Sydney residents, and in particular to the mother-country (England), was as follows:

> *To the Public. The principal object of this Work is to remove the erroneous and discreditable notions current in England concerning this City, in common with everything else connected with the Colony. We shall endeavour to represent Sydney as it really is - to exhibit its spacious Gas-lit streets, crowded by an active and thriving population - its Public Edifices, and its sumptuous Shops, which boldly claim a comparison with those in London itself: and to shew that Colonists have not been inattentive to matters of higher import, we shall display to our Readers the beautiful and commodious Buildings raised by piety and industry for the use of Religion. It is true, all are not yet in a state of completion; but, be it remembered, that what was done gradually in England, in the course of many centuries, has been effected in the comparatively short period of sixty years. Our object, in setting forth this Work, is one of no mean moment; and we trust that every Australian, whether this be his native or adopted country, will heartily bid us 'God speed!' Sydney, July 14, 1848.*

The publication was fortnightly, consisting of two illustrations with explanatory letterpress. Each issue was to show a "finished etching of one of the principal edifices" and a front elevation of one of the principal streets to the extent of about 250 yards, giving an exact representation of each house in the range. They were produced on fine Demy quarto paper and were priced at 1/- to subscribers and 1/6d to non-subscribers. A facsimile edition of the complete work was published in 1878, and re-issued in 1882. Finally, an annotated facsimile edition was published in 1962 by Ure Smith Pty. Ltd., of Sydney, entitled *Sydney in 1848*, by Joseph Fowles. It is from that work that the numbered assemblage on the previous page has been extracted, and much of the information gathered.

On the western side of Pitt Street near the King Street intersection was a building numbered (4) in the next illustration. It was occupied by G.H. Hamilton, with signage: *Oil Colour, Chemist and Druggist and Italian warehouse.* The right-hand portion of the building was used by S. Peek & Co's stores, a firm of wine merchants and wholesale grocers who conducted a Grocery and Tea warehouse in George Street.

A few doors away towards King Street was a large building which included a shop occupied by a bookseller and stationer named Moffit. He was one of those who sold Fowles' publications. Next to his shop on the corner of King Street was Edward Samuell's *Liverpool Arms.* On the opposite corner was the *Elephant and Castle* (1), and a row of four nondescript odd-shaped buildings, all of which are shown on the $5 note.

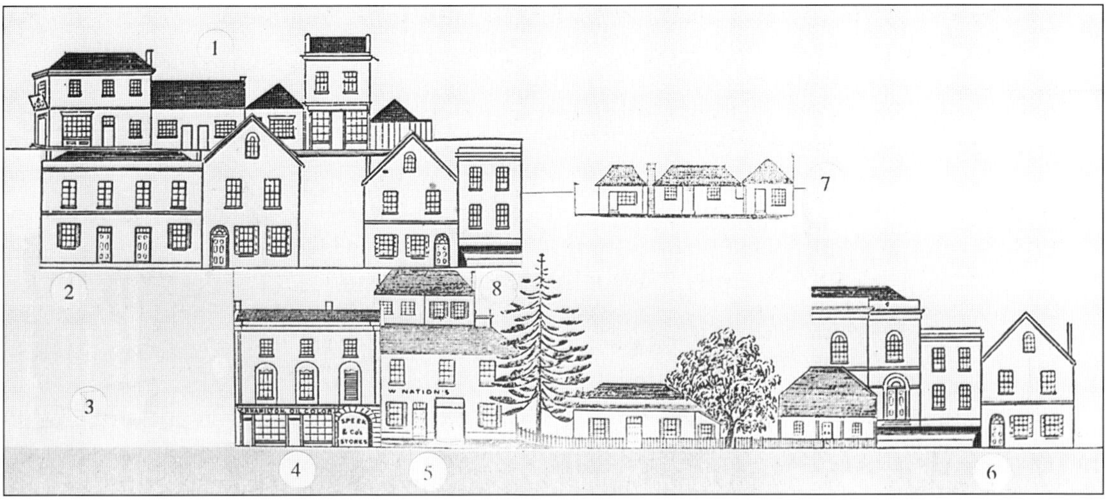

Fig. 204. Sydney in 1848, re-assembled as on the $5 note.

The second row of houses (2 in the illustration above) on the note includes (as the pointed-roof building on the left) the premises which had been occupied by Joseph Fowles himself, at 5 Harrington Street. On the right of this row is a portion of St. Philips Infant School. The small houses between the two main groups of buildings have been inserted by the note's designer to fill a gap which appeared in the original drawings. The right side of (2) has been inverted at (6) on the note, and includes a further portion of St. Philips Infant School. Fowles' house (inverted) again appears on the right.

If Joseph Fowles had looked out his front windows he would have seen a pine tree across the road, to the left of which was a printing office run by W. Nation. This is depicted at (5) on the note, except that the designer of the note (Gordon Andrews) has substituted the name *G. Andrews, Plumber.* As there is no *G. Andrews,* Plumber, mentioned in *Sydney in 1848,* it can only be assumed that the designer has not only honoured Fowles by featuring his premises twice on the note, but perpetuated his own name on the note as a small reward for having designed it.

Between the printing office and the pine tree was a building occupied by Byers and Lockhead. A picket fence then surrounded the tree and two houses to the right which were separated by another tree. The row of small houses (7, on the note) appear to originate from Pitt Street, but these have been inverted on the note, and a portion of another house immediately to the left of the three houses has also been inverted and placed on the note (8). The buildings (3, on the note), do not appear to be in *Sydney in 1848* and may have been improvised as space-fillers.

After publication of his works, Fowles moved to various addresses, according to contemporary directories, including 45 King Street, 273 Pitt Street and Glebe Road. To the public and private schools in N.S.W. he described himself as a master of drawing. He died at Forest Lodge, Sydney, in 1878, having spent forty years of his life in the Colony's first city. His *Sydney in 1848* did not cover the whole of the city of his time, but what has been proven by today's experts is his absolute integrity as a recorder of Sydney buildings as they really appeared. His claim to fame is not as he believed at the time, his painting, but his work *Sydney in 1848* which has allowed succeeding generations to see the Sydney that was, and will never be, again. Reference and further reading: *Sydney in 1848* by Joseph Fowles, Ure Smith Pty. Ltd., Sydney, 1962.

When a decision was made to introduce the polymer $5 note (released in 1992) the Queen's effigy, having disappeared after the $1 note ceased in 1984, was reintroduced on the front, and the old and new Parliament Houses, Canberra, appeared on the back. There was a public outcry about Chisholm's removal at the time. The Reserve Bank later pointed out, that at the time the paper note was being considered, the design panel had shortlisted Elizabeth Macarthur, Mary Reiby, Nellie Melba, Daisy Bates, Caroline Chisholm and Dame Mary Gilmore. Three of those were later featured on the new polymer notes, Dame Mary Gilmore on the back of the $10 in 1993, Mary Reiby on the front of the $20 in 1994 and Nellie Melba on the front of the $100 note in 1996. In 2001 a new design commemorating 100 years of Federation will be issued featuring Henry Parkes and Catherine Helen Spence.

$5 "COMMONWEALTH OF AUSTRALIA" NOTES

Serial numbering "Gothic" type. No notes were printed or issued with Coombs-Wilson signatures.

V.105

Signatures

H.C. Coombs Governor, Reserve Bank of Australia.
R.J. Randall Secretary to the Treasury.

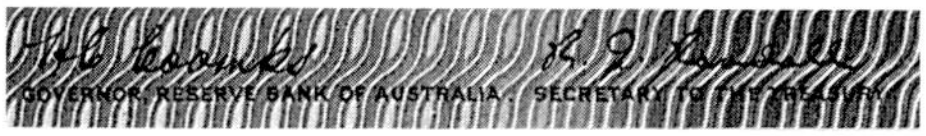

Fig. 205. Signatures and titles, Coombs-Randall $5 (V.105).

Issued 29 May, 1967.

Serial numbers NAA 000001 - NCS 600000. Printed 57,600,000.

Star notes ZNA 00001* - ZNC 04000*. Printed 204,000.
See Fig. 350.

V.106

Signatures

J.G. Phillips Governor, Reserve Bank of Australia.
R.J. Randall Secretary to the Treasury.

Fig. 206. Signatures and titles, Phillips-Randall $5 (V.106).

Issued October, 1969.

Serial numbers NCS 600001 - NGS 999999. Printed 84,400,000.

Star notes ZNC 04001* - ZND 05619* Printed 101,619.

V.107

Signatures **J.G. Phillips** Governor, Reserve Bank of Australia.
F.H. Wheeler Secretary to the Treasury.

Fig. 207. Signatures, titles and legal tender clause, Phillips-Wheeler (Commonwealth) $5 (V.107).

Issued October, 1972.

Serial numbers NGT 000001 - NKG 504000. Printed 55,504,000.
No star notes were issued from this signature combination onwards.

From 27 September, 1974, notes with "AUSTRALIA" replacing "COMMONWEALTH OF AUSTRALIA" were issued. See Second type, following.

Fig. 208. Back, sheet of 24 $5 "Australia" notes.

V.108-111 $5 FIVE DOLLARS

Type Second. "AUSTRALIA".

Issued 27 September, 1974 to July, 1992.

Signatures Phillips - Wheeler, Knight - Wheeler, Johnston - Stone, Johnston - Fraser, Fraser - Higgins, Fraser - Cole. Other details as in the First type.

Serial numbers NKG 504001 - QPG 999999.

Printed 978,068,318, plus uncut notes and Collector Issues.

Fig. 209. Front, $5 note. Second type (V.108).

FRONT AND BACK

All main design details and features are the same as in the First type with the following exceptions. "AUSTRALIA" replaced "COMMONWEALTH OF AUSTRALIA" at the top in larger lettering than previously, and the legal tender clause was changed to read "This Australian note is legal tender throughout Australia and its Territories." Background design and details remained the same as those in the First type.

Fig. 210. Back, $5 note. Second type (V.108).

$5 "AUSTRALIA" NOTES

V.108

Signatures — **J.G. Phillips** Governor, Reserve Bank of Australia.
F.H. Wheeler Secretary to the Treasury.

Fig. 211. Signatures, titles, legal tender clause, Phillips-Wheeler (Australia) $5 (V.108).

Issued 27 September, 1974.

Serial numbers NKG 504001 - NQT 999999. NLL not used. Printed 97,496,000. "Gothic" serial numbering. "Centre thread". Metallic security thread approximately 70 mm from the left edge of the front.

Sheet content 24 NKG uncertain, then NKH-NLK, NLN-NNP, NNQ-NPR, NPS-NQT.

V.109

Signatures — **H.M. Knight** Governor, Reserve Bank of Australia.
F.H. Wheeler Secretary to the Treasury.

Fig. 212. Signatures and titles, Knight-Wheeler $5 (V.109).

Variety (a) "Gothic" serial numbering, "Centre thread". Metallic security thread approximately 70 mm from the left edge of the front.

Issued April, 1976.

Serial numbers NQU 000001 - NVC 999997. Printed 96,000,000.

Sheet content 24 NQU-NRV, NRX-NSY. With (b), NSZ-NUA, NUB-NVC.

Variety (b) "Gothic" serial numbering. "Side thread". Metallic security thread approximately 55 mm from the left edge of the front.
Serial numbers and totals included in variety (a).

Sheet content 24 With (a), NSZ-NUA, NUB-NVC.

Variety (c) "OCR-B" serial numbering.

Issued About December, 1978.

Serial numbers NVD 000001 - NXE 999999. NXF to NYG, serial numbers 000001 to 132987 only. Printed 27,191,688.

Sheet content 24 NVD-NXE. With V.110, NXF-NYG.

NUS 634840

Fig. 213. "Gothic" serial numbering.

NVZ 263800

Fig. 214. "OCR-B" serial numbering.

From July, 1976, all paper despatched by the Note Printing Branch's suppliers had the security thread positioned in an area approximately 55 mm from the left edge of the front. The change was made to avoid the natural fold area which, because of the close proximity of the metallic thread, caused undue wear and tearing.

V.110

Signatures	**H.M. Knight**	Governor, Reserve Bank of Australia.
	John Stone	Secretary to the Treasury.

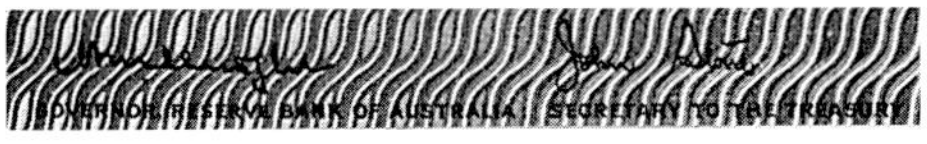

Fig. 215. Signatures and titles, Knight-Stone $5 (V.110).

Issued First despatched from Note Issue Department, August, 1979.

Serial numbers
NXF to NYG, numbers 133001 to 999999 only.
NYH 000001 - NZZ 999999.
PAA 000001 - PDT 999999. Printed 137,073,952.
"OCR-B" serial numbering. Prefixes beginning "O" were not used.

Sheet content 24 With V.109, NXF-NYG, then NYH-NZJ, NZK-PAL, PAN-PBP, PBQ-PCR, PCS-PDT.

V.111

Signatures	**R.A. Johnston**	Governor, Reserve Bank of Australia.
	John Stone	Secretary to the Treasury.

Fig. 216. Signatures and titles, Johnston-Stone $5 (V.111).

Issued May, 1983.

Serial numbers
PDU 000001 - PKE 999999.
PKF to PLG, numbers 000001 to 060500 only. (060501-061000 not used).
"OCR-B" serial numbering. Printed 121,331,000.

Sheet content 24 PDU-PEV, PEX-PFY, PFZ-PHA, PHB-PJC, PJD-PKE.
With V.112, PKF-PLG.

The first type of serial numbering in decimal notes was "Gothic No. 18". In 1978 the style of numbering was changed to "OCR-B" and remained on all paper decimal notes until they were discontinued. This signature combination began with "OCR-B" serial numbering.

On 26 August, 1988, through Note Printing Branch's Newsletter No. 3, it was advised that $5 notes were currently being printed with "Gothic" serial numbering, and $20 and $50 notes with "OCR-B" numbering. The temporary change was made to enable production flexibility (it was later stated that those denominations were urgently required and the regular machines were unavailable). The $20 note was also temporarily printed with "Gothic" serial numbers.

V.112

Signatures — **R.A. Johnston** Governor, Reserve Bank of Australia.
B.W. Fraser Secretary to the Treasury.

Fig. 217. Signatures and titles, Johnston-Fraser $5 (V.112).

Variety (a) "OCR-B" serial numbering.

Issued March, 1985.

Serial numbers
PKF to PLG, numbers 061001 to 999999 only.
PLH 000001 - PXA 999999.
PXB to PYC, numbers 158501 to 999999 only.
QBK 000001 - QDE 999999.
QDF to QFA, numbers 303001 to 999999 only.
Printed 234,731,952.

Sheet content 24 With V.111, PKF-PLG, then PLH-PNJ, PNK-PPL, PPN-PQP, PQQ-PRR, PRS-PST, PSU-PTV, PTX-PUY, PUZ-PXA. With variety (b), PXB-PYC.

Variety (b) "Gothic" serial numbering.

Issued July, 1988.

Serial numbers
PXB to PYC, numbers 000001 to 158500 only.
PYD 000001 - QBJ 999999.
Printed 75,803,928.

Sheet content 24 With variety (a), PXB-PYC, then PYD-PZE, PZF-QAG, QAH-QBJ.

Sheet content 40 QBK-QDE, then with V.113, QDF-QFA.

V.113

Signatures — **B.W. Fraser** Governor, Reserve Bank of Australia.
C.I. Higgins Secretary to the Treasury.

Fig. 218. Signatures and titles, Fraser-Higgins $5 (V.113).

Issued — December, 1990.

Serial numbers — QDF 000001 - QGV 999999.
QGX to QJR, numbers 763001 to 999999 only.
Printed 103,959,880.

Sheet content 40 — With V.112, QDF-QFA, then QFB-QGV, then with V.114, QGX-QJR.

Fig. 219. Uncut vertical pair of Fraser-Higgins $5 notes.

Fraser-Higgins $5 notes were also sold in uncut, unpackaged form to collectors (80,000 notes).

4,000 vertical pairs were offered through mail order in April, 1991. Serial letters on the pairs were either QDZ-QEA, QEB-QEC, QED-QEE, QEF-QEG, with numbers from 000001 to 001000 only. They were sold at $62.50 for matched serial numeral pairs (e.g. two pairs of two notes) and were all cut from the vertical centres of sheets. See previous illustration. Further reading: *The Future of Uncut Pairs,* Michael Vort-Ronald, *Australian Coin Review,* November, 1991.

3,000 blocks of four were first sold in Sydney at a coin fair on 17 & 18 November, 1990, with serial letters QDF to QDY and QEH to QFA, numbers 000001 to 000375 only, at $50 per block. The first 100 of each of the top left and top right blocks bearing the intaglio printing plate identification number on the selvege were sold specially framed at $75 each.

Block number 000001 including prefix QFA was donated for auction for the Numismatic Association of Australia (N.A.A.), realising $4,250.
Further reading: *Collectors Cut-up over Uncut Notes,* Michael Vort-Ronald, *Australian Coin Review,* December, 1990.

5,000 blocks of four were offered through mail order and dealers in December, 1990. The notes had serial letters QDF to QDY, and QEH to QFA, with numbers 001501 to 002000 only, at $50 per block.

1,000 horizontal half sheets of 20 notes were offered through mail order in December, 1990, with serial letters QDF to QEV or QDK to QFA, serial numbers 001501 to 002000 only, at $250 per half sheet.

500 full sheets were also offered with serial letters QDF to QFA, serial numbers 001001 to 001500 only, at $500 per sheet.

V.114

Signatures **B.W. Fraser** Governor, Reserve Bank of Australia.
A.S. Cole Secretary to the Treasury.

Fig. 220. Signatures and titles, Fraser-Cole $5 (V.114).

Issued September, 1991.

Serial numbers QGX to QJR, numbers 000001 to 763000 only.
QJS 000001 - QLL 999999.
QLN to QPG, numbers 401001 to 9999999 only.
Printed 84,479,920. See also, Collector Issues, Chapter 9.

Sheet content 40 With V.113, QGX-QJR, then QJS-QLL, QLN-QPG.

20,000 notes with Fraser-Cole signatures were also sold as uncut vertical and horizontal pairs and blocks of four. The left note in the horizontal pairs, top note in the vertical pairs and top left note in the blocks of four had an overprint in red:

"25TH ANNIVERSARY
1967-1992"

All notes were numbered with serial letters XXV (Roman figure 25) out of sequence, and serial numbers were printed 500 apart on the notes in each pair or block. A number 000001 vertical pair and horizontal pair were specially framed by N.PA. and auctioned.

Fig. 221. Uncut horizontal pair of Fraser-Cole $5 notes.

3,000 horizontal pairs were sold at a coin fair in Melbourne on 11 & 12 July, 1992, at $32.50 each. A further 1,000 pairs were sold by mail order. See illustration above.

1,500 vertical pairs were issued in Adelaide on 5 & 6 September, 1992, with a coin fair overprint on their folders, at $32.50 each. A further 500 folders without the overprint on the folder were offered by mail order at $32.50 each, plus post. See next illustration.

Fig. 222. N.P.A. framed "No. 1" vertical pair XXV $5 notes, re-auctioned 1999 for $230.

Further reading: *Rent-a-Queue Returns to Melbourne,* and *Adelaide's First International Coin Fair,* Michael Vort-Ronald, *Australian Coin Review,* September, 1992, and October, 1992, respectively.

1,500 blocks of four were sold at a coin fair in Sydney on 21 & 22 November, 1992, at $65 per block, with a further 500 by mail order. The number 000001 of each was donated to the N.A.A. with the blocks framed, and sold at a dinner on 29 November, for $1,050. Further reading, *The Last Caroline Chisholm Issue,* Michael Vort-Ronald, *Australian Coin Review*, December, 1992.

From 7 July, 1992, the paper $5 note was replaced by a new polymer note. See Chapter 13.

Fig. 223. Front, sheet of 24 $5 notes.

Fig. 224. Front, sheet of 40 $5 notes.

V.125-128 $10 TEN DOLLARS

Type First. "COMMONWEALTH OF AUSTRALIA"

Issued 14 February, 1966 to September, 1974.

Size 155 mm x 77.5 mm.

Watermark The profile of Captain James Cook is on the left side of the front, facing right. See Fig. 101. A metallic security thread runs vertically through the note approximately 70 mm from the left edge of the front.

Signatures Coombs - Wilson, Coombs - Randall, Phillips - Randall, Phillips -Wheeler.

Serial numbers SAA 000001 to TBB 999999. ZSA 00001* to ZSJ 48004*.

Printed 470,000,000.

Fig. 225. Front, $10 note. First type (V.125).

FRONT

Main print: Blue-black intaglio. 142 mm x 69 mm.

A portrait of Francis Howard Greenway is on the right side. In the centre and behind Greenway are buildings and architecture of his period. At the top is "COMMONMWEALTH OF AUSTRALIA" and a "10" is in each top corner. The buildings are an assemblage of Greenway's architectural work. Under the signature titles at the bottom is the legal tender clause "Legal tender throughout the commonwealth of Australia and the Territories of the Commonwealth".

Background print: Dry offset using four colours. 147 mm x 69 mm.

In the horizontal centre are 87 straight blue-green lines which vary in thickness on the left, producing three "glows". The background pattern around the head of Greenway and behind the remainder of the design consists of vertical wavy blue lines, in between which are blue-green lines. In the vertical centre they rainbow to orange and khaki, and colouring the face of Greenway are greenish vertical lines.

1,500 blocks of four were sold at a coin fair in Sydney on 21 & 22 November, 1992, at $65 per block, with a further 500 by mail order. The number 000001 of each was donated to the N.A.A. with the blocks framed, and sold at a dinner on 29 November, for $1,050. Further reading, *The Last Caroline Chisholm Issue,* Michael Vort-Ronald, *Australian Coin Review*, December, 1992.

From 7 July, 1992, the paper $5 note was replaced by a new polymer note. See Chapter 13.

Fig. 223. Front, sheet of 24 $5 notes.

Fig. 224. Front, sheet of 40 $5 notes.

He reached Sydney on 7 February, 1814, and was employed by Governor Macquarie in reporting on Government buildings then nearing completion. Some of those buildings Greenway criticised in scathing terms for their architectural shortcomings and structural weaknesses. In March, 1816, Macquarie appointed him Civil Architect at a salary of three shillings a day.

Between 1816 and 1820, Greenway planned and superintended the erection of a number of public buildings, the first of architectural excellence built in Australasia. They included, 1818 - Macquarie Lighthouse, 1819 - The Convict Barracks in Queen Square, Sydney, Port Macquarie in 1821, and St. James Church in 1824. Eventually it was suggested by others that his style of work was "too grand for an infant colony", and he ceased to be Civil Architect in November, 1822.

He was Australia's first fully-qualified architect, and his work has been admired by succeeding generations. He died just prior to 26 September, 1837, the cause and exact date of his death are unknown, as is his place of burial.

Further reading: *Australian Encyclopaedia,* 3rd Edition, 1977, Sydney. The Grolier Society of Australia; *Francis Greenway, His Life and Times,* M.H. Ellis, Angus & Robertson, 1978.

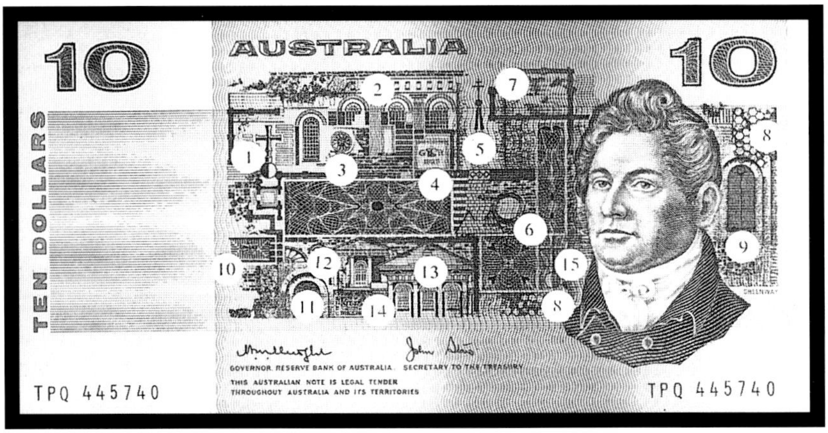

Fig. 227. Front, $10 note. Greenway's architectural works.

GREENWAY'S ARCHITECTURAL WORKS

The front of the $10 note bears a portrait of Francis Greenway and engravings of portions of historic buildings in Sydney and Windsor, New South Wales. Although the assemblage of architectural work on the note was said to be Greenways, some additions by later architects were included. The building featured most is that of St. James (Anglican) Church, Sydney. Other buildings from which features have been included on the note are the Supreme Court, Hyde Park Barracks, the Obelisk in Sydney, and St. Matthew's Church, Windsor. Interwoven are random outlines of building plans.

Fig. 228. St. James Church, Sydney, 1981.

Fig. 229. St. Matthew's Church, Windsor, 1981.

St. James Church, Queen's Square, Sydney.

The foundation stone was laid on 7 October, 1819, not for a church, but for a courthouse. Governor Macquarie had planned a Cathedral in George Street to be named St. Andrews, but because of the expense involved, Commissioner Bigge prompted him to abandon its construction and instead the projected courthouse became St. James Church. The church is located in King Street, at the southern end of Phillip Street, near the northern end of Hyde Park in the centre of the city, facing Macquarie Street.

By 1820, building had progressed sufficiently for the Governor to place a commemorative plaque high on the outside of the eastern wall. In 1822, an unofficial service was held. Regular services began in 1824, and have continued ever since.

Near the top left of the note (2) is a portion of the east end of the church showing three windows in typical Greenway style. The engraving has reduced the number of glass panes and omitted the inner brickwork arch. The columns between the present windows are plain and not fluted as in the engraving, and no such columns exist elsewhere in St. James.

To the bottom left of these three windows on the note is another window, possibly placed at random. It seems to be an engraving of the type of window in the west side of the tower of St. Matthew's Church, Windsor.

Near the bottom centre of the note (13 in Fig. 227) the vestry from the eastern end of the church appears, showing the top portion only of the three windows and the roofline. This was not built by Greenway. It is an accurate drawing of the present-day east end of the church, the lower part and roofline of which were built by John Verge in 1832. The original east end designed by Greenway contained very tall lancet windows. The circle in the gable has been enlarged and appears separately at (6). The inscription in the circle is "St. James Church, Erected A.D. 1820 L. Macquarie Esq. Governor."

The portico on the north side of the church off King Street is featured at (12). Shuttered windows (9) and (11) from possibly the tower under the spire appear near bottom left and centre right. Above (11) is a portion of an oval window typical of Greenway's work, and to the right of it, another random window.

The spire (5) shown on the note is an engraving similar to the spire of today, but not as it was designed and first built by Greenway. The original spire was wider and joined onto the tower in a different way. It was sheathed with lead and copper bands and was fairly plain. This spire became unsound and was replaced by Varney Parkes in 1892, who also added a small portico in a new tower entrance. The new spire is copper sheathed with a more ornate design. The small triangular corner supports (broaches) were added to give additional bracing to the centre mast of the spire.

For an official explanation of apparent discrepancies in the design of the note, see end of section about the Supreme Court, following.

St. Matthew's Church, Windsor.

St. Matthew's Anglican Church in Moses Street, Windsor, was erected under the direction of Henry Kitchen on a site chosen by Governor Macquarie when he established the town of Windsor on the Hawkesbury River in 1810, approximately 56 km from Sydney, via Parramatta. The foundation stone was laid by him on 11 October, 1817, after he deposited a "holey dollar" in a bottle under the stone. That night the dollar was stolen. Other dollars were placed under the stone, but these too, were stolen. Thus the church was commenced without the silver basis which Macquarie apparently believed would ensure its survival. Two years later the walls had to be pulled down to the foundations because of the defective materials used, and a building of much larger dimensions designed by Francis Greenway was commenced using the best materials available. The first sermon was conducted on 18 December, 1822. This is St. Matthew's Church of today.

The cross and orb, (1) and (15) on Fig. 227, is from the top of the church tower at the western end. The tower was originally copper, but it was replaced by stainless steel in the 1960s. The cross and orb is a very large and heavy wooden structure, and after the restoration it was replaced on the tower by helicopter.

A porch added to the south side of the church in 1857 obscured Macquarie's large commemorative stone depicted at (4) on the note, and it was removed and placed on the outer wall of the porch. The stone has a large crown between "G" and "R", below which is the inscription "St. Matthew's Church, Erected A.D. 1820. L. Macquarie Esq. Governor". The date shown on the stone on the note is 1825. The original foundation stone, dated 11 October, 1817, can still be seen in the foundation at the south-western corner of the church, with a convict marker to its left.

The engraving of Greenway on the $10 note was probably based on what is believed to be a self-portrait in the possession of, and part-reproduced by courtesy of, the Mitchell Library, Sydney. See next illustration. This unsigned pencil drawing, oval-shaped, thirteen inches by nine and three quarters of an inch, was presented to the library in 1948 by Greenway's grand-daughter, Mrs. C.E. Irving. The drawing is very faint and is possibly the only authentic portrait of Greenway.

Fig. 226. Francis Howard Greenway.

Francis Howard Greenway.

Francis Howard Greenway was Christened in Bristol, England, on 20 November, 1777, and was trained as a painter and architect in Bristol and London. In 1805, he joined his two brothers in establishing a firm that undertook extensive speculative building from his designs. Four years later, after a collapse in the building trade, the partners were declared bankrupt. In 1812, Greenway was charged with having forged an endorsement on a contract, and upon pleading guilty, was sentenced to death on 28 March, 1812. His sentence was later commuted to transportation to New South Wales for 14 years.

He reached Sydney on 7 February, 1814, and was employed by Governor Macquarie in reporting on Government buildings then nearing completion. Some of those buildings Greenway criticised in scathing terms for their architectural shortcomings and structural weaknesses. In March, 1816, Macquarie appointed him Civil Architect at a salary of three shillings a day.

Between 1816 and 1820, Greenway planned and superintended the erection of a number of public buildings, the first of architectural excellence built in Australasia. They included, 1818 - Macquarie Lighthouse, 1819 - The Convict Barracks in Queen Square, Sydney, Port Macquarie in 1821, and St. James Church in 1824. Eventually it was suggested by others that his style of work was "too grand for an infant colony", and he ceased to be Civil Architect in November, 1822.

He was Australia's first fully-qualified architect, and his work has been admired by succeeding generations. He died just prior to 26 September, 1837, the cause and exact date of his death are unknown, as is his place of burial.

Further reading: *Australian Encyclopaedia,* 3rd Edition, 1977, Sydney. The Grolier Society of Australia; *Francis Greenway, His Life and Times,* M.H. Ellis, Angus & Robertson, 1978.

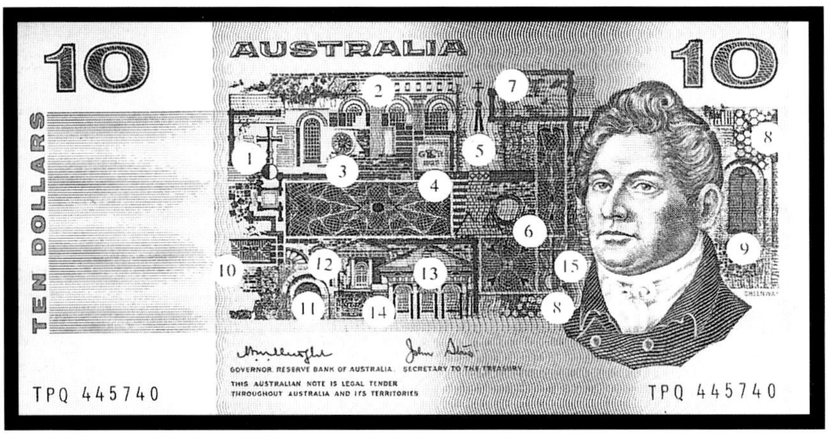

Fig. 227. Front, $10 note. Greenway's architectural works.

GREENWAY'S ARCHITECTURAL WORKS

The front of the $10 note bears a portrait of Francis Greenway and engravings of portions of historic buildings in Sydney and Windsor, New South Wales. Although the assemblage of architectural work on the note was said to be Greenways, some additions by later architects were included. The building featured most is that of St. James (Anglican) Church, Sydney. Other buildings from which features have been included on the note are the Supreme Court, Hyde Park Barracks, the Obelisk in Sydney, and St. Matthew's Church, Windsor. Interwoven are random outlines of building plans.

St. Matthew's also became the final restring place of the man featured on the back of the $100 note, John Tebbutt, who was interred in the family crypt in the grounds of this church in 1916, not far from the foundation stone (see bottom illustration). Tablets on the photograph are for John Tebbutt, (the astronomer), his wife Jane (died March 21, 1903) and Mary Alice Tebbutt, died May 12, 1910, aged 48 years. See also, John Tebbutt - $100 notes.

Fig. 230. St. Matthews Church, Windsor, 1981.

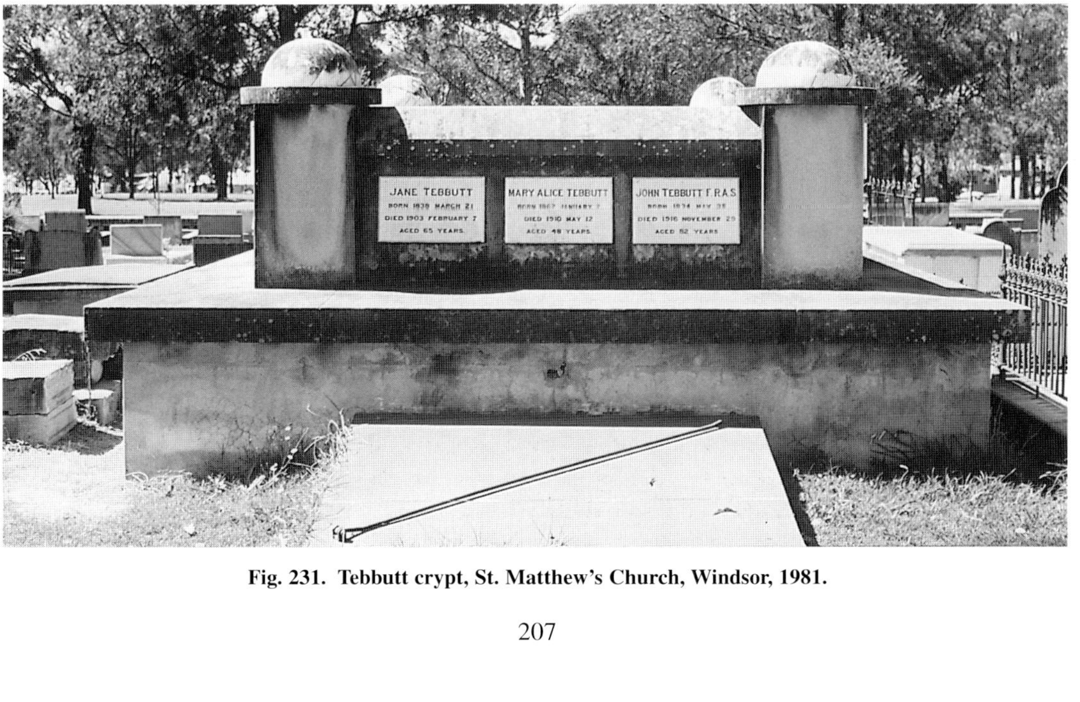

Fig. 231. Tebbutt crypt, St. Matthew's Church, Windsor, 1981.

Supreme Court, Sydney.

The Supreme Court, situated on the corner of King and Elizabeth Streets, Sydney, next to St. James Church, is not fully considered to be the work of Greenway because others took over its construction before it was half finished and introduced changes which completely altered Greenway's original design.

At the top right and bottom left of the portrait of Greenway on the note (8) is a honeycombed effect said to be hexagonal paving from around the courthouse. There is such paving at present between the southern side of St. James Church, and the court buildings. According to church officials, this paving is not original, and was added around 1900. This style of paving is not known elsewhere around the present Supreme Court in Sydney, or the courthouse at Windsor.

Near the bottom left (10) and (14) are cast vents from around the courthouse, Sydney. Vents as in (10) are visible in the walls of the courthouse alongside the St. James Road Court entrance, but none of the type as in (14) are visible. It is likely that these vents are of a different period to Greenway.

The New South Wales Government of Public Works stated in May, 1981:

> *Francis Greenway design on ten dollar note. As no known original drawings are available (with the exception of certain details), it is apparent that the artist used pictorial material from the later period as reference for his design. It is most certain that Greenway did not pave the surrounding area with the type of bitumastic hexagonal paving shown on the bank note as this form of paving was unknown at the time and the vents are obviously from the same Victorian Period as are also other elements in the design.*
>
> *In short, the artist has recorded Greenway's buildings complete with their natural additions over the years, but this in no way detracts from the intrinsic fact that their original fabric was by Greenway.*

Hyde Park Barracks.

Hyde Park Barracks is situated immediately north of the northern end of Hyde Park, Queen's Square, Sydney. The barracks was designed to provide accommodation for convicts employed on Government projects in Sydney and took two years to build. A trial occupation took place on 20 May, 1819, but the building was not formally occupied until its official opening by Governor Macquarie on 4 June, 1819. Macquarie was so pleased with the building that at its opening he announced an absolute pardon for Greenway, thus restoring the former convict to full citizenship.

A large clock (3) is contained in the pediment at the entrance facing Queen's Square. It was said to be a gift from King George III to the Colony, but this has not been verified. The clock was fully imported, having been made by the famous Villiamy Family, Royal clockmakers, in London. It was installed by J. Oatley, who was paid 75 pounds and received a 300-acre land grant for the work which later became the nucleus of the suburb Oatley. Under the clock is inscribed "L. Macquarie Esq Governor 1817". Except for a short period in 1984 when it was overhauled under a National Estate Grant, the clock has kept time continuously since it was installed in 1819.

Fig. 232. Hyde Park Barracks, Sydney, 1981.

Various later occupants of the barracks were female immigrants, Irish orphans, the infirm, destitute women, and various Government Offices such as Master in Lunacy. In more recent years the barracks were used as District Law Courts. It has since been restored as a museum of Sydney's social history and of convict life.

Obelisk, Macquarie Place, Sydney.

This hand-hewn sandstone obelisk was erected in 1818 by order of Governor Macquarie, at a cost of 120 pounds. It served as a point from which all public roads and distances were to be measured to the interior of the colony. Other small relics in the triangular park containing the obelisk include the anchor of H.M.S. *Sirius* (of the First Fleet) which was wrecked on 19 March, 1890, at Point Ross, Norfolk Island.

Most of one of the inscriptions (next illustrated) appear near top centre (7, on Fig. 227), and immediately to the right of (12) is a repeat of the first part of the same inscription.

All of these buildings and the obelisk have survived to the present day. They have either been faithfully restored, or restored to as near as possible to their former Colonial appearance.

At the time of their construction, or soon afterwards, they were criticised for their extravagance, but they remain today as testimony to the vision of Macquarie and the skill of Greenway. Together, they gave the young Colony its first buildings of excellence.

References: Photographs of all buildings and the obelisk by the author. *The Early Australian Architects and their Work,* by Morton Herman, 2nd edition, 1970, Angus and Robertson. Special thanks to Professor K.J. Cable for initial advice and consultation.

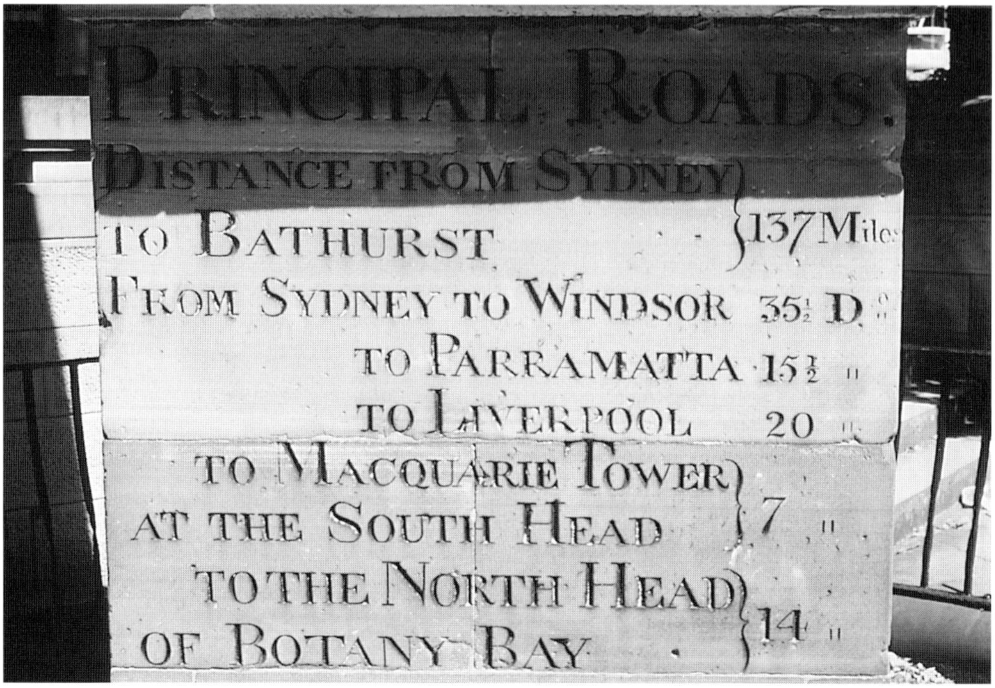

Fig. 233. Obelisk inscription used on the front of the $10 note.

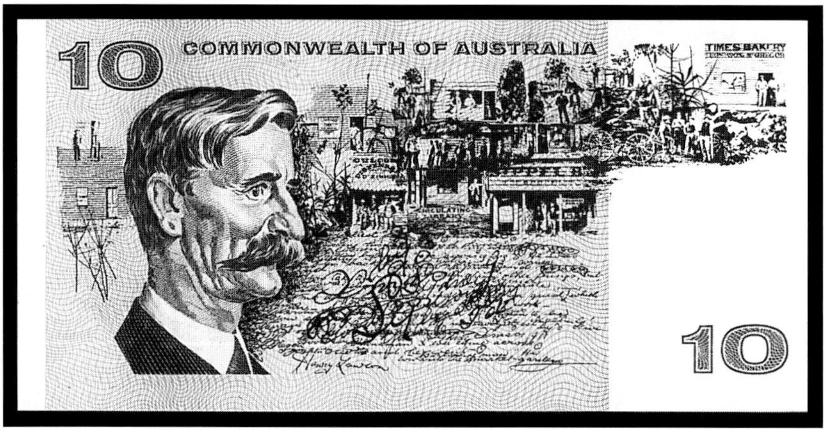

Fig. 234. Back. $10 note. First type. (V.95).

BACK

Main print: Blue-black intaglio. 142 mm x 66 mm.

The profile of Henry Lawson appears on the left, surrounded by a background composed of photographs of his time and of personal letters and manuscripts. The building "TIMES BAKERY" is at top right. "COMMONWEALTH OF AUSTRALIA" is along the top and the figure "10" is at top left and bottom right. The initials of Gordon Andrews appears in the clump of twigs to the left of the portrait. At the bottom is a re-arrangement by the designer of random lines and words from the manuscripts of Lawson held in the Mitchell Library, Sydney. See Fig. 235 for Intaglio printing.

Part of the text, written at Christmas time, 1911, appears to be:

> *...and he went on "no savaying". He was bright enough in other things, but in the matter of the six quid which I regarded as a loan to be returned to a man who made it by the hardest kind of work - Ah Loo was the "no savayingest" Chinaman I ever came across...*

The above transcript seems to be a variation of a story contained in a school text book *Henry Lawson: Stories for Senior Students,* selected by Colin Roderick, Angus and Robertson, Sydney, 1962. In that book is the story about a Chinese vegetable gardener Ah See, the son of Ah Soon, who delivered vegetables by horse and cart. In this book the story ends *...but when I wanted him to take and send the six pounds, he didn't "savvy", and he went on "no savvying.* The same story is in *A Fantasy of Man, Henry Lawson Complete Works* 1901-1922 edited by Leonard Cronin, and published by Warwick Jacobson, 1984 (at page 500).

Fig. 235. Back, $10 note, main print (Intaglio) only (error note).

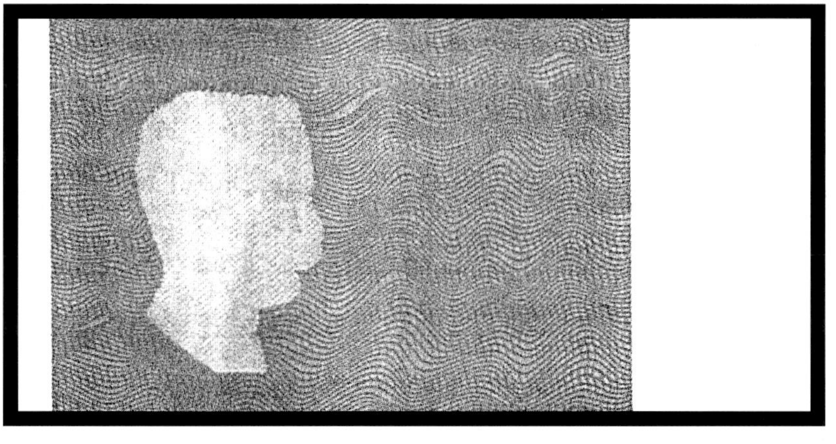

Fig. 236. Back, $10 note, background print (Simultan) only (error note).

Background print: Dry offset in six colours. 110 mm x 77.5 mm.
Around the portrait of Lawson, and behind the buildings and writings, the main background pattern consists of vertical wavy blue and blue-green lines, widening at regular intervals to form "pods". In addition, there are horizontal wavy fluctuating lines. On the left near the vertical centre of the note the background colours rainbow to orange and khaki. See fig. 236. Extensive forging of this type occurred 1966/67 in the signature combination of Coombs-Wilson (see Chapter 12).

Fig. 237. Henry Lawson

The illustration of Henry Lawson above was probably the one from which the profile on the note was based, then reversed. The original drawing by Sir Lionel Lindsay is in the possession of the Mitchell Library, Sydney, and is reproduced by courtesy of Peter Lindsay, son of the artist.

Henry Lawson

Henry Lawson was born in a tent near Grenfell, New South Wales, on 17 June, 1867. His father, a Norwegian, born Nils Larsen, later assumed the name of Peter, and changed his name to Lawson when the birth of Henry was registered. Peter Lawson took up a selection at Eurunderee, N.S.W. His weatherboard cottage was demolished about 1950, leaving only a brick chimney, which has since been surrounded by local stonework. This cottage now serves as a memorial to his son Henry. In 1876 Henry attended his first school at the age of nine. His hearing was affected at an early age and he had a miserable home life. Eventually his parents separated, and since he could learn little at school, he never learnt to spell efficiently.

Henry Lawson had lived in poor country where selectors slaved for a wretched living, and his experiences were to colour the whole of his later literary work. At the age of fifteen he left Eurunderee for Sydney with his mother after the separation of his parents. There he became apprenticed as a carpenter's improver. At the age of seventeen he was earning 30/- a week and attending night school. He moved to Melbourne in the hope of finding a cure for his deafness but, unable to do so, eventually returned to Sydney. He did not just see the slums and how the poor lived, he was most of his life "one of the poor", and "wished that he could write".

In June 1887, the Sydney *Bulletin* printed four lines of a poem he had submitted and advised him to try again. In October that year *Song of the Republic* was published, and by Christmas, two other poems. Lawson's first story *His Father's Mate* was published in the *Bulletin* on 22 December, 1888. In 1892 he went to western N.S.W. and carried his swag for six months doing odd jobs, and much of his experiences were included in his writings.

He tried gaining employment in New Zealand, but returned to Sydney. By 1894, his *Short Stories in Prose and Verse* was published by his mother in a poorly printed volume of 96 pages. In April, 1896, he married, and after various travels and published works, went to England in 1900. In his later years he had trouble with alcohol and eventually separated from his wife in about 1903. Lawson was a tall, good looking man in his youth. Shy, diffident and very sensitive, he was a convinced socialist as a young man and always passionately concerned about the under-dog. His gift of narration was unfailing, giving him the foremost place in Australian literature as a writer of short stories. His writings have preserved the moods and hardships of the period. He died 2 September, 1922, and was given a State funeral to Waverley Cemetery, Sydney. Further reading: *Australian Encyclopaedia, 3rd Edition,* 1977, Sydney, The Grolier Society of Australia. *Henry Lawson*, the Grey Dreamer, by Denton Prout.

Gulgong, New South Wales.

The profile of Henry Lawson on the back of the $10 note is accompanied by actual scenes of his period. The accurate depiction of those scenes was made possible by two men over a century ago, and the re-discovery in 1951 of a large number of negatives on glass, forming part of what is now known as the ***Holtermann Collection.***

Bernard Otto Holtermann was born in Hamburg, Northern Germany, on 29 April, 1838. Although unable to speak English, he travelled to Australia at the age of 20 years. After various jobs he was drawn to the goldfields, but it was not until he had been in Australia for ten years that his name was to become well known for his part-ownership of the Star of Hope Mine, at Hill End. It was, however, the addition of Mark Hammond to the mining venture, with his new ideas on how to operate the mine which brought fame and fortune to its owners. In the early hours of 19 October, 1871, a final charge for the shift set off in the mine, disclosed a veritable wall of gold. When finally brought to the surface the main specimen of gold (with some quartz and slate) measured four feet nine inches (1.45 metres) high, two feet two inches (.66 metres) wide and averaged four inches (10 cm) in thickness. It weighed 630 lbs. and the actual gold content was estimated in excess of 3,000 ounces.

Stimulated by rich finds on Hawkins Hill in the Star of Hope and other mines, an era of reckless speculation followed, and by the end of the year, 1,500 claims had been staked out, and the population of Gulgong and its satellite villages had risen to 20,000.

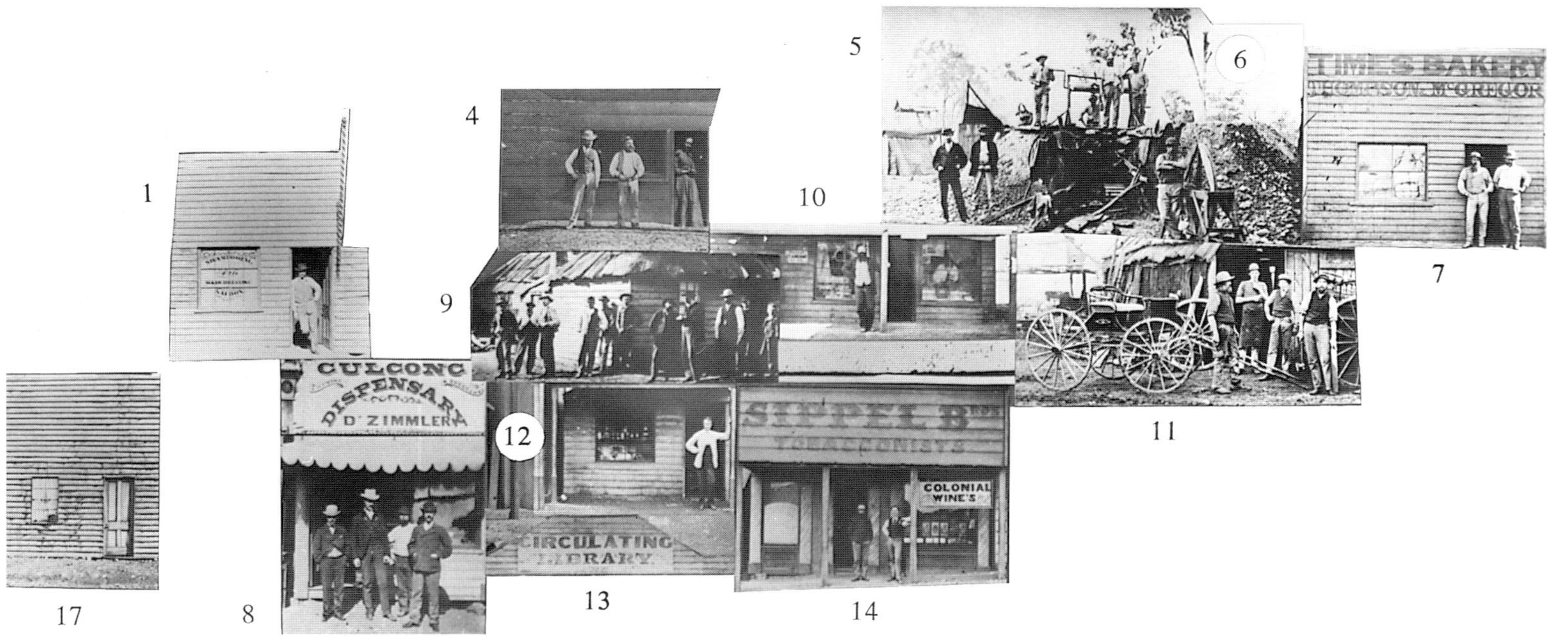

Fig. 238. Photographs from the Holtermann Collection re-assembled as on the $10 note.

The size of the population supported three newspapers and sixty hotels. Thus was born a town, but it was the work of another man, Beaufoy Merlin, which preserved it as it was for succeeding generations - through the art of photography.

Henry Beaufoy Merlin was born in England in 1830. By 1866, he had established himself in Victoria as a field or travelling photographer operating under the name of "Australasian & American Photographic Company". He had with him a young and able assistant, Charles Bayliss. Merlin, as did other photographers of his time, travelled with a fully-equipped horse-drawn caravan which was virtually a darkroom on wheels. He used what was called the collodion method for his photography.

The collodion or wet-plate emulsion process of Frederick Scott Archer emerged in the 1850s with the introduction of albumen printing paper, a type of soft printing paper which made excellent prints and multiple copies possible from the contrasty negatives of that time. Despite the immense advantages, the collodion process suffered from a grave hindrance. It was purely a chemical restriction - the negative had to be coated, exposed while still "wet" and then processed, all within half an hour or less - for once the collodion dried out, the silver nitrate crystallised, and the image was destroyed.

The "A & A Photographic Company" travelled to New South Wales and remained in Hill End for three months where it was present to photograph Holtermann's Nugget. After Hill End, Merlin shifted to Gulgong, several days travel to the north. He photographed virtually everything, and certainly no town within a matter of months of its formation, was so thoroughly photographed during this period. The prints produced were in *carte-de-visite* form exposed on quarter plate three and one quarter inches (82 mm) x four and a quarter inche (108 cm) glasses, but the customer actually received a considerably smaller picture which averaged two and a quarter inches (57 mm) x three and three quarters of an inch (95 mm), for just over a shilling. The reduction was due to the exigencies of the hand-coating procedure, and the need for accurate trimming prior to mounting.

Photography had long fascinated Holtermann, and it was his new-found wealth that was to enable him to fulfil his ambition to collect, and exhibit overseas, a great series of photographs showing the life and development of commerce and industry throughout N.S.W. and Victoria. Impressed by Merlin's work, he offered him the task of undertaking this extensive photographic work on his behalf. This Merlin set out to do, but before he could complete the task, he died of pneumonia on 27 September, 1873. He was betrayed by his great love, the wet-plate process. The continual inhalation of the deadly potassium cyanide in the closely-confined quarters of the coating caravan no doubt contributed greatly to his untimely death.

The photography for Holtermann's Great Exposition was continued by Charles Baylis, who had been Merlin's assistant. Later, Holtermann was to build a mansion in Sydney with a very high tower, from which he would take giant photographs, bigger than had ever been seen, or thought possible. These he took to Philadelphia for the 1876 Exhibition, where he gained a first award for photography.

Holtermann died on 29 April, 1885, aged 47, but before his death he purchased the *carte-de-visite* negatives of Hill End and Gulgong. These, together with the other larger negatives used for his exhibitions, were stored and preserved by his descendants, to be "re-discovered" in 1951. They are now housed in the Mitchell Library, Sydney. Hill End was proclaimed a Historic site in 1967, and the National Parks and Wildlife Service has restored much of the town as a tourist attraction.

Fig. 239. Back, $10 note - Gulgong in 1872.

Many of the individual scenes accompanying the portrait of Lawson on the note are identifiable from photographs in the Holtermann Collection as originating in Gulgong. In the previous illustration, the scenes have been numbered and identified as follows: The five-digit numbers in brackets refer to the Mitchell Library reference numbers for the particular photographs.

(1) One of the town's barbers, Thomas B. Scurrah, standing in the doorway of his Shampooing and Hairdressing Saloon which was situated on the south side of Mayne Street, just east of Medley Street (18142).

(2)(3)(16) Unidentified.

(4) John Lewis, tailor, had a shop on the west side of Herbert Street, between Bayly and Little Bayly Streets (18124). The woman standing in the doorway has been transposed from a doorway of a Tobacconist shop (C.Caps) (18154) which sold wine, and bread for four pence a loaf. It was located on the south side of Mayne Street between Herbert and White Streets. The sign "Colonial Wines" from under the window of this shop appears to have been transposed to the window of the shop at (14).

(5)(6) A group of men standing at a mine head, possibly the Caledonian Mine. The man standing at the top is next to a hand-operated windlass, and at his feet is a rawhide bucket. A hand-operated ventilation fan serviced the mine (18412).

(7) Perhaps the best-recognised building on the note is that of Thompson and McGregor's "Times Bakery". Originally one block north of Lynne Street, the proprietors moved to a new and substantial stone building in the centre of Gulgong when the shopping area contracted southward. The new building now forms part of the Gulgong Pioneer Museum (18362).

(8) Dr. Charles Zimmler's Gulgong Dispensary, north side of Mayne Street (18289) between Herbert Street and White Street. See also (12).

(9) A group of men standing in front of a bark-roofed hut (18365).

Fig. 240. Original photographs of Gulgong from the Holtermann Collection, adapted for the $10 note.

(10) Donald McDonald's Circulating Library. The roof of the library appears at (13) (18359).

(11) A group of people standing by a carriage in front of a carriagemaker's shop situated on the south side of Mayne Street (18120), next door to G. Matthews' Lachlan Brewery (18115).

(12) The bottom half of the dispensary which included "Young Mr. White" in the doorway has been transposed from (8) (18289). The American Tobacco Warehouse and Fancy goods Emporium (18149) is situated in Mayne Street on the south side, between Medley and Herbert Streets. The bottom portion which included four men, has been transposed to the bottom of the Gulgong Dispensary. The outside of the "Warehouse" has been preserved as it was originally, and can still be seen on its original site at Gulgong.

(14) Sippel Bros. Tobacconists, was located on the east side of Herbert Street between Mayne and Queen Streets (18177).

(15) Text from Lawson's manuscript, as previously described in Henry Lawson section.

(17) A weatherboard house in Gulgong (18316). Only the left window and door have been featured on the note. Many buildings depicted on the note, including this one, clearly show the pine-board facings typical of the period - constructed from material brought across by bullock dray from Dubbo.

There were three banks in Gulgong at the time; the Australian Joint Stock Bank, north-east corner of Herbert and Queen Streets; the Bank of New South Wales, south-west corner of Mayne and Herbert Streets and the Oriental Bank on the north side of Mayne Street, nearly opposite the Bank of New South Wales. Most of the Holtermann photographs were taken of premises in Mayne Street and Herbert Street. Herbert Street was the main north-south street in Gulgong with Mayne Street being the main east-west street. Travelling north along Herbert Street from Mayne Street, the east-west streets crossing it were Queen Street, Bayly Street, Little Bayly Street, Belmore Street, Little Belmore Street and Lynne Street, one block beyond which the village of Gulgong became Black Lead, 1.5 km N.N.E. of the Gulgong Post Office. .

Without doubt, Gulgong can claim to have been the *town on the $10 note.*

References and further reading: *Gold and Silver, Photographs of Australian Goldfields from the Holtermann Collection,* Keast Burke, Penguin Books, 1977; *Written in Gold,* Eileen Maxwell, Gulgong Pioneer's Museum and Historical Society, Gulgong 1975; Map of Gulgong 1872 with location of premises with cross references to Holterman photographs, compiled by Leonard D. Reid.

The grouping of nine small photographs on the previous page is from glass negatives in the Holtermann Collection, taken at Gulgong in 1872, and now in the possession of the Mitchell Library, which holds Copyright and gave permission for their inclusion in this book. The numbers on the individual photographs refer to the previous listing.

Serial numbering "Gothic" style, as in Fig. 250.

V.125

Signatures **H.C. Coombs** Governor, Reserve Bank of Australia.
Roland Wilson Secretary to the Treasury.

Fig. 241. Signatures and titles, Coombs-Wilson $10 (V.125).

Issued 14 February, 1966 to September, 1974.

Serial numbers SAA 000001 - SDR 168000. Printed 77,168,000.

Star notes ZSA 00001* - ZSD 36000*. (See V.126). Printed 336,000.

V.126

Signatures **H.C. Coombs** Governor, Reserve Bank of Australia.
R.J. Randall Secretary to the Treasury.

Fig. 242. Signatures and titles, Coombs-Randall $10 (V.126)

Issued October, 1967.

Serial numbers SDR 168001 - SFR 300000. Printed 48,132,000.

Star notes ZSD 36001* - ZSE 100000*. Printed approximately 167,000.
(star notes possibly commenced at ZSD 33001).

V.127

Signatures **J.G. Phillips** Governor, Reserve Bank of Australia.
R.J. Randall Secretary to the Treasury.

Fig. 243. Signatures and titles, Phillips-Randall $10 (V.127).

Issued October, 1968.

Serial numbers SFR 300001 - STG 999999. Printed 223,700,00.

Star notes ZSF 00001* - ZSJ 48004*. Printed 348,004.

V.128

Signatures	**J.G. Phillips**	Governor, Reserve Bank of Australia.
	F.H. Wheeler	Secretary to the Treasury.

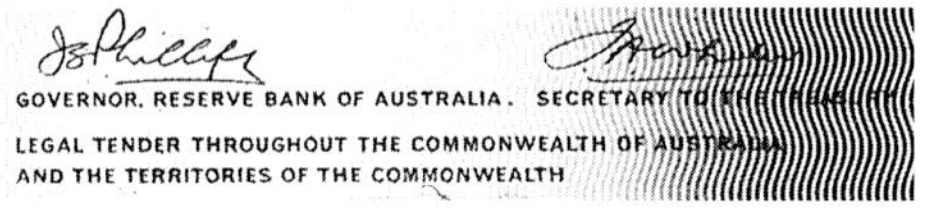

Fig. 244. Signatures, titles, legal tender clause, Phillips-Wheeler (Commonwealth) $10 (V.128).

Issued	November, 1972.	
Serial numbers	STH 000001 - TBB 999999.	Printed 121,000,000.
	No star notes were issued from this signature combination onwards.	

From 19 September, 1974, notes with “AUSTRALIA” replacing “COMMONWEALTH OF AUSTRALIA” were issued. See Second type.

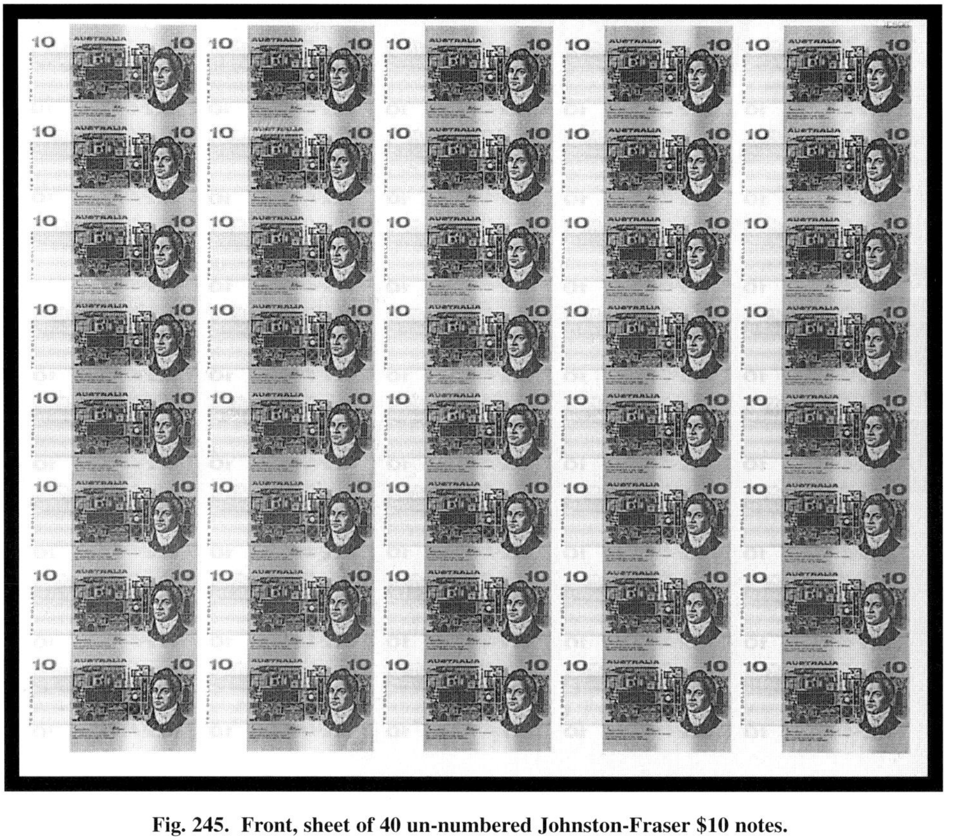

Fig. 245. Front, sheet of 40 un-numbered Johnston-Fraser $10 notes.

V.129-136 **$10** **TEN DOLLARS**

Type Second "AUSTRALIA".

Issued 19 September, 1974 to November, 1993.

Signatures Phillips - Wheeler, Knight - Wheeler, Knight - Stone, Johnston - Stone, Johnston - Fraser, Fraser - Higgins, Fraser - Cole. Other details as in the First type.

Serial numbers TBC 000001 - UZZ 999999. MAA 000001 - MRR 999999.

Printed 1,265,959,091, plus Uncut notes and Collector Issues.

Fig. 246. Front, $10 note. Second type (V.129).

FRONT AND BACK

All main design details are the same as in the First type with the following exceptions. "AUSTRALIA" replaced "COMMONWEALTH OF AUSTRALIA" at the top in larger lettering than previously, and the legal tender clause was changed to read "This Australian note is legal tender throughout Australia and its Territories." Background design and details remained the same as those in the First type, although some later issues had a paler yellow rainbowing effect in the centre.

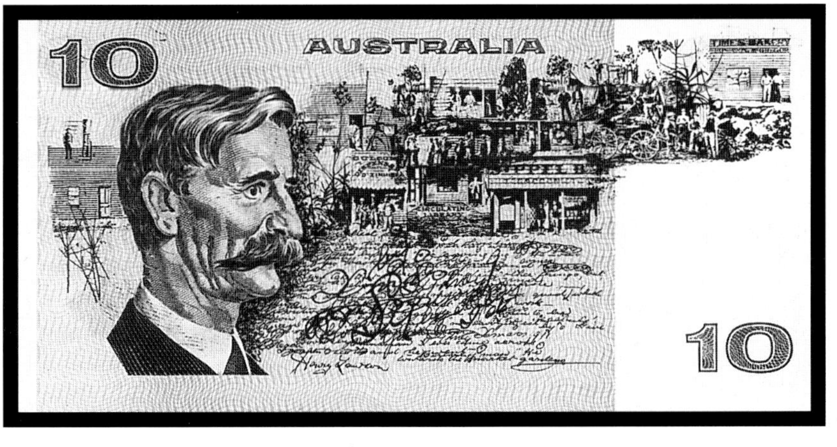

Fig. 247. Back. $10 note. Second type (V.129).

$10 "AUSTRALIA" NOTES.

V.129

Signatures — **J.G. Phillips** Governor, Reserve Bank of Australia.
F.H. Wheeler Secretary to the Treasury.

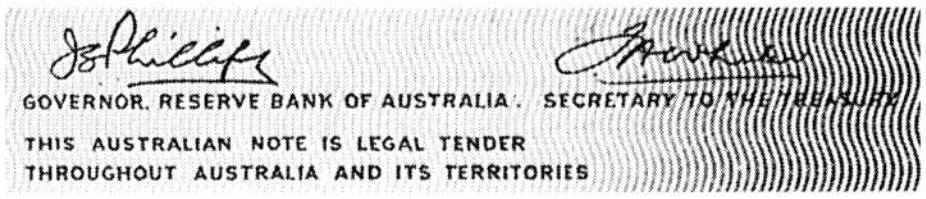

Fig. 248. Signatures, titles, legal tender clause, Phillips-Wheeler (Australia) $10 (V.129).

Issued 19 September, 1974.

Serial numbers TBC 000001 - TEL 999999. Printed 75,000,000.
"Gothic" serial numbering. "Centre thread". Metallic security thread approximately 70 mm from the left edge of the front.

Sheet content 24 Prefixes uncertain to TBE, then TBF-TCG, TCH-TDJ, TDK-TEL.

V.130

Signatures — **H.M. Knight** Governor, Reserve Bank of Australia.
F.H. Wheeler Secretary to the Treasury.

Fig. 249. Signatures and titles, Knight-Wheeler $10 (V.130).

Issued May, 1976.

Serial numbers TEN 000001 - TPC 999924. Printed 167,999,924.

Variety (a) "Gothic" serial numbering. "Centre thread". Metallic security thread approximately 70 mm from the left edge of the front.

Sheet content 24 TEN-TFP, TFQ-TGR, TGS-THT.

Variety (b) "Gothic" serial numbering. "Side thread". Metallic security thread approximately 55 mm from the left edge of the front.

Sheet content 24 THU-TJV, TJX-TKY, TKZ-TNA, TNB-TPC.

From July, 1976, all paper despatched by the Note Printing Branch's suppliers had the security thread positioned in an area approximately 55 mm from the left edge of the front. The change was made to avoid the natural fold area which, because of the close proximity of the metallic thread, caused undue wear and tearing.

The type of serial numbering for $10 notes changed in the next signature combination. For an explanation of the reasons for the change and technical details, see V.90.

TPL 168100

Fig. 250. "Gothic" serial numbers.

TUB 985510

Fig. 251. "OCR-B" serial numbers.

V.131

Signatures — **H.M. Knight** Governor, Reserve Bank of Australia.
John Stone Secretary to the Treasury.

Fig. 252. Signatures and titles, Knight-Stone $10 (V.131).

Variety (a) "Gothic" serial numbering.

Issued First despatched from Note Issue Department June, 1979.

Serial numbers TPD 000001 - TTL 999999. Printed 96,000,000.

Sheet content 24 TPD-TQE, TQF-TRG, TRH-TSJ, TSK-TTL.

Variety (b) "OCR-B" serial numbering.

Issued May, 1981.

Serial numbers TTN 000001 - TXT 999999. Printed 72,000,000.

Sheet content 24 TTN-TUP, TUQ-TVR, TVS-TXT.

V.132

Signatures — **R.A. Johnston** Governor, Reserve Bank of Australia.
John Stone Secretary to the Treasury.

Fig. 253. Signatures and titles, Johnston-Stone $10 (V.132).

Issued October, 1983.

Serial numbers TXU 000001 - UCC 999926. Printed 95,999,926.
"OCR-B" serial numbering. "Side thread".

Sheet content 24 TXU-TYV, TYX-TZY, TZZ-UBA, UBB-UCC.

V.133

Signatures — **R.A. Johnston** Governor, Reserve Bank of Australia.
B.W. Fraser Secretary to the Treasury.

Fig. 254. Signatures and titles, Johnston-Fraser $10 (V.133).

Issued February, 1985.

Serial numbers UCD 000001 - UYG 999999. UYH to UZZ, MAA to MAC, numbers 524001 to 999999 only. Printed 419,039,560.

Sheet content 40 UCD-UDY, UDZ-UFT, UFU-UHP, UHQ-UKJ, UKK-UNE, UNF-UQA, UQB-URV, URX-UTR, UTS-UVL, UVN-UYG. With V.135, UYH-MAC.

In 1988 a polymer $10 note was issued to commemorate the Bicentenary of Australia. It was printed and issued at the same time as the paper notes were being printed and issued, but the general (undated) AB series was restricted to issue only in that year (V.134). See Chapter 13.

V.135

Signatures — **B.W. Fraser** Governor, Reserve Bank of Australia.
C.I. Higgins Secretary to the Treasury.

Fig. 255. Signatures and titles, Fraser-Higgins $10 (V.135).

Issued December, 1989.

Serial numbers UYH to UZZ, MAA to MAC, numbers 000001 to 524000 only.
MAD 000001 - MFP 999999.
MFQ to MHJ, numbers 624001 to 999999 only. Printed 148,999,847.

Sheet content 40 With V.134, UYH-MAC, then MAD-MBY, MBZ-MDT, MDU-MFP.
With V.136, MFQ-MHJ.

An unknown quantity of sheets with this signature combination was accidentally mixed with sheets in the next signature combination and received serial numbers in the range of Fraser-Cole, i.e. with serial prefixes from MFQ to MHJ with numbers below 624001.

At the Hobart Coin Fair in May 1991 uncut pairs of $10 notes with Fraser-Cole signatures were sold to the public. After the fair it was discovered that 20 pairs (40 notes) had Fraser-Higgins signatures. They were numbered MGH/MGJ, MGK/MGL, MGN/MGP, MGQ/MGR, with serial numbers 000106 to 000110.

The incident was explained in a story in the July, 1991, *Australian Coin Review* by Peter Hutchison, titled *The Higgins Production Error - More Excitement Than My Fair Lady,* and a pair was illustrated in colour on the front cover of that edition. The following is extracted:

> *...It seems that the order went in for uncut sheets of Fraser and Cole $10 notes to be released in pairs and later, in blocks-of-four. During the printing process some sheets must have become spoiled. The production team replaced the spoiled sheets with some from a reserve stack......with Fraser/ Higgins signatures......the matching blocks of four have been taken out of the release scheduled for the Melbourne Coin Fair.*

> A letter of reply published on 13 May, 1992, from Alan Flint, Manager (Gallery) and Numismatic Curator, Note Printing Australia included:

> *It is not possible to indicate how many sheets were mixed up, but it is unlikely that the number would have been large, given that Fraser/Higgins had been exhausted, barring a few sheets, possibly spoils.*

One of the Fraser-Higgins $10 pairs in the Fraser-Cole range sold in auction on 27 August, 1991, realising $8,525.

But the story did not end there. In December, 1991, a Sydney bank employee who had a habit of fanning through new notes looking for errors, discovered a run of three Fraser-Higgins $10 notes in the middle of a section of Fraser-Cole notes. All notes were consecutively numbered. He then located corresponding serial numbers in other sections of notes and eventually five "sets" of nine notes were located. Each "set" had serial numbers 568853 to 568861, with the three centre notes numbered 568856, 7, 8 being Fraser-Higgins and the remainder, Fraser-Cole. The five "sets" had serial prefixes MGS, MGT, MGU, MGV and MGX. Set MGT sold in auction in March, 1994, for $3,300. Further reading *Australian Accidental Banknotes* by Harold Peake, Buderim, Queensland, 1994, and *$10 mixup*, by Michael Vort-Ronald in the *Australian Coin Review*, May and June, 1992.

Fig. 256. Front, Fraser-Higgins $10 note within the Fraser-Cole serial number range.

Other single notes located in circulation with Fraser-Higgins signatures in the Fraser-Cole serial number range have included MFT 105328, MFV 490113, MFY 469571 and 462979, MGB 105582 and MGD 489278. As notes were printed 40 to a sheet it means that at least six sheets of 40 notes would have been numbered out of sequence with Fraser-Higgins signatures - probably more.

V.136

Signatures — **B.W. Fraser** Governor, Reserve Bank of Australia.
A.S. Cole Secretary to the Treasury.

Fig. 257. Signatures and titles, Fraser-Cole $10 (V.136).

Issued — May, 1991 to 31 October, 1993.

Serial numbers — MFQ to MHJ, numbers 000001 to 624000 only.
MHK 000001 - MPV 999999.
MPX to MRR, numbers 477001 to 999999 only.

Sheet content 40 — With V.135, MFQ-MHJ, then MHK-MKE, MKF-MNA, MNB-MPV, MPX-MRR.

Printed 165,879,960, plus 12,000 in sheets. See also, uncut notes, following, and Collector issues, Chapter 9.

V.137-144 — Reference numbers not used.

Fraser-Cole notes were extensively marketed in uncut form and were specially numbered out of sequence in the range MFQ - MHJ 600001 to 601000. They were issued as follows:

4,000 vertical pairs loose inside the publication *Note Printing in Australia* and a numbered certificate, at a cost of $65 per pair. 3,000 were sold at the Hobart Coin Fair on 11 & 12 May, 1991 and 1,000 vertical pairs through the *Australian Coin Review* in August, 1991, without certificates. It was oversubscribed and a ballot was held to allocate the notes. In both cases, they were sold as either a single pair or two pairs with matching numerals. The issue was a hurried one as an alternative to a proposed issue of $5 notes in perspex at the coin fair and this may have contributed to the former mixup of Fraser-Higgins/Fraser-Cole notes. All pairs were from the vertical centres of sheets and bear prefixes MGH/MGJ, MGK/MGL, MGN/MGP and MGQ/MGR only.

The number 600001 centre two pairs were retained for Reserve Bank Archives. Melbourne dealers Downies purchased the specially framed top and bottom number one pairs at a gala dinner and auction for $9,500. Proceeds of the auction went to the Numismatic Association of Australia.

4,000 blocks of four from the left side of the sheets were sold at $130 per block in a special folder with a copy of *Note Printing in Australia.* 3,000 were sold at the Melbourne Coin Fair on 13 & 14 July, and 1,000 by mail order.

Another number 600001 block of four was specially framed by Note Printing Australia and sold at a gala dinner to Downies for $7,700, and was later offered for sale at $7,700. The remaining number 600001 blocks were retained in Reserve Bank Archives. Proceeds of the auction went to the N.A.A. All blocks used prefixes MFQ - MGG or MGJ - MHJ. Melbourne No. 1 block re-auctioned in August, 1999, for $126.50.

4,000 blocks of four from the right side of the sheets were sold in a similar fashion, 3,000 at the Sydney Coin Fair on 16 & 17 November, 1991, and 1,000 by mail order in January, 1992. The top left note in each block of four was overprinted in black with "INTERNATIONAL COIN FAIR 16/17 November 1991". This was the first time a paper note had been overprinted for collectors.

A maximum of four blocks per customer allowed the purchaser to have matching serial numerals on all four blocks at a cost of $520.

One of the number 000001 blocks was specially framed by N.P.A. and auctioned for the N.A.A.The framed block sold for $4,000. See Figs. 259 and 260. Further reading: *Rent-a-crowd and the Melbourne Coin Fair,* and *The Future of Uncut Blocks,* Michael Vort-Ronald, *Australian Coin Review* August, 1991, and December, 1991, respectively.

Some collectors discovered minor creasing in the paper (caused during printing) of some bottom corner blocks issued in Sydney. As the faulty blocks were part of a matching set of four blocks, they did not wish to obtain just any block replacement as it would not match. To keep faith with its customers, Note Printing Australia accepted back the damaged blocks, and reprinted other blocks with the same serial numbers. The reprinting had to wait until a new shipment of paper was received from Portals and the next scheduled $10 production run. The reprinting took place in June, 1992, and the replacement blocks were forwarded in September. In effect, those reprinted and renumbered blocks became replacement notes without stars.

The long delay in replacing the creased blocks had been caused by the urgency to print the new plastic $5 in time for its July 7 release. The same machines were used to print on the same paper stock, but because of the time in between the original printing and the replacements, different printing plates were used. The difference is visible in the reprinted blocks, referred to by Harold Peake as defective reprints.

The defective reprints contained "traffic lights" (colour registration dots) on the back of the notes which had a gap between them and the bottom edge of the main body of the Simultan printing which has a "saw-tooth" edge. On the original printings, the "traffic lights" touched the main body of the Simultan (background) printing, which had a straight edge. See Fig. 261.

The original blocks had metallic security threads 160 mm apart compared with 152 mm apart on the defective reprints. The positioning of the coin fair overprint was also slightly different. There is a colour variation in the yellow rainbowing in the centre of the reprinted notes, and other minor differences. Some of the reprinted notes did not have plate identification letters.

N.P.A. would not confirm the number of blocks reprinted, but it probably did not exceed 40. An extraordinary amount of time and effort went into the printing of the defective reprints, the ownership of which deserves a premium, but none have been sold at auction as yet to establish a base price.

After the accidental inclusion of Fraser-Higgins $10 notes with Fraser-Cole prior to numbering, and the subsequent issue of 20 uncut pairs of Fraser-Higgins notes in Hobart, the corresponding blocks were removed by N.P.A. from blocks intended for sale and replaced by other blocks from replacement sheets specially renumbered with the same numbers as those withdrawn.

One of the right hand bottom blocks returned by Harold Peake with the damage (termed crazing) was a block with serial number 600106, In due course it was replaced with another block bearing the same serial number. In essence, the serial number block 600106 was originally printed as part of a Fraser-Higgins sheet which was mixed up with Fraser-Cole sheets and received Fraser-Cole numbering. It was removed (and later destroyed) and replaced by another block with Fraser-Cole signatures and numbered the same. When it was replaced for Harold Peake with a fresh printing with Fraser-Cole signatures and the original serial numbers, it became a replacement of a replacement. Harold, who did the research on the defective reprints, now believes he has the only block of four notes with serial numbers which have been printed three times (signature reprint). Further reading: *Replacement Notes without Stars,* Michael Vort-Ronald, *Australian Coin Review,* June, 1993 and *Australian Accidental Banknotes,* by Harold Peake.

300 uncut full sheets of (40) Fraser-Cole $10 notes were sold by tender in May, 1994. They had prefixes from MPX to MRR, and were specially numbered out of sequence with numbers 000001 to 000300. The higher the bid the lower the number received. Successful tenders ranged from $829 to $3,100, the average tender being $981. Sheets with numbers 000001 and 000002 were later privately cut up and sold as singles. Further reading: *King of the Uncuts,* Michael Vort-Ronald, *Australian Coin Review,* August, 1996.

From 1 November, 1993, the paper $10 note was replaced by a new polymer design. See Chapter 13.

Fig. 258. Uncut vertical pair of Fraser-Cole $10.

Fig. 259. No. One block of $10, Melbourne.

Fig. 260. No. One block of $10, Sydney.

The two top illustrations show the placement of the Overprint on the Sydney Defective Reprints (top), and the normal Sydney Blocks (below).

The two bottom illustrations are of the Reverse Sides of the Defective Reprint (left) with saw tooth edge, and Sydney Block (right) with straight bottom edge - by far the easiest method of idenifying these two Varieties.

Fig. 261. Sydney overprint and traffric light variations, $10 defective reprints.

V.145-148 $20 TWENTY DOLLARS

Type First. "COMMONWEALTH OF AUSTRALIA".

Issued 14 February, 1966 to August, 1974.

Size 160 mm x 80 mm.

Watermark The profile of Captain James Cook is on the left side of the front facing right. See Fig. 101. A metallic security thread runs vertically through the note approximately 70 mm from the left edge of the front.

Signatures Coombs - Wilson, Coombs - Randall, Phillips - Randall, Phillips -Wheeler.

Serial numbers XAA 000001 to XGY 960000. **Printed** 146,960.000.
ZXA 00001* to ZXA 62500*.

Fig. 262. Front, $20 note. First type (V.145).

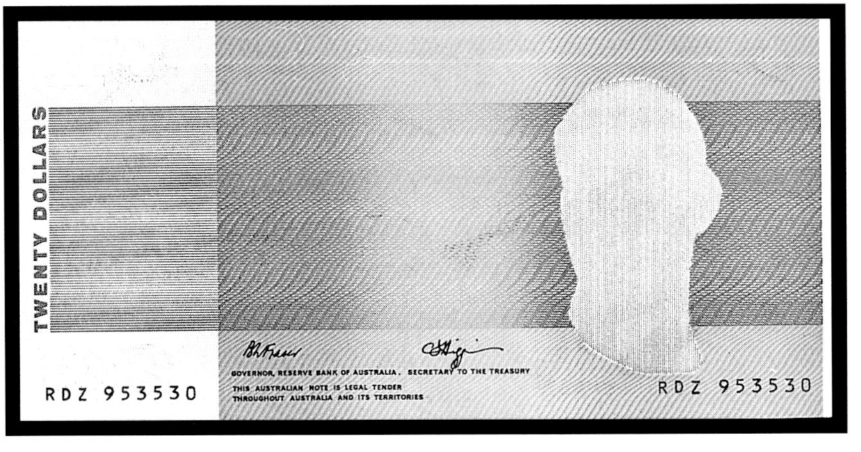

Fig. 263. Front, $20 note, background (Simultan) printing (error note).

FRONT

Main print: Red-black intaglio. 147 mm x 72 mm.

On the right side is a portrait of Sir Charles Kingsford Smith. In the centre of the note are pendulum tracings symbolic of wings. At the top is "COMMONWEALTH OF AUSTRALIA" and "20" is in each top corner. At the bottom, under the signature titles, is the legal tender clause "Legal tender throughout the Commonwealth of Australia and the Territories of the Commonwealth".

Background print: Dry offset in six colours. 153 mm x 80 mm.

Across the horizontal centre are 89 khaki lines, varying in thickness in three places to produce "glows". The background pattern behind the pendulum tracings and around the portrait consists of diagonal wavy lines in white, khaki and red. Above and below the main background pattern the colours change to red and white only, and in the vertical centre the colours rainbow to yellow and orange. The next illustration of Air-Commodore Sir Charles Kingsford Smith is reproduced from the frontispiece of his book *The Old Bus*, published in Melbourne in 1932. It appears to be the picture from which the portrait on the note was engraved. See Fig. 262 and 264.

Charles Edward Kingsford Smith

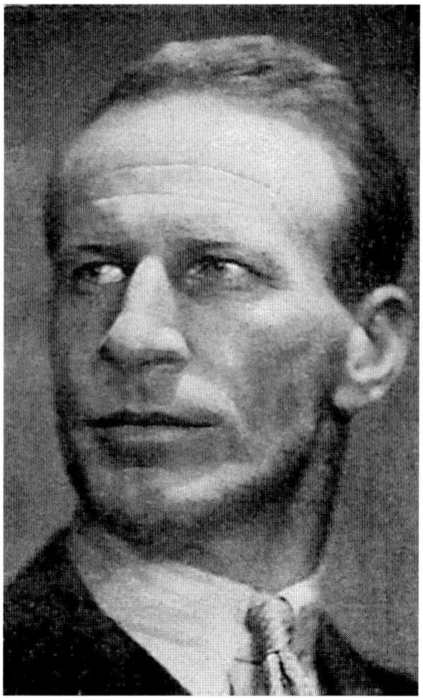

Fig. 264. Air Commodore Sir Charles Kingsford Smith.

Charles Edward Kingsford Smith was born at Hamilton, (Brisbane), on 9 February, 1897, the fourth son of William Charles Smith and Catherine Mary Smith (nee Kingsford). In 1915, on his 18th birthday, he enlisted in the AIF, but transferred to the Royal Flying Corps and was Commissioned there in 1917. After three months' service with a fighter squadron in France, during which he was awarded the Military Cross, he was wounded in the foot and rendered unfit for operational flying.

After the war he spent a year in California in "Flying Circuses" and flying for films.

In 1926 he purchased two small Bristol aeroplanes and flew to Sydney from Western Australia. There he was joined by another pilot, Charles T.P. Ulm. Together they made a round-Australia flight in ten days and five hours, halving the previous record.

In July, 1927, with Ulm, he went to California in search of a suitable aircraft in which to make a trans-Pacific flight. With financial assistance he purchased an airframe of a Fokker monoplane that had been used in the Arctic by the South Australian explorer Sir Hubert Wilkins. The machine was re-equipped and re-engined and named the *Southern Cross*.

On 31 May, 1928, Kingsford Smith, with Ulm as second pilot, and two Americans, H. Lyon as navigator and J. Warner as radio operator, took off from Oakland, San Francisco in the *Southern Cross*. They crossed the Pacific in three stages, Honolulu, Fiji and then Brisbane, arriving on 9 June, 1928. Honours and gifts were bestowed on the fliers, the amount of subscriptions being over 20,000 pounds.

He made two other memorable flights in the *Southern Cross* in 1928 - from Point Cook, Victoria to Perth, the first non-stop flight across Australia, and from Richmond N.S.W. to Christchurch, New Zealand, and back, the first West-East and East-West crossing of the Tasman Sea by air.

In June, 1929, he flew from Sydney to London in record time, 12 days and 18 hours, and in June, 1930, he concluded his circumnavigation of the world by flying from Ireland to New York via Newfoundland, and thence to San Francisco. Later in 1930 he flew solo from England to Darwin in an Avro Avian machine in just under 10 days, establishing a record for flight over that route by a light aircraft. Between 1930 and 1935 he was engaged in airmail services between Australia and England. In October, 1934, with P.G. Taylor in the *Lady Southern Cross*, he made the first west-east crossing of the Pacific. Eventually the *Southern Cross* was sold to the Commonwealth Government to become a national relic.

On 6 November, 1935, Kingsford Smith and a companion, J.T. Pethybridge, left England in the Lockheed Altair previously used on the trans-Pacific flight, to fly to Australia. On 7 November, the machine took off from Allahabad, India, for Singapore, and was not seen again. One of the aircraft's wheels was washed up on the coast of Burma in 1937.

The *Southern Cross* was not only the first aeroplane to fly across the Pacific Ocean but the *Old Bus,* as "Smithy" called it, was the first aeroplane to circumnavigate the World by crossing the equator twice. These accomplishments, together with the first crossing of the Tasman Sea, were amongst the main record-breaking flights by the *Southern Cross,* a modified Dutch Fokker F7B/3m. It is now on display at Brisbane's Eagle Farm Airport. In all, *Southern Cross* completed 13 famous flights between January, 1928 and June, 1935.

Sir Charles Kingsford Smith occupies a unique place in the history of aviation in Australia for he was a pioneer of aerial routes and services, both within the Commonwealth and between the Commonwealth and Europe and North America. He was 38 years old at the time of his presumed death. Reference: *Australian Encyclopaedia,* 3rd Edition 1977, Sydney, The Grolier Society of Australia.

Fig. 265. "Smithy" and Sir Hubert Wilkins, California, 1928.

For a different viewpoint on "Smithy" and the history of the Southern Cross and its former owner Sir Hubert Wilkins, see: *Smithy and the Southern Cross,* Michael Vort-Ronald, *Australian Coin Review,* May, 2000. Further reading: *Charles Kingsford Smith the World's Greatest Aviator,* Pedr Davis, Paul Hamlyn 1977; *Sir Charles Kingsford Smith...The Southern Cross Story*, (reprint of The Old bus) Rigby, 1978 and *Smithy,* Ian Mackersby, Little, Brown & Company, 1998.

Fig. 266. "Smithy" and *Southern Cross* in Holland just prior to the June, 1930, Atlantic Ocean crossing.

Fig. 267. *Southern Cross Replica*, August, 1987.

Southern Cross Replica

Early in 1977, John Pope, an Adelaide Commercial Pilot and former Chief Flying Instructor, decided to "do something creative, like building an aeroplane". He chose to build a replica of the Southern Cross. After two years of planning he sought support for his idea from the Federal Government. Following a Technical Feasibility meeting in April, 1979, the concept was considered worthy of Federal Government support, subject to the setting up of a legal Trust to raise the balance of the monies needed to complete the Replica. The Federal Government made an initial grant of $150,000 followed by a further grant of $50,000. In December, 1979, a Company was formed and called Famous Australian Aircraft Pty. Ltd. (FAA), and in February, 1980, the fund-raising trust was formed and called the Southern Cross Museum Trust.

FAA was forced to lay off its building team in August, 1980, and again in November, 1981. The replica then endured a long period of 44 months "in limbo" during which time, no construction took place. Work resumed in mid-1985 and the first flight took place on 14 August, 1987. The title to the aircraft was then transferred to the Federal Government on 3 September, 1987, and flight operations were then leased to the Southern Cross Museum Trust. Late in 1996, the Trust advised the Federal Government that it would not be renewing the lease. By this time the Federal Government had decided to divest itself of the replica and numerous expressions of interest were submitted. South Australia, with the support of its State government, was successful.

The new custodian of the Southern Cross Replica is the Southern Cross Replica Assoc. Inc. which is contactable on phone (61 8) or (08) 8555 1259. The photograph of Southern Cross Replica, courtesy of the Southern Cross Museum Trust, was taken in August, 1987.

It is a "simple" aircraft which ran off three engines with a top speed of 100 miles (160 km) per hour. The replica is a ten-seater. The original seats were wicker, but those on the replica are metal framed and bolted to the floor, as required by safety regulations. The extra weight necessitated larger fuel tanks and slightly larger engines, and modifications were made to the shock absorbers.

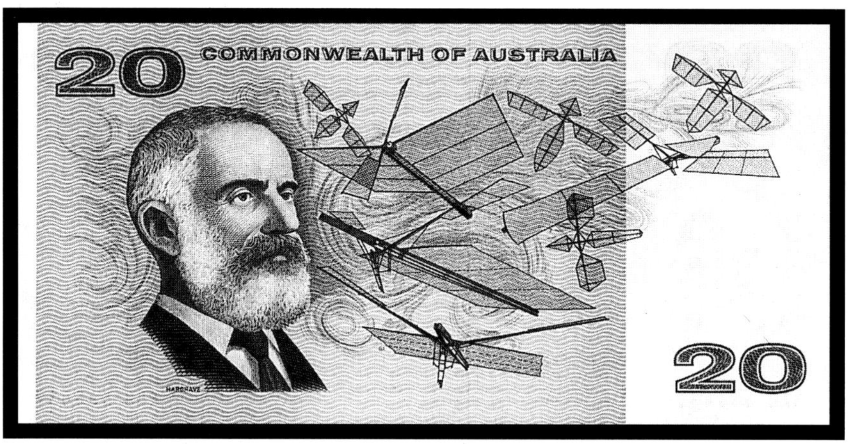

Fig. 268. Back, $20 note. First type (V.145).

BACK

Main print: Red-black intaglio. 146 mm x 69 mm.

The portrait of Lawrence Hargrave is on the left and drawings of some of his India-rubber powered flying machines and kites are portrayed alongside him. Across the top is "COMMONWEALTH OF AUSTRALIA" and at top left and bottom right is "20". The initials of Gordon Andrews are to the left wing of the bottom drawing. See Fig. 269 for an example of the Simultan printing printing phase.

Background print: Dry offset in four colours. 115 mm x 80 mm.

Surrounding the portrait of Hargrave and behind the drawings is a continual background of horizontal wavy lines, alternating orange and red with white lines in between, rainbowing in the vertical centre to yellow and khaki. See Fig. 270.

Fig. 269. Back, $20 note, main print (Intaglio) only (error note).

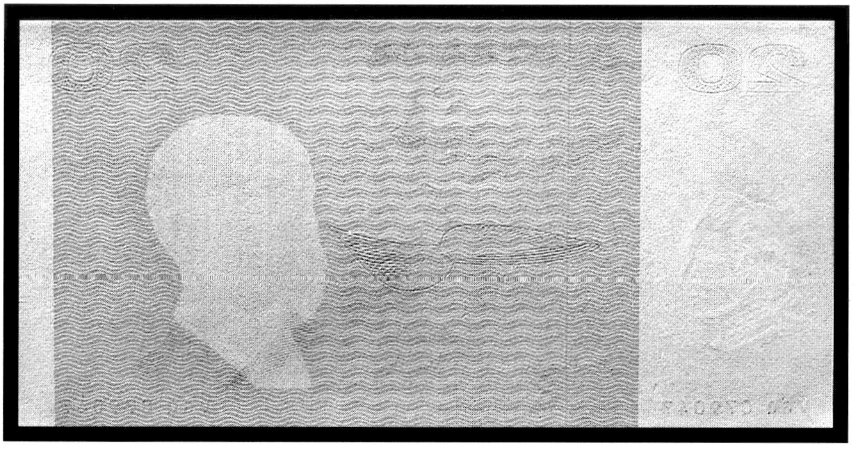

Fig. 270. Back, $20 note, background print (Simultan) only (error note).

Lawrence Hargrave was born at Greenwich, England, on 29 January, 1850. In 1865 he arrived in Sydney where he served as an apprentice in the engineering shops of the Australasian Steam Navigation Company. Between 1875 and 1876 he accompanied various expeditions to New Guinea. In July, 1877, he was elected a member of the Royal Society of New South Wales.

From 1878 to 1883, he was Extra Observer (Astronomical) at Sydney Observatory. He retired at the age of 33 years to devote the remainder of his life to research work and, in particular, to the problems connected with human flight. He commenced his investigations by close study of the movements of snakes and fish, and by observing the action of seawaves and air currents. From 1884 to 1892, he experimented with monoplane models constructed of a framework of light wood and paper. Some were propelled by means of flapping wings and some by a primitive airscrew. The motive power was at various times, clockwork, rubber bands in tension, and compressed air.

In 1889 he invented a radial rotary engine. Although it was only operated by compressed air, the idea was later copied in Europe, and internal combustion engines of this type played a vital role in early European aviation.

At the beginning of the 1890s Hargrave's experiments had shown him that stability in the air and motive power were the major obstacles to man-powered flight. He began a series of experiments with kites in a wide range of types, and in 1893, invented a multi-celled kite from which he evolved his famous cellular or box kite. Four of these kites lifted him 16 feet (about 5 metres) off the Stanwell Park beach on 12 November, 1894, an event which received wide publicity overseas.

Fig. 271. Lawrence Hargrave.

The illustration of Lawrence Hargrave was probably the one from which the portrait on the note was based. It originated from a photograph (by an unknown photographer) in the possession of and reproduced by courtesy of, the Mitchell Library, Sydney.

It was his cellular supporting surface that the French were to turn to in desperation when they learned of the Wrights' first flight in a powered flying machine on 17 December, 1903. The stability of Hargrave's invention enabled Santos Dumont to make the first powered flight in Europe three years later.

In a paper read to the Royal Society of New South Wales on 3 June, 1885, he stated that he had experimented with nearly 50 models and had been making further experiments with trochoided planes. The *Sydney Morning Herald* reported the next day that a demonstration before the Royal Society the previous night ....*The machines flew from his hand, the motive power used being India-rubber bands. The bodies of the machines were flat and made of paper, as were the wings. After leaving the hands of Mr. Hargrave the machines flapped their wings with lifelike motion and covered a distance of 20 or 30 feet....*

In his quest for a suitable power source he designed and constructed 36 engines of many types, operated by compressed air, steam and petrol. He was deprived of the opportunity of powered flight by his inability to obtain the necessary output from his engine propeller combinations.

He always refused to patent any of his inventions, believing that they should be common property for the benefit of mankind. For the remainder of his life he concentrated on other fields including wave-propelled vessels and a one-wheeled car. He also devised plans for improving the port of Sydney. He died in hospital after an illness, on 6 July, 1915.

Fig. 272. Back $20 note depicting Hargrave's flying machines.

The majority of Hargrave's aeronautical constructions were sent to the Technological Museum in Munich in 1910. The few that were not destroyed in World War II, were generously donated to the Museum of Applied Arts and Sciences in Sydney. They, together with other items and records, provide a complete and unique collection of the wide range of the work of Lawrence Hargrave.

Models numbered 1,2,3, and 7 on the previous illustration were probably engraved from an old photograph taken about 1885 which contained eight variations of his early models. See illustration below. Model 5 on Fig. 272 is probably Hargrave's sixth flying machine designed for free flight. It was flapper propelled, and flew 120 feet in level flight on 27 June, 1886. It is now in the Museum of Applied Arts and Sciences, Ultimo (Sydney).

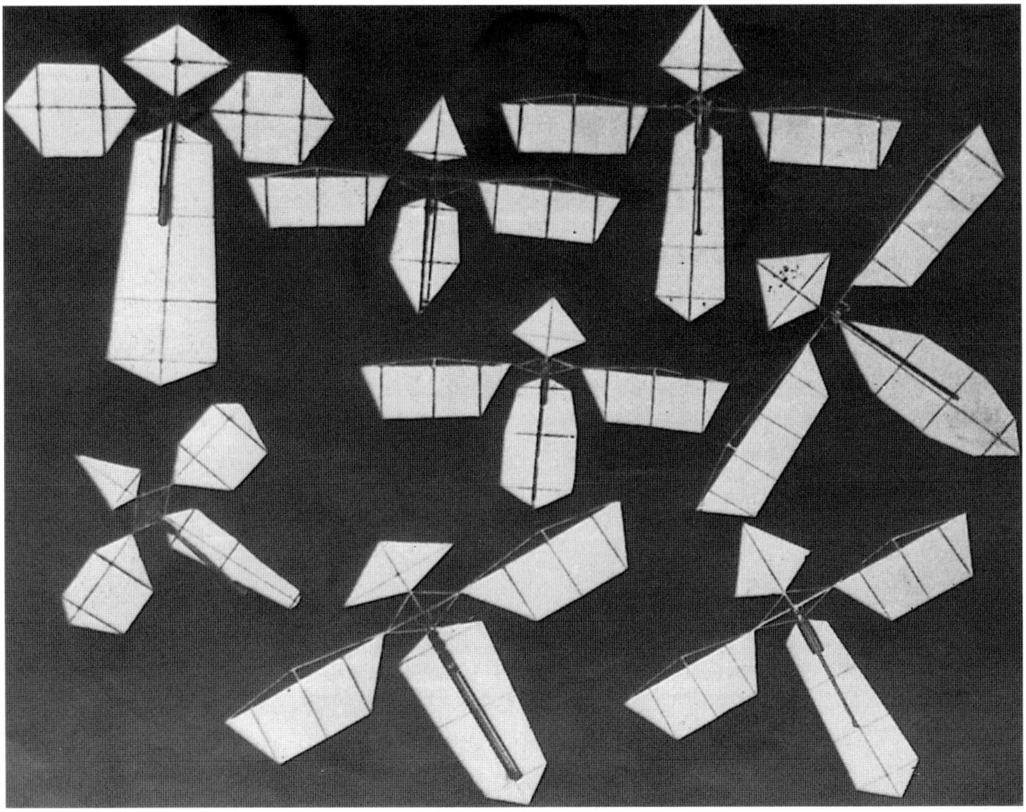

Fig. 273. Hargrave's early models

Model 8 on Fig. 272 is Hargrave's 11th flying machine designed for free flight. It was flapper propelled, weighed 1.28 lbs. and was powered by 24 rubber bands. It flew 230 feet on 24 September, 1887. He called it experiment H. It was modified twice, having flown 209 feet on 8 August, and on 28 September, 203 feet (experiments J and K). See illustration next page.

Hargrave developed an arrangement of small ivory pulleys over which cords ran from the ends of India-rubber bands to two toggles with centres fixed to the two steel cranks that moved the flappers.

Model 6 on Fig. 272 depicts the development of Hargrave's flapper-driven India-rubber powered model flying machines, showing the hollow main spar, the arrangement of the 48 India-rubber bands (24 on each side), the pulley location and the toggle winder with the cranks operating the flapper arms, This model, his 14th flying machine designed for free flight, weighed 33 and a half ounces and flew 270 feet on 15 November, 1887 (experiment L). Its flight was reported to the Royal Society on 7 December, 1887.

Model 4 on Fig. 272 is Hargrave's 19th and last India-rubber powered propeller-driven flying machine. Using 48 India-rubber bands, this two lb. weight model flew 120 feet on 31 January, 1889. Its propeller was 28 inches (71 cm) in diameter, with a pitch of seven feet four inches (2.235 metres), and was fitted with nine inch (23 cm) blades. Its achievement was reported to the Royal Society on 7 August, 1889.

He went on to experiment with larger models powered by compressed air motors, and later, experiments with supporting surfaces. He designed several full-sized flying machines, but they were not built, because the many engine propeller combinations constructed to drive them, did not deliver the necessary power.

Fig. 274. Hargrave's 11th flying machine designed for free flight.

The world owes much to Lawrence Hargrave as a pioneer of aviation experimentation. To anyone fortunate enough to gain access to his original papers housed in the Museum of Applied Arts and Sciences, the dedication of Hargrave is soon apparent from the many pages of detailed notes, observations and theories.

Reference and further reading: *Lawrence Hargrave Papers,* Volume 2, pages 109, 113, 191 and 337. *Lawrence Hargrave, Explorer, Inventor and Aviation Experimenter,* W. Hudson Shaw and Olaf Ruhen, Cassell Australia, 1977.

Serial numbering "Gothic" type, see Fig. 285.

V.145

Signatures

H.C. Coombs	Governor, Reserve Bank of Australia.
Roland Wilson	Secretary to the Treasury.

Fig. 275. Signatures and titles, Coombs-Wilson $20 (V.145).

Issued 14 February, 1966.

Serial numbers XAA 000001 - XBP 1000000. Printed 34,000,000.
No star notes printed in this signature combination.

V.146

Signatures

H.C. Coombs	Governor, Reserve Bank of Australia.
R.J. Randall	Secretary to the Treasury.

Fig. 276. Signatures and titles, Coombs-Randall $20 (V.146).

Issued 16 September, 1968.

Serial numbers XBQ 000001 - XBS 200000. Printed 2,200,000.
No star notes printed in this signature combination.

V.147

Signatures

J.G. Phillips	Governor, Reserve Bank of Australia.
R.J. Randall	Secretary to the Treasury.

Fig. 277. Signatures and titles, Phillips-Randall $20 (V.147).

Issued October, 1968.

Serial numbers XBS 200001 - XEU 999999. Printed 65,800,000.

Star notes ZXA 00001* - ZXA 62500*. Printed 62,500.

V.148

Signatures — **J.G. Phillips** Governor, Reserve Bank of Australia.
F.H. Wheeler Secretary to the Treasury.

Fig. 278. Signatures, titles and legal tender clause, Phillips-Wheeler (Commonwealth) $20 (V.148).

Issued October, 1972.

Serial numbers XEV 000001 - XGY 960000. Printed 44,960,000.
No star notes printed or issued from this signature combination onwards.

From 20 August, 1974, notes with "AUSTRALIA" replacing "COMMONWEALTH OF AUSTRALIA" were issued. See Second type, following.

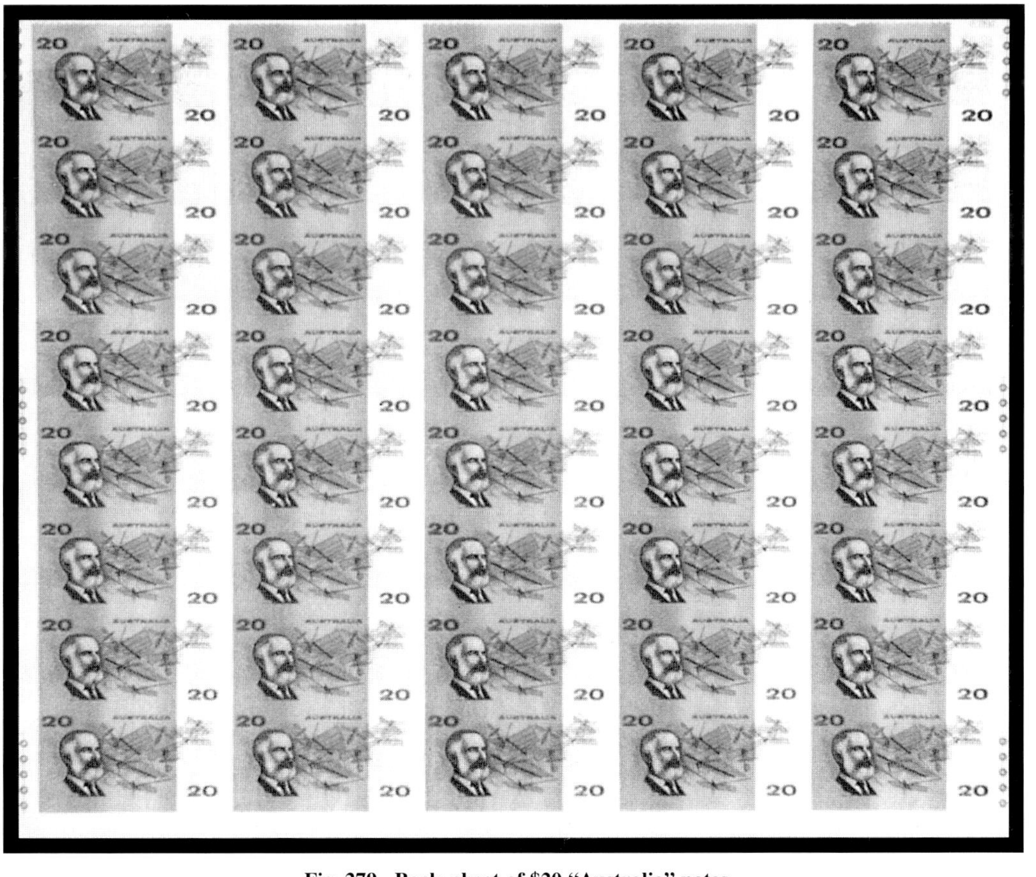

Fig. 279. Back, sheet of $20 "Australia" notes.

V.149-157 $20 TWENTY DOLLARS

Type	Second. "AUSTRALIA".	
Issued	20 August, 1974 to October, 1995.	
Signatures	Phillips - Wheeler, Knight - Wheeler, Knight - Stone, Johnston - Stone, Johnston - Fraser, Phillips - Fraser, Fraser - Higgins, Fraser - Cole, Fraser - Evans.	
Serial numbers	XGY 960001 - XZZ 999999. EAA 000003 - EZZ 999999. AAA 000001 - ADK 999999.	VAA 000001 - VZZ 999999. RAA 000001 - RZZ 999999. Plus Uncut notes and Collector notes.
Printed	1,661,970,048 plus Uncut notes and Collector notes.	

Fig. 280. Front, $20 note, Second type (V.149).

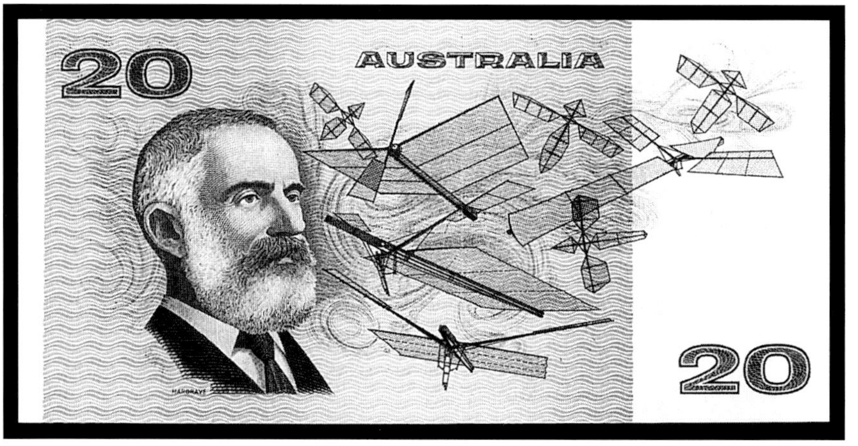

Fig. 281. Back, $20 note, Second type (V.149).

FRONT AND BACK

All main design details and features are the same as the First type with the following exceptions. "AUSTRALIA" replaced "COMMONWEALTH OF AUSTRALIA" at the top, in larger lettering than previously, and the legal tender clause was changed to read "This Australian note is legal tender throughout Australia and its Territories." Background design and details remained the same as those in the First type.

$20 "AUSTRALIA" NOTES

V.149

Signatures — **J.G. Phillips** Governor, Reserve Bank of Australia.
F.H. Wheeler Secretary to the Treasury.

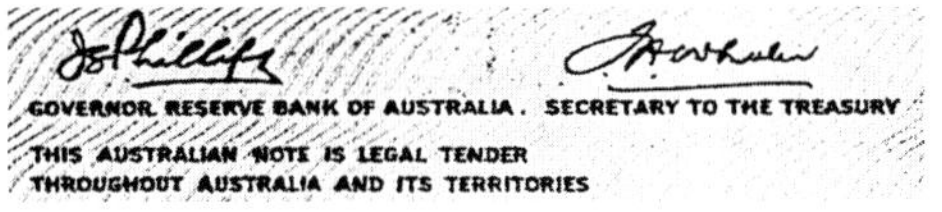

Fig. 282. Signatures, titles and legal tender clause, Phillips-Wheeler (Australia) $20 (V.149).

Issued — 20 August, 1974.

Serial numbers — XGY 960001 - XLH 999999. Printed 73,040,000.

Sheet content 24 — XGY and XJD uncertain, then XHA-XJC, XJE-XKF, XKG-XLH.

V.150

Signatures — **H.M. Knight** Governor, Reserve Bank of Australia.
F.H. Wheeler Secretary to the Treasury.

Fig. 283. Signatures and titles, Knight-Wheeler $20 (V.150).

Issued — December, 1975.

Serial numbers — XLJ 000001 - XUZ 999905. Printed 167,999,905.

Variety (a) — "Gothic" serial numbering. "Centre thread". Metallic thread approximately 70 mm from the left edge of the front.

Sheet content 24 — XLJ-XNK, XNL-XPN, XPP-XQQ, XQR-XRS.

Variety (b) — "Gothic" serial numbering. "Side thread". Metallic thread approximately 55 mm from the left edge of the front.

Sheet content 24 — XRT-XSU, XSV-XTX, XTY-XUZ. Changeover from (a) to (b) uncertain.

From July, 1976, all paper despatched by the Note Printing Branch's suppliers had the security thread positioned in an area approximately 55 mm from the left edge of the front. The change was made to avoid the natural fold area which, because of the close proximity of the metallic thread, caused undue wear and tearing.

V.151

Signatures — **H.M. Knight** Governor, Reserve Bank of Australia.
John Stone Secretary to the Treasury.

Fig. 284. Signatures and titles, Knight-Stone $20 (V.151).

Variety (a) "Gothic" serial numbering.

Issued First despatched from Note Issue Department, June, 1979.

Serial numbers XVA 000002 - XZZ 999999.
VAA 000001 - VDQ 999999. Printed 165,000,000.
The allocation of serial prefixes for $20 was initially XAA - XZZ. "Y" having been used for the $50 and "Z" for the $100, the $20 denomination then reverted to VAA - VZZ, and others, following. XZZ and VAA prefixes were issued in October, 1980. The style of serial numbering for $20 notes changed in this signature combination. For explanation, see V.90.

Sheet content 24 XVA-XXB, XXC-XYD, XYE-XZF, XZG-VAH, VAJ-VBK, VBL-VCN, VCP-VDQ.

VDG 340413

Fig. 285. "Gothic" serial numbering.

VEJ 912800

Fig. 286. "OCR-B" serial numbering.

Variety (b) "OCR-B" serial numbering.

Issued The first notes were in a consignment to Adelaide on 28 May, 1982. Issued July, 1982.

Serial numbers VDR 000001 - VFU 999999.
VFV to VGX, serial numbers 000001 to 539500 only.
Printed 60,948,000.

Sheet content 24 VDR-VES, VET-VFU. With V.152, VFV-VGX.

V.152

Signatures — **R.A. Johnston** Governor, Reserve Bank of Australia.
John Stone Secretary to the Treasury.

Fig. 287. Signatures and titles, Johnston-Stone $20 (V.152).

Issued — October, 1983.

Serial numbers — VFV to VGX, numbers 668001 to 999999 only.
VGY 000001 - VQK 999931. Printed 143,999,931.
"OCR-B" serial numbering.

Sheet content 24 — With V.151, VFV-VGX, then VGY-VHZ, VJA-VKB, VKC-VLD, VLE-VNF, VNG-VPH, VPJ-VQK.

V.153

Signatures — **R.A. Johnston** Governor, Reserve Bank of Australia.
B.W. Fraser Secretary to the Treasury.

Fig. 288. Signatures and titles, Johnston-Fraser $20 (V.153).

Variety (a) "OCR-B" serial numbering.

Issued — February, 1985.

Serial numbers — VQL 000001 - VZZ 999999.
EAA 000003 - EJX 999999.
ELA to ENB, numbers 000001 to 863000 only.
ENC 000001 - EVH 999999.
EVJ to EYD, numbers 667001 to 999999 only.
Series "E" commenced about July, 1986. Printed 390,305,960.

Sheet content 24 — VQL-VRN, VRP-VSQ, VSR-VTS, VTT-VUU, VUV-VVX, VVY-VYS, VYT-EAN, EAP-ECH, ECJ-EED, EEE-EFZ, EGA-EHU.
With (b), EHV-EJX, EJY-EKZ.

Sheet content 40 — ENC-EPX, EPY-ERS, ERT-ETN, ETP-EVH. With V.154, EVJ-EYD.

Variety (b) "Gothic" serial numbering.

Issued May, 1988.

Serial numbers EJY 000001 - EKZ 999999.
ELA to ENB, numbers 863001 to 999999 only. Printed 27,287,952.

Sheet content 24 With (a), EHV-EJX, EJY-EKZ, then ELA-ENB.

"Gothic" serial numbers were printed as a temporary measure to produce urgently needed notes at a time when the "OCR-B" numbering machines were occupied.

V.154
Signatures **M.J. Phillips** Deputy Governor, Reserve Bank of Australia.
B.W. Fraser Secretary to the Treasury.

Fig. 289. Signatures and titles, Phillips-Fraser $20 (V.154).

Issued August, 1989.

Serial numbers EVJ to EYD, numbers 000001 to 028500, and 100001 to 667000 only.
(numbers 028501 to 100000 were not used). Printed 23,820,000.

Sheet content 40 With V.153, EVJ-EYD.

This was the first time that the facsimile signature of a Deputy Governor of the Reserve Bank of Australia (or of the previous Commonwealth Bank of Australia) had signed an Australian note.

It occurred because the then Secretary to the Treasury (B.W. Fraser) was unable to take up his position as Governor of the Bank for approximately three months.

A limited series of uncut notes was produced in this signature combination, as follows:

36 blocks (strips) of ten notes (5 x 2) were sold by Note Printing Australia through mail order in May, 1990, at $500 per block. A ballot was held to distribute the notes as the offer (which included 72 blocks of four $50 notes) was hugely oversubscribed. Apparently over $400,000 had to be sent back to collectors who missed out. These were restricted to nine sheets serially numbered 000002 to 000010, with prefixes EVJ to EYD. Sheet with 000001 was retained by N.P.A.

Fig. 290. Block of ten Phillips-Fraser uncut $20 (V.154).

V.155

Signatures	**B.W. Fraser**	Governor, Reserve Bank of Australia.
	C.I. Higgins	Secretary to the Treasury.

Fig. 291. Signatures and titles, Fraser-Higgins $20 (V.155).

Issued December, 1989.

Serial numbers EYE 000001 - EZZ 999999. RAA 000001 - RHF 999999.
RHG to RKB, numbers 657501 to 999999 only.
Printed 207,698,380, plus 40 in an uncut sheet.

Sheet content 40 EYE-EZZ, RAA-RBU, RBV-RDQ, RDR-RFK, RFL-RHF.
With V.156, RHG-RKB.

One full sheet of 40 notes was donated by the Reserve Bank to charity and auctioned in Sydney on 23 February, 1990, for $38,500, the proceeds going to the Financial Markets Foundation for Children. It was taken from a normal production run with serial letters RAA to RBU, numerals 001092, and handsigned by the signatories.

V.156

Signatures	**B.W. Fraser**	Governor, Reserve Bank of Australia.
	A.S. Cole	Secretary to the Treasury.

Fig. 292. Signatures and titles, Fraser-Cole $20 (V.156).

Issued	August, 1991.
Serial numbers	RHG to RKB, numbers 000001 to 657500 only. RKC 000001 - RZU 999999. RZV to RZZ, AAA to ABQ, numbers 884001 to 999999 only. Printed 350,939,960, plus 7,600 uncut notes.
Sheet content 40	With V.155, RHG-RKB, then RKC-RLX, RLY-RPS, RPT-RRN, RRP-RTH, RTJ-RVD, RVE-RXZ, RYA-RZU. With V.157, RZV-ABQ.

A total of 7,600 notes in this signature combination were also sold as uncut pairs and blocks. Only the tops and bottom of sheets were used (which displayed plate numbers from the tops or "traffic lights" at the bottom) as follows:

Fig. 293. Fraser-Cole gold numbered uncut pair $20.

100 vertical pairs with gold coloured serial numbering were sold for $98 each at the Melbourne Coin Fair on 17 July, 1993, limit of two per person. The pairs were numbered A 000001 and B 000001 to A 000100 and B 000100.

1,400 red numbered vertical pairs were sold for $85 each at the Melbourne Coin Fair on 17 & 18 July, 1993, limit two per person. The red pairs were numbered from A 000101 and B 000101 to A 001500 and B 001500.

700 red numbered vertical pairs were sold for $85 each through mail order in the *Australian Coin Review* in August, 1993. They were numbered from A 001501 and B 001501 to A002200 and B 002200. Limit two per person.

100 blocks of four with gold coloured serial numbers were sold for $165 each at the Melbourne Coin Fair on 17 July, 1993, limit one per person. They were numbered from C-D-E-F 000001 to C-D-E-F 000100.

450 blocks of four with red numbering were sold for $148 each at the Melbourne Coin Fair on 17 & 18 July, 1993. They were numbered from C-D-E-F 000101 to C-D-E-F 000550.

350 blocks of four with red numbering were sold by mail order for $148 each through the *Australian Coin Review* in August, 1993, limit one per person. They were numbered from C-D-E-F 00550 to C-D-E-F 000900.

1 full sheet of notes was sold at a charity auction for $40,000.

Further reading: *Media Coverage Ensured Fair Success,* by Michael Vort-Ronald, *Australian Coin Review*, August, 1993.

V.157

Signatures **B.W. Fraser** Governor, Reserve Bank of Australia.
E.A. Evans Secretary to the Treasury.

Fig. 294. Signatures and titles, Fraser-Evans $20 (V.157).

Issued December, 1993.

Serial numbers RZV to RZZ, AAA to ABQ, numbers 000001 to 884000 only.
ABR to ADK, numbers 611001 to 999999 only.
Printed 50,919,960, plus 10,000 in uncut sheets.
See also, Collector Issues, Chapter 9.

Sheet content 40 With V.156, RZV-ABQ, then ABR-ADK.

250 full sheets were sold by tender in March 1995. They were the last of the full production sheets of the paper $20 notes, numbered from 000001 to 000250 with serial letters ABR to ADK, 40 notes per sheet. Sheets with notes numbered 000001 and 000002 were later cut up privately and sold as singles.

The tender for number 000001 was $5,300 and the average tender $1,454.
Note ADK (the last serial prefix of $20 paper notes) 000001 sold at auction on 28 January, 1996, for $4,900. It is illustrated below, still in sheet form.

Further reading: *The King is Dead,* and *Note Printing Australia Collector Folders,* and *The Cut-Up Uncuts,* Michael Vort-Ronald, *Australian Coin Review,* August, 1996, and December, 1994, and March, 1996, respectively.

See also, Collector Issues, Chapter 9.

V.158-164 Reference numbers not used.

On 31 October, 1994, the newly-designed polymer note was issued and the paper notes progressively phased out. They were not immediately withdrawn because many automatic teller machines had still not been converted to use polymer notes. See Chapter 13.

Fig. 295. Number 000001 of the final $20 prefix.

V.165-173 $50 FIFTY DOLLARS.

Type	First. "AUSTRALIA".
Issued	9 October, 1973 to October 1995.
Size	165 mm x 82.5 mm.
Watermarks	Profiles of Captain James Cook appear on the left side of the front with two full profiles in the centre and a half profile above and below. Each profile is in vertical line, alternating in dark and light watermark. See Fig. 99.
Signatures	Phillips - Wheeler, Knight - Wheeler, Knight - Stone, Johnston - Stone, Johnston - Fraser, Phillips - Fraser, Fraser - Higgins, Fraser - Cole, Fraser - Evans.
Serial numbers	YAA 000001 - YZZ 999999. WAA 000001 - WYQ 999999. WYR to WZZ and FAA to FAB, numbers 412501 to 999999 only.
Printed	919,809,604, plus Uncut notes.

Fig. 296. Front, $50 note. First type (V.165).

FRONT

Main print: Black, brown and green intaglio. 152 mm x 75 mm.
On the right side of the note appears a portrait of Lord Howard Walter Florey. The remainder of the main print depicts motifs illustrating laboratory research and academic life. Under the signature titles appears the legal tender clause "This Australian note is legal tender throughout Australia and its Territories". At the top "AUSTRALIA" appears with "50" in each top corner. The initials of Gordon Andrews are 8 mm directly above "FLOREY".

Background print: Dry offset using six colours. 158 mm x 82.5 mm.
A series of wavy cross hatching in light goldish-green is over the horizontal centre of the note, as well as orange horizontal lines, giving an all-over gold appearance. "Medallioning" is in the centre above and below which are a series of diagonal wavy lines and colours alternating orange and two light greens. Near the vertical centre the background colours rainbow turquoise and green. See Fig. 297.

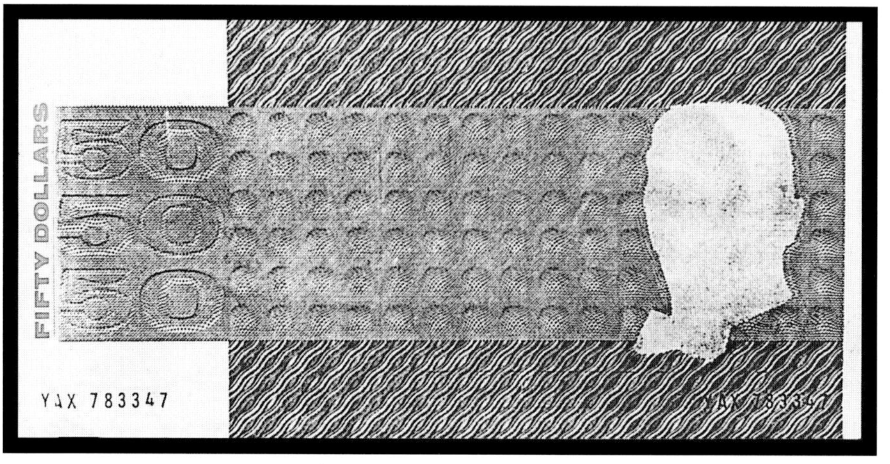

Fig. 297. Front, $50 note, background (Simultan) printing only (error note).

Lord Howard Walter Florey.

Howard Walter Florey was born at Malvern (Adelaide) on 24 September, 1898, the son of Joseph Florey, boot manufacturer, and Bertha Mary Florey (nee Wadham), but his birth certificate was written as Walter Howard (Florey). He studied medicine and gained his Bachelor's degree at Adelaide University. A brilliant student, he was awarded a Rhodes Scholarship and in 1921, went to Oxford. There he took his Batchelor of Science degree and later received several fellowships. He became a Fellow of Gonville and Caius College at Cambridge, where he took the position of Huddersfield Lecturer in Special Pathology, and was Freedom Research Fellow at the London Hospital.

At the age of 33 years he was appointed Joseph Hunter Professor of Pathology at the University of Sheffield. In 1935 he became Professor of Pathology and head of the Sir William Dunn (inscribed DVNN in the foundation stone featured on the front of the note) School of Pathology at Oxford. It was in this year that he began his famous collaboration with Professor Chain, a refugee from Nazi Germany. Together they and their team of research workers were to develop a discovery which had lain unused since 1929, the chance discovery by Dr. Alexander Fleming that certain bacteria were destroyed by a mould which had contaminated one of his cultures of staphylococci germs. Fleming later shared the Nobel Prize which came to Florey and Chain in 1945 for their penicillin work.

Fleming was a bacteriologist, but a biochemist was needed to reduce his mould to a stable salt. In short, it would not keep. Professors Florey and Chain thought differently. In 1929 Florey had been investigating lysozyme (also discovered by Fleming), a substance found in the human body, in the white of an egg and in plants. Lysozyme set Florey and Chain on the trail of anti-bacterial substances. Eventually Florey and his assistants succeeded in extracting penicillin as a yellow powder.

Florey's wife Mary Hayter (whom he married in 1926) also a Doctor from Adelaide, helped him throughout his researches. The use and demand for penicillin rapidly increased. Without penicillin, pneumonia, diphtheria, meningitis and venereal diseases were often fatal. With the drug, post-operative infections could be controlled and the hazards of surgery greatly reduced.

Fig. 298. Sir Howard Florey, F.R.S.

In 1944, Florey visited Russia, talking about penicillin, and visited Australia and New Zealand. That year he was knighted, and the Australian Government asked him to plan a school of medical research for the Australian National University in Canberra. His plans for the school, to be known as the John Curtin School of Medical Research, took 13 years to fulfil. In March, 1958, he flew from England to open the 1.25 million pound ($2.5 million) school.

Apart from his Nobel Prize in 1945 (which was shared with Fleming and Chain), he became a Commander of the Legion of Honour in 1946, and was awarded the U.S.A. Medal for Merit in 1947. He held many other foreign decorations and was an honorary member of many world Medical Societies. In 1960, he became the first Australian President of the Royal Society. He was Provost of the Queen's College, Oxford from 1962. In 1963, the new Howard Florey Laboratory of Experimental Physiology was dedicated in Melbourne. In 1965 he was created a Life Peer, as Baron Florey of Adelaide and Marston, and became a member of the Order of Merit.

Although still based at Oxford, he was made Chancellor of the Australian National University. His hair was silver-grey, brushed severely back from his forehead. His wife Mary Ethel Hayter (nee Reed) died in 1966, and in 1967 he married Mrs. Margaret Jennings, his colleague at the Sir William Dunn School. He died in his seventieth year on 21 February, 1968, and was buried at Marston near Oxford. His latest work had been on new antibiotics, the cephalosporins, designed to supplement the work of penicillin.

The world owes a great debt to the discoverer of penicillin, Alexander Fleming, but another, and possibly greater debt, is owed to the man who took Fleming's discovery from the confines of the science laboratory where it had lain unused as a scientific oddity for many years, and turned it into a healing antibiotic drug with world-wide application. This man was Howard Florey, Baron of Adelaide and Marston.

The Florey Research Fund was established to fund medical research in the Medical School of the University of Adelaide. In March, 1996, a tiny spore of the original mould from 1928 sold at Sothebys in England, for $46,000. The original glass plate used by Fleming is preserved in his laboratory at St. Marys' Hospital in London, but he gave two tiny specimens to his assistant Dan Stratful, who in turn gave one to his secretary Diane Huntingford, who decided to sell it.

A public opinion poll was conducted by *The Advertiser* (Adelaide) where it was announced on January 1, 2000, that Lord Florey was voted the South Australian of the past Century. Later, in other surveys, he was voted Australian of the last century.

Further reading: *Rise Up to Life,* Lennard Bickel, Angus and Robertson, 1972 (later republished as *Florey – The Man who made Penicillin*, Sun Books P/L, 1983); *Howard Florey: Penicillin and After,* Trevor I Williams, Oxford University Press, 1984; *The (London) Times, obituary,* 23 February, 1968; *The Florey Portfolio Launch,* (by Michael Vort-Ronald), *Australian Coin Review,* November, 1995. See Fig. 316.

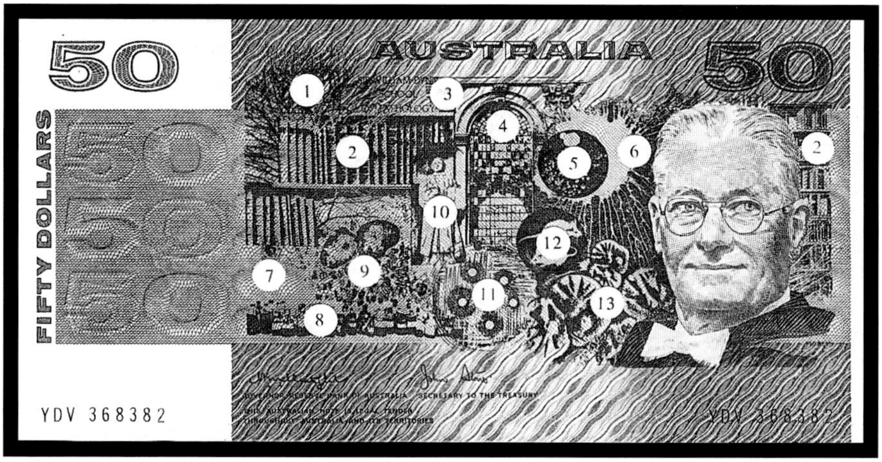

Fig. 299. Oxford University and pathology on the $50 note.

Situated within the City of Oxford, 63 miles by rail from London, Oxford University dates back to the 12th century. It now consists of many buildings and colleges, including the Queen's College, founded in 1341 by Robert of Eglesfield, Chaplain to Queen Philippa.

A wide range of photographs was taken by Christopher Ridley of the Queen's College and The Sir William Dunn School of Pathology at Oxford University for use in the preparation of the design for the $50 note. The following details from the previous illustration are represented on the note.

1. A tree at Oxford University.
2. Books in the Queen's College library - two views.
3. The inscription over the entrance to the Sir William Dunn School of Pathology.
4. A window of the library as viewed from the Fellow's Garden, Queen's College.
5. A culture plate showing the dissolution of staphylococci and microorganisms of globular shape which tend to grow in clusters. They cause morbid conditions such as boils, carbuncles and abscesses.
6. Polymorphonuclear leucocyte from normal human blood, white blood cells which are an important factor in the defence mechanism in the body. Counts of white blood cells are one of the clinical procedures in the diagnosis of leukemia and infectious diseases.
7. Bacteria colonies, microscopic single-cell organisms which occur in enormous numbers everywhere in nature, including plants and animals.
8. Chemical bottles in the laboratory of the Sir William Dunn School of Pathology.
9. A rat, taken from an illustration of *Self-not Self, Cellular Immunology Book 1,* by Sir Macfarlane Burnet, O.M., F.R.S., Nobel Laureate.
10. One of a series of statues in niches around the Fellow's Garden, Queen's College.
11. Subculture sensitivity test, a test conducted by placing a specimen from a patient into a culture medium to produce a subculture. Small paper discs impregnated with various identifiable antibiotics are placed with the subculture which is then incubated and examined for indications of sensitivity to the various antibiotics, thus eliminating much trial and error in treatment.

12. Swiss albino mice bred in large numbers for research work in testing the effects of penicillin on numerous diseases then deadly to man.

13. *Penicillium notatum,* the growth which resulted from a spore which fell on Fleming's plate and attracted his attention by disintegrating some staphylococci. Fleming initiated investigation into the mould and preserved it, later to be studied by Florey and others.

Fig. 300. Back, $50 note, First type (V.165).

Fig. 301. Back, $50 note, main (Intaglio) printing only (error note).

BACK

Main print: Blue-black, brown and green intaglio. 152 mm x 70 mm.
On the left is a portrait of Sir Ian Clunies Ross. "AUSTRALIA" is at the top, and "50" at top left and bottom right. Surrounding the portrait is a theme of research into the environments of Earth and outer space. See Fig. 301.

Background print: Dry offset in four colours. 118 mm x 82.5 mm.
The background design is a series of diagonal wavy lines in lime green and orange, rainbowed to turquoise and pale green near the vertical centre.

Ian Clunies Ross

Ian Clunies Ross, K.B., C.M.G., D.C.V.Sc., D.Sc., A.R.C.V.S., LL.D., F.A.A. was born on 22 February, 1899, at Bathurst, New South Wales, the fourth and youngest son of William John Clunies Ross and his wife Hannah Elizabeth.

He entered the Faculty of Agriculture at the University of Sydney in 1917, but next year transferred to Veterinary Science because he wanted to work with animals. He graduated B.V.Sc. with Honours in 1921 and the following year was appointed a Walter and Eliza Hall Veterinary Research Fellow. This enabled him to spend some time overseas, much of which was spent working on internal parasites of animals.

He returned to Sydney and resumed research in parasitology, in particular the hydatid parasite, the liver fluke and the dog-tick. In 1926 he became Parasitologist to the Council for Scientific and Industrial Research (CSIR). He married Janet Leslie Carter on 6 October, 1927, and in 1929 and 1930 they lived in Japan where he studied research methods in parasitology.

From 1931 to 1937 he was Officer-in-charge of the McMaster Animal Health Laboratory in Sydney. By 1937, he had published some 50 scientific papers, some of which extended to substantial booklets.

In November, 1940, he was appointed Professor of Veterinary Science at the University of Sydney. Three years later he was elected Commonwealth Chairman of the Australian Institute of International Affairs and in 1943, was appointed Director of Scientific Personnel in the Commonwealth Directorate of Manpower, as well as Adviser on the Pastoral Industry to the Department of War Organization of Industry. His task was to see that trained people were used to maximum advantage for the war effort.

In May and June, 1945, arrangements were made for him to be released from the University to assist CSIR in making plans for new sheep and wool-textile research. In May 1949, CSIR was reconstituted to become the Commonwealth Scientific and Industrial Research Organization (CSIRO) and he was appointed its Chairman. He was made a C.M.G. and knighted in 1954.

His qualities as a public speaker were exceptional. The Universities of Sydney and Melbourne reached their hundredth birthdays in 1952 and 1954 respectively, and he was called upon to give the centenary oration for each. He was generally able to speak to any group that wanted to hear him. His appointment book for 1957, in which nearly two months were absorbed by the Murray Committee visits alone, revealed over 70 engagements, apparently including speeches and broadcasts.

Ian Clunies Ross was later described by his son as a good, but not a great, scientist, even though the term "scientist" was not used during his father's time. Yet clearly the task of leading CSIRO was one that he did with great success. He lost no opportunity in bringing scientific discoveries to public notice and did everything possible to see that they were applied quickly.

Fig. 302. Sir Ian Clunies Ross

The photograph above, used for the artwork for the $50 note, was one of two poses taken by Jan De Boer (c. 1969) to update Sir Ian's official photograph for his passport and for use by the press. This photograph was supplied and reproduced by courtesy of the CSIRO.

The Royal Agricultural Society of England awarded him its gold medal, and the Royal Society of New South Wales its James Cook Medal. He died on 20 June, 1959, aged 60 years, whilst still Chairman of the CSIRO. Nearly 1,000 people attended a memorial service to Sir Ian in Scots Church, Melbourne, on 22 June.

At various times he was: Member, Australian delegation, League of Nations Assembly; Australian Member of Council, International Chamber of Commerce; Chairman, Commonwealth Council, Australian Institute of International Affairs; Fellow of the Senate, Sydney University; Member of Council, Scotch College, Melbourne; Member of Council, Melbourne University and Deputy Chancellor; and Member of Council, Australian National University.

His grandfather, Robert Clunies Ross, a sea captain born in the Shetland Islands, was a brother of the John Clunies Ross who settled with his family and crew on the Cocos-Keeling Islands in 1826-7.

References and further reading: *Ian Clunies Ross* by A.L. Clunies Ross, *Records of the Australian Academy of Science.* Volume 3, number 3/4, November, 1977; *Ian Clunies Ross, Memoirs and Papers,* Oxford University Press, Melbourne, 1961; *Clunies Ross Australian Visionary,* L.R. Humphreys, The Miegunyah Press, Melbourne, 1998: *Ian Clunies Ross. A Biography,* Marjory O'Dea, Hyland House, Melbourne, 1997.

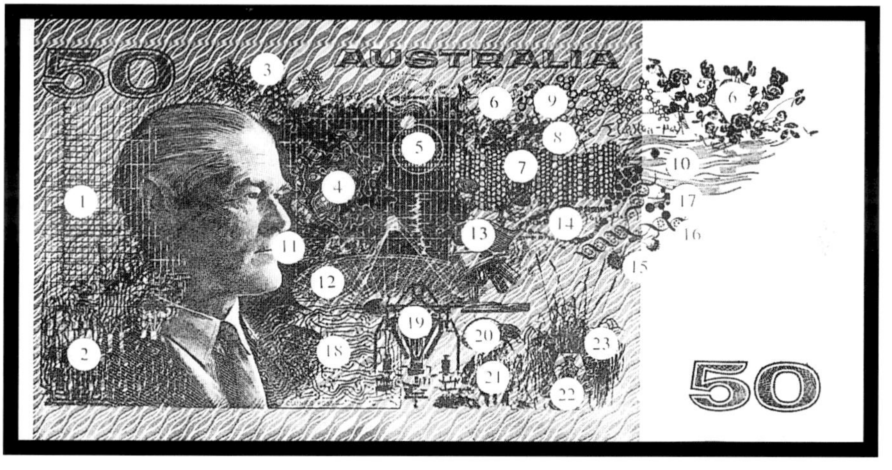

Fig. 303. Back, $50 note depicting Space and soil sciences.

The topics featured on the back of the $50 note are:

1. Pulsating radio source C.P. 1919. The description of this radio source refers to Cambridge Pulsar 19hr. 19min. right ascension. This, the first pulsar observed, was detected in 1967 by a radio telescope at the Mullard Radio Astronomy Observatory near Cambridge. It emits a radio pulse every 1.33730113 sec.
2. Transistors in computer circuitry.
3. Snow crystals - some of the infinite variety of six-pointed, star-like crystals comprising frozen precipitation.

4. The Large Magellanic Cloud. This cloud is one of the nearest galaxies to our galactic system (200,000 light years away). Both the Large and Small Magellanic Clouds are visible to the naked eye from the Southern Hemisphere.

5. Radio heliograph picture of the Sun. The former CSIRO Solar Observatory at Culgoora, N.S.W. included a radio heliograph which consisted of 96 dish-shaped aerials, each 13.7 metres across and are spaced in a circle with a diameter of 3 km. Each dish is automatically steered to follow the Sun. Radio signals from the Sun are picked up by the aerials, amplified, and then carried along overhead transmission lines which converge on the central observatory where pictures of the radio corona of the Sun can be displayed on a T.V. tube at the rate of one per second. Disturbances transmitted from the Sun to Earth exert a significant influence on the outer atmosphere of the Earth. The first Sun-bursts recorded by the radio heliograph were on 2 September, 1967.

6. Subterranean clover - an introduced leguminous plant recognized by Amos William Howard at Wistow near Mount Barker, South Australia, in the 1890s. The species buries its seeds in the soil, but its most important attribute is that the nodules on its roots are able to take nitrogen from the air and convert it into nitrates for its own enrichment and that of non-leguminous plants growing nearby. The sowing of Mount Barker subclover (as it was then called) in a wide range of environments lifted production of animals, and crops such as cereals, enormously, particularly in the acid soils of southern Australia.

7. Cellular structure of a plant. Among the cell compartments of green plants are cell-walls and chloroplasts (No. 10) which contain the green pigment chlorophyll. This is able to absorb light energy and use it to carry out chemical reactions by the process of photosynthesis to form carbohydrates.

8. Random formulae.

9. Alpha helix of a protein molecule (amino acid). Free amino acids are found in living cells, as well as in the body fluids of higher animals in varying amounts. They are the building blocks for protein synthesis.

10. See 7.

11. Gridded paper with superimposed random notations. The background design is gridded paper used in recording radio sources, with superimposed random notations and signals. Virtually every object in the sky is a source of at least weak radio emission, the most prominent source being the Sun itself.

12. Radio Telescope, Parkes, New South Wales. This telescope was commissioned on 31 October, 1961. Originally the parabolic reflector was constructed of an inner section of welded thick steel plate and an outer zone of woven, high-tensile, galvanised steel wire. Later, part of the outer zone was replaced with special perforated aluminium panels and, in 1975, the inner 17 metres of the dish were clad with a continuous aluminium skin. Radio telescopes are aerials for collecting feeble radio signals (sometimes only a billionth of a watt) and focusing them onto a radio amplifier and recorder for computer analysis. Radio astronomy allows probing more deeply into the remotest depths of space than is possible with optical telescopes, and enables penetration through clouds of dust. This telescope, operated by the Australian National Radio Astronomy Observatory, CSIRO, was a prime station for the link between Earth and the lunar module for the Moon landings of various American Apollo Missions.

Fig. 304. The 64-metre Radio Telescope, Parkes, N.S.W., 1984.

Other work being carried out at Parkes includes the study of quasars and pulsars, mapping the Milky Way and the magnetic fields of other galaxies. The telescope is the largest of its kind in the Southern Hemisphere, and was the main instrument to receive information from the Giotto Space-probe as it flew through the tail of Halley's comet in 1986. The Parkes Telescope is featured in the above illustration.

13. High-powered optical microscope.

14. Giant chromosomes - thread-like bodies within a cell, visible through a microscope. The amounts in each organism can aid identification e.g. Man has 48.

15. *Leucaena leucocephala* - a protein-rich herb. Proteins are initially involved in all life processes, some as enzymes, others as haemoglobin, but most ubiquitously as body tissue.

16. Stylized version of D.N.A. molecule replication. Deoxyribonucleic acid (D.N.A.) of a cell occurs in the nucleus of a component of the chromosomes. The ability to manipulate genetic material has depended on several comparatively recent discoveries. As a result of modern knowledge, plants and animals can be modified genetically to maintain or increase disease resistance, improve yield, accelerate growth, improve the protein quality in the food products, and so on.

17. Alanine - one of the amino acids. See also, 9.

18. Printed circuitry in a computer.

19. One-kilogram standard balance. The signing of the Treaty of the Metre in 1875 established an international Bureau of Weights and Measures to define suitable standards for measuring such things as length, mass and volume. The international standard for mass was defined as the kilogram.

20. Oribatid mite which forms a major component of the fauna of the surface soil and litter of pastures and forests where it contributes to the breakdown of vegetable debris. Their population density may reach many thousands per square metre.

21. Surface soil (see above).

22. *Drosophila melangaster* - a fly used by geneticists for cross-fertilization.

23. *Phalaris hybrid.* Its use as a grass in the southern pastures of Australia increased pasture production considerably, as the plant grows profusely. A hybrid which is strong and resistant to disease was developed by CSIRO by crossing two types of Canary grass. The CSIRO hybrid is better suited to Australian conditions and therefore grows even more profusely. Also, its seed heads are less prone to shattering before harvest, and it is more digestible by cud-chewing animals. Though perennial, phalaris does not grow in winter - one of its major shortcomings. Drought resistance is one of its particular attributes, hence it flourishes in country where the rainfall is too low for ryegrass and other grasses, which otherwise would be preferable.

There is now an Ian Clunies Ross Memorial Foundation which recognises people for their ongoing, outstanding contribution to the application of science and technology for the benefit of Australia. With assistance from major sponsors, the foundation awards include a medallion featuring Clunies Ross and the wording "The Clunies Ross National Science and Technology Award". The 1997 awards were presented at a dinner held in conjunction with the official opening of the Queensland Clunies Ross Centre for Science and Industry.

Further information: Chapter 2 - Designing the notes, and Press Releases in Chapter 3 - Informing the public.

$50 "AUSTRALIA" NOTES
No notes printed or issued with "Commonwealth of Australia".

V.165

Signatures — **J.G. Phillips** Governor, Reserve Bank of Australia.
F.H. Wheeler Secretary to the Treasury.

Fig. 305. Signatures and titles, Phillips-Wheeler $50 (V.165).

Issued — 9 October, 1973.

Serial numbers — YAA 000001 - YAU 696000. Printed 17,696,000.
"Gothic" serial numbering. "Centre thread".
Metallic security thread approximately 70 mm from the left edge of the front. The lowest serial number available to the public was YAA 000011 which was purchased by the then Treasurer, Frank Crean.
However, most of the first 1,000 of each of the decimal paper notes were retained in archives, and later used in the 25th Anniversary Collections ($1, $2, $10, $20) and Triple Anniversary Collections ($5, $50 and $100). See, Collector Issues, Chapter 9.

Sheet content 24 — YAA-YAU.

V.166

Signatures — **H.M. Knight** Governor, Reserve Bank of Australia.
F.H. Wheeler Secretary to the Treasury.

Fig. 306. Signatures and titles, Knight-Wheeler $50 (V.166).

Issued — December, 1975.

Serial numbers — YAV 000001 - YCZ 999913. Printed 47,999,913.

Variety (a) — "Gothic" serial numbering. "Centre thread". Metallic security thread approximately 70 mm from the left edge of the front.

Sheet content 24 — With (b), YAV-YBX.

Variety (b) — "Gothic" serial numbering. "Side thread". Metallic security thread approximately 55 mm from the left edge of the front.

Sheet content 24 — With (a), YAV-YBX, then YBY-YCZ.

From July, 1976, all paper despatched by the Note Printing Branch's suppliers had the security thread positioned in an area approximately 55 mm from the left edge of the front. The change was made to avoid the natural fold area which, because of the close proximity of the metallic thread, caused undue wear and tearing.

V.167

Signatures — **H.M. Knight** Governor, Reserve Bank of Australia.
John Stone Secretary to the Treasury.

Fig. 307. Signatures and titles, Knight-Stone $50 (V.167).

Issued 29 March, 1979.

Serial numbers YDA 000001 - YHH 999999. Printed 96,000,000.
Notes YDA 000001 - YDA 000101 were retained as specimens.
"Gothic" serial numbering. "Side thread". Metallic security thread approximately 55 mm from the left edge of the front.

Sheet content 24 YDA-YEB, YEC-YFD, YFE-YGF, YGG-YHH.

V.168

Signatures — **R.A. Johnston** Governor, Reserve Bank of Australia.
John Stone Secretary to the Treasury.

Fig. 308. Signatures and titles, Johnston-Stone $50 (V.168).

Issued January, 1984.

Serial numbers YHT 000001 - YNS 999547. Printed 87,999,547.
"Gothic" serial numbering. Notes with "OCR-B" serial numbering in this signature combination restricted to specimen notes only.

Sheet content 24 YHJ-YJK, YJL-YKN, YKP-YLQ, YLR-YNS.

V.169

Signatures — **R.A. Johnston** Governor, Reserve Bank of Australia.
B.W. Fraser Secretary to the Treasury.

Fig. 309. Signatures and titles, Johnston-Fraser $50 (V.169).

Variety (a) "Gothic" serial numbering (see Fig. 285).

Issued December, 1985.

Serial numbers YNT 000001 - YTB 999999. Prefixes YTC to YUD not used.
YVG to YXH, numbers 000001 to 474500 only.
Printed 107,388,000.

Sheet content 24 YNT-YPU, YPV-YQX, YQY-YRZ, YSA-YTB. With (b) YVG-YKH.

Variety (b) "OCR-B" serial numbering (see Fig. 286).

Issued July, 1988.

Serial numbers YUE 000001 - YVF 999999.
YVG to YXH, numbers 212501 to 999945 only.
Numbers 000001 to 212500 not used. Printed 40,898,680.

Sheet content 24 YUE-YVF. With (a) YVG-YXH.

V.170

Signatures — **M.J. Phillips** Deputy Governor, Reserve Bank of Australia.
B.W. Fraser Secretary to the Treasury.

As with the $20 denomination, this was the first time that Australian notes bore the facsimile signature of a Deputy Governor. The temporary change was made because of the three month's delay in Mr. Fraser (then Secretary to the Treasury) taking up his appointment as Governor.

Fig. 310. Signatures and titles, Phillips-Fraser $50 (V.170).

Issued September, 1989.

Serial numbers YXJ to YYU, numbers 000001 to 009500, 010001 to 060000 and 100001 to 999999 only. Numbers 009501 to 010000 and 060001 to 100000 not used. Printed 23,027,976.

Sheet content 32 YXJ-YYU.

72 blocks of four notes were sold by Note Printing Australia through mail order in May, 1990, at $500 per block (along with 36 blocks of Phillips-Fraser $20 notes - see V.154).

N.P.A. retained sheet number 000001 with serial letters YXJ to YYU. The remaining nine sheets were cut into blocks of four with numbers 000002 to 000010, and prefixes:

YXJ	YXT	YYC	YYL
YXK	YXU	YYD	YYN
YXL	YXV	YYE	YYP
YXN	YXX	YYF	YYQ

(Top blocks)

YXP	YXY	YYG	YYR
YXQ	YXZ	YYH	YYS
YXR	YYA	YYJ	YYT
YXS	YYB	YYK	YYU

(Bottom blocks)

V.171

Signatures

B.W. Fraser Governor, Reserve Bank of Australia.
C.I. Higgins Secretary to the Treasury.

Fig. 311. Signatures and titles, Fraser-Higgins $50 note (V.171).

Issued May, 1990.

Serial numbers YYV 000001 to YZZ 999999. WAA 000001 - WBS 999999.
WBT to WDD, numbers 860001 to 999999 only.
This was the first time that the letter W had been used for general circulating decimal notes. Printed 68,479,904.

Sheet content 32 YYV-WAF, WAG-WBS. With V.172, WBT-WDD.

V.172

Signatures

B.W. Fraser Governor, Reserve Bank of Australia.
A.S. Cole Secretary to the Treasury.

Fig. 312. Signatures and titles, Fraser-Cole $50 (V.172).

Issued August, 1991.

Serial numbers WBT to WDD, numbers 000001 to 860000 only.
WDE 000001 - WNX 999999.
WNY to WQH, numbers 298501 to 999999 only.
Printed 241,967,776.

Sheet content 32 With V.171, WBT-WDD, then WDE-WEQ, WER-WGB, WGC-WHN, WHP-WJZ, WKA-WLK, WLL-WNX. With V.173, WNY-WQH.

V.173

Signatures **B.W. Fraser** Governor, Reserve Bank of Australia.
E.A. Evans Secretary to the Treasury.

Issued December, 1993.

Fig. 313. Signatures and titles, Fraser-Evans $50 (V.173).

Serial numbers WNY to WQH, numbers 000001 to 298500 only.
WQJ 000001 - WYQ 999999.
WYR to WZZ, FAA to FAB, numbers 412501 to 999999 only.
Printed 188,351,808, plus 4,000 in uncut sheets. Serial letters FAA and FAB had previously been used on $2 notes in 1966.

Sheet content 32 With V.172, WNY-WQH, then WQJ-WRU, WRV-WTF, WTG-WUS, WUT-WXD, WXE-WYQ, WYR-FAB.

Notes with this signature combination were issued in uncut form:

250 vertical pairs with red numbers were sold at the Perth coin fair on 20 August, 1994, at $250 each, limit one per person. The notes were numbered E 000001 to E 000250 and F 000001 to F 000250. Number 000001 pair was auctioned in July, 1994, and the $1,100 proceeds donated by N.P.A. to the Princess Margaret Children's Hospital, Perth. See Fig. 314.

1,250 vertical pairs with black serial numbers at $190 each, limit two per person. 750 pairs were sold at the Perth coin fair on 20 & 21 August, 1994, and 500 by mail order in August. The notes were numbered from E 000251 to E 001500 and F 000251 to F 001500.

250 blocks of four with red serial numbers were sold at the Perth coin fair on 20 August, 1994, at $350 each, limit one per person. They were numbered A,B,C,D 000001 to 000250. Number 000001 block was auctioned in July, 1994, for $2,600, and the proceeds donated by N.P.A. to the Royal Childrens Hospital, Melbourne.

750 blocks of four with black numbers at $290 each, limit two per person. 500 were sold at the Perth Coin Fair on 20 & 21 August, 1994, and 250 by mail order in August.

125 sheets of 32 notes were sold by tender in March, 1996. The notes were numbered out of sequence at WYR - WZZ, FAA - FBB, numbers 000001 to 000125. The top price paid was over $20,000 for the number 000001 sheet, with the average tender being $2,376. Sheets with numbers 000001 and 000002 were later privately cut up and sold as consecutive pairs of single notes. Further reading: *King of the Uncuts,* Michael Vort-Ronald, *Australian Coin Review,* August, 1996.

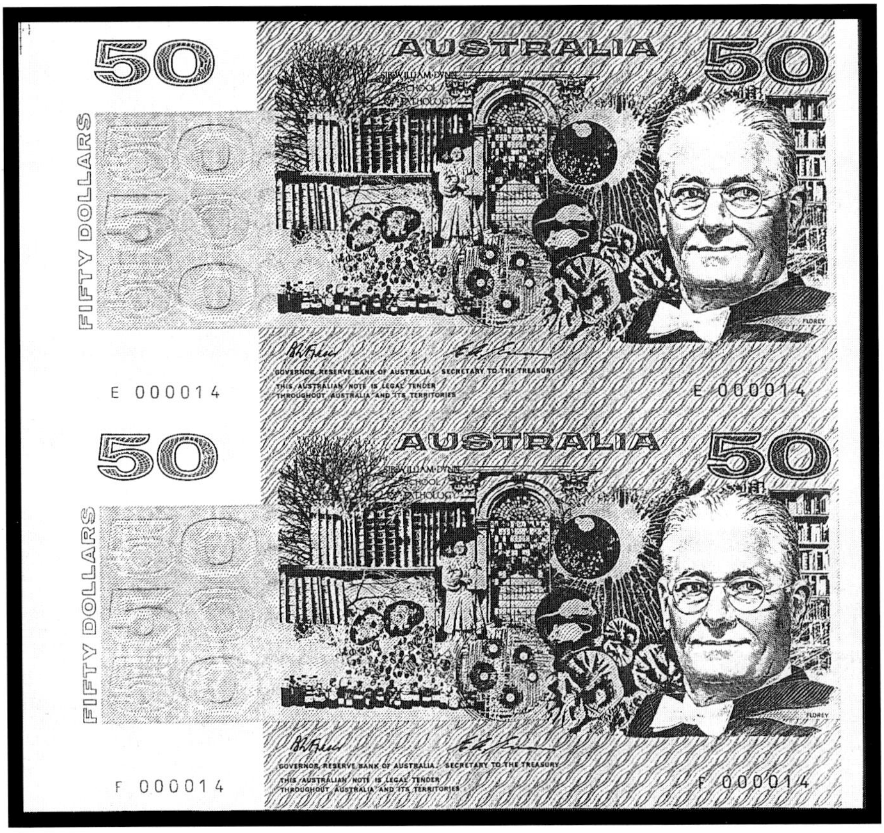

Fig. 314. Uncut vertical pair of Fraser-Evans $50 notes.

On 4 October, 1995, the newly designed polymer $50 note was issued and the paper notes were then progressively phased out. They were not immediately withdrawn because many automatic teller machines had still not been converted to using polymer notes. See chapter 13.

Fig. 315. Front, sheet of 24 un-numbered Johnston-Fraser $50 notes.

Fig. 316. Assoc. Professor Robert Bauze receiving Collector Issue
Florey Portfolio No. 1 from N.P.A.s John Tsoucalas, 1995.

V.185-188

Denomination **$100** ONE HUNDRED DOLLARS

Type First. "AUSTRALIA".

Issued 26 March, 1984, to May, 1996.

Size 172 mm x 82.5 mm.

Watermarks Profiles of Captain James Cook appear on the left side of the front, with two full profiles in the centre alternating vertically in dark and light watermark, and a half profile above and below. See Fig. 99.

Signatures Johnston - Stone, Johnston - Fraser, Fraser - Higgins, Fraser - Cole.

Serial numbers ZAA 000001 to ZLD 999999. **Printed** 221,842,984.

Fig. 317. Front, $100 note. First type (V.185).

Fig. 318. Front, $100 note, main (Intaglio) print only (error note).

FRONT

Main print: Black, brown and green intaglio. (See previous illustration). 162 mm x 74 mm. The main feature in black intaglio is a portrait of Sir Douglas Mawson in the centre of the note. On the left side of the note is a large geometrical pattern consisting of alternating fine lines. It is based on crystal forms and is related to traditional banknote fine-line scroll features. The pattern is symbolic only and does not represent any particular crystal shape. However, if copied, it produces a moire pattern - distorting the fine lines. It alternates in green, black and brown intaglio. At top left and top right is a large "100", the figures on the left alternating in black and brown, and those on the right in brown and black. "ONE HUNDRED DOLLARS" occurs vertically in black over the geometric pattern in the region of the metallic security thread embedded in the paper.

Fig. 319. Sir Douglas Mawson, 1931.

The portrait of Sir Douglas Mawson on the $100 note was taken from a photograph by J. Frank Hurley on board the *Discovery* upon its return from the Antarctic in 1931. The previous illustration and the group photograph on board the *Discovery* are by courtesy of the Mawson Institute for Antarctic Research, University of Adelaide (now the Mawson Antarctic Collection). The group photograph was reproduced from the original glass negative, and the portrait enlarged from the same negative and used to produce the photograph from which the note portrait was designed.

"Australia" is in smaller letters in black intaglio at bottom right. Behind the portrait are drawings of rock strata formations alternating in black, brown and green intaglio. The initials of the designer "HW" are on the right side of the note under the top strata formation. The bottom rock strata formation on the note is a cross section drawing based on typical formations in the Flinders Ranges, South Australia.

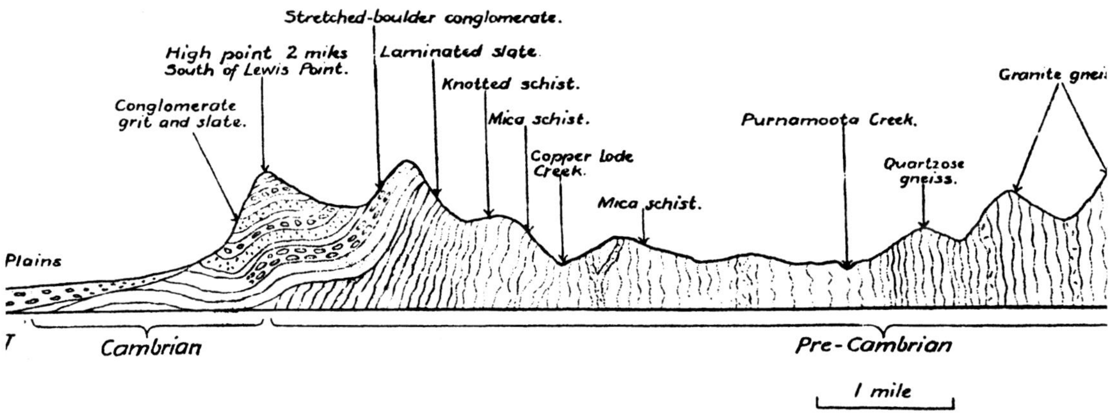

Fig. 320. Rock strata formation, Lewis Point Region, Barrier Range.

The top rock strata formation on the note appears to be a drawing of a cross section of the main portion of the Barrier Range, between The Paps and Lewis Point, in the neighbourhood of Euriowie, South Australia, illustrating the character of folding. The original drawing appeared in a paper by D. Mawson, D.Sc., B.E., *Geological Investigations of the Broken Hill Area,* published in *Memoirs of the Royal Society of South Australia Incorporated,* Volume II, part 4, in which Mawson wrote:

> *In the folded Cambrian strata observed, looking to the south from the ridges in the vicinity of Lewis Point, an unusually instructive picture meets the eye. The rock features are the more obvious on account of the absence of vegetation and soil. Particular horizons can be singled out and traced by the naked eye through the convolutions incorporated in the above section. Northward of The Paps the main anticline flattens out and the range dwindles in consequence.*

The middle section shown in Fig. 321 was based on strata formations of the Munyallina Beds-Mount Warren Hastings region of the Flinders Ranges, South Australia. The area is near the Arkaroola-Mount Painter tourist resort commenced by the late Reg Sprigg, who was one of Mawson's former students. The cross section drawing is from an illustration in a paper by D. Mawson, K.B., D.Sc., F.R.S., read on 11 October, 1934, and published in *Transactions of the Royal Society of South Australia,* Volume 58, pp 187-196, 1934, under the title *The Munyallina Beds: A late-Proterozoic Formation.*

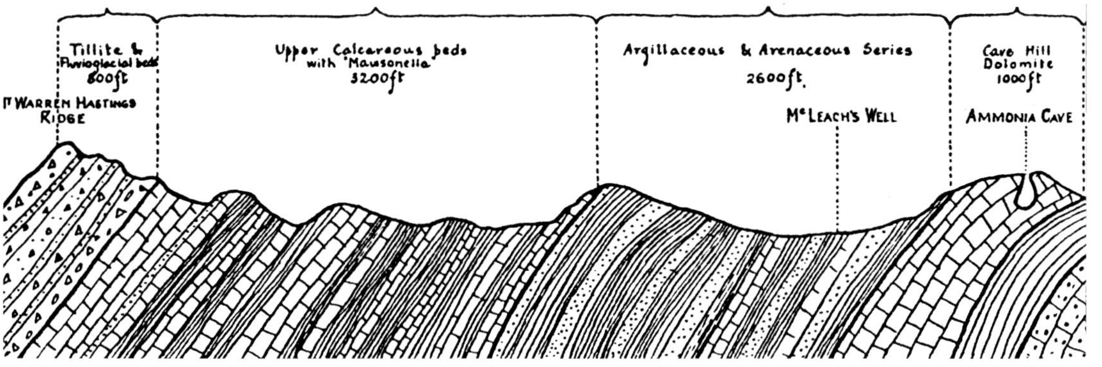

Fig. 321. Rock strata formations, Mt. Warren Hastings Region, Flinders Ranges.

Mawson studied this region in 1924 and again in 1929. The actual portion used for the design on the note is from McLeach's Well at Arkaroola Creek, to Mount Warren Hastings. Lake Frome is further to the east. Mawson wrote:

> *When I crossed the horizon in 1924, on the trek from McLeach's Well to Mount Painter, time did not permit of our recording detailed measurements. It was noted merely that we had crossed massive glacial conglomerate beds before descending a steep slope leading to a tributary stream of the Bolla Bollana Creek...*

Fig. 322. Looking southeast from the top of Mount Painter, 1972.

He concluded that the Munyallina beds appeared to represent a continuous series estimated to total about 12,400 feet in thickness, and that the climatic record ranged from severe glacial to probably warm arid conditions, and again glacial within the period of deposition of those beds. A late-Proterozoic age was assigned to them.

The author of this book, as a mineral collector, knows the area well and has climbed Mount Painter several times. The previous illustration, from the top of Mount Painter, looking East, shows the country traversed by Mawson, with Lake Frome in the background. This area is now a part of the Arkaroola Resort and Wildlife Sanctuary founded by Reg Sprigg. It is situated about 129 km east of Copley (which is 267 km north of Port Augusta), South Australia.

Background print: Dry offset in nine colours. 164 mm x 83 mm.
The background printing consists of a range of background colours including blue, green, mauve, grey, red and brown to produce a combination of 26 colours. The signatures, titles and legal tender clause are in blue at bottom left in the watermark area. In the other denominations designed by Gordon Andrews, these form part of the intaglio design. One small departure from the wording in the legal tender clause in lower denominations is the use of "&" instead of "AND" to reduce the length of the line. The use of blue signatures and titles was to inhibit photocopying and photography which finds blue difficult to reproduce.

The remainder of the background design consists of a series of different coloured lines and patterns showing fine parallel diagonal lines and alternating fine wavy lines in various colours. They are designed to be suggestive of Antarctic auroral lights, a phenomenon in which Mawson was interested.

During the British Antarctic Expedition of 1908, Mawson made it his business to personally observe every auroral display possible between the hours of 8.00 a.m. and midnight. The nightwatchman had orders to waken him at any other time if there was any notable display. On 4 June, 1908, Mawson witnessed an aurora which he described in the following terms:

> *A brilliant auroral display concurrently with mild blizzard conditions. An intensely illuminated curtain formed the main part of the aurora and stretched across the zenith, trending N.W. For a short period a red selvage appeared below. Ripples of luminescence travelled from end to end at a wild and rapid pace. When the excitation travelled more slowly and in a more concentrated fashion the jerky effect is best described as a pulsation. The building up of the curtain by vertical filaments, exactly as the teeth are arranged in a comb, was well illustrated.... This particular curtain remained strongly illuminated for 10 minutes; it then faded, and had disappeared in 30 minutes.*

Mawson read a paper on 13 July, 1916, before the Royal Society of South Australia, which later published it as *Transactions and Proceedings* (before it), Volume XL, 23 December, 1916.

The next illustration is from a photograph taken just before midnight during the winter of 1981, by Peter G. Jacob, a postgraduate student at the Mawson Institute for Antarctic Research, University of Adelaide.

Fig. 323. An Aurora, Mawson Base, Antarctica, 1981.

Sir Douglas Mawson.

Douglas Mawson, O.B.E., B.E., D.Sc., F.R.S., F.A.A., Professor of Geology and Minerology, was born in Bradford, Yorkshire, England, on 5 May, 1882. In 1884 his parents took him and his brother William, to Australia. He graduated as a Bachelor of Engineering (Mining) in 1901 at the University of Sydney where he met and was influenced by the eminent geologist T.W. Edgeworth David, one of whose interests was the process of glaciation. In 1903, Mawson joined a geological survey of the New Hebrides (Vanuatu). In 1904 he completed his Science degree (specialising in Geology) and graduated in 1905.

His interests in glaciation later took him to South Australia where he became lecturer in mineralogy and petrology at the University of Adelaide. In 1908, with Professor Edgeworth David and other scientists, he accompanied Shackleton to Antarctica.

In 1910, a part-time prospector named William Greenwood brought a piece of green rock to Mawson which he had found near Mount Painter in the northern Flinders Ranges in South Australia. Mawson identified it as Torbernite, a uranium ore. Greenwood formed the Radium and Rare Earths Company to mine the deposits. Mawson bought shares and became the company's consultant.

He again visited the Antarctic, as leader of the Australasian Antarctic Expedition of 1911-14. While exploring inland, his two companions perished, and during his journey of 300 miles (480 km) he also nearly died when he fell into a crevasse on 17 January, 1913. In his book *The Home of the Blizzard* he wrote:

> *...Exhausted, weak and chilled (for my hands were bare and pounds of snow had got inside my clothing) I hung with the firm conviction that all was over except the passing. Below was a black chasm; it would be but the work of a moment to slip from the harness, then all the pain and toil would be over. It was a rare situation, a rare temptation - a chance to quit small things for great - to pass from the petty exploration of a planet to the contemplation of vaster worlds beyond. But there was all eternity for the last and, at its longest, the present would be but short. I felt better for the thought....*

In 1914 Mawson was knighted and also awarded the King's Polar Medal with two bars, the Founder's Medal of the Royal Geographical Society, and the first David Livingstone Centenary Medal of the American Geographical Society. The same year he married Francisca Adriana (Paquita) Delprat, (19/8/1891 - 25/5/1974), and in 1915, published his two-volume book, *The Home of the Blizzard.*

From 1916 to 1919, he served with the British Ministry of Munitions, later receiving an O.B.E. for his work.

He had strong feelings about the desirability of Australia changing to a metric system. In 1919 he wrote to the Prime Minister, Mr. Hughes, suggesting that the sovereign could be kept as the major unit with florins becoming tenths, and shillings as half-florins. Another coin of nickel or silver worth about two and a half pence was suggested as one hundredth of the major unit, with the halfpenny being one fifth of that coin.

He became Professor of Geology at the University of Adelaide in 1921, and was elected a Fellow of the Royal Society in 1923. As a geologist he made an essential contribution to the knowledge of the geology of Australia, and to the development of geological thought. His work in the Broken Hill district, together with his early discoveries in the radium-bearing areas of Mount Painter and Radium Hill were outstanding contributions to economic geology and mineralogy.

In 1929 he was the leader of the British, Australian and New Zealand Antarctic Research Expedition (B.A.N.Z.A.R.E.) which left Capetown on 19 October aboard the vessel *Discovery*, which had been made available by the British Government. The chief patron of the expedition was Mr. MacRobertson after whom Mawson later named an extensive new land area discovered. The expedition arrived back at Melbourne on 8 April, 1930. As a result of that expedition, extensive new areas of the Antarctic were charted, deducing evidence that it was a portion of a great continental mass which occupied the major portion of the region. Large areas were claimed for the Crown. Several tons of rock and mineral specimens were collected. About 1,000 deep-sea soundings were recorded and extensive hydrological data secured. Extensive biological studies were made and a whale fishery discovered off the coast of Enderby Land, worth far more than the cost of the expedition. His official report to the Commonwealth Parliament was presented on 21 May, 1930.

In the summer of 1930-31 he again returned to the Antarctic. He revisited his old base at Commonwealth Bay and from magnetic observations, calculated the considerable movement of the Magnetic Pole since 1909. From the air he observed and named Princess Elizabeth Land.

The next illustration was taken aboard the *Discovery* in 1931. Those in the photograph were:

Back Row:	A.J. Williams, Wireless Officer, R.N.
	A.L. Kennedy, Physicist.
	H.O. Fletcher, Assistant Biologist.
	S.A.C. Campbell, Flt. Lieut. R.A.A.F., Chief Pilot.
	R.A. Falla, Ornithologist.
	J. Bonus Child, Third Officer.
	R.G. Summers, Meteorologist.
Centre Row:	W.J. Griggs, Chief Engineer.
	Dr. W.W. Ingram, Medical Officer.
	Capt. K.N. MacKenzie, Master, R.R.S. *Discovery.*

Fig. 324. Members of the BANZARE on board the *Discovery* in 1931. Sir Douglas Mawson, Leader, is near the centre, wearing a balaklava.

Centre Row:	Sir Douglas Mawson, Leader.
	Prof. T. Harvey Johnston, Chief of Scientific Staff, and second in command.
	W.R. Colbeck, Second (and Navigating) Officer.
Front Row:	A. Howard, Hydrologist.
	K.E. Oom, Lieut. R.A.N., Cartographer.
	E. Douglas, R.A.A.F., Second Pilot.
	B.F. Welch, Second Engineer.
	Absent on duty at the bridge was the Chief Officer, A.M. Stanton.

In 1932, Mawson became President of the Australasian Association for the Advancement of Science. His continuing Antarctic activities were largely responsible for the ceding to Australia in 1933 of Britain's Antarctic claims between the 45th and 160th eastern meridians (but excluding part of Adelie Land).

He was active in the establishment of the first Australian National Antarctic Research Expedition in 1947, and an Antarctic Division of the Department of External Affairs in 1948. In 1952, the Mawson Laboratory, School of Geology, University of Adelaide was named in his honour. On 13 February, 1954, the first permanent Australian station to be set up on the Antarctic continent was established by Phillip Law, and named in honour of Sir Douglas Mawson.

Sir Douglas died at his Brighton (Adelaide) home on 14 October, 1958, aged 76 years. On 16 October he was given a Commonwealth State Funeral at St. Jude's Church, Brighton. His coffin was draped with the Australian Blue Ensign which he had used to proclaim the territory he had claimed in the name of King George V on his 1929-31 expedition. He was buried in the church cemetery (established 1854) behind St. Jude's at Brighton, a simple granite slab later marking his grave in Section L30 / 1B. His wife Paquita was buried in the same grave in 1974.

On 15 April, 1961, the Mawson Institute for Antarctic Research at the University of Adelaide was inaugurated by the Prime Minister, Mr. Menzies, to house Sir Douglas Mawson's private Antarctic library, his diaries and other papers. It is now the Mawson Antarctic Collection.

In June, 1997, Sydney coin dealers International Numismatics advertised for sale specially framed $100 notes personally countersigned by the signatories B.W. Fraser and A.S. Cole, for $6,950 each. A certificate with the frame advised that only 50 were produced to assist the AAP Mawson's Hut Foundation Appeal to raise funds for the conservation of the historic huts at Cape Denison, on Commonwealth Bay, which was used as a base by the Australasian Antarctic Expedition of 1911-14, led by Sir Douglas Mawson. The certificate was signed by Sir William Deane, Governor General; John Howard, Prime Minister; Sir Edmund Hillary, Antarctic Explorer and Conquerer of Mount Everest and Peter Costello, Federal Treasurer.

The South Australian Museum on North Terrace, Adelaide, closed for nearly a year (after 142 years of opening almost daily) to enable the installation of new exhibitions of international stature including the "Australian Aboriginal Cultures Gallery" and "In the Footsteps of Sir Douglas Mawson". Reopened in April 2000, it now focuses on the scientific information that Mawson acquired, and shows his life, his adventures, his success in taking science to extreme environments and the scope of his achievements. The display includes many photographs, and computer interactives to help explain the sciences that Mawson was interested in.

A new book by Philip Ayres was published by Miegunya Press in 1999, *Mawson, a life,* which, according to a review in the *Adelaide Advertiser* by Chris Brice on 11 September, 1999, suggests that it presents *a complex man standing aloof from those he led, who largely based his leadership on the example of "working like a Trojan" - a mortal whose flaws and frailties only serve to make him even more fascinating.*

The print of Sir Douglas Mawson used to illustrate this book was later used for the front cover of Lennard Bickel's paperback reprint of *This Accursed Land.*

References and further reading:

B.A.N.Z.A.R.E. 1929-30. *Geographical Journal,* Vol. 80, No. 2, pp. 101-131, 1932.
Sir Douglas Mawson Anniversary Volume (preface) University of Adelaide, 1952.
The Winning of Antarctica. Mawson's BANZARE Voyages 1929-31, based on the Mawson Papers, A. Grenfell Price, Angus & Robertson, 1962.
Mawson of the Antarctic, Paquita Mawson, O.B.E., Longmans, 1964.
Douglas Mawson, The Survivor, David Parer and Elizabeth Parer-Cook, Allela Books, 1983.
Press Release, Reserve Bank of Australia, 20 March, 1984.
Reserve Bank of Australia Currency magazine, April, 1984, *The Bank's Baby* by Ron Stuart and *My Design on Money* by Harry Williamson; May, 1984, *The $100 Launch, and How did they make that commercial?* Articles in the *Australian Coin Review* by Michael Vort-Ronald, *Tracing the Footsteps of Sir Douglas Mawson,* November, 1999, and *The Neglected $100 Heroes,* April, 1986.

Fig. 325. N.P.A. line drawing of Sir Douglas Mawson.

Fig. 326. N.P.A. line drawing of John Tebbutt.

Fig. 327. Back, $100 note. first type (V.185).

BACK

Main print: Blue, brown and grey intaglio. 157 mm x 71 mm.

The main feature is a portrait of John Tebbutt in the centre of the note. The portrait is believed to have been engraved from the photograph in Fig. 331, which was probably taken not long before his death in 1916.

Fig. 328. Back, $100 background (Simultan) printing only (error note).

Background print: Dry offset in nine colours. 126 mm x 83 mm.

The background design consists of many colours, including mauve, blue, green, red, beige and purple. On the left of the note is a step-like pattern in alternating colours with a concentrated diagonal band suggestive of a comet in the night sky. The remainder of the background design consists of a series of geometric fine-lined designs in various pastel shades.

On the left side of the note is a reproduction of the wooden observatory built by John Tebbutt himself in 1863. The building had a slate roof. Over the years the building was destroyed by dry rot and white ants and none of the building has been in evidence since the early 1930s. Reproduced below is an early lithograph showing the building on the left, and the fence shown no longer exists. However, his second and third observatories are still at Windsor, New South Wales, 57 km from Sydney. The public can view them from the outside, but there is now a privately operated restaurant and function centre alongside, and internal tours can only be arranged by appointment by telephoning (02) 4577 8546.

Fig. 329. Early lithograph of John Tebbutt's first, third and second observatories.

To the right of Tebbutt on the note is a red-brick observatory built in 1879. The buildings depicted are reproduced in a mixture of blue and brown intaglio. At the bottom right of the right side window of the brick observatory are the very small letters "JM", possibly the initials of the engraver, John Mackie. The buildings featured on the note were architecturally surveyed and drawn for the note by Phillip Cox and Associates of New South Wales.

The next illustration (Fig. 330) is an old photograph of the brick observatory which includes another brick structure on the left, erected in 1864, which no longer stands. The main brick observatory on the right was erected mainly because a new telescope purchased by John Tebbutt was too large and heavy to install in the existing observatory.

On the right of the note is "100" at the top in blue and brown intaglio, and at the bottom "Australia" is in black and brown intaglio. The printing of serial numbers on the back was a radical change, as all serial numbers on the lower denominations have always been printed on the fronts. Because of this, the serial number sequence runs backwards when viewed from the numbered sides in new sections of notes. Printed in a separate operation by letterpress, the serial numbers are black at top left and blue at bottom right, both in "OCR-B" style.

Fig. 330. Early photograph of John Tebbutt's third and second observatories, c. 1916.

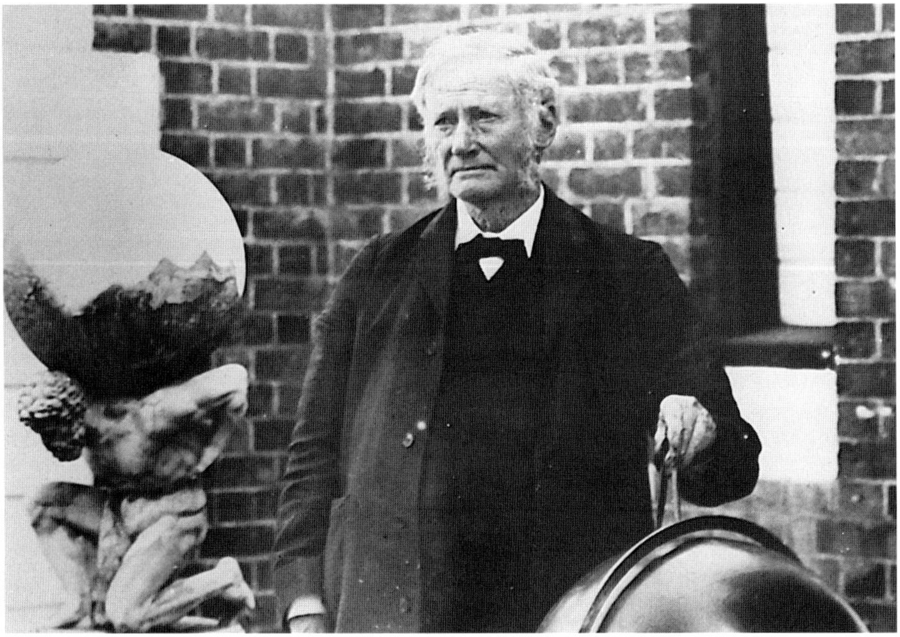

Fig. 331. John Tebbutt c. 1916.

John Tebbutt.

John Tebbutt was born on 25 May, 1834, at Windsor, New South Wales, the only son of John Tebbutt (1794-1870) and Virginia Tebbutt, (nee Saunders). His grandfather, also John Tebbutt (1763-1844), arrived in Australia aboard the convict ship *Nile* with his wife Ann Tebbutt (nee Halfpenny), and three children, in 1801, as free settlers and settled in the Hawkesbury River District as farmers.

John Tebbutt the astronomer, was a pioneer in Australian astronomy. In his book *Astronomical Memoirs* (published in 1908) he explained the origin of his work in the following terms after much discussion with his old friend and tutor, Edward Quaife:

> *...owing to this circumstance and the reading of some popular contributions to astronomy by Mr. Hind the well known London astronomer, it dawned on me that the universe was really mechanism of the highest order, and being, as I have already said, mechanically inclined, I began to turn my attention to celestial mechanism. Thus began my love for astronomy, and I became fired with an ambition to do real work in its behalf...*

His first attempt at celestial observation was in May, 1853, when he observed a comet by means of an ordinary marine telescope and a celestial atlas. These observations, with accompanying sketches, formed the first entries in his journal. The first astronomical communication he published appeared in the *Sydney Morning Herald* concerning sunspots which occurred on 11 May, 1854.

On 8 September, 1857, he married Jane Pendergast at St. Matthew's Church, Windsor. He was the first discoverer of the grand comet of May, 1861, now known as Tebbutt's Comet (1861 II), and went on to discover several comets, including a notable one in 1881, the orbits of which he computed from his own observations. In 1862, he refused the position of Government Astronomer for New south Wales after the resignation of W. Scott.

His valuable contributions, both observational and mathematical, appeared in many of the most important astronomical publications in Europe and America, and from 1863 to 1896, he published extensive meteorological observations. In 1867, he won a silver medal at the Paris Universal Exhibitionfor his paper *On the present progress and present state of astronomical science in New South Wales,* published in Sydney in 1871. In 1873, he became a Fellow of the Royal Astronomical Society, London.

In 1879 he erected the brick observatory, and from 1887, he privately published each year an account of his work. He devoted his time, money and energy to the advantage of astronomical knowledge in Australia in a thoroughly earnest and practical manner. By the time he announced his relinquishing of the work at the age of 70 years, he had made regular and systematic observations of some 1,400 occulations of stars by the Moon, including double stars. His work was so recognised that his observatory was placed on the list of principal working observatories in the national ephemerides of Great Britain, France, Germany and the United States. He was also on the distribution lists of the principal astronomical and meteorological institutions of the world.

In 1905, the Royal Astronomical Society of London awarded him the Hannah Jackson (nee Gwilt) Gift and Medal of the Society. He handed the gift of 25 pounds to the New South Wales Branch of the British Astronomical Association, of which he had been elected first president. In 1908, 371 publications were listed to his credit, covering over 50 years of work in the fields of astronomy and

Fig. 332. Tebbutt's Hannah Jackson Gwilt medal.

meteorology. He died at Windsor on 29 November, 1916, and was buried in the cemetery of St. Matthew's Church, Windsor (see Francis Greenway and the front of the $10 note and Fig. 231).

Reference and further reading: *Astronomical Memoirs,* John Tebbutt, 1908; Press Release, Reserve Bank of Australia, 20 March, 1984; *The Neglected $100 Heroes,* Michael Vort-Ronald, *Australian Coin Review,* April, 1986.

Fig. 333. John Tebbutt's second observatory, 1984.

$100 NOTES "AUSTRALIA".

Serial numbering "OCR-B".

V.185

Signatures

	R.A. Johnston	Governor, Reserve Bank of Australia.
	John Stone	Secretary to the Treasury.

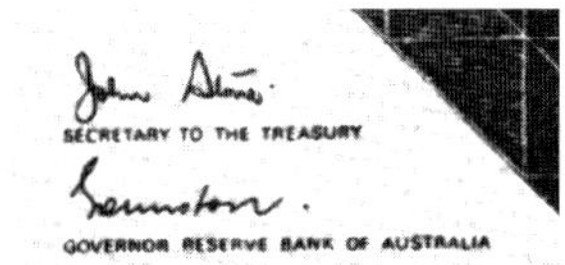

Fig. 334. Signatures and titles, Johnston-Stone $100 (V.185).

Issued 22 March, 1984.

Serial numbers

ZAA 000001 - ZBB 999999.
ZBC to ZCD, numbers 864501 to 999966 only.
The first 2,500 notes were set aside for undisclosed purposes.
From those notes, the first 1,000 notes were later chosen for the Triple Anniversary Collection, see Collector Issues, Chapter 9.
Printed 27,251,160.

Sheet content 24 ZAA-ZBB.

V.186

Signatures

	R.A. Johnston	Governor, Reserve Bank of Australia
	B.W. Fraser	Secretary to the Treasury.

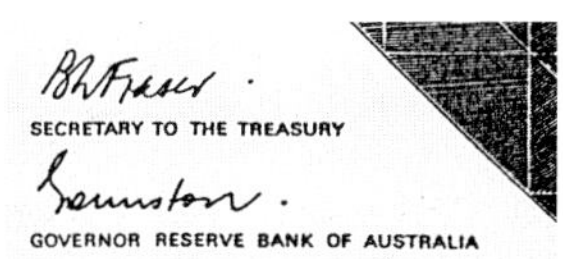

Fig. 335. Signatures and titles, Johnston-Fraser $100 (V.186).

Issued December, 1985.

Serial numbers

ZBC to ZCD, numbers 000001 to 864500 only.
ZCE 000001 - ZEH 999999.
ZEJ to ZFU, numbers 555501 to 999999 only.
Printed 82,971,920.

Sheet content 24 ZBC-ZCD, ZCE-ZDF, ZDG-ZEH.

Sheet content 32 With V. 187, ZEJ-ZFU.

V.187

Signatures **B.W. Fraser** Governor, Reserve Bank of Australia.
C.I. Higgins Secretary to the Treasury.

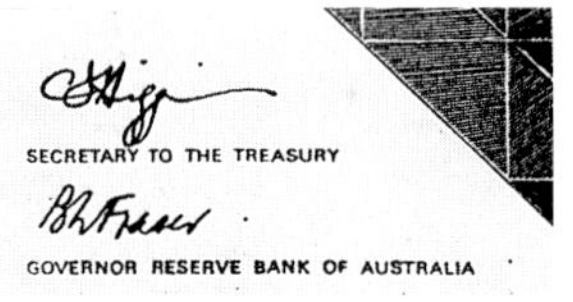

Fig. 336. Signatures and titles, Fraser-Higgins $100 (V.187).

Issued June, 1990.

Serial numbers ZEJ to ZFU, numbers 000001 to 555500 only.
ZFV 000001 - ZHF 999999.
ZHG to ZJS, numbers 945501 to 999999 only.
Printed 51,519,936.

Sheet content 32 With V.186, ZEJ-ZFU, then ZFV-ZHF. With V.188, ZHG-ZJS.

V.188

Signatures **B.W. Fraser** Governor, Reserve Bank of Australia.
A.C. Cole Secretary to the Treasury.

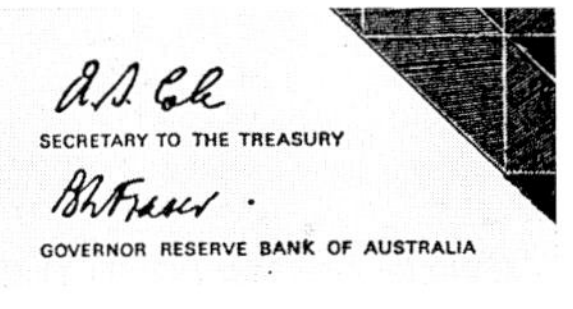

Fig. 337. Signatures and titles, Fraser-Cole $100 (V.188).

Issued April, 1992.

Serial numbers ZHG to ZJS, numbers 000001 to 945500 only.
ZJT to ZLD, numbers 071501 to 999999 only.
Printed 59,999,968.

Sheet content 32 With V.187, ZHG-ZJS, then ZJT-ZLD.

This signature combination was also issued in uncut form.

300 pairs with red serial numbers at $350 per pair, limit one per person, were sold by mail order ballot in August, 1995. Serial numbers were E 000001 - E 000300 and F 000001 - F 000300.

700 pairs with two black serial numbers were sold at $295 per pair, limit two per person. 350 were sold at the Melbourne Coin Fair on 15 & 16 July, 1995, and 350 by mail order in August, 1995. Serial numbers were E 000301 - E 001000 and F 000301 - F 001000. Circulating notes had one blue and one black serial number with three prefix letters.

150 blocks of four with red serial numbers at $595 per block, limit one per person, were sold by mail order ballot in August, 1995. Serial numbers were A, B, C, D, numbers 000001 - 000150.

Number 000001 pair and block were auctioned by Noble Numismatics for the N.A.A. and raised $1,500 and $2,800 respectively, which was donated to the British Astronomical Association, N.S.W. branch.

500 blocks of four with two black serial numbers were sold at $495 per block, limit two per person, 300 at the Melbourne Coin Fair on 15 & 16 July, 1995, and 200 by mail order in August, 1995. Serial numbers were A, B, C, D, numbers 000151 - 000650. Circulating notes had one blue and one black serial number with three prefix letters.

75 sheets of 32 notes were sold by public tender in March, 1997. The notes had prefixes ZJT to ZLD and were numbered out of sequence at 000001 to 000075.

On 15 May, 1996, the new polymer $100 notes were issued and the paper notes withdrawn. See Chapter 13.

Fig. 338. Backs, sheet of 24 un-numbered $100 notes.

Chapter 8: STAR REPLACEMENT NOTES

Notes found to be faulty after the printing processes were marked while still in sheet form, and later withdrawn by hand after guillotining, to be replaced by a note bearing a "star" (asterisk) after each serial number. For illustrations of checking and error marking, see Printing Errors, Chapter 10.

The insertion of the star note was to indicate that the break in the numerical sequence was due to the removal of a faulty note. The serial numbers of the star notes bore no relationship to the serial numbers of the notes being replaced, but their inclusion allowed the section (100 notes) to commence at one and finish at an even hundred.

Fig. 339. Checking a section of 100 $20 notes.

Fig. 340. Don Dunn, Chief Cashier of the Commonwealth Bank's Head Office in Sydney, holding up a random sample of $1 notes for the Press on 14 January, 1966. The front note held is a star replacement note.

Further reading: Articles by Michael Vort-Ronald in the *Australian Coin Review, The Rarest Decimal Star Notes,* April, 1999 (in which the last serial letter of the $2* should read ZFS), *$20 Starnotes Dazzle Like a 1930 Penny*, April, 1997 and *Star collection - and how it began,* May, 1983.

The use of star replacement notes continued on from the replacement notes in the ten shilling, one pound and five pound notes after conversion to decimal currency on 14 February, 1966. An actual star was no longer used, but a six-pointed asterisk (*). The first decimal star notes to appear were in the $1, $2 and $10 notes with the signature combination of Coombs-Wilson. This was followed on 29 May, 1967, with the introduction of the $5 note with signatures Coombs-Randall. Star notes in the $20 denomination did not commence until late in the Phillips-Randall issues in about 1971. For a sequence of more than five error notes, or for top and bottom notes in a hundred, the correct serial numbers were made up without any indication that they were in fact, replacement notes.

This only applied to notes in numerical sequence (consecutive), for if the faulty notes were scattered, there could still be a high concentration of star notes in a section e.g. the author of this book once located 17 consecutive star notes (Phillips-Randall $1) scattered through one section of new notes.

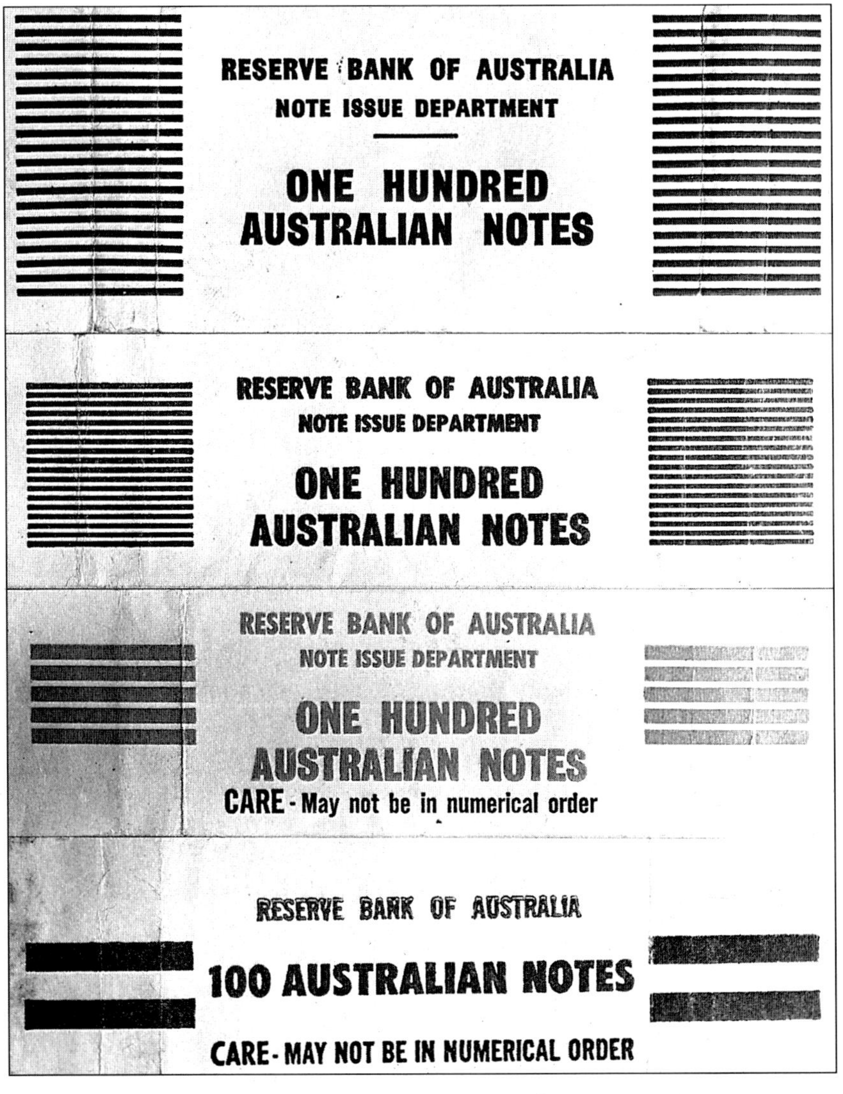

Fig. 341. Section wrappers $20 (1966 and 1970), $5 (1971) and $2 (1972).

The use of star notes was discontinued from 1972, and from the signature combination Phillips-Wheeler (Commonwealth) onwards, they were no longer used. Prior to the adoption of star replacement notes in the $20 denomination, substituted notes were numbered by means of a hand press with the same serial number as the spoiled notes they replaced.

The ever-increasing volume of new notes being printed to replace old notes made the continuance of the star note system impracticable. Faulty notes are now marked by note checking staff while still in sheet form and not removed. After guillotining in reams of 500, the notes are processed through an electronic counter with a cros-field scanning head which counts the notes into sections of 100.

As the notes pass through, any marked with the special ink pen react with the scanning head and are diverted into another area and their serial numbers recorded. The count then goes on until there are 100 notes in the section, regardless of how many breaks in numerical sequence. Thus a section could commence at 123456 and finish at 123567 (indicating 12 notes removed). There can also be a complete change of sequence in a section with the end of one stack of 500 notes and the beginning of another.

With the change in the system of replacing faulty notes it was considered necessary to advise handlers that the notes may not be in numerical sequence. Around each section of notes during the star replacement note era was a paper wrapper printed in the same colour as that particular denomination. It was similar to those used prior to decimal currency. There were several types of wrapper:

Type 1. The number of horizontal bars on each side of the text equalled the denomination. 50 mm wide. See Fig. 340 for illustration of notes with wrappers in place.

Type 2. As in Type 1, but 38 mm wide, and $20 wrappers only had 18 bars each side.

Type 3. As in Type 2, but CARE - *May not be in numerical order* printed underneath text in red for all denominations except the $20, which had this inscription printed in blue.

Type 4. Size as in Type 2 and 3, but *NOTE ISSUE DEPARTMENT* omitted. *100 AUSTRALIAN NOTES* replaced *ONE HUNDRED AUSTRALIAN NOTES* and the CARE etc. line. The $20 wrapper again had 20 bars either side of the wording and the new $50 wrapper when introduced from 1973 was printed in black with 25 diagonal lines from two directions, producing a criss-cross pattern on either side of the wording.

Paper section wrappers were later replaced by a clear to grey unprinted plastic wrapper.

Ten note sections were then put into a bundle of 1,000 notes and separately labelled. Ten bundles (10,000 notes) were then put into a shrink pack and separately labelled again. These are illustrated in Chapter 4: Printing the notes.

Precise information regarding the issues of the decimal star notes was made available by the Note Issue Department, Reserve Bank of Australia, from which it was possible to calculate the total printings of each signature combination. By dividing such figures into the known totals produced in the ordinary series, ratios of ordinary notes to star notes were obtained and included in the following listings.

ONE DOLLAR STAR REPLACEMENT NOTES

Fig. 342. Front, $1 star replacement note (V.65S).

V.65S

Signatures H.C. Coombs - Roland Wilson.

Fig. 343. Signatures and titles, Coombs-Wilson $1 (V.65S).

Serial numbers ZAA 00001 - ZAF 35000. Printed 535,000.

Average One star note to every 243 ordinary issue.

V.66S

Signatures H.C. Coombs - R.J. Randall.

Fig. 344. Signatures and titles, Coombs-Randall $1 (V.66S).

Serial numbers ZAF 45001 - ZAH 17000. Printed 172,000.

Average One star note to every 219 ordinary issue.

V.67S

Signatures J.G. Phillips - R.J. Randall.

Fig. 345. Signatures and titles, Phillips-Randall $1 (V.67S).

Serial numbers ZAH 17001 to ZAQ 100000. Printed 683,000.
Serial letter combinations ZAI, ZAO, ZAM were not used.

Average One star note to every 438 ordinary issue.

TWO DOLLAR STAR REPLACEMENT NOTES

Fig. 346. Front, $2 star replacement note (V.85S).

V.85S

Signatures H.C. Coombs - Roland Wilson.

Fig. 347. Signatures and titles, Coombs-Wilson $2 (V85S).

Serial numbers ZFA 00001 - ZFH 18299. Printed 718,299.
Serial numbers ZFH 15600-16000, 16600-17000, 17400-18000 not issued.

Average One star note to every 268 ordinary issue.

V.86S

Signatures H.C. Coombs - R.J. Randall.

Fig. 348. Signatures and titles, Coombs-Randall $2 (V.86S).

Serial numbers ZFH 19001 - ZFK 89000, excluding ZFI. Printed 270,000.

Average One star note to every 281 ordinary issue.

V.87S

Signatures J.G. Phillips - R.J. Randall.

Fig. 349. Signatures and titles Phillips-Randall $2 (V.87S).

Serial numbers ZFK 89001 - ZFS 96107. Printed 607,107.
Serial letter combinations ZFM and ZFO were not used.

Average One star note to every 779 ordinary issue.

FIVE DOLLAR STAR REPLACEMENT NOTES

Fig. 350. Front, $5 star replacement note (V.105S).

V.105S

Signatures H.C. Coombs - R. J. Randall

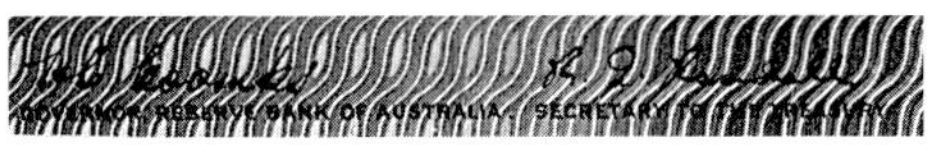

Fig. 351. Signatures and titles, Coombs-Randall $5 (V.105S).

Serial numbers ZNA 00001 - ZNC 04000. Printed 204,000.

Average One star note to every 282 ordinary issue.

Only two notes with ZSD (Coombs-Randall) have appeared in auctions.

Further reading: Articles in the *Australian Coin Review* by Michael Vort-Ronald,: *Star collection - and how it began,* May, 1983; $20 *Starnotes Dazzle Like a 1930 Penny,* April 1997; *The Rarest Decimal Star Notes,* April, 1999. A full set of 50 serial letters is illustrated on the back cover.

V.106S

Signatures J.G. Phillips - R.J. Randall.

Fig. 352. Signatures and titles, Phillips-Randall $5 (V.106S).

Serial numbers ZNC 04001 - ZND 05619. Printed 101,619.

Average One star note to every 831 ordinary issue.

Fig. 353. Front, $10 star replacement note (V.125S).

V.125S

Signatures H.C. Coombs - Roland Wilson.

Fig. 354. Signatures and titles, Coombs-Wilson $10 (V.125S).

Serial numbers ZSA 00001 - ZSD 36000. Printed 336,000.
Final serial number uncertain, see V.126S below.

Average One star note to every 230 ordinary issue.

V.126S

Signatures H.C. Coombs - R.J. Randall.

Fig. 355. Signatures and titles, Coombs-Randall $10 (V.126S).

Serial numbers ZSD 36001 - ZSE 100000. Printed 164,000.
The dividing line between this and the previous signature combination is uncertain as Coombs-Randall notes have been seen with serial numbers ZSD 33131 and 33132. Authorities state that the relevant records may have been destroyed, and thus they are unable to recheck. At least five other notes in auctions have had numbers between the ZSD 33132 and ZSD 36001, and no verifiable Coombs-Wilson star note has been seen above ZSD 33132, so the dividing line is likely to be around ZSD 33001.

Average One star note to every 258 ordinary issue.

TEN DOLLAR STAR REPLACEMENT NOTES

V.127S
Signatures J.G. Phillips - R.J. Randall.

Fig. 356. Signatures and titles, Phillips-Randall $10 (V.127S).

Serial numbers ZSF 00001 - ZSJ 48004, excluding ZSI. Printed 348,004.

Average One star note to every 643 ordinary issue.

TWENTY DOLLAR STAR REPLACEMENT NOTES

Fig. 357. Front, $20 star replacement note (V.147S).

V.147S
Signatures J.G. Phillips - R.J. Randall.

Fig. 358. Signatures and titles, Phillips-Randall $20 (V.147S).

Serial numbers ZXA 00001 - ZXA 62500. Printed 62,500.

Average One star note to every 1,053 ordinary issue.

Star replacement notes in the the $20 denomination were restricted to Phillips-Randall issues because this denomination did not commence to use stars until late in 1970, and star notes were discontinued in the following year. Star notes in the other denominations in the Phillips-Randall series terminated before the end of their series, therefore those averages may also fail to give a true indication of the frequency of spoils and thus star replacements at that time.

Chapter 9: COLLECTOR ISSUES CONTAINING PAPER NOTES

Collector Issues are defined as officially issued general-circulation notes which are modified by overprinting or different serial numbers, and sold to collectors or as souvenirs at a premium over face value. Joint Issue products were issued with Australia Post or the Royal Australian Mint.

Notes which were not modified, but formed part of special issues or collections, are included in the N.P.A. Special Anniversary Collections below, or in Miscellaneous Issues. Uncut pairs, blocks, sheets and half-sheets of paper notes are included in the listings of general circulating notes.

Where a folder or portfolio contained a paper and a plastic note, they are included. Issues confined to polymer notes only, are omitted, and will be listed in a future book, *Australian Polymer Banknotes.*

Collector Issues are grouped as under:

A. Commemorative folders.
- (1) $20 80th anniversary of first Commonwealth note.
- (2) $5 30th anniversary folder (Famous Fives).

B. Last and first portfolios. Paper and polymer notes, matching red serial numbers.
- (1) $5 Portfolio included, although it has no paper note.
- (2) $10 Rare Edition Collector Portfolio.
- (3) $20 Rare Edition Collector Portfolio.
- (4) $50 Rare Edition Collector Portfolio.
- (5) $100 Rare Edition Collector Portfolio.

C. Special N.P.A. Anniversary Collections.
- (1) $1, $2, $10, $20. 25th Anniversary Collection, notes from the first 1,000, with the equivalent pre-decimal notes from the last 1,000. Matching end numbers.
- (2) $5, $50, $100. Triple Anniversary Collection. Notes from the first 1,000, matching serial numerals.

D. Joint issue portfolios.
- (1) $20 Hargrave Centenary.
- (2) $50 Florey 50th Anniversary of Nobel Prize.
- (3) $20 Kingsford Smith Centenary.

E. Miscellaneous issues.
- (1) $2, $5, $10. Bicentenary Coin & Note Collection. Joint issue with Royal Australian Mint.
- (2) $5 Note in perspex.
- (3) $2 Note folders.
- (4) $5, $10, $20, $50, $100. First day of issue folders.

Part A: Commemorative Folders.

Fig. 359. Front, 80th anniversary of first Commonwealth note, $20 Collector Issue (CA1).

In 1993, 5,500 Fraser-Cole $20 notes were overprinted and issued in special folders to commemorate the 80th anniversary of the first Commonwealth note. Note Printing Australia's *To Be Noted* in the *Australian Coin Review,* June, 1993, gave the background to the issue:

> *....The linking of 1913 serial numbers with those of 1993 was seen as the main feature. Printing both styles on the one note would be a first. In addition, there has never been a red serial number on a decimal note before, nor only the one prefix letter, "M" as used in 1913. An overprint commemorating the 80th Anniversary would complete the printing of the note.*
>
> *After numerous meetings, it was concluded that in order to undertake this work, many production oddities would be necessary to complete the desired printing. Some of these included ordering new numbering wheels to be manufactured in England for both the 1993 OCR-B type face and the set similar to that used on the first distinctive note in 1913. These wheels would take four weeks to make and as time was getting short, it was decided to have two new wheels consigned to us by D.H.L.*
>
> *In the meantime, full sheets of numismatic quality twenty dollar notes - forty per sheet - were prepared and cut into horizontal strips with a half note beneath the bottom edge of each note. The strips were guillotined into single notes with the extra piece to act as a "gripper" or leading edge. This action was necessary to prevent marking the finished product. This part of the note would be trimmed off afterwards. ...The serial numbers for each of the 5,500 notes were printed separately on a flat-bed machine in lieu of our huge rotary presses used for current high speed note production....*
>
> *....The prefix letter "M" used in 1913 and the vertical overprint....were printed in one run. Then, after a drying period, the two different serial number styles were printed in a separate run....*

CA1.	**$20**	**80th anniversary of the first Commonwealth note.**

Signatures B.W. Fraser - A.C. Cole.

Serial numbers M 000001 - M 005500. Printed 5,500.

Special features Vertical red overprint on left front "80TH ANNIVERSARY / First Commonwealth Note / 1913 - 1993". Red serial numbers, 1913 style medium seriffed on the left and 1993 style OCR-B numbering on the right.

Issued Brisbane Coin Fair 8 & 9 May, 1993, and by mail order in June, 1993.

Number M 000001 was raffled at the coin fair on 9 May, 1993.

(a) Numbers M 000002 - M 000500 were sold at the coin fair on 8 May, at $78 each in a special folder, limit 4 per person.

(b) Numbers M 000501 - M 003000 were sold at the coin fair on both days at $49 each in a folder, limit 4 per person.

(c) Numbers M 003001 - M 005500 were sold by mail order in June, 1993, at $49 each, limit 4 per person.

Major Australian Medal, Coin and Banknote fairs are conducted by the N.A.A. (Numismatic Association of Australia) and A.N.D.A. (Australasian Numismatic Dealers Association) and others annually in Sydney and Melbourne, and less frequently in Brisbane, Hobart, Adelaide and Perth. "Special Products" such as uncut notes and portfolios were released at the fairs where collectors have queued for up to a week on the footpath (sleeping out overnight) to obtain the lowest numbered special products. Further reading: Reports in the *Australian Coin Review,* as per various references given.

Fig. 360. A queue at a N.A.A. coin fair in Melbourne, July, 1995.

Fig. 361. Front, "famous fives" overprinted paper note (CA2a).

CA2. $5 30th anniversary of decimal currency folder (Famous Fives).

Three overprinted notes were issued in a special folder to commemorate the 30th Anniversary of the issue of the first $5 note in 1967. Sometimes referred to as the "Famous Fives", the folder contained a paper note, the first polymer note and the recoloured polymer note. Each note was overprinted with "First issued" and the date.

Signatures	(a) Paper $5,	Fraser-Cole.
	(b) First polymer $5	Fraser-Cole.
	(c) Recoloured polymer $5	Fraser-Evans.

Serial numbers
(a) Various numbers from the final print run.
(b) Last prefix, EA 93.
(c) First prefix, AA 95.

Special features
Overprinted at top right with the first day of issue.
1,000 red numbered and overprinted and 1,500 black numbered and overprinted of each.

(a) "First issued 29 May 1967".
(b) "First issued 7 July 1992".
(c) "First issued 24 April 1995".

Issued
September, 1995 by mail order at $85 for red (Premium), limit two per order, or $45 for black (Deluxe), limit 4 per order (plus post).

Number One folder was auctioned by Noble Numismatics and the proceeds of $780 donated by Note Printing Australia to the Guide Dog Association of Victoria.

Fig. 362. Front, paper note from Last and First $10 portfolio (CB2).

Part B: Last and First portfolios.

To commemorate the issue of each of the NNS (New Note Series) polymer notes, Note Printing Australia produced 900 limited edition portfolios each of the $10, $20, $50 and $100 notes, sold as Rare Edition Collector Portfolios. Each portfolio contained a NNS polymer note on the right and a paper note on the left. Both notes bore the same serial number in red. A $5 portfolio was also issued, but with a first coloured polymer note and a recoloured polymer $5 note. While the $5 did not contain a paper note, it is included here for the sake of completeness.

CB1. Denomination **$5** Total produced, 900.

Issued June, 1995, by mail order ballot at $195 per portfolio.

Signatures B.W. Fraser - E.A. Evans.

Serial numbers Old coloured polymer $5 EA 93 500101 to EA 93 501000. Recoloured $5 EA 95 500101 to EA 95 501000, overprinted with date of issue "24 April 1995" in red. Both notes in each portfolio had matching numerals.

CB2. Denomination **$10** Total produced, 900.

Issued November, 1993, by mail order ballot at $295 per portfolio.

Signatures Paper note B.W. Fraser - A.C. Cole.
Polymer note B.W. Fraser - E. A. Evans.

Serial numbers Both notes AA 93 000101 - AA 93 001000 in red.
Polymer note overprinted with "1 November 1993" in red. See also, page 303.
Some serial numbers on the paper notes were mismatched. See Error Notes, Chapter 10, and *Rarest of the Rare,* Michael P. Vort-Ronald, *Australian Coin Review*, February, 1994. See Fig. 411.

CB3.

Denomination **$20** Total produced, 900.

Issued November, 1994, by mail order ballot at $350 per portfolio.

Signatures B.W. Fraser - E. A. Evans.

Serial numbers Both notes AA 94 000101 - AA 94 001000 in red.
Polymer note overprinted with “31 October 1994” in red.

Number One portfolio (with serial numbers 000101) was auctioned by Noble Numismatics and the $2,200 proceeds donated by N.P.A. to the Royal Flying Doctor Service. Number 100 portfolio (000200) was also auctioned and $489 donated to the Key Centre for Women’s Health.

Fig. 363. $50 paper note from Last/First portfolio (CB4).

CB4.

Denomination **$50** Total produced, 900.

Issued November, 1995, by mail order ballot at $395 per portfolio.

Signatures B.W. Fraser - E.A. Evans.

Serial numbers Both notes AA 95 00101 - AA 95 001000 in red.
Polymer note overprinted with “4 October 1995” in red.

Number One Portfolio was auctioned by Noble Numismatics and the proceeds of $4,100 donated by N.P.A. to the Point McLeay Community Council (where David Unaipon was born and his people still live). Number 100 was auctioned and $400 donated to the Elsie Women’s Refuge, Sydney.

Fig. 364. $100 Last and First portfolio (CB5).

CB5.

Denomination	**$100** Total produced, 900.
Issued	June, 1996, by mail order ballot at $495 per portfolio.
Signatures	Paper note B.W. Fraser - A.C. Cole. Polymer note B.W. Fraser - E.A. Evans.
Serial numbers	Both notes AA 96 000101 - AA 96 001000 in red. Polymer note overprinted with "15 May 1996" in red.

Number One portfolio was auctioned by Noble Numismatics for $2,700 and the proceeds donated by N.P.A. to the Melba Memorial Conservatorium of Music. Number Two was auctioned for $1,140 and the proceeds donated by N.P.A. to the Museum of Lillydale, Victoria.

Dame Melba was buried at Lilydale. Lillydale was the "old" spelling for the name of the town.

Both the paper notes and the polymer notes used in the $10 to $100 Last and First portfolios had matching red serial numbers in the style used on the polymer notes - the left side number was in "Modern Extended" and the right side "Buch Grotesk". "No. 1" $10 portfolio was auctioned in November, 1994, for $2,200 and again in August, 1999, for $253.

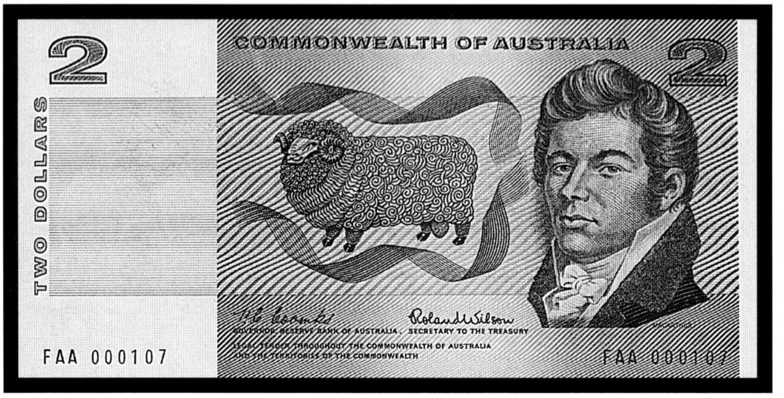

Fig. 365. Front, $2 note, serial number under 1000 - type as used in 25th Anniversary Collection.

Part C: Special N.P.A. Anniversary Collections.

CC1. 25th Anniversary of Decimal Currency Rare Banknote collection.

In 1991, Note Printing Australia released the 25th Anniversary of Decimal Currency Rare Banknote Collection by public tender. A total of 800 sets were sold containing one each of the Ten Shilling, One Pound, Five Pound and Ten Pound notes from the last 1,000 notes printed, the last three digits in the serial numbers matching. The sets also contained one each of the $1, $2, $10 and $20 notes from the first 1,000 decimal notes printed. All notes had matching serial numbers which also matched the end numbers of the pre-decimal notes. Successful bids ranged from $1,864 to $10,664 - the higher the bid, the lower the serial numbers. The total amount tendered was $1,590,340.90.

While the notes were not overprinted or modified in any way, they were matched from Note Printing Australia archival material and are thus unique as sets. They were largely the creation of Alan Flint, N.P.A.s Numismatic Sales Manager (now retired).

The final number of sets was determined by the number of sets with the last three digits matching which could be made up from the 1,000 of each of the notes held. If one note was spoiled or damaged in any way it prevented the other notes with the same last numbers being used. There were no star replacement notes located during the exercise. The lowest numbered set contained notes with serial numbers 000020. Sets were then hand numbered 1 to 800 from the lowest decimal notes to the highest. Two un-numbered sets were retained for archival purposes.

The $2 note illustrated above (and a $1 note 000123 illustrated at Fig. 149) were two of the notes which had been extracted from the 1,000 notes prior to this exercise and thus a set with note numbers 000107 or 000123 was not possible.

The hides from 251 cattle were required for the finely-grained leather chosen for much of the packaging. The finish, known as Brisbane Black, was selected so that a silver embossed title and image of Captain James Cook could be added as appropriate to the 25th (silver) Anniversary. The jewel boxes containing the books were made by Sylvia Shaw & Company of Cowra, N.S.W. and the books of 44 pages were manufactured by Sprintpak Pty. Ltd.

Note designer and engraver Bruce Stewart had recently retired from N.P.A. and many "forgotten" and original note designs from the 1950s were located in his work area. Many of them were included in the album, together with their decimal counterparts, and the text was written by Alan Flint.

Three of the four last serial number prefixes in the pre-decimal notes were only available in these sets.

Fig. 366. 25th Anniversary Collection.

CC2. Triple Anniversary Rare Collector Edition.

In 1994, N.P.A. produced the logical sequel by making 800 sets available with the three decimal notes not issued in the original anniversary collection - the $5 issued in 1967, $50 in 1973 and $100 in 1984. The three denominations were issued in matching numbered sets in a similar fashion to the previous sets, and again sold by public tender. Not all of those sets had the same numbers as the former sets. The average tender was $1,527.61.

Reference and further reading: *An Heirloom and an Investment Without Parallel,* Michael Vort-Ronald, *Australian Coin Review*, December, 1998 - January, 1999.

Fig. 367. Back, $20 note, Lawrence Hargrave Centenary overprint (CD1a).

CD1.

Special event	To commemorate the centenary of Hargrave's flight experiments. Joint Issue with Australia Post containing a special pane of stamps.
Denomination	$20.
Signatures	B.W. Fraser - E.A. Evans.
Serial numbers	Serial number prefix ADK (last prefix).
Special features	Overprinted with "Lawrence Hargrave Centenary Portfolio (number)". Overprinted (a) number 0001 - 1000 in red, and (b) 1001 - 5000 in black.
Issued	19 November, 1994, by Note Printing Australia at the Sydney Coin Fair, 250 red overprinted at $175 per portfolio and 250 by mail order. Australia Post, 500 by mail order ballot. 19 November, 1994, by Note Printing Australia at the Sydney Coin Fair, 1,250 black overprinted at $95 per portfolio, and 750 by mail order. Australia Post 2,000 at selected post offices and by mail order. Total produced, 1,000 red overprinted notes and 4,000 black overprinted notes.

Number One portfolio was auctioned by Noble Numismatics in November, 1994, and the $1,793 proceeds donated by N.P.A. to the Powerhouse Museum for restoration work on Hargrave's remaining kites. It was resold by auction in March, 2000, for $690.

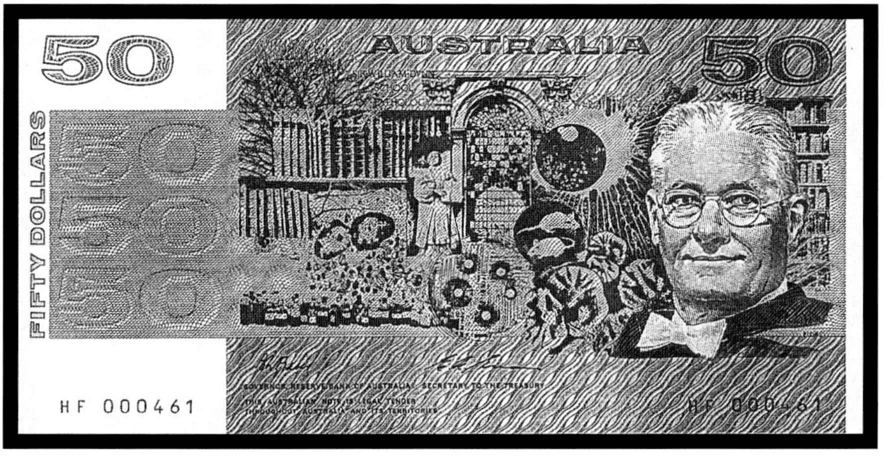

Fig. 368. Front $50 note, Howard Florey commemorative with special prefix (CD2).

CD2.

Special event	50th anniversary of Lord Howard Florey's Nobel Prize.
Denomination	$50. Total produced, 1,000 red numbered and 2,500 black numbered.
Signatures	B.W. Fraser - E.A. Evans.
Serial numbers	HF 000001 - HF 001000 (red), HF 001001 - HF 003500 (black).
Special feature	Serial numbers in red or black on the note with prefix HF (for Howard Florey), and a special pane of stamps. Joint issue with Australia Post.
Issued	500 by special ballot on 6 November, 1995, by Australia Post at $199 per portfolio with red serial numbers, and 500 by post and dealer allocation by Note Printing Australia in November, 1995. Limit one per customer. 2,500 black numbered notes at $129 per portfolio, 1,250 by N.P.A. and 1,250 by Australia Post in blocks of 100, limit two per customer.

Number One portfolio was presented at the launch of the portfolio in Adelaide on 3 November, 1995, at the South Australian Museum. See Fig. 316. The portfolio was auctioned by Noble Numismatics on 24 November, 1995 and the $2,400 proceeds donated by N.P.A. to the Florey Research Fund. Further reading: *The Florey Portfolio Launch* (by Michael Vort-Ronald) *Australian Coin Review,* November, 1995.

Note number HF 000461 illustrated above is a note specially numbered to replace a damaged note from a Florey portfolio. At the time of the launch, Florey's children, Dr. Paquita McMichael and Professor Charles Florey, lived in Scotland. Lord Florey is honoured by a memorial plaque adjacent to that of naturalist Charles Darwin in Westminster Abbey.

Fig. 369. Overprinted $20 note from Sir Charles Kingsford Smith Centenary Portfolio (CD3).

CD3.

Special event Centenary of the birth of Sir Charles Kingsford Smith.

Denomination $20. Total produced, 4,000.

Signatures B.W. Fraser - E.A. Evans.

Serial numbers Last $20 prefix letters ADK.

Special features Vertical red overprint on the right side of the front of the note "Sir Charles Kingsford Smith Centenary". Joint issue with the Royal Australian Mint containing a special Kingsford Smith $1 silver proof coin.

Issued May, 1997, by mail order or dealer allocation at $129 per portfolio. N.P.A. and R.A.M. shared allocations in blocks of 100 e.g. N.P.A. 000001 - 000100, R.A.M. 000101 - 000200 etc. The R.A.M. sent invitations to their mail order customers to apply for a portfolio from the 1,500 available. The actual allocation was then decided by random selection.

Number One portfolio was auctioned by Noble Numismatics and the $1,150 proceeds donated by N.P.A. to the Sudden Infant Death Foundation.

Sir Charles Kingsford Smith's aircraft the *Southern Cross* is permanently on display at Brisbane's Eagle Farm Airport and is sometimes confused with the Vickers Vimy aircraft which is on public display at the Adelaide Airport. The Vickers Vimy G-EAOU in Adelaide was flown by South Australian brothers Sir Keith and Sir Ross Smith and crew from England to Australia in late 1919, the first aviators to perform the feat.

Part E: Miscellaneous Issues.

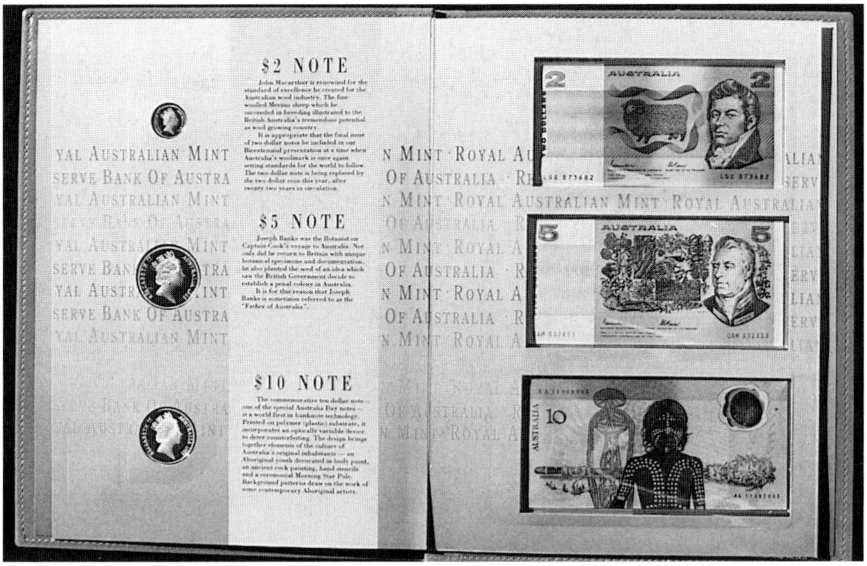

Fig. 370. 1988 Bicentennial Coin & Note Collection (CE1a).

CE1

Special event 1988 Bicentennial Coin & Note Collection.

Special features Joint issue by the Royal Australian Mint and Reserve Bank of Australia (Note Printing Australia). Proof $2, $5 and $10 coins, $2 and $5 paper notes and the dated polymer $10 Bicentenary note.

Signatures All notes had the facsimile signatures of R.A. Johnston and B.W. Fraser.

Proof coins $2, 1988 designed by Horst Hahne, $5 new Parliament House, and Bicentenary silver $10, both designed by Stuart Devlin.

Serial numbers $2 with final prefix LQG.
$5 Gothic serial numbering QAH 000001 - QAH 025000.
The serial number of the $5 note was the number of the set.
$10 polymer Bicentenary, AA (dated) issue.

Issued (a) Melbourne International Coin Fair 16 & 17 July, 1988, 4,980 (QAH 000020 - QAH 005000) were sold at $120 each with a coin fair ribbon and "Royal Australian Mint" on the bottom of the slip-case at the front. The first 20 were archived or presented to V.I.P.s.

(b) 20,000 (QAH 005001 - QAH 025000) were sold by mail order at $120 each, plus post. These did not have ribbons, and had "Royal Australian Mint" and "Reserve Bank of Australia" at the bottom of the slip-case.

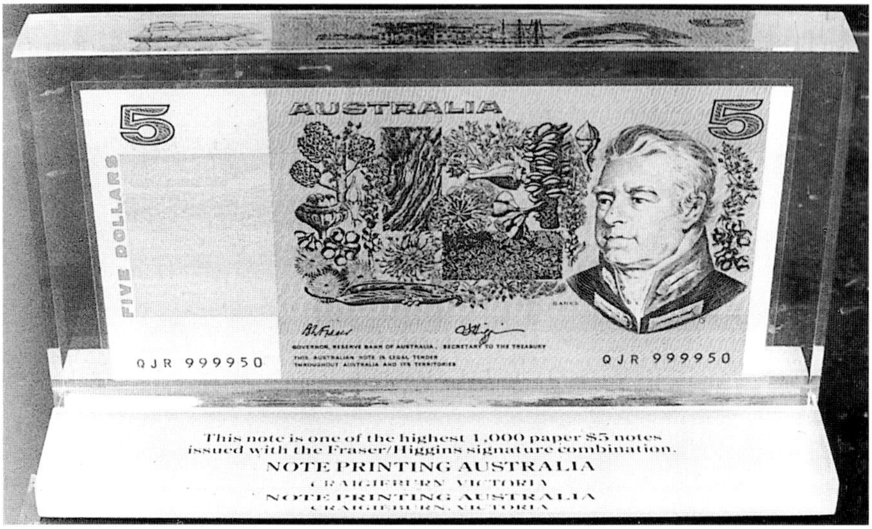

Fig. 371. $5 note in perspex - Fraser-Higgins (CE2).

CE2.

Special event One of the highest 1,000 numbered Fraser-Higgins $5 notes.

Special features $5 note officially sealed in perspex.

Signatures B.W. Fraser - C.I. Higgins.

Serial numbers In the range of QJR 000001 - QJR 999999. Issued 999.

Issued October, 1991, by mail order at $67.50 each, plus postage.

It was anticipated that these notes would be the last of the paper $5 with the issue of the new polymer notes expected around April, 1991. The notes were encapsulated in perspex with an inscription to that effect and were intended for release at the Hobart Coin Fair.

When it was realised that a further printing of paper $5 notes with Fraser-Cole signatures would be necessary because of production problems with the polymer $5 note, the product was withdrawn and uncut $10 Fraser-Cole pairs issued at the coin fair instead.

Later, the original inscription was cut off the bottom of the perspex block and a new base fitted with the inscription:

This note is one of the highest 1,000 paper $5 notes issued with the Fraser-Higgins signature combination. NOTE PRINTING AUSTRALIA / Craigieburn, Victoria.

Note Printing Australia also produced the 1988 Bicentenary dated polymer $10 note in three variations of the perspex sizes. Other notes were privately produced in perspex, but those issues are separately numbered.

CE3.

Special event — $2 notes from the final printing to commemorate the replacement of the $2 note by a coin.

Special features — None - issued in a green coloured folder using notes originally intended for general circulation.

Signatures — R.A. Johnston - B.W. Fraser.

Serial numbers — At random from the final print run, LNG to LQG (last prefix).

Issued

(a) 1988 through branches of the Reserve Bank of Australia or by mail order at $4.50 per folder, plus post.

500 specially overprinted folders were released at each coin fair listed below, at $8 each:

(b) 11 & 12 May, 1991, Hobart.
(c) 13 & 14 July, 1991, Melbourne.
(d) 16 & 17 November, 1991, Sydney, LQG (final) prefixes.
(e) 5 & 6 September, 1992, Adelaide.
(f) 8 & 9 May, 1993, Brisbane.
(g) 20 & 21 August, 1994, Perth.

Special "First day of issue" folders were produced for the introduction of the polymer notes:

CE4.

(a)	$10	1988	Single polymer note with overprinted date "26 JANUARY 1988", AA prefixes sold at $14 (general circulation notes had AB prefixes). Johnston-Fraser signatures. Total printed approximately 800,000.
(b)	$5	1992	Paper note from final print run and polymer note overprinted "7 JULY 1992" in purple. The folder sold for $19, or $20 with embossed first day of issue on the cover. Fraser-Cole signatures. Note Printing Australia staff were presented with a personal $5 new note at a special function on 7 July, in recognition of the successful result of the new product, the first of the NNS (New Note Series) polymer notes.
(c)	$10	1993	Paper note from final print run with polymer note overprinted with "1 NOVEMBER 1993" and date in purple, sold for $36 per folder. A similar folder with paper final prefix MRR and black numbers and date sold for $49 (illustrated next page). Paper note, Fraser-Cole signatures, polymer note, Fraser-Evans signatures. Total black dated folders, 9,000.
(d)	$20	1994	Paper note with final prefix ADK and polymer note overprinted with "31 OCTOBER 1994" sold for $69, or a single dated polymer note for $36. Paper note and polymer note, Fraser-Evans signatures. 5,000 double note folders and 25,000 single dated polymer note folders were issued.

(e) $50 1995 Paper note with final prefix FAB and polymer note overprinted with "4 OCTOBER 1995" sold for $129, or a single dated polymer note for $66. Paper note and polymer note, Fraser-Evans signatures. A total of 3,500 double note folders and 7,000 single note folders were issued.

(f) $100 1996 Paper note with final prefix ZLD and polymer note overprinted with "15 MAY 1996" sold for $240, or a single dated polymer note for $120. Paper note, Fraser-Cole signatures, polymer note, Fraser-Evans signatures. A total of 2,000 double note folders and 3,000 single note folders were issued.

Fig. 372. $10 first day of issue folder, black date and numbers on polymer note (CE4c).

Further reading: Articles in the *Australian Coin Review:*
A new Banknote Series is Born, Michael Vort-Ronald and Jolyon Sykes, July, 1992;
A New Note Series is Born, Michael Vort-Ronald, November 1993;
$10 Banknote Issues, November, 1993; Michael Vort-Ronald;
Red & Black & Purple & Blue .....& My View, Klaus Ford; December, 1993.
Further articles by Michael Vort-Ronald, *A New Note Series is Born - Part II,* January, 1994;
N.P.A. Collector Folders, December, 1994; *The Florey Portfolio Launch,* November, 1995.

Chapter 10: PRINTING ERRORS

There are four main stages of note production:

(1) Background (Simultan) printing on both sides at the same time.
(2) Main (Intaglio) printing, on the backs, and then on the fronts.
(3) Serial numbering.
(4) Guillotining into individual notes.

Printing errors are set out in that general order:

(1) Background (Simultan) printing errors.
  (a) No background print
  (b) Fadeout of background print
  (c) Obstructions to background print
  (d) Set off or wet ink transfer

(2) Main (intaglio) printing errors.
  (a) No main printing
  (b) Fadeout or ink starvation
  (c) Print obstructions
  (d) Set off or wet ink transfer
  (e) Ink smudging

(3) Serial numbering errors.
  (a) No serial numbers
  (b) One serial number
  (c) Mismatched numbers
  (d) Missing digits
  (e) Inverted serial numbers
  (f) Numbers on the wrong side (back)
  (g) Identical serial numbers

(4) Folding errors.
  (a) Corner folds
  (b) Corner flaps
  (c) Tear flaps

(5) Miscellaneous errors.
  (a) Registration shifts
  (b) Creasing
  (c) Inverted paper (watermarks)
  (d) Metal thread missing or duplicated
  (e) Repairs during printing
  (f) Printing plate faults

ALL NOTES DESCRIBED OR ILLUSTRATED WERE LOCATED IN CIRCULATION OR IN BANKS INTENDED FOR CIRCULATION.

There are three main circumstances in which error notes reach circulation, plus a fourth (unconfirmed) reason.

- A The error was not detected during inspection.
- B The error was detected, but not error marked.
- C The error was marked, but not detected during electronic counting.
- D Unfinished notes misappropriated during production (unconfirmed).

When printing errors were located, there were two different types of marking the notes for later withdrawal.

- (a) First type error marking - large purple inverted tick.
  See next illustration and also, Figs. 376 and 393.
- (b) Second type error marking - vertical orange line.
  See illustration below and Figs. 385, 395, 404, 421, 430.

Fig. 373. First type decimal error marking.

Fig. 374. Second type decimal error marking.

Printing errors on currency notes are not uncommon. All types of printing produces "spoils", and notes are no exception. The chance of a note becoming spoiled during note production is more likely because the same sheet of paper is printed upon separately four times, which increases the chances of an error occurring anywhere on any one piece of note paper. No matter how much care is taken or how modern the equipment, spoils always have, and probably always will, occur.

On average a rate of two to four per cent spoilage can occur during note printing. Probably 99% of those are located and do not reach circulation. Possibly one per cent of 100 to 200 million notes could still mean a lot of spoils can reach circulation, but up to 98% of those could be considered of a minor nature and within tolerance and acceptable for issue. Nevertheless, a considerable amount of "errors" are still located, but when divided among a population of say, 20 million, it is understandable that the finders of such notes can believe that their "find" is rare. Rarity depends on the nature and extent of the error, the numbers of such notes in circulation, and the condition of the notes.

Fig. 375. Note examiners at work. About 2,000 sheets per shift are checked.

The inspection of notes took place in a separate area of Note Printing Australia (formerly the Reserve Bank of Australia's Note Printing Branch). The section could employ 40 people or more (mostly women) who were responsible for the final quality control. Each person was issued with a ream of 500 sheets of notes at a time, and about four reams were checked for faults and imperfections by each person during a shift. Any spoils found were marked with a felt pen in the manner shown in the two previous note illustrations. The ink in these pens was made on site.

The first type error marking (large inverted purple tick - Fig. 373) was designed to be easily located after the notes were guillotined, by checkers who fanned a section of notes like the pages of a soft-covered book, and substituted a star replacement note for the faulty note withdrawn. See Fig.339.

The second type error marking (vertical orange line) was to facilitate withdrawal during electronic counting. Many of the error notes illustrated have either of these two types of marks. Where a faulty note with one of these markings has reached circulation, it could be that the shelf-life of the machine readable ink failed and the note so marked was therefore not detected. See Fig. 374.

The first decimal errors to be located were reported in the Adelaide *News* of 16 February, 1966, two days after the release of the new decimal notes. Coombs-Wilson $2 notes were discovered in the King William Street branch of the Commonwealth Savings Bank with the "A" of "BANK" missing in the signature title of H.C. Coombs. It is believed 80 went into circulation before bank staff discovered the error, and the remainder was purchased by bank staff. Two such notes bore serial numbers FCJ 290448 and 9. A similar error has been observed in a Coombs-Wilson $2 note (FCH 408097) where the top portion of the "B" in "BANK" was missing.

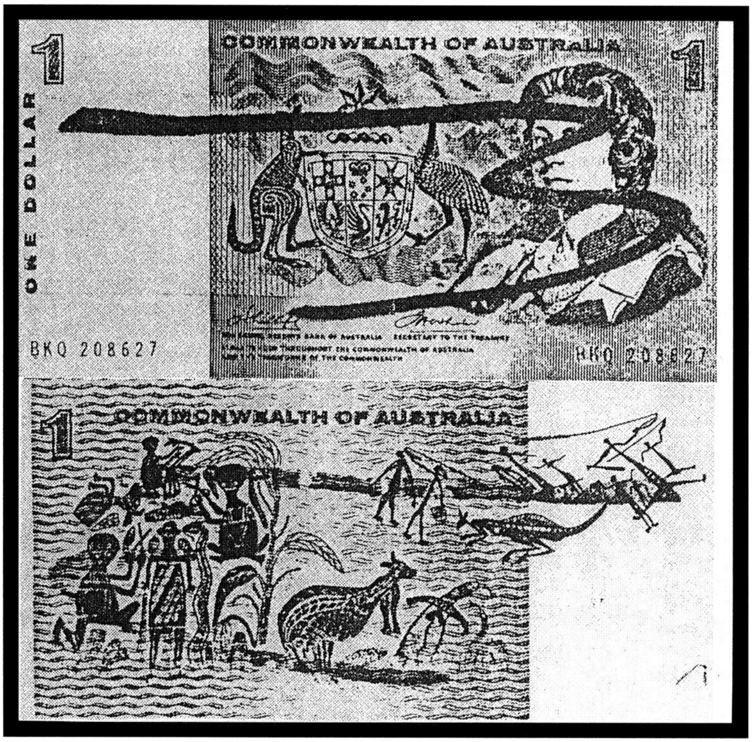

Fig. 376. A note examiner's mark which has soaked through the note.

The illustration above, from *Australian Coin Review,* December, 1984, shows a variation to the checker's mark which was applied because of the fadeout at the bottom on the back of the note.

Collectors and researchers benefit from misprinted notes reaching circulation because it helps to explain the various printing processes and better illustrates the components of the designs.

BACKGROUND SIMULTANEOUS (SIMULTAN) PROCESS PRINTING ERRORS

Missing printing phase (no multicoloured background print).

Fig. 377. Front, no background (Simultan) printing.

Fig. 378. Back, no background (Simultan) printing.

A possible cause for this type of error is two sheets sticking together through the offset printing press. Several "pigeon pairs" as illustrated above were located, and are included in the listings of known "missing printing phase" notes on the next page. Examples of the same type of error in other denominations have been included in the main sections for those notes to illustrate the actual printing phases described. In some cases, a very large corner fold or paper obstruction can be the cause. Further reading: *Twin Dogs and Pigeon Pairs,* Michael Vort-Ronald, *Australian Coin Review,* February, 1992. Two dollar notes (illustrated at Figs. 166 and 174) located without the Simultan (background) printing could also indicate that the sheet missed the Simultan printing stage (on both sides) altogether.

The following decimal paper notes have been observed **missing the Simultan printing** (on one side only, unless indicated otherwise). As the error is usually a sheet fault, there is a potential for there to be anywhere from 24 to 45 notes of the same error with the same serial numerals, but different serial letter prefixes. For that reason, the list is set out by numeral order.

$1	Phillips-Wheeler (Australia)	Back	021768	BQY, BRA, BRB, BRJ, BRN, BRQ, BRV, BSA.
$2	Johnston-Fraser	Front and back	928654	KUB (Figs. 166, 174), KUK, KUR. KUN had traces of yellow at the bottom.
$2	Phillips-Wheeler	Front	999976	(folding error)
$2	Johnston-Stone	Back	420859	KPQ (no print at all).
$2	Johnston-Fraser	Back	180369	KTA, KTE, KTL, KTN.
			200918	KYA.
			720103	KXC, KXD, KXH, KXD, KYH, KYK.
			928654	KUB.
$5	Knight-Wheeler	Back	477955	
$5	Johnston-Stone	Back	059731	PHE
			176295	PHC, PHG.
$5	Johnston-Fraser	Front	057131	PNS, PPL.
$5	Johnston-Fraser	Back	057131	PPV, PHE.
			629032	PQL, PQN.
$5	Fraser-Higgins	Front	185301	QFD, QFE (both sides).
			185302	QFD, QFE, QFG, QFH (both sides).
			198532	QDF, QDK, QDL, QDN, QDP, QDQ, QDR, QDT, QDU, QDV.
$5	Fraser-Higgins	Back	028506-7-8-9-0-1	QDG
			198533	QDK, QDL, QDN, QDQ, QDR, QDV.
			347285	QFD, QFE, QFF, QFG, QFL, QFP, QFU, QFV, QGE, QGF, QGL, QGU.
$10	Johnston-Fraser	Back	309968	UFU, UGC, UGP, UHB, UHH, UHL.
			992053	UFU, UFY, UGB, UGF, UGJ, UGV,UVX, UVY.
$10	Fraser-Cole	Back	058885	MND, MNE, MNL, MNV, MNZ, MPA, MPB, MPC, MPJ, MPN, MPU, MPV.
			149434	MKR, MND, MNE.
			309968	UGC, UGP, UHJ, UHL.
			992053	UGB, UGF, UGJ, UGX, UHJ, UHL.

No Simultan printing - continued.

$20	Fraser-Higgins	Back	627594	RGF, RGG, RGJ, RGS, RGT.
$20	Fraser-Higgins	Front and back		Surfers Paradise auction, September 1998, Lot 432, serial numbers not stated.
$50	Fraser-Higgins	Back	139350	YZX.
			740702	WAN, WAP, WAT, WBE, WBJ, WBK.
$100	Johnston-Stone	Front	508595	ZAC, ZAD, ZAR, ZAY.
$100	Johnston-Fraser	Front	032283	ZDD.
			165353	ZFF.
			750543	ZER, ZES, ZFF, ZFU, ZNF.
$100	Fraser-Higgins	Front	336921	ZFS.
			750543	ZER, ZES.

Fadeout of background print.

Fig. 379. Fadeout of Simultan print at top.

The $20 note illustrated above has a 2 mm wide fadeout of the background design at the top of the note on the front and a faint fadeout in the same area on the back. This type of fault is possibly due to a low ink level in the duct or reservoir. Notes observed:

$20	Johnston-Stone	VKY 960187, 960195, 960199, 962738.
		VNP 886056 (different gradual fadeout on top third).

Other notes with larger areas of background (Simultan) fadeout observed:

$1	Knight-Stone	Front	CZH 463298.

Larger areas of simultan fadeout - continued.

$2	Johnston-Fraser	Front and back	JUN 928654.
$10	Johnston-Fraser	Back	UHP 373792.
$20	Johnston-Stone	Front	VNP 886056.
$20	Johnston-Fraser	Back	EFN 640507.
$100	Johnston-Fraser	Front (no signatures)	ZBJ 856753.

Fig. 380a. Front, $100 note, Simultan printed signatures and titles missing.

Fig. 380b. Front, $100 note showing Intaglio fadeout with Simultan printed signatures and titles remaining.

Fig. 381. Obstructions to background Simultan printing.

Obstructions to background printing

The two notes illustrated above have large white angular sections of unprinted areas possibly caused by large pieces of paper lodging on the sheets prior to the printing of the background stage or a folded sheet occurring within a ream, either from the note paper maker or when the paper was counted "in house" for accountability before printing of the background stage was commenced. The sheet may have become unfolded, or the foreign matter dislodged which allowed the main design to be printed over the blank spaces.

Fig. 382. Paper obstruction to Simultan and Intaglio printing.

The note illustrated above had a piece of paper (or tape) lodged on the paper prior to both main printing phases, firstly the background (Simultan) printing, and later the main (Intaglio) printing. The piece of paper later dislodged and left a white unprinted portion underneath.

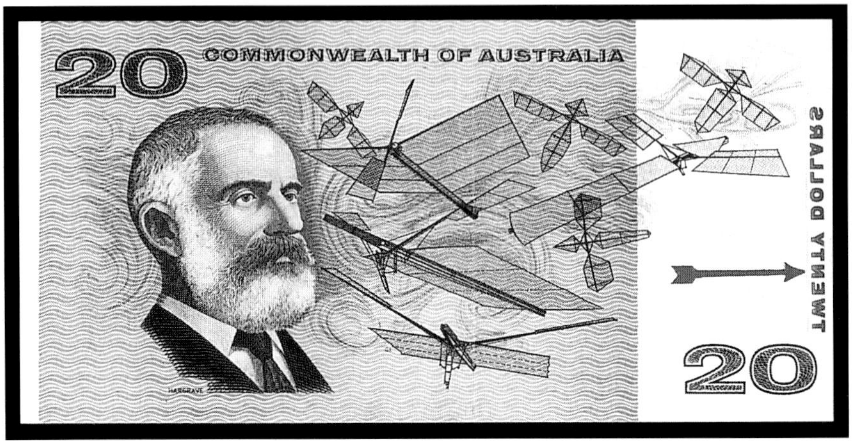

Fig. 383. Inverted background printing (set off) on a portion of a $20 note.

Set off or wet ink transfer of background printing.

The note illustrated above shows an inverted "TWENTY DOLLARS" which gives an initial appearance of having soaked through from the other side of the note. However, the inks used for the background design are quick drying and the paper is of sufficient quality to prevent the ink from soaking through. One explanation might be that the ink transferred onto a roller and back during a run through the Simultan machine. Notes observed:

$20 Phillips-Wheeler (Commonwealth)	XFR 002443
$20 Phillips-Wheeler (Australia)	XKL 659045, 659046.

A Johnston-Fraser $20 (VRR 6629973) has also been observed as below, with the background design of the front set off on the back of the note and later printed normally, giving a rich red appearance to the note. Only one note has been observed, although it would have been a sheet fault.

Fig. 384. Back, $20 with full Simultan set-off (reversed printing).

MAIN PRINT (INTAGLIO) PRINTING ERRORS

Missing printing phase (no raised printing).

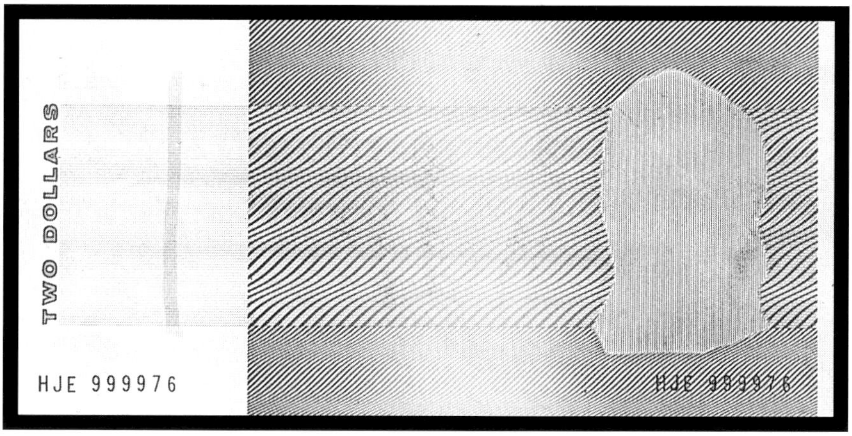

Fig. 385. Front, $2 note without Intaglio printing.

Fig. 386. Back, $20 note without Intaglio printing.

Notes which reach circulation without any raised (intaglio) printing on one side (or occasionally on both sides) are usually a sheet fault due to two sheets sticking together through the press or a blocked ink duct. The $2 note illustrated above is the result of a folding error where a large corner has folded over and the inside of the fold missed the printing phase. See also, folds and flaps. Examples of missing printing phases in other denominations have been included in the main circulating note sections to illustrate the actual printing phases described.

The following decimal paper notes have been observed **missing the Intaglio printing** (on one side only, unless indicated otherwise). As the error is usually a sheet fault, there is a potential for there to be anywhere from 24 to 45 notes (depending on sheet content) of the same error with the same serial numerals, but different serial letter prefixes. For that reason, the list is set out in numerals order.

$2	Phillips-Wheeler (Australia)	Front	999976	HJE (illustrated - folding error).
$2	Johnston-Stone	Back	288364	KJJ, KJP, KJQ, KJV, KJX.
			420859	KPP, KPQ, KQF.
			420860	KQF.
			420861	KQF.
			826564	KNC.
			921747	KBN.
$5	Knight-Wheeler		477955	prefix not stated
$5	Johnston-Stone	Front	438756	PLL, PLJ, PND, PNE.
			495291	PKB, PKK, PKG, PKL, PKT, PLG.
		Back	059731	PHT.
			059783	PHE.
			106945	PJJ.
			176295	PHG, PHP, PJC.
			560601	PJF, PJG, PJQ, PJV.
			928170	PPC.
$5	Johnston-Fraser (OCR-B)	Front	438756	PLJ, PLL, PLZ, PND, PNE.
		Back	928170	PPC.
$10	Fraser-Higgins	Back	959168	MGS.
$10	Fraser-Cole	Front	149434	MKH, MKK, MKU.
		Back	058885	MPB.
$20	Knight-Stone	Back	079047	VGQ, VGX.
$20	Johnston-Stone	Back	802410	VFX, VGB.
$20	Fraser-Higgins	Front	953530	RDS, RDU, RDX, RDZ.
		Back	927168	RDR.
$20	Fraser-Evans	Front	633947	ABH (very faint).
$50	Knight-Wheeler	Front	783347	YAX. (See fig. 297).
$50	Fraser-Cole	Front	885726	WFT (70%).
		Back	071388	WFJ, WFK.
			071583	WFJ.

Missing intaglio printing phase - continued -

$100	Johnston-Stone	Back	865230 ZBH.
			866043 ZBB.
$100	Johnston-Fraser	Front	165353 ZFF.
$100	Fraser-Cole	Back	014247 ZHG, ZHS.

Fig. 387. Front, Intaglio fadeout - omitting signatures.

Intaglio fadeouts.

The typical fadeout occurs at the bottom of the note with an uneven edge to the printing. The fadeout can range from 10% to 60% of the intaglio print missing and is possibly due to a starvation of ink at the end of the sheet, or something on the paper which prevented the ink from adhering. Where this type of fault occurs on the front of notes from $1 to $50, the signatures and legal tender clause are omitted because they were initially part of the intaglio print. Signatures on the $100 are part of the background (Simultan) design. Notes observed with intaglio fadeout are as follows:

$1	Phillips-Wheeler (Commonwealth)	Front	551365 BEV.
			902441 BEE.
		Back	208627 BKQ.
			832124 BKK.
			906003 BKJ.
$1	Knight-Wheeler	Front	979967 CEC.
$1	Johnston-Stone	Front	435029 DGZ.
$2	Johnston-Fraser	Back	119276 KTH.
			987313 KSD.

Fig. 388. Back, $5 fadeout of Intaglio printing.

Intaglio ink fadeouts - continued.

$5	Phillips-Wheeler (Commonwealth)	Back	471524 NJK.
$5	Knight-Wheeler	Back	713770 NUP.
$5	Johnston-Stone	Front	482781 PEV.
		Back	106945 PJH.
			768929 PHG.
$5	Johnston-Fraser	Front	970140 PHV, PJC.
		Back	028505 QDF, QDH.
			028506 QDF.
			028507 QDF.
			028508 QDF, QDH.
			028512 QDJ.
			028521 QDG, QDH.
			028524 QDG, QDH.
			028525 QDG, QDJ.
			028527 - 31 QDJ.
			028523 - 35 QDG, QDH, QDJ.
			766356 PNC.
			946080 PJC.
$10	Knight-Stone	Back	511263 TXT.
			813692 TVK.
$10	Johnston-Fraser	Front and back	245690 UGV.
		Back	071120 UDY.

Intaglio ink fadeouts continued.

$20	Knight-Wheeler	Front	511263 XTC. 529866 XSU.
$20	Knight-Stone	Back	101563 VES. 235962 VED. 381837 VFF. 759487 VEK. 820838 VFU.
$20	Johnston-Stone	Front and back Back	886056 VNP. 207639 VKH. 709772 VLZ.
$20	Phillips-Fraser	Back	454152 EXV.
$20	Fraser-Cole	Front	129273 RRL.
$50	Phillips-Wheeler (Australia)	Back	411454 YAF.
$50	Knight-Wheeler	Front	138136 YLB. 967962 YLB.
$50	Knight-Stone	Back	814324 YGN.
$50	Johnston-Stone	Front	074905 YJZ. 117031 YKU, YLB. 138136 YLB. 144542 YLQ. 182577 YHQ, YJD. 426637 YKU. 511303 YJZ (Fig. 387). 529494 YKN. 571267 YJD. 606481 YJZ. 688668 YLH. 695084 YLQ. 746749 YKV. 967962 YLB.
		Back	287588 YJZ, YKF. 550105 YJK. 819253 YNS. 899292 YNK. 952601 YNS.

Intaglio ink fadeouts continued.

$50	Johnston-Fraser	Front	695084	YLQ.
		Back	096607	YQJ.
$50	Fraser-Higgins	Front	707586	YZZ.
		Back	139350	WAF.
			606378	WAE.
			606379	WAE.
$50	Fraser-Cole	Back	975128	WJR.
$50	Fraser-Evans	Back	555503	WUJ.
$100	Johnston-Stone	Front	055671	ZAU.
			595026	ZAU.
			668878	ZBB.
			712023	ZAN.
			740393	ZAU, ZBB.
			842699	ZAG.
			857753	ZBJ.
$100	Johnston-Stone	Back	055670	ZAU, ZAV.
			287588	YJZ.
			413702	ZBB.
			892748	ZDF.
$100	Johnston-Fraser	Back	007373	ZDF.

Print obstructions - mostly to main (Intaglio) printing.

Fig. 389. $5 with paper obstruction to Intaglio printing.

Print obstructions - continued.

Fig. 390. $5 with tape obstruction to Intaglio printing.

Fig. 391. $10 with cotton obstruction to Intaglio printing.

Fig. 392. $20 with blotchy areas in Intaglio design - substance on paper preventing adherence.

Print obstructions - continued.

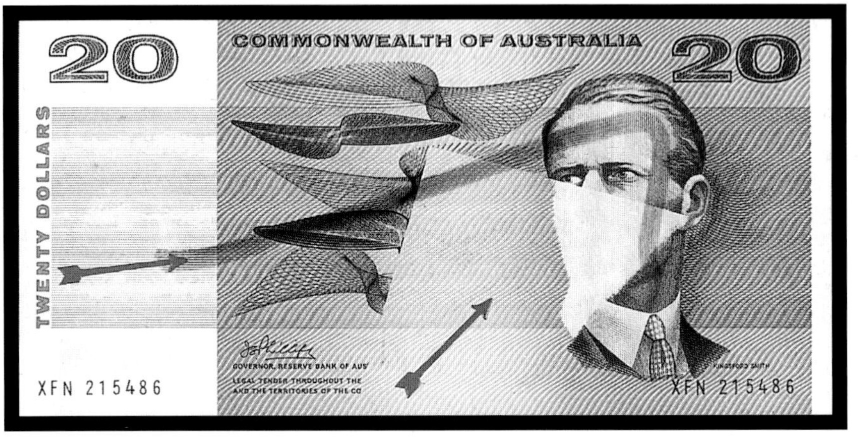

Fig. 393. $20 with paper obstruction to Intaglio printing, error marked.

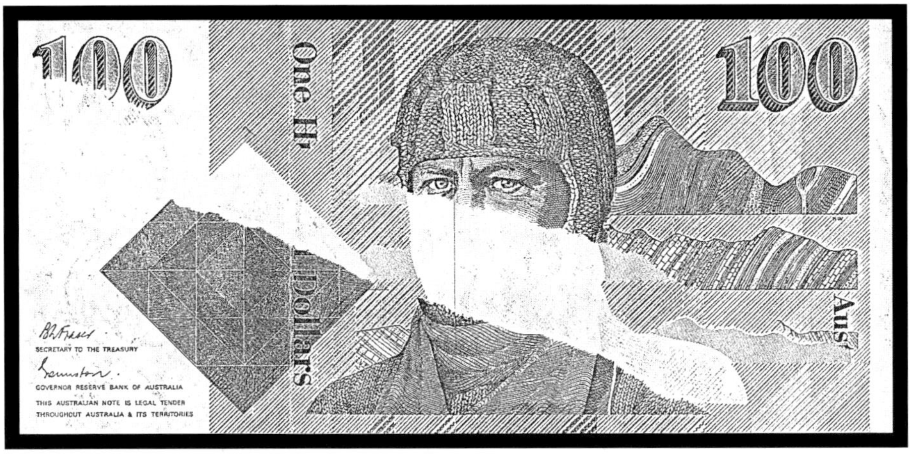

Fig. 394. $100 with obstruction to Intaglio printing.

Ink faults.

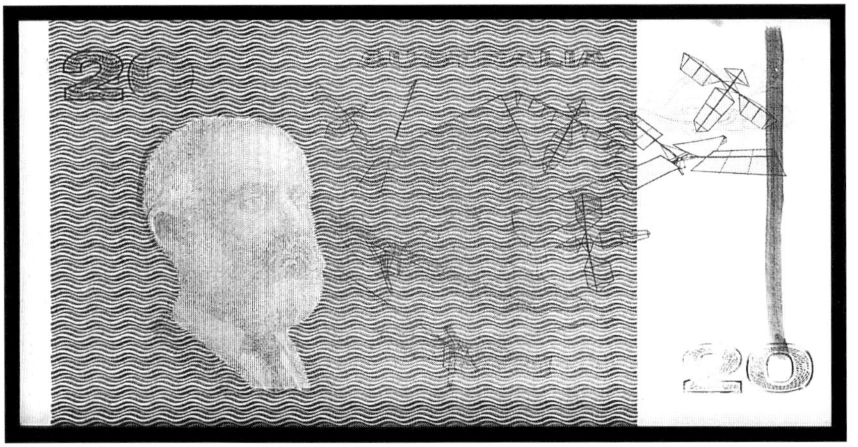

Fig. 395. $20 with faint Intaglio printing - error marked.

Ink faults continued.

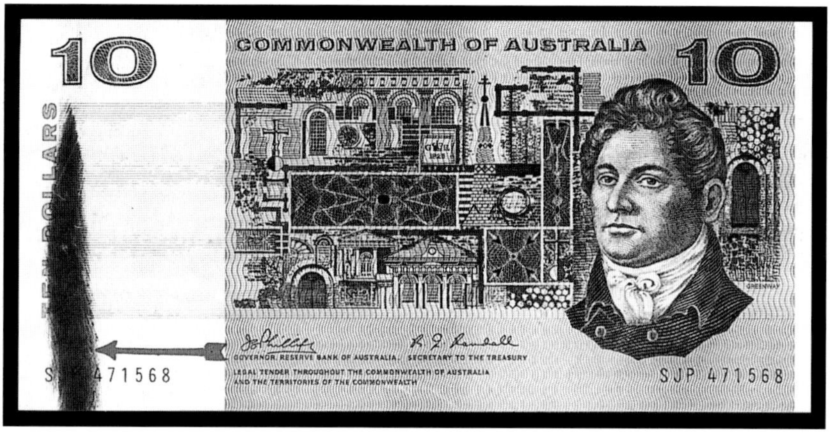

Fig. 396. $10 with large ink smudge.

Fig. 397. $50 note with large cotton-waste ink blob on forehead of Florey.

Fig. 398. $50 with major ink spill/smudge.

Set-off or wet ink transfer of Intaglio ink.

The Intaglio process uses a heavy butter-like ink which fills the printing plate "graves" by covering the whole plate with ink. The surplus ink is then wiped from the surface of the printing plate and the notes in sheet form are printed at great speed under tonnes of pressure, forcing the paper into the recesses of the plate to receive a raised-up ink image on the paper in varying thicknesses as the printed design. This is considered a security feature, as the raised design can be felt with the fingers, easily distinguishing genuine notes from those illegally printed by the offset process or photocopied note facsimiles.

Fig. 399. Common set off errors - inverted denomination figures.

Fig. 400. $1 and $50 with set offs at the bottom, from the backs of other notes.

Because of the thickness of the Intaglio ink, it remained wet for a considerable time. Before the development of quick-drying inks, "tissues" (or "blankets") were placed between the sheets to prevent set off. See Fig. 79. If the sheet was absent, or folded over, a set off or wet ink transfer error note could occur on the next sheet. Backs were printed first, then the fronts. Set off was usually confined to one side only. Depending on how dry the ink was at the time it came into contact with the back of another sheet, a faint or full transfer could occur. The most common set off error was a single inverted denomination figure, probably caused by a corner of a "tissue" or an actual sheet folding over during handling. See fig. 399.

The perfect registration of the printing can give the impression that the ink has soaked through the paper, but that is not the case. Before quick-drying inks, this type of error was quite common, particularly with a single inverted denomination figure on the top right of the back.

Fig. 401. Set off error - full faint ink transfer.

Fig. 402. Set off error, full wet ink transfer.

SERIAL NUMBER ERRORS

No serial numbers.

Four types of "no serial number" notes have been located in circulation.

A. No numbers at all.
B. No machine numbers, with a large six-digit number stamped on the note by hand.
C. No numbers on the front, with numbers on diagonally on the back resulting from a corner fold.
D. No machine numbers, with a number written on with ball point pen.

Fig. 403. $2 without serial numbers.

Notes observed without serial numbers: (Type A).

$1	Knight-Stone.	
$2	Phillips-Wheeler (Australia)	located between new notes HDR 690906 and HDR 690909, illustrated above.
$2	Knight-Wheeler, Knight-Stone, Johnston-Stone.	
$5	Knight-Stone.	
$10	Coombs-Wilson, Johnston-Stone.	
$20	Coombs-Wilson, Fraser-Higgins, Fraser-Cole, Johnston-Fraser.	
$50	Fraser-Higgins, Fraser-Cole.	
$100	Johnston-Fraser.	

Some of the above may have been insufficiently described in auctions, and apply to another category.

The next type occurs when a sheet of notes fails to receive numbers at all. It is not practical to separately number the sheet and place it back in the ream of sheets, so a note examiner applied a large six-digit hand stamped number to each note on the sheet not printed with its actual number. The number is that which would have been on the notes in the sheet, but without a prefix. When electronically counted, the number of each note withdrawn would register between other notes, indicating the prefix.

Fig. 404. $5 with no machine serial numbers, number hand-stamped.

No serial numbers - hand stamped numbers - notes observed:

$2	Knight-Stone	169674
$2	Johnston-Fraser	781315
$5	Knight-Wheeler	356382, 356440, 356454, 466109, 466124 (NTZ), 477955.
$5	Knight-Stone	562555
$5	Johnston-Fraser	510081
$10	Johnston-Fraser	455061, 455062.
$20	Knight-Wheeler	195221
$50	Johnston-Stone	598906
$50	Fraser-Higgins	756920

Where one note without printed serial numbers is located, it is likely that there could be from 24 to 45 other notes from the same sheet also without proper serial numbers. These would not necessarily be found together after guillotining, but be distributed with other prefixes due to the method of numbering.

Fig. 405. Serial numbers on the back due to folding error.

No serial numbers observed - numbers or part numbers on the back from a folding error.

\$5	Knight-Wheeler	NTJ 743918
\$5	Fraser-Higgins	??C/QFL/QFK/QFB 980531 (illustrated above).
\$10	Knight-Wheeler	TKZ 533764
\$20	Knight-Stone	part on back
\$20	Fraser-Higgins	RCE 475533
\$20	Fraser-Cole	RNE 6

There have been some instances of notes in circulation without machine numbers, but with numbers written on them by ball point pen.

\$2	Knight-Wheeler	HQP 808693 (with examiner's pen mark).
\$5	Fraser-Cole	QHY 536591
\$10	Johnston-Stone	TLC 720219 (hand cut).

Several \$10 notes were located in circulation with Knight-Wheeler signatures and a handwritten serial number on the left side front. They may have been stolen. There has also been instances where an unnumbered note has been found by a member of the public and hand numbered to facilitate its use. Numbers observed:

\$10	Knight-Wheeler	TFF, TFG, TFL, 480323. TFG, TEZ 480325.

Fig. 406. $20, no left side serial number.

One Serial Number.

Numerous notes have been observed with only one serial number. Usually the left side number is missing, but care should be taken to examine the area where the number should be to check that it has not purposely been erased, thus leaving the paper thinner in the area. Any attempt to erase the right side number would interfere with the background printing. Notes observed with **no left side number:** Serial numbers marked * signify number or part number on the back from a folding error.

$1	Coombs-Wilson	ACX 392749.
$1	Phillips-Wheeler (Australia)	BQR 068339.
$1	Knight-Stone	*CYR 751125.
$2	Coombs-Wilson	*FDF 892945.
$2	Phillips-Randall	GAP 238918, GCE 712380.
$2	Phillips-Wheeler (Commonwealth)	HBE 499497.
$2	Knight-Stone	JEH 612946. *JKB 4.
$2	Johnston-Fraser	LFN 717128, 761133, 920666.
$5	Phillips-Wheeler (Commonwealth)	NHG 342979, NJV 351824.
$5	Knight-Stone	PBV 255550, *PCY 773027.
$5`	Johnston-Fraser	PXG 858721.
$5	Fraser-Higgins	QFL 970785, QGX 843997.
$10	Coombs-Wilson	*SAY 849845.

No left side serial number - continued.

$10	Phillips-Wheeler (Commonwealth)	STU 998549.
$10	Knight-Wheeler	TET 208443, 208446, TFU 123258 TGY 143385, *TKZ 533764.
$10	Johnston-Stone	UCC 469186.
$10	Johnston-Fraser	USE 778213.
$20	Phillips-Wheeler (Australia)	XJK 487977 (illustrated previous page).
$20	Knight-Stone	VAQ 685724.
$20	Johnston-Fraser	*VVB 473942, EQF 413510.
$20	Fraser-Cole	RNE 227079, *RTS 745237 *49762.
$20	Fraser-Evans	RZU 869463.
$50	Knight-Stone	YEG 515957.
$50	Johnston-Stone	YJS 002452, YLX 0050623, YXS 035372.
$50	Phillips-Fraser	*YXJ 242893.
$50	Fraser-Higgins	WBN 814542, WBT 398652.
$50	Fraser-Cole	WEZ 749241, *853359, WGJ 250356, WGK 046462, WKH 652488, *WLL 248786, WLL 265372.
$100	Johnston-Stone	*ZAN 417678, ZAU 019630.
$100	Johnston-Fraser	*ZDN 700885.
$100	Fraser-Higgins	ZES 499911.
$100	Fraser-Cole	*ZHG 158890, *ZHQ 034158, *ZHQ 034163, *ZHQ 505049.

No right side serial number,

$2	Coombs-Wilson	*FGQ 414857, FHA 059491.
$2	Phillips-Randall	GHD 259592.

Fig. 407. $10, no right side serial number.

$5	Phillips-Randall	NED 771772.
$10	Coombs-Randall	SFB 670038, 716996, SFR 229081 (illustrated).
$10	Johnston-Stone	UAZ 210816. UAZ 469186 (paper obstruction).
$20	Johnston-Fraser	*VRH 493510.
$20	Fraser-Higgins	RGZ 706783 (five digits missing). *RKB 748138.
$50	Knight-Stone	YEY 775831, YFC 018725.
$100	Johnston-Fraser	ZFT 687345.

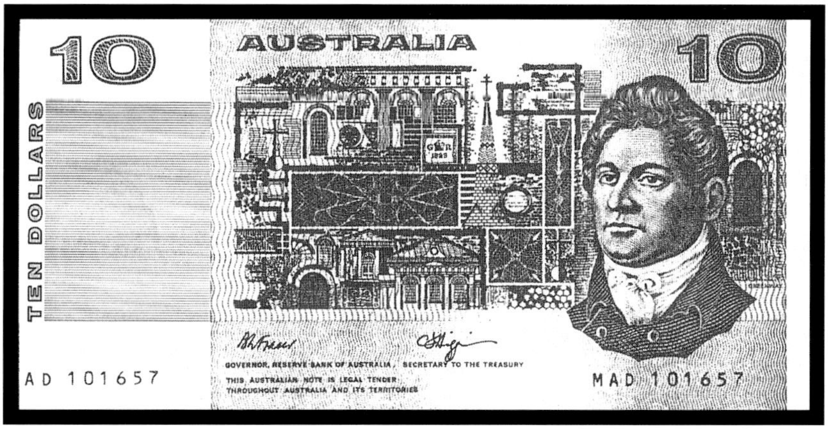

Fig. 408. Registration shift of serial numbers.

Fig. 409. $10 with mis-matched serial numbers.

Mis-matched serial numbers.

Notes with serial numbers which are not the same on each side are termed mis-matched serial number notes. They are caused by the band in a numbering box failing to turn when due, resulting in one or more digits of the serial numbers which do not match. Notes observed:

$1	Coombs-Wilson	ACT 249090	249190
$1	Phillips-Randall	AJK 987924	997924
		ALC 339531	336531
$1	Phillips-Wheeler (Commonwealth)	BKH 770500	ECA 770500
$1	Knight-Wheeler	BZJ 317853	317858
$1	Knight-Stone	DEG 263455	263445
$2	Coombs-Wilson	FBS 960516 - 17 - 18 / 860516 - 17 - 18.	
		FDU 990313	999313
		FEH 379017	370017
		FGA 186214	196214 - 303, 503, 513, 514, 515, 516, 527, 528, 530, to FGA 186534 - 196534.
		FHD 247872	247871.
$2	Coombs-Randall	FPJ 999444	998444
$2	Phillips-Randall	GFC 015760	005760
		GHA 999003	GHB 999003
		GHA 999003	GHB 999004
		GHB 999003	GHB 999004

Mis-matched serial numbers - continued.

$2	Knight-Wheeler	HNF 100434	200434
		HNF 200250	100250
$2	Knight-Stone	JRA 326714	326713
		JRA 326714	326715
$2	Johnston-Stone	KGC 265147	265146
		KGR 265546	265545
		KGY 266366	266367 + correct note 266366
		KGY 320055	320056
$2	Johnston-Fraser	LLN 691275	691274 - 284/3, 314/3, 365/4, 475/4.
$5	Phillips-Randall	NEC 124482	124486
$10	Coombs-Randall	SFA 039711	039716, 712/716, 713/716, 714/716, 715/716, sold with correct note 716/716.
$10	Phillips-Wheeler (Australia)	SVJ 999734	998734 - 735, 736, 737.
		TDP 818240	818259
		TDP 818242	818259
$10	Knight-Stone	TVD 867847-8-9	857847-8-9
		TVD 868207	858207 (illustrated).
$10	Fraser-Cole (Last/First portfolio)	AA 93 009266-67-76	000266-67-76. See Fig. 411.

(Further reading: *Rarest of the Rare,* Michael Vort-Ronald, *Australian Coin Review*, February, 1994).

$20	Knight-Wheeler	XQR 815208	815206
		XQR 815208-9-10	815207-8-9
$20	Johnston-Fraser	ESK 953634-5	953635-6
$20	Fraser-Evans	AAZ 585249	585250
$50	Johnston-Stone	YLP 909413	909412
$50	Johnston-Fraser	YUE 394140	283140
$50	Fraser-Cole	WDU 199189	199179
		WFG 760225	760226
		WFZ 684888	684887

Mis-matched serial numbers - continued.

$100	Johnston-Stone	ZBS 233973	333983
		ZBT 969227	969237
		ZBT 969293	969303
$100	Johnston-Fraser	ZFY 861251	VFX 86125- (vertical shift)
		ZGG 747599	743599
		ZGG 897966	997966
$100	Fraser-Higgins	ZEQ 064177	ZHQ 064177
		ZGG 955098	965098
		ZGV 747603	744603
		ZGV 747621	746625
		ZGV 747656	744656
		Then 747/746 with end numbers 806-7-8-9-	830-1-4-9, 840-5-7-8, 863-4.
		ZJA 591259	ZJB 591259
		ZJG 951937	961937
		ZJG 953233	963233
		ZJG 955098	965098
		ZJG 955826	965826
		ZKL 916505	916504
$100	Fraser-cole	ZJJ 148973	ZJK 148973
		(vertical shift - illustrated below)	

Fig. 410. $100 with serial numbers out of registration and therefore mis-matched.

Mis-matched serial numbers - continued.

Fig. 411. Mis-matched serial numbers, $10 note from Last/First portfolio.

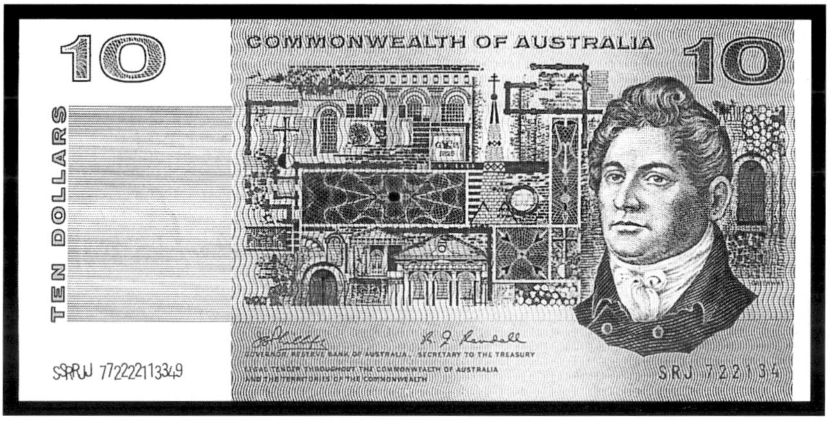

Fig. 412. $10 note with two different left side serial numbers.

Fig. 413. $20 note with two different sets of serial numbers from a vertical registration shift.

Missing digits.

A missing digit on a note is characterised by a portion of the digit above and below the space in the serial number, caused by the numbering band failing to fully turn and jamming in between digits. The next illustration shows the top note is correct, but a missing digit occurred in the next nine notes then righted itself in the bottom note. For a left side digit missing, check to make sure that a digit has not been purposely erased, by holding the note up to the light to make sure the paper is not thinned.

A variety of reasons can cause missing or misaligned digits, as per the other illustrations, following.

Fig. 414. Consecutive run of nine missing serial number digits.

Missing digits or part of serial numbers can occur through corner folding, registration shifts, fadeouts, and paper obstructions. Some of the notes observed with missing digits resulted from jammed numbering box bands.

$1	Coombs-Wilson	ADE 564881 to 9 (illustrated at Fig. 414). ADE 569883-6-7-8.
$10	Knight-Wheeler	THK 006059
$20	Johnston-Fraser	EAS 289999
$20	Fraser-Cole	RJK 280517, RJR 280507, 508 and 517.
$50	Knight-Stone	YEG 518957
$100	Fraser-Higgins	ZHK 949996

Fig. 415. Portions of serial numbers missing.

Fig. 416. Gap in serial number and excess paper due to creasing.

Inverted serial numbers.

Notes with the serial numbers printed upside down and near the top of the note are usually the result of a sheet of notes being put back upside down on the stack of sheets after inspection, part-way through the full production process. The sheet remained upside down during the numbering. The fault was detected by examining staff if stamped with a number, but those without the stamped number were not detected during inspection. Notes observed:

$50	Fraser-Cole	WQE 784400-1; WQF 784376-7-8; WQG 784797 & 9.
$50	Fraser-Higgins	YZR 756920 (illustrated below) and YZU 756920.

Fig. 417. $50 with upside down serial numbers, with examiner's number.

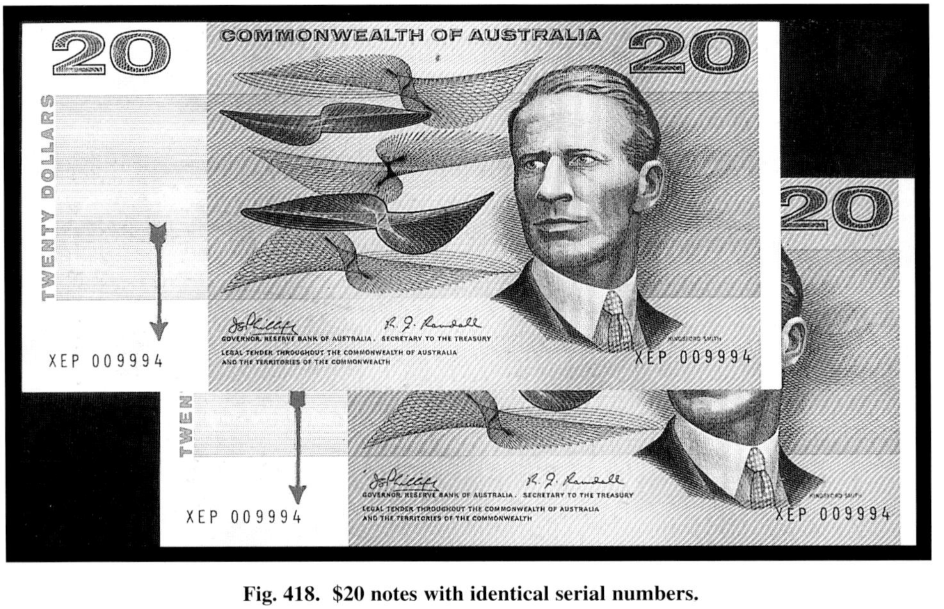

Fig. 418. $20 notes with identical serial numbers.

The two $20 notes illustrated at Fig. 418 are the only known pair of Australian paper notes with identical serial numbers. The reason for the duplication is not known. Thousands of English one pound notes had identical numbers in 1977, and in the same year, two New Zealand ten pound notes were sold at auction with identical serial numbers of AL 078055. It is also believed that batches of US $1 notes had also been printed with the same number prior to 1985.

FOLDING ERRORS

Folding errors are usually confined to a top corner of a sheet (the leading edge during printing), but can also occur on bottom corners. They can vary from a couple of centimetres to a whole note folded over. Depending on when this occurs, print can end up missing from the background printing stage, the Intaglio process or the serial numbering. The fault is characterised by a straight line of demarcation of the printing stage. The next illustration shows minor folds caused by a corner folding over prior to the Intaglio printing and serial numbering.

Fig. 419. Fronts, minor corner fold errors.

Fig. 420. Major corner fold - missing Intaglio printing.

A corner fold can stay in place during another stage of printing, as per the next note. The corner was was straightened out and was guillotined amongst other sheets. When refolded, the note shows the additional unprinted area which was previously the border of the sheet before trimming the selvedge off (see Uncut notes). The bottom illustration shows two notes from the top right of a sheet with a very large corner fold printed over.

Fig. 421. Major corner fold - overprinted.

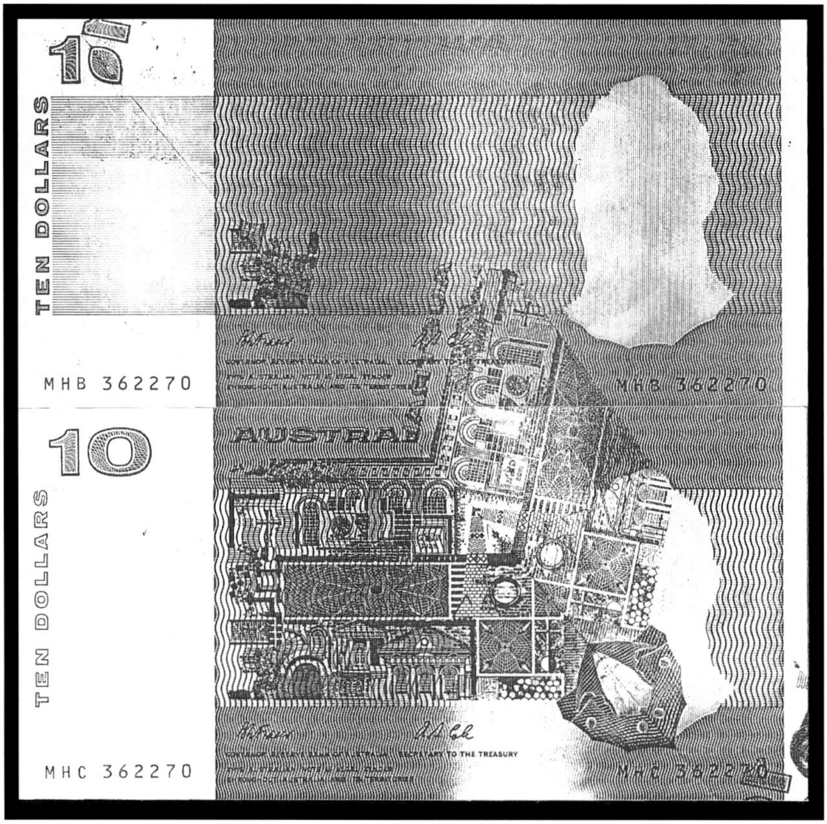

Fig. 422. Two vertically consecutive notes with the same large corner fold error.

Further reading on two previous notes illustrated: *Fraser-Cole Phenomena,* Michael Vort-Ronald, *Australian Coin Review,* November, 1992. Below are four consecutive "dog-eared" corner flaps. The fifth corner fold was cut off during guillotining as the "neck" of the folds gradually diminished.

Fig. 423. Consecutive run of "dog-eared" corner folds.

Fig. 424. Front, $100 with corner flap printed.

Fig. 425. Back of $5 note, flap printed.

Tear Flaps

A tear flap is caused by the sheet catching on some part of the machinery as it passes through the printing press, folding over the damaged portion so that the area is printed on over the damage, and unprinted underneath. In the case of the $100 next illustrated, the tear crumpled from the top selvedge and was partly printed on.

Fig. 426. Tear Flap.

The next illustration shows a major tear damage as viewed from three perspectives. The note with the fold still folded, the unfolded note from the front and the unfolded note from the back.

Fig. 427. Three perspectives of a major tear flap error note.

Registration shifts.

The printing of notes first involves a pass through a Simultan printing press to print the coloured background designs on both sides, and later, the Intaglio press for the back main print, and the same process again later for the fronts. Relatively blank spaces, particularly behind the portraits, are left during the Simultan printing to give a whiter shade to the faces after the Intaglio printings. If the sheet feeds through the presses too early or too late, the designs can be out of register with one another, and the registration shift note occurs. Being a sheet fault, all of the notes on the sheet would have the same error. This can result in a shadow or halo to the portrait to the left, right, above or below. Minor registration shifts are illustrated below. Usually the shift is on one side only, but it can occur on both. Very minor registration shifts allow notes to be within certain acceptable tolerances.

Fig. 428. Relatively minor registration shifts on fronts of notes.

Fig. 429. Relatively minor registration shifts on backs of notes.

The next three illustrations show a major registration shifts to the left, and major vertical shifts.

Fig. 430. Major registration shift of the Intaglio to the left.

Fig. 431. Major vertical Intaglio registration shift down on the front.

Fig. 432. Major vertical Intaglio shift down on the back.

In the previous illustrations the Intaglio printings were off-line. In Fig. 433 the Simultan background print is off-line to the left and the Intaglio printing is in the correct position. A vertical registration shift which occurred during the printing of serial numbers on the backs of the paper $100 notes, or the new polymer notes, can result in the serial number from the next note appearing, to create a "mis-matched serial number note", which is really a registration error. See Fig. 410.

Fig. 433. Front, registration shift of the Simultan printing to the left.

Creasing

Notes are printed in sheets and fed through heavy printing presses at the rate of 40 to 60 thousand sheets an hour, and under tonnes of pressure. Under those conditions, if the paper encounters an impediment to its passage through the machine, a crease can occur in the paper. If this occurred before it reached the Simultan printing plates, then the paper remained unprinted inside the crease. If it occurred during or after the Simultan printing, the paper could then remain creased and be printed on by the Intaglio process. The crease then remains closed until handling loosens it and the error is apparent. If guillotined with a crease, the edge of the note will be uneven after the crease is flattened out.

Fig. 434. Multiple creases, no Simultan printing on creases.

Fig. 435. Creases with Simultan design, but unprinted by Intaglio.

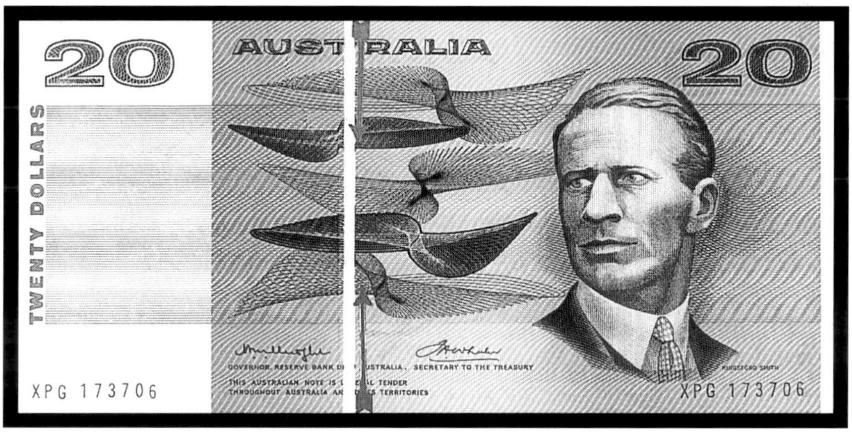

Fig. 436. Vertical crease alongside the metallic thread, unprinted.

Inverted paper

If blank paper sheets are fed into the machines upside down, or as supplied by the note paper maker, the watermarks are not visible on the left (because they were amongst the design on the right) and the metallic security thread ends up "on the wrong side". Being a sheet error, all notes with the same serial numerals would be affected. (The $20 notes mostly turned up in Queensland). Notes observed:

$5	Knight-Stone	527644	NZB (upside down)
$10	Coombs-Wilson	153692	SCE
		163692	SCF
		506093	SCL
$10	Coombs-Randall	179261	SFD

Inverted paper (watermarks) - continued.

$10	Phillips-Randall	353838	SLN
$20	Johnston-Fraser (OCR-B)	132057	EVD
		489525	ERZ, ESZ
		489622	ERS
		489637 & 8	ETA
		526831	ERX
		544735	ERS
		544779	ESL
		544907	ERZ
		544908	ERX
		544910	ESV
$20	Fraser-Higgins	697181	EYE
		697186 & 7	EYH
$50	Phillips-Fraser	100726	YXP

It is also believed that this fault occurs in other denominations. Collectors who have notes in their collections with serial numbers close to those listed above should check to see if the watermarks are visible in the usual position on the left front of their notes. If not, inverted paper is possible - or maybe a forgery could be detected.

Prominent watermarks were seen in $2 and $5 notes resulting in a heavy raised appearance to the watermark of Captain James Cook. An explanation given was that although the weight of the paper remained the same, there may have been a very slight reduction in the thickness of the paper, resulting in buckling.

Printing plate faults

The note below shows a large diagonal crack in the intaglio printing resulting from a cracked pressure plate behind the engraved plate.

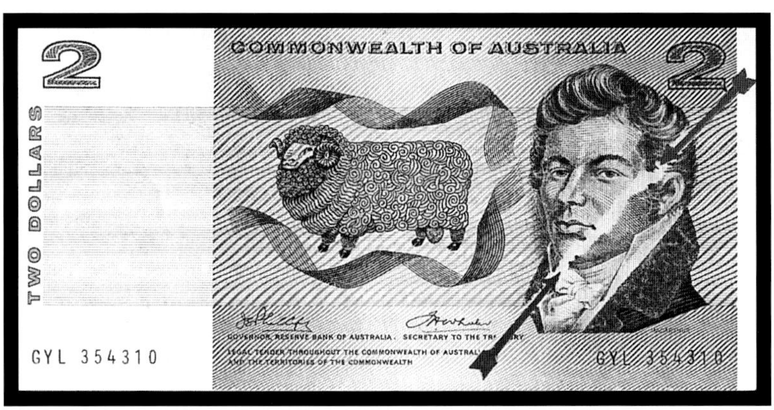

Fig. 437. Break in intaglio printing from a cracked pressure plate.

Metallic thread faults

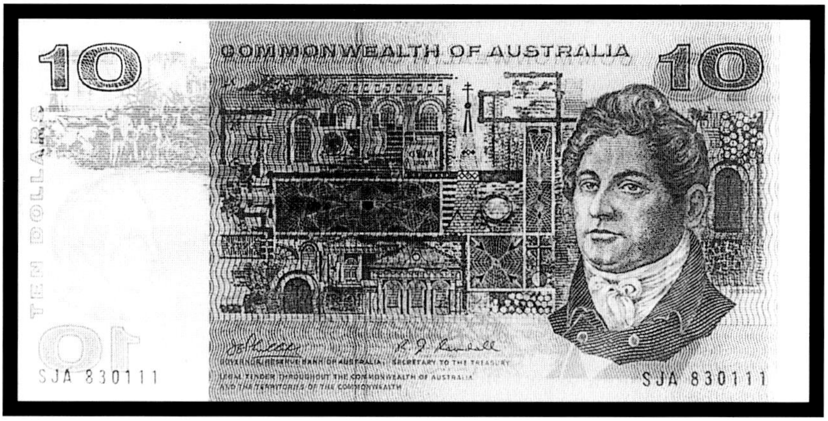

Fig. 438. Two metallic security threads (looking through note).

Various metallic security thread faults have been observed:

$2	Johnston-Stone	Two threads	KPL 892270	(one stray on front)
$20	Knight-Stone	Two Threads	XVB 857732	(one stray on front)
$10	Phillips-Randall	Two parallel threads	SJA 830111	(illustrated above)
$10	Coombs-Wilson	No metallic thread	SDQ 790396	(beware of forgeries)

Fig. 439. $20 with metallic thread on the surface and printed on.

Fig. 440. Repaired during printing.

The $2 note above has a large piece of yellow tape over a ragged tear which was repaired prior to the Intaglio printing and was thus printed on. It remained there to provide for accountability during production and the whole sheet therefore processed and printed, and for the later withdrawal of the damaged note after inspection.

The note below has no right side number and the number HJJ 865900 on the left. What may be faint and blurred serial numbers are repeated diagonally three times from centre bottom to top left. On the top left of the back is a faint HHZ8. The condition of the note suggests that it may have been jammed in the numbering machine.

Fig. 441. Damage during printing of serial numbers.

MINOR FAULTS AND NON FAULTS

Faint or slightly out of line serial number digits are often found. Notes cut off centre are not uncommon, and it is only when there is a portion of a design missing, with a corresponding portion of the design from the next note present, that this could be considered significant.

Notes with a dip along the top and bottom edges to the region of the metallic thread are due to the extra thickness of a section of notes in the region of the thread which raises the stack of notes up.

Bad cutting was more prevalent in the $50 and $100 notes, usually on the top edge in the region of the watermark area, which was apparent as a slight buckling and/or raised portion on the top edge and a corresponding dip in the bottom edge. The continuous watermarks on the $50 and $100 notes made a ream higher in this general area which needed extra clamping pressure before being guillotined.

Some notes, more noticeably in the Phillips-Wheeler (Australia) $10 and $20, had parallel sides and top and bottom edges, but no strict right angles on the corners, resulting in uneven white borders.

Breaks in the metallic security threads of 1 mm were common. Faint wet ink transfers of small portions of notes were fairly common, as were serial numbers with digits slightly out of alignment.

Slight registration shifts could produce faint white lines around portraits, and minor spot blemishes were sometimes apparent in the background design.

In Johnston-Stone $20 notes, whole sections (of 100 notes) with prefix VGX were located with very small grey dashes in the form of a cross, in the bottom right corner of the front, possibly as guillotining guidelines.

Sometimes the pressure of the intaglio printing caused severe buckling of the paper. These and other minor faults were more of a faulty note, rather than a collectable printing error - too minor to pay a premium for, and not perfect enough to place in a general circulation note collection.

Non-errors.

Partly green $5 notes, (or $5 notes with green serial numbers), and partly blue $2 notes are usually due to exposure to sunlight for a prolonged period or contact with washing detergents etc. which affect the chemical composition of some of the colours, interwoven with other colours that are not affected to the same degree.

Notes which have come into contact with petroleum-type solvents (such as leaving underneath linoleum for years) can end up with reddish black inverted portions of designs or the appearance of the ink having soaked through the paper.

Fig. 442. Cancelling a ream of $10 notes by drilling.

Fig. 443. $2 "confetti" from the bank note drill in the Hobart branch of the R.B.A.

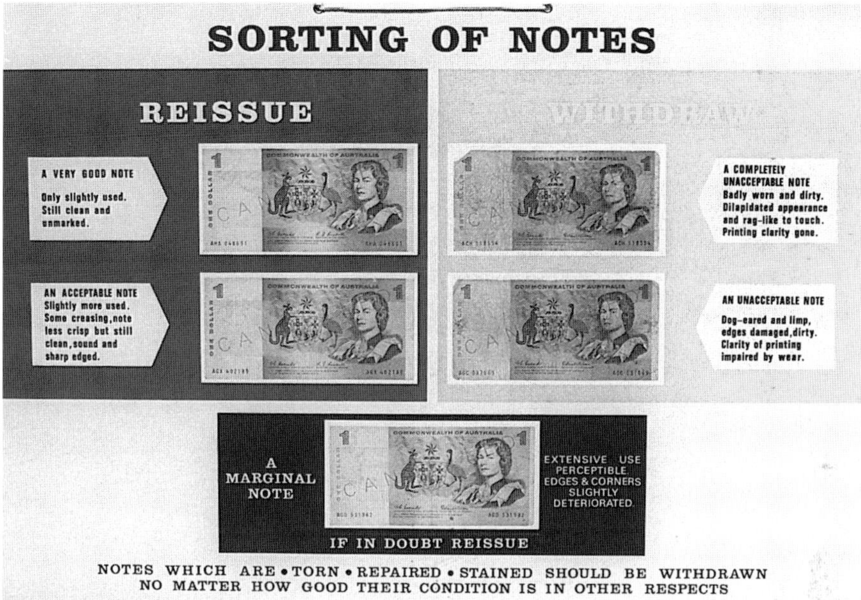

Fig. 444. R.B.A. board issued to banks as a guide to sorting and withdrawing notes.

As notes became worn, torn or dirty, a process of separation, cancellation and eventual destruction took place. Up to 400,000,000 notes per year were destroyed, and their places taken by new notes. The new polymer notes which began to replace the paper notes from 1992 lasted far longer than their paper predecessors, requiring less notes to be printed, thus less to be taken out of service and rejected.

The separation process began in the trading banks. Any notes found excessively dirty, worn or damaged, were put to one side during normal teller transactions, or later, as duties permitted. The "soiled notes" were generally referred to as "mutes". See illustration above for sorting guidelines.

In 1976 the Reserve Bank of Australia tested a new system of re-usable plastic note containers each holding 500 notes and sealed to obviate the "middleman" counting previously undertaken by the Reserve Bank. The system went Australia-wide in early 1977. The principle was that the contents of a properly sealed container could be accepted as correct without having to be counted by the Reserve Bank or any other bank branches while it was enroute from one bank to another.

Strict rules applied. Only notes which were counted by the sending branch were to be included in consignments to the Reserve Bank, and were to be prepared as follows:

(1) Sections of 100 pieces (notes) - each denomination was to be made up of flat sections of 100 notes, each section to be banded with a self-adhesive paper strap showing the bank or branch name, teller's identification and date.

(2) Amalgamations of sections - where quantities were sufficient, five sections (of 100 notes) of the one denomination (except $50) were to be firmly secured by thick or doubled elastic bands near each end and placed in the container, (a) $1 and $2 notes to be placed on edge, facing the front and (b) $5, $10 and $20 notes were to be placed flat, face up in the note container.

Fig. 445. Reserve Bank re-usable note container.

The note containers (as above) were to be packed by two officers who were to maintain the notes under their joint control until the containers were sealed (as detailed below) and despatched. $50 notes and quantities of less than 500 notes in other denominations were not to be placed in the containers. The minimum units for consignment were 500 $1 or $2 notes, or 100 each of $5, $10 or $20 notes. Soiled notes (extracted by tellers as unfit notes) were not permitted to be sent in the containers.

When sealing the note containers a locking strap was passed down through the slot in the container catch and a special self-adhesive seal prepared showing the total value and denomination of notes, a legible bank/branch stamp and the date. A special manilla tag was placed under the locking strap and the seal placed over the locking strap and manilla tag which was then signed by the two officers packing the container, their signatures to extend from the seal onto the manilla tag. Properly sealed containers were then accepted as correct enroute, and there were special instructions on how to open the containers and advise any discrepancies. The system lasted for some years before it was discontinued.

Mutilated notes were something different. The term applied to notes which, although mutilated by tearing or missing portions, still had value. To make a claim for reimbursement for mutilated notes, the following applied:

(a) If the portion of the note presented for payment was about half, but less than two thirds, half value was paid.
(b) If the portion was two-thirds or more of the note, full face value was paid.
(c) Note pieces were treated as being pieces of different notes, unless it was clear that they were pieces of the same note.
(d) Unless there were exceptional circumstances, all payments on mutilated note claims were based on visual evidence of notes. Any chemical analysis was only used to support the assessment of the processor. Serial numbers of notes were no longer used to make assessments of the value.
(e) Claims were presented on Statutory Declarations which required information on how the note(s) became mutilated and what happened to any missing portion/s.

Fig. 446. A "mutilated" note.

Fig. 447. Solving a mutilated note puzzle.

There have been many interesting mutilated note claims, of which the following are but two examples.

A cafe proprietor made a claim for half of a $50 note ($25). It transpired that a customer had torn a $50 note in half and presented one half to the waitress to pay for his meal, adding that if she would go out with him later, he would give her the other half of the $50 note. The waitress was the cafe owner's wife who duly declined the offer. The customer, apart from offending both the "waitress" and her husband, had committed two offences, one major and one minor. In tearing the note in half he had deliberately mutilated a banknote, and in tendering half a note he had failed to pay for his meal (with legal tender).

A small group of electricity linesmen had been working in a paddock. During the morning their pay packets were delivered to them. It was a warm day, and after their lunch the men dozed off. One of the workers awoke to see a goat completing its lunch - their pay packets. In desperation the men contacted the farmer and purchased the goat, which then met a premature end. The contents of the goat's stomach were collected, coins and all, and their claims were duly paid in full.

Claims over the years have included notes cooked in the oven, found shredded in rat's nests or stuck into a solid mass from being buried. In most cases, if the "evidence" is carefully collected, claims for reimbursement can be successful.

In country areas where a Commonwealth Trading Bank was represented, soiled notes were cleared through that bank. If there was no Commonwealth Bank in the area, then the banks sent their soiled notes direct to the Reserve Bank of Australia. In the cities and suburbs, banks sent notes direct to the Reserve Bank of Australia on a daily basis.

After soiled notes were separated by the tellers, the $2 to $20 notes were accumulated, counted into even hundreds, and then forwarded. In smaller branches with small cash stocks, the $50 and $100 notes were forwarded in multiples of ten to avoid undue depletion of cash holdings. For many years, the most convenient way to forward notes was by registered post, the packets of notes being tied up in a special way and wax sealed with the imprint of the forwarding bank. If the parcel arrived intact, but was deficient, then the sender was believed responsible. If the parcel arrived with the wax seals broken, and money was missing, then it was likely to have been interfered with in transit.

To render soiled notes unusable, the first decimal notes were cancelled as per the next illustration. The $10 note has the signatures of Coombs-Randall, dating it at around 1968. It was part of a consignment of cancelled notes enroute to Note Issue Branch of the Reserve Bank in Fitzroy (Melbourne) Victoria, by train. The train derailed and caught fire, and many of the burnt notes were scattered around the scene and souvenired by onlookers, as was apparently the one illustrated below.

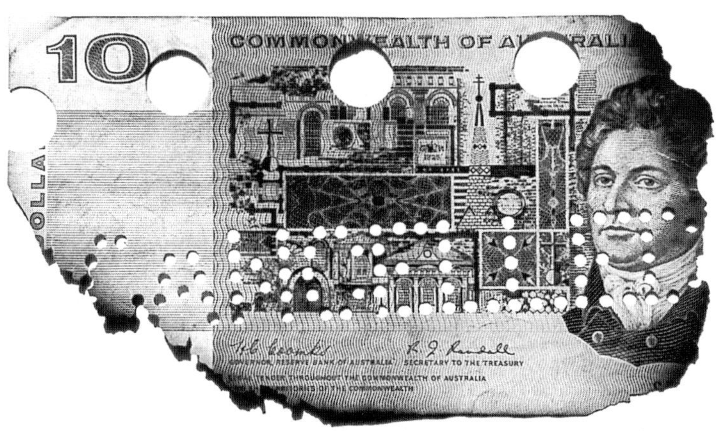

Fig. 448. Cancelled and partly burnt $10 note, First type cancellation.

Later the "LE" near the end of "CANCELLED" was omitted from the perforation to permit more convenient hand counting as will be described later.

Smaller bank branches used hand-operated perforating machines which perforated up to 30 notes at a time, with five holes as per the illustration following.

Later, three large holes only were drilled, so positioned that any half of a cancelled note would show at least one hole, if not two, and therefore be incapable of being presented for payment (as a mutilated note).

The Reserve Bank branches also had large machines capable of punching twelve large holes through a section of 100 notes at a time. The resultant banknote "confetti" residue from one of those machines is illustrated in Fig. 451.

Possession of a cancelled note by an unauthorised person may be regarded as possession of a stolen note, the property of the Reserve Bank of Australia, or, in the case of an unauthorised cancellation, possession of a mutilated note.

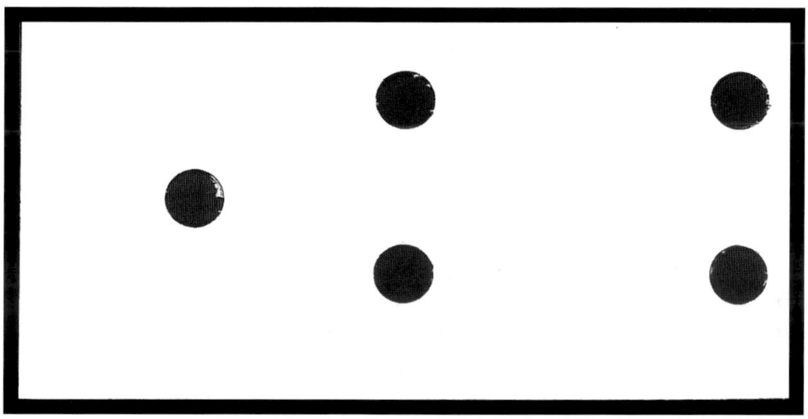

Fig. 449. Second type cancelling for decimal notes.

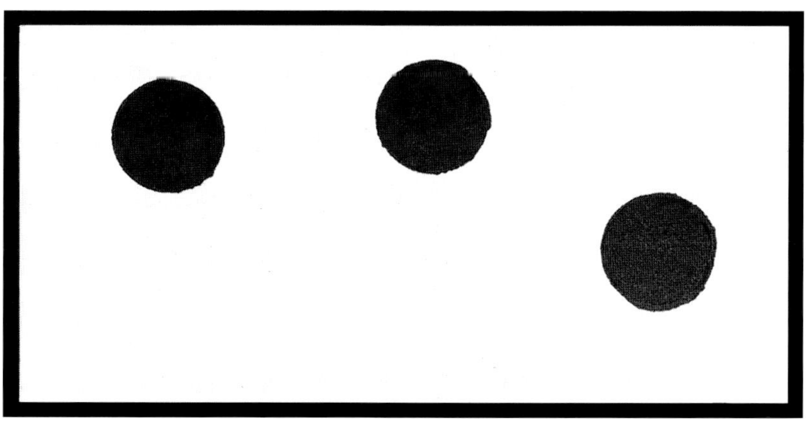

Fig. 450. Third type cancelling for decimal notes.

Fig. 451. Banknote "confetti" from the cancelling machine of the Reserve Bank branch in Adelaide.

During printing of notes, any sheets found to be faulty, or due for destruction, were also cancelled by drilling, as per Fig. 442. They were then kept in sheet form for audit purposes (checking and counting) and were eventually destroyed under triple control.

Fig. 452. Burn Count Room personnel at work in the 1970s.

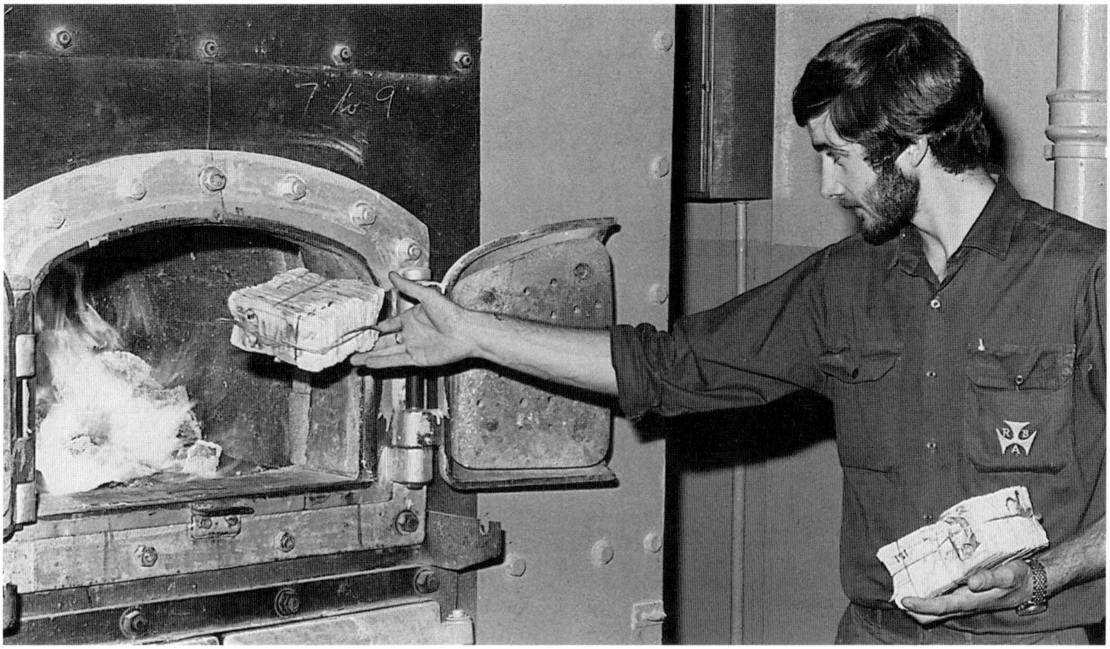

Fig. 453. Throwing notes into the furnace - 1970s, Fitzroy.

The "old system" of examining notes took place at the various branches of the Reserve Bank by various means, including testing by ultraviolet light which would reveal any counterfeits produced on non-banknote (mould made) paper. Each section of notes (100) was then guillotined vertically about 30 mm from the right side of the front. That procedure produced a clean sharp edge on the notes which then facilitated fan-counting on vacuum-operated counting machines. The "LE" in "CANCELLED" was removed so as to not interfere with the guillotining.

Fig. 454. South-eastern view of Note Printing and Issue Branch at Fitzroy.

After checking and counting, the offcuts were shredded, bagged, and destroyed. The remaining portions of cancelled notes were then forwarded to Note Printing and Issue Branch at Fitzroy and later

Craigieburn, Victoria, for eventual destruction by burning. The safe disposal of destroyed notes was a long-standing problem, and many different methods were tried over the years in an attempt to achieve complete and safe destruction. In some instances, shredded paper notes were buried in rubbish dumps as burning was, and still is, considered environmentally undesirable. With the introduction of polymer notes, notes for destruction were mixed with other plastics for recycling.

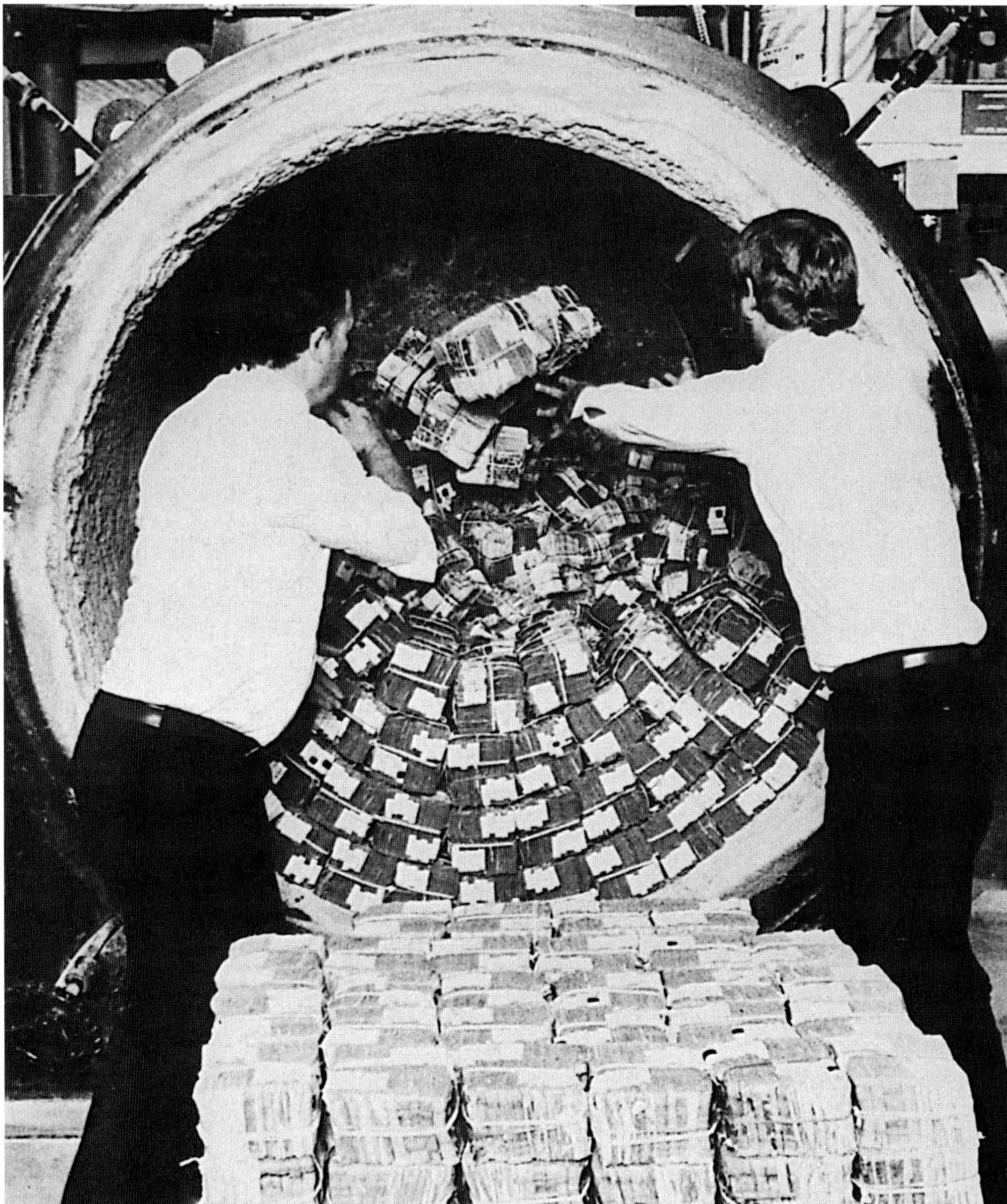

Fig. 455. Throwing notes into the incinerator at Craigieburn. Approximately one million notes were destroyed each day.

In December, 1980, a special unit was installed on a trial basis in the Cash Department of the Reserve Bank, Sydney. The system, known as CVCS (Currency Verification, Counting and Sorting), was manufactured by Recognition Equipment Incorporated, Dallas, Texas, U.S.A. Its performance was impressive, and it was purchased at the end of the trial period.

The CVCS system incorporated three basic components: an electro-mechanical processing machine, a Visual Display Unit (VDU) terminal and a teletypewriter. The following functions could be performed at rates up to 1,200 notes per minute:

1. Counting the notes, and identifying a shortage or surplus, and the lodging bank.
2. Checking denominations and authenticity of the notes.
3. Sorting notes into: fit for issue, and unfit for issue.
4. Restrapping of fit notes into sections of 100 for reissue.
5. On-line shredding of unfit notes.

Notes were at first shredded, as per Fig. 460. Later, this was modified to "granulating" which shredded the notes into much smaller irregular pieces which compacted much more efficiently and thus saved space. See Fig. 461.

Fig. 456. Shredded notes from a commercial shredding machine, 1987.

Notes suspected of being counterfeit, and notes which failed to meet other criteria, were diverted into a separate pocket for manual examination and counting. The initial CVCS machines had been modified to process notes from $1 to $10. A second machine to process higher denominations was delivered to Sydney in July, 1981. Two further machines were purchased for Sydney, three for Melbourne and two for Brisbane. Eventually, each branch of the Reserve Bank had one or more of these units which processed one denomination at a time. Bent corners were straightened and heavily taped and stapled notes turned around so they protruded out of the main stack. Special header cards, which replaced identifying straps, were placed between each section.

The notes were then stacked into the machine and automatically fed through numerous sensors. The turned-around notes were manually removed by the operator (prior to the bulk of the notes going through the sensors) and placed in the reject pocket.

The sensors checked the genuineness of each note, recognised and ejected incorrect denominations, counterfeits and composite notes. Rejected notes included those affected by washing detergent, doubles (notes passing through the equipment together) and those with turned-up corners (also counted as doubles). After hand counting, the rejected notes were then fed through a normal commercial-type shredder. See Fig. 456.

When sorting the notes into fit and unfit, adjustable standards could mean up to two thirds of the notes not being reissued. The unfit notes, having been verified as genuine, passed through the shredder which cut them lengthways into 2 mm wide strips. They were then fed by vacuum hoses to a large compactor where they were mixed with water, compressed into a mulch-like material, and later buried.

A final reconciliation was then carried out by balancing the totals of reissuable (fit) notes, CVCS destroyed notes, and the rejected notes, using a combination of manual and electronic counting.

By May, 1994, 22 CVCS systems had been installed Australia-wide, and some upgrading of the machines was deemed necessary, as reported in a statement released by the Reserve Bank on 11 February, 1993:

> *....This upgrading primarily involved upgrading the overall fitness and multi-item detector capabilities. This required substantial redevelopment/replacement of the C.V.C.S. software and hardware including new and improved detectors for assessing the extent of soiling of notes, for measuring mechanical fitness (such as missing corners) and for detecting when two or more notes are stuck together. Adaption of the systems to facilitate processing of notes with clear areas was also required.*
>
> *Specifically, the upgrade enables the Bank to:*
>
> 1. *Process plastic as well as paper notes.*
> 2. *Implement and control a national fitness standard for notes to be reissued following C.V.C.S. processing (independent of the standard of notes being processed). The improved soil fitness detector scans notes and categorizes them into sixteen pre-determined soil fitness levels, and only selects, for reissue, notes above a pre-selected soil level. Each C.V.C.S. system consistently classifies notes at any time during processing.*
> 3. *Improve detection of multiple notes and notes with mechanical faults. The system can now accurately and consistently identify the following mechanical defects: holes larger than 6.5 square mm, open tears to a depth of 2.5 mm, folded and/or missing corners larger than 12.5 square mm and sticky tape larger than 25 square mm.*
> 4. *Reduce the premature destruction of fit notes and further reduce the reissue of unfit notes.*
> 5. *Have an option to destroy or reissue notes with folded corners which are otherwise fit.*

Reserve Bank of Australia statement re CVCS continued -

6. *Interface a new authentication/denomination detector for the new series notes.*
7. *Install new detectors in the future at minimum cost and disruption by providing a flexible software/hardware infrastructure.*

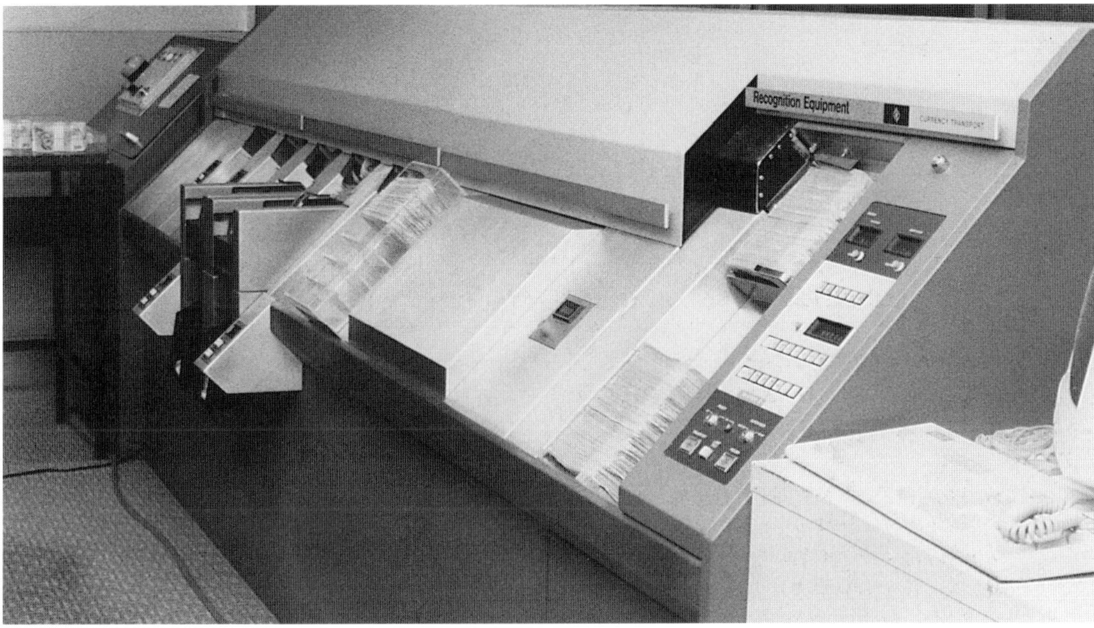

Fig. 457. Currency, Verification, Counting and Sorting machine (C.V.C.S.).

Fig. 458. Notes being fed into the C.V.C.S. machine.

Fig. 459. Notes on their way to the granulator in the C.V.C.S. machine.

Fig. 460. Shredded notes from a C.V.C.S. machine in 1987. Notes are now granulated.

Fig. 461. Granulated paper $5 notes from a C.V.C.S. machine.

Fig. 462. Notes passing through sensors for counting and vereification in the C.V.C.S. machine.

Fig. 463. Fit notes being strapped into sections of 100 in the C.V.C.S. machine.

A technician from the developer, Recognition Equipment Incorporated was in attendance to service and maintain the systems. Each C.V.C.S. machine weighed approximately 1.5 tonnes, was nearly four metres long, one metre wide and one and a half metres high. Second-generation new equipment at that time could cost from $500,000 to $2 million each.

Further reading: articles by Michael Vort-Ronald in *Australian Coin Review, Automated system now 'cleans up' notes,* February, 1987, and *Development of the C.V.C.S. Systems,* May, 1994.

Chapter 12: FORGERIES

The first coloured pictures of the new decimal notes were published by the *Australian Women's Weekly* of January 26, 1966. On the front cover were the fronts of a $1, $2, $10 and $20 note. On page three were the respective backs. The pictures were partly overlapped by decimal coins. On page three, the pictures were accompanied by *...Permission to photograph the notes in color (never previously allowed) was given with the stipulation that they be reproduced at least five percent bigger or smaller. Ours are smaller...* See Figs. 39 *and* 40.

Apparently not small enough - some dishonest people cut out the pictures and spent them. Some even glued the fronts and backs together, and were able to pass them as genuine notes, even though they had pictures of coins on them. In effect, the "notes" passed became Australia's first decimal forgeries.

Possibly as a result, for many years permission to publish banknotes in colour was not allowed in any scale, and even black and white reproductions had to be at least one third larger or one third smaller than genuine notes. Technically, even a colour photo of a banknote on a tea towel was not allowed. So strict were the rules, that an entire issue of a monthly magazine was ordered to be destroyed in March 1981 because there were some black and white photos of notes in it which were too close to the actual size of the notes.

Now the onus is on any person reproducing a note illustration not to produce anything capable of misleading someone else into believing it to be a genuine note. See also, Laws affecting notes, Chapter 14.

Fig. 464. Front, $10 forgery, Coombs-Wilson.

The first serious decimal forgeries were $10 notes circulated in late 1966 with the signature combination of Coombs-Wilson. On 24 December, 1966, the Governor of the Reserve Bank of Australia, issued a Press Release which was repeated in the form of an advertisement (reproduced on the next page). It was rather ironic that Greenway on the front of the $10 note (better known as a Master Stone Mason) was himself at one time convicted of forgery and transported to Australia for his crime. These forgeries prompted the Reserve Bank to find a new material on which to print notes, but it took 22 years to successfully mass-produce the first polymer (Bicentenary $10) note in 1988.

[*Advertisement*]

WARNING—

Forged $10 Notes

The Governor of the Reserve Bank of Australia, Dr. H. C. Coombs, warned the public to be on guard against counterfeit $10 notes which have been detected in circulation so far in Melbourne. He said some of the forged notes had been recovered but he emphasised that special care was necessary as the forgeries closely resembled the genuine note. Dr. Coombs said some characteristics of the counterfeit note are as follows:

PAPER

The paper used in the counterfeit note has a waxy feel quite unlike the characteristic feel of the genuine note. Apparently it has been treated with some kind of coating and this has given the counterfeit notes a distinct solvent-like smell.

METALLIC THREAD

There has been an imitation of the metallic security thread on the forged note, but held to the light it does not stand out anywhere near as clearly as on the genuine note. In fact, on some of the forgeries it is difficult to see at all. The public should therefore look for the distinctive vertical thread as a test of the genuineness of the note.

WATERMARK

There is a good imitation of the watermark on the forgeries but it does not have the clarity of the genuine watermark. A characteristic of most of the forgeries examined is that when the note is laid flat that portion of the watermark overlapping the bottom of the panel on the left side of the note appears as a light brown mark.

PRINTING

In general the printing closely resembles the genuine note but on careful examination there are deficiencies. The forged note feels somewhat smooth and its main features are less distinct and slightly grey by comparison with a genuine note.

In particular on the front the wording "Ten Dollars" is somewhat blurred and the numerals "10" are somewhat blotchy, especially on the right side of the note.

On the back the background color printing lacks the clarity and definition of the genuine note, especially to the left of the portrait of Lawson. In a genuine note this is a pattern of fine interweaving, but in most of the forgeries it appears as rather coarse blue and white vertical wavy lines.

Fig. 465. $10 forgery warning advertisement, 1966.

By February, 1967, more than "$140,000 worth" of forged $10 notes had been located by police and banking authorities. In 1967, a total of 1,533 forged notes had been passed in Victoria alone. A major scare and threat to the currency ensued. They were passed in other States as well.

> ***Press release:*** *20 February 1968.*
>
> *Counterfeit $10.00 notes.*
>
> *The Secretary of the Reserve Bank of Australia, Mr. A.C. McPherson, said today that, to help the public recognise $10 counterfeit notes, the Bank had produced a small pocket-size pamphlet setting out a full description of the counterfeit and ways to detect it. With the co-operation of the banks, the pamphlet will be available to the public at all bank branches throughout Australia as soon as distribution can be completed. (See next page)*
>
> *Mr. McPherson said that counterfeit $10 notes were still being detected at present mainly in Sydney. He advised the public to continue to give particular scrutiny to any $10 notes tendered to them.*

In a press statement released on 11 March, 1968, the Governor of the Reserve Bank stated that the Bank had decided to pay rewards totalling more than $3,000 to a number of persons who had volunteered information regarding the counterfeit $10 notes which were first detected in Melbourne in December, 1966. In each instance the information given had been of material assistance in investigations into the counterfeiting.

Fig. 466. Back, $10 Coombs-Wilson forgery.

On 21 May, 1971, a batch of 1,750 was handed to police. The week before that, another batch of 500 was handed in. The forgeries used various combinations of serial letters or numbers to produce 80 different serial numbers - as detailed in the next illustration. The quickest means of detecting one of the forgeries was the "TIMES BAKERY" on the back at top right. The walls of the building were wooden planked and represented by horizontal black lines. On the genuine note the right side of the lines were even on the vertical edge. On the forgeries, they were uneven. The forgeries also fluoresced white under long-wave ultraviolet light and the "watermark" darkened, while in genuine notes, this did not occur.

RESERVE BANK OF AUSTRALIA

REWARD

FORGED NOTES

SUBSTANTIAL REWARDS of up to **$10,000** will be paid by the RESERVE BANK OF AUSTRALIA for information leading to the apprehension and conviction of persons responsible for the forging of Australian notes or the uttering or the unlawful possession of forged Australian notes. Rewards of smaller amounts will be paid to persons who supply information which assists in the investigation.

ANY PERSON with this information should communicate immediately with the Police.

J. G. PHILLIPS
GOVERNOR
RESERVE BANK OF AUSTRALIA

RESERVE BANK OF AUSTRALIA

COUNTERFEIT NOTES

COUNTERFEIT $10 NOTES

BE ON YOUR GUARD

THE COUNTERFEITS HAVE THE FOLLOWING SERIAL NUMBERS:—

SAE—280178	SAN—280231	SAV—280023	SAZ—280170
280231	280708	280231	280231
527178	527406	527023	527170
527406	527708	527406	527406
756178	756414	756023	756170
756414	756708	756414	756414
817082	817082	817023	817082
817178	817708	817082	817170
SBE—178082	SBN—280231	SBV—023082	SBZ—170082
178231	280708	023231	170231
178406	527406	023406	170406
178414	527708	023414	170414
280178	708082	280023	280170
280231	708231	280231	280231
527178	708406	527023	527170
527406	708414	527406	527406
756178	756414	756023	756170
756414	756708	756414	756414
817082	817082	817023	817082
817178	817708	817082	817170

MEMORISE THE LETTERS SA AND SB FOLLOWED BY E,N,V OR Z.
Check very carefully notes with any of these letters.

If you cannot see a distinct vertical metallic thread when the note is held to the light, the note is counterfeit.
If there appears to be a metallic thread, check for other faults
● Waxy, smooth feel ● Imitation watermark — on front only
● Irregular edge on "Times Bakery" ● Coarse vertical patterns of blue and white wavy line on back.

IF YOU DETECT A COUNTERFEIT NOTE INFORM THE POLICE IMMEDIATELY

RETAIN THIS CARD FOR READY REFERENCE

Published by Reserve Bank of Australia

Fig, 467. The $10 (Coombs-Wilson) forgery card, 1968.

It is believed that only about 4,500 of the counterfeits passed into circulation. The two men who printed them each received a 10-year prison sentence, and the plate-maker, seven years, but authorities believe that the main perpetrator has still not been caught.

In Brisbane, on 29 April, 1971, a home was raided and authorities seized an offset printing machine from a room underneath. They took possession of zinc plates that could be used to forge $10 and $2 notes. A total of 225 forged $10 and 1,477 forged $2 notes was also found. The $10 notes were of a new type of forgery first discovered circulating in Brisbane in January of that year.

In June, 1971, a further eight men were arrested in connection with forged tax stamps and $10 notes and 2,790 forged $10 notes were located in the boot of a car in Queensland.

Three forged $20 notes were found in one week in New South Wales. They had Knight-Wheeler signatures and all bore the serial number XQB 531364. They were of relatively poor standard, but the colours closely matched those of the genuine note. They had a waxy feel and the printing was slightly blurred. The name *Kingsford Smith* was not distinct and a faint printed line was substituted for the metallic strip. The front of the note had a printed simulation of a watermark and the printing across the top lacked definition and was smudgy. The back of the note had a reddish-black denomination figure at top left, and at bottom right it was smudgy and lacked definition.

In 1980, $20 and $50 notes were located which had been made up of sliced sections from a number of other notes. The originals had been rejoined and the "spare" pieces used to manufacture additional notes, resulting in forgeries which were 16 mm shorter. Up to 50 such notes had been found in Melbourne by August of that year, and an 18 year old man appeared in the Sydney court on 12 September, 1980, charged with the forgery and uttering of the notes. (Called composite notes).

On 12 August, 1983, five men appeared in a Melbourne court charged with forging and possessing $50 notes to the approximate street value of $3 million, and with having uttered $30,000, knowing it to be forged. One man was later charged with having made a printing plate. The offences occurred at Long Gully, Victoria, between 12 July and 12 August, 1983. The court appearances followed two police raids code-named "Operation Anvil" in the Bendigo area.

The month after the introduction of the $100 note in March, 1984, two $100 notes were passed in Melbourne shops. They were photocopies pasted together and coloured in with pencils. The next month a man was located by police in Port Pirie S.A. after he had duplicated 30 copies of the $100 note on both sides of the paper.

In August, 1984, forged $100 notes totalling $300,000 were recovered in a North Melbourne lane, and on 6 August, 11 notes were found with heroin. The forged notes bore serial numbers DBR 429250 to DBR 429254. Serial numbers of genuine notes commenced with a "Z", and the signatures, titles and legal tender clause are blue. Photocopy forgeries render the signatures and legal tender clause black.

From January to September, 1991, the Federal Police Currency Squad seized more than $3.2 million in counterfeit Australian notes and a little more in fake American currency. Two men were charged with possessing counterfeit $50 and $100 notes "worth" more than $3.2 million in January, 1991.

In February, 1992, Federal police were looking for a young couple who used forged $50 notes to buy jewellery valued at more than $6,000. 145 of the forgeries had been passed bearing one of the following serial numbers: WCU 073027, WCL 259820, WCZ 430485, WEE 493985 or WEJ 296803.

The Bulletin of May 19, 1992, reported that numerous forged $50 notes had circulated with serial numbers starting with YOZ 427 - thousands of dollars worth having been passed over a six month period until the murder-suicide of a suspect and his girlfriend in Sydney on April 26, 1991. Police were also looking for the printer of fake $100 notes with serial number prefixes ZDU and ZEX. Further reading: *Suckers for a suss buck,* Martin Warneminde, *The Bulletin,* May 19, 1992.

In 1993, a number of forged $100 notes were passed in Melbourne suburbs. They contained a watermark and a metallic thread. After about $5,000 in counterfeits had been circulated, a house in Box Hill was raided and forged notes to the "value" of $164,000 were discovered, together with enough paper to forge another $2.2 million. On February 18, 1994, Eddy Grant pleaded guilty to counterfeiting $164,950 in Australian $50 and $100 notes, and uttering $5,400 in $100 notes. Most of the forgeries passed through the banks undetected and were not discovered until they reached the C.V.C.S. machines in the Reserve Bank of Australia. The colour reproduction was perfect, and all notes had different serial numbers. Further reading: *Eddie the Forger,* Michael Vort-Ronald, *Australian Coin Review*, May, 1994, and *Master forger lived in luxury, Sunday Herald Sun,* February 20, 1994.

In 1993, some forged $20 notes were located with serial numbers RUB 619711, and $10 forgeries with serial numbers MLK 483617. Other $10 forgeries discovered in June of that year had serial numbers MPC 758652, MKZ 574494 and MPF 346239.

In late 1995-early 1996, up to $250,000 in forged $100 notes had been distributed in Sydney. They were named "the Teacher's series" after the credit union where they first appeared. There was not as much detail on them as the genuine notes, and they had a printed line instead of a metallic strip.

The introduction of polymer $20 notes from 1994, $50 notes from 1995 and $100 notes from 1996 drastically reduced the incidents of forgeries of Australian notes, although large quantities of foreign notes (mostly American $100 bills) have also been forged in this country.

The Australian Federal Police Currency Squad is responsible for;

Conducting or coordinating the investigation of currency and currency related offences in Australia.
The collection, recording and dissemination of information on counterfeiting in general, both nationally and internationally.
Liaison with the United States Secret Service with respect to counterfeit United States currency, and,
Arranging the expert examination and final disposal of all counterfeit currency.

If you suspect you have been handed a counterfeit banknote, it should be placed in a plastic bag or envelope as soon as possible with a minimum of handling (to preserve any fingerprints) and it should then be reported to the AFP Currency Squad immediately on (03) 9607 7777, or to your nearest police station.

ADM 489

RESERVE BANK OF AUSTRALIA

REWARD

COUNTERFEIT AUSTRALIAN NOTES

SUBSTANTIAL REWARDS of up to $50,000 will be paid by the RESERVE BANK OF AUSTRALIA for information leading to the arrest and conviction of persons responsible for the counterfeiting of Australian notes or the uttering or the unlawful possession of counterfeit Australian notes.

ANY PERSON with information should communicate immediately with the nearest Police Station or the Australian Federal Police, Currency Branch. The information and its source will be treated as strictly confidential.

B. W. FRASER
GOVERNOR
RESERVE BANK OF AUSTRALIA

Fig. 468. Reserve Bank of Australia reward notice.

Chapter 13: POLYMER NOTES

While this volume is principally a study of the paper decimal note issues, it is appropriate to give a brief introduction to the polymer notes that replaced them. A much more detailed study of the polymer notes will be presented in a future volume, *Australian Polymer Banknotes.*

The first polymer note was issued for the 1988 Bicentenary and first released on the day after "Australia Day" (26 January, 1988) on the 27th January. It was issued alongside the paper $10 as a commemorative issue, not a replacement of the existing $10.

The New Note Series (NNS) polymer notes later replaced the existing paper notes as under:

$5	7 July, 1992.	$20	24 October, 1994.	$100	15 May, 1996.
$10	11 November, 1993.	$50	4 October, 1995.		

A recoloured $5 polymer note was issued on 24 April, 1995, after persistent complaints from the public that the original pastel colours used on the $5 were hard to distinguish from the NNS $10, especially in poor lighting conditions.

While the Bicentenary $10 incorporated an OVD (Optically Variable Device) of Captain Cook, the NNS notes incorporated a clear window with white design features in the window. Metallic threads were no longer used, nor the watermark, but the NNS notes did incorporate something similar to a watermark in the form of a Coat-of-Arms which was visible within the design when held up to light.

The Bicentenary $10 was also issued in July, 1988, in a souvenir folder for $14 with the overprinted date of issue as 26 JANUARY 1988. Serial number prefixes were AA. General circulation notes had AB prefixes. Souvenir folders were also produced for the NNS notes as they were issued:

$5	Paper note, and polymer note with date overprinted 7 JULY 1992 in purple.
$5	Recoloured, portfolio with old and new polymer notes, the recoloured note overprinted with date 24 APRIL 1995 in red.
$10	Last and first portfolio, paper and polymer notes with matching red serial numbers and date on polymer note in red.
	Folder with paper note, and polymer note with date overprinted 1 NOVEMBER 1993, in black, and black serial numbers (normal issues used blue serial numbers).
	As above, but serial number and overprint in purple.
$20	Last and First portfolio as in $10.
	Folder with paper note, and a polymer note with date overprinted 24 OCTOBER 1994 in black.
	Folder with single overprinted polymer note.
$50	As in the $20 note, but with date 4 OCTOBER 1995 in black.
$100	As in the $20 note, but with date 15 MAY 1996 in green.

Later, there were various commemorative issues and joint issues. Those containing only polymer notes will be dealt with in detail in *Australian Polymer Banknotes.* Those including a paper note are listed in the relative paper sections of general circulating issues of this book, and Collector Issues, Chapter 9.

Fig. 469. Front, Bicentenary polymer $10, basic colours blue, green and orange-yellow.

Issued 27 January, 1988 to 31 December, 1988.

Size 155 mm x 77.5 mm.

Security features OVD (Optically Variable Device) featuring Captain James Cook.
Wave pattern "watermark", see-through registration and micro-printing.

Signatures R.A. Johnston - B.W. Fraser.

Designer Sydney graphic designer, Harry Williamson.

Front HMS "Supply" in Sydney Cove with a medley of people.

Back Aboriginal Youth, with a Morning Star Pole by Aboriginal artist Yumbulul. Other background designs are from original Aboriginal works commissioned by the Reserve Bank of Australia.

Fig. 470. Back, Bicentenary polymer $10, basic colours blue-black, orange and purple.

NNS POLYMER $5 - FIRST COLOUR

Fig. 471. Front, first polymer $5, basic colour purple.

Issued	7 July, 1992.
Size	130 mm x 65 mm.
Security features	Transparent window with a white gum flower. Micro-printing, see-through registration, Coat-of-Arms "watermark" and fluorescent chequerboard patch and serial number (white and cream).
Signatures	B.W. Fraser - A.C. Cole, B.W. Fraser - E.A. Evans.
Designer	Bruce Stewart, Chief Designer at Note Printing Australia.
Front	Her Majesty, Queen Elizabeth II, and gum leaves and flowers.
Back	The old and new parliament houses, Canberra, A.C.T.
Delayed issue	The original date of issue was forecast for May, 1991, but was delayed until July, 1992, because of a number of technical problems.

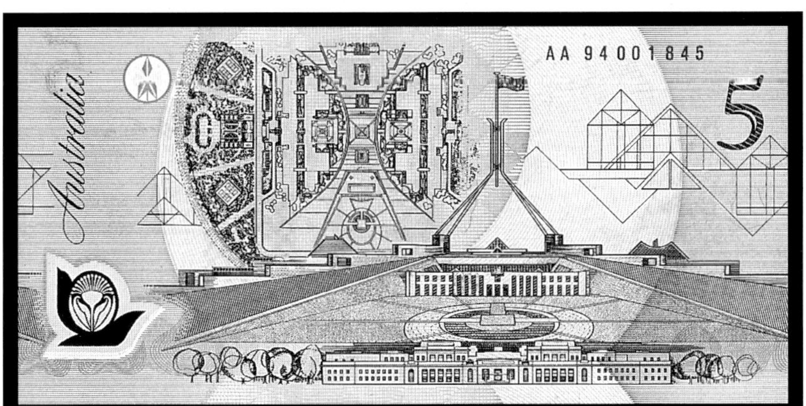

Fig. 472. Back, first polymer $5, basic colour purple.

Fig. 473. Front, recoloured polymer $5, basic colour mauve.

Issued 24 April, 1995.

Size 130 mm x 65 mm.

Security features As in the previous NNS $5.

Additional features Style of the denomination figure changed, and orientation bands added. Solid white fluorescent patch.

Signatures B.W. Fraser - E.A. Evans, I. Macfarlane - E.A. Evans.

Designer Bruce Stewart, Chief Designer at Note Printing Australia.
Basic colour changed from purple to mauve to help distinguish it from the NNS $10 issued in 1993.
All other details as in the first polymer $5 issue.
In 2001, the centenary of Federation, a new $5 polymer note will be issued featuring Henry Parkes "The father of Federation" and Catherine Helen Spence, journalist, novelist and social worker.

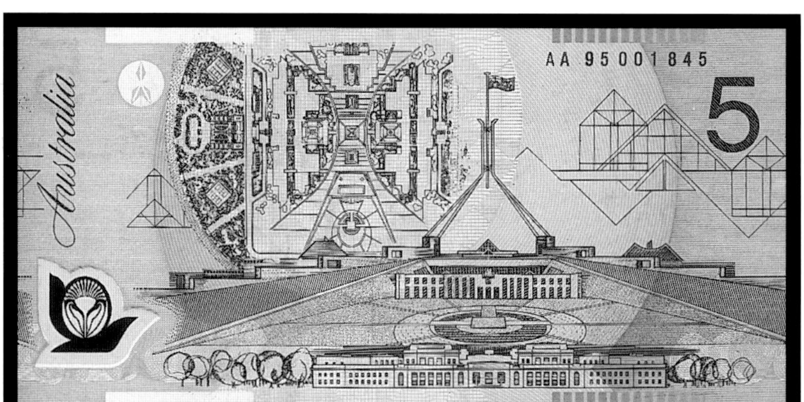

Fig. 474. Back, recoloured $5, basic colour mauve.

NNS POLYMER $10

Fig. 475. Front, NNS polymer $10, basic colour blue.

Issued 1 November, 1993.

Size 137 mm x 65 mm.

Security features Transparent window with a white windmill. Micro-printing, see-through registration, Coat-of-Arms "watermark" and fluorescent serial numbers (blue).

Signatures B.W. Fraser - E.A. Evans, I. Macfarlane - E.A. Evans.

Designer Melbourne-based graphic designer, Max Robinson.

Front Andrew Barton (Banjo) Paterson (1864-1941), poet and ballad writer, author of *Waltzing Matilda* and *The Man from Snowy River.*

Back Dame Mary Gilmore (nee Cameron, 1865-1962), poet, patriot and tireless campaigner against injustice and deprivation.

All of the Australian polymer denominations have "see through" registration. When held up to light, half of a pattern on one side lines up exactly with the other half of the pattern on the other side.

Fig. 476. Back, NNS polymer $10, basic colour blue.

Fig. 477. Front, NNS polymer $20, basic colour red.

Issued 31 October, 1994.

Size 144 mm c 65 mm.

Security features Transparent window with a white compass. Micro-printing, see-through registration, Coat-of-Arms "watermark" and fluorescent denomination patch and serial numbers (yellow).

Signatures B.W. Fraser - E.A. Evans, I. Macfarlane - E.A. Evans.

Designer Graphic designer, Garry Emery.

Front Mary Reibey (nee Haydock 1777 - 1855), originally transported to Australia for seven years for horse-stealing, she married, and with her husband, carried on with the family businesses. After his death in 1811, enterprises expanded into warehouses and shipping.

Back Reverend John Flynn (1880 - 1951), founder of the Australian Inland Mission and the Royal Flying Doctor Service.

Fig. 478. Back, NNS polymer $20, basic colour red.

NNS POLYMER $50

Fig. 479. Front, NNS polymer $50, basic colour gold.

Issued	4 October, 1995.
Size	151 mm x 65 mm.
Security features	Transparent window with the stars of the Southern Cross in white. Micro-printing, see-through registration, Coat-of-Arms "watermark" and fluorescent denomination patch and serial numbers (yellow).
Signatures	B.W. Fraser - E.A. Evans, I. Macfarlane - E.A. Evans.
Designer	Melbourne-based graphic designer Brian Sadgrove.
Front	David Unaipon (1872 - 1967), inventor and first published Aboriginal writer, who was awarded a Coronation Medal in 1953 for his achievements.
Back	Dame Edith Dircksey Cowan (nee Brown 1861 - 1932), social worker and first female member of an Australian Parliament. For her various activities, including her role with Red Cross in WWI, she was awarded an O.B.E. in 1920.

Fig. 480. Back, NNS polymer $50, basic colour gold.

NNS POLYMER $100

Fig. 481. Front, NNS polymer $100, basic colour green.

Issued 15 May, 1996.

Size 158 mm x 65 mm.

Security features Transparent window with a white Lyrebird. Micro-printing, see-through registration, Coat-of-Arms "watermark" and fluorescent denomination patch and serial numbers (yellow).

Signatures B.W. Fraser - E.A. Evans, I. Macfarlane - E.A. Evans.

Designer Bruce Stewart (former) Chief Designer with Note Printing Australia.

Front Dame Nellie Melba (Helen Porter Armstrong nee Mitchell 1861-1931), soprano opera singer, appointed a D.B.E in 1918 and a G.B.E. in 1927.

Back Sir John Monash (1865 - 1931) soldier, engineer and administrator. He was knighted in 1918, and after the war led the State Electricity Commission of Victoria for 10 years until his death. See also, page 42.

Fig. 482. Back, NNS polymer $100, basic colour green.

Chapter 14: LAWS AFFECTING CURRENCY

The information contained in this chapter is intended only as an indication of some of the laws affecting currency. It is recommended that copies of the relevant Acts be consulted if further, more detailed information, is required.

The Currency Act, 1963 (Act No. 67 of 1963), assented to on 30 October, 1963, repealed the *Coinage Acts of 1909, 1936 and 1947.* The Act established the monetary unit as the dollar with the cent being one hundredth of a dollar, and listed the cent equivalents of pence as shown in Fig. 63.

It set Legal Tender for five, ten, twenty or fifty cents for payment of an amount not exceeding $5 and for other coins (one and two cents) for an amount not exceeding twenty cents. It made arrangements for the introduction of the Decimal Currency System, set out the powers of the Treasurer and established the Decimal Currency Board and its Constitution. Part VI, Miscellaneous, specified the prohibition of other than official coins and gave the standard composition of coins.

The Currency Act, 1965 (No. 95 of 1965) as amended, repeated much of the 1963 Act above, expanded upon it, and added legal tender for coins greater than fifty cents, but less than $10 - for payment of an amount not exceeding 10 times the face value of a coin of the denomination concerned. For coins of $10 - payments not exceeding $100, and for coins of another denomination - for payment of any amount.

The **Reserve Bank Act, 1959** (Act number 4 of 1959 as amended) repealed the *Commonwealth Bank Acts* of 1945, 1948, 1951 and 1953. Part II sets out the Constitution, policy and management of the Reserve Bank of Australia. Part III deals with the Reserve Bank Board and the Governor and Deputy Governor of the Bank. Part IIIA covers the Payments System Board and Part IV, Central banking. Part V relates to The Note Issue, some Sections of which follow:

Section	Summary
32	Defines an Australian note as a note issued under the *Australian Notes Act 1910,* under Part VII of the *Commonwealth Bank Act 1911,* under Part VI of the *Commonwealth Bank Act 1945* or under this Part as in force at any time.
34	The Bank has power to issue, re-issue and cancel Australian notes.
35	Notes may be issued for $1, $2, $5, $10, $20, $50, or $100 or in any other denomination that the Treasurer, by instrument in writing published in the (Government) *Gazette,* determines.
36	Lists pre-decimal notes from Ten shillings to One thousand pounds and gives their decimal equivalents from One dollar to Two thousand dollars.
37	Notes shall bear the signature of the Secretary to the Treasury or of such other officer of the Department of the Treasury as the Treasurer directs, and the signature of the Governor or, if the Governor so directs, of the Deputy Governor, or an officer of the Bank, specified by the Governor. Signatures may be in the handwriting of those persons or may be made by engraving or by any other process determined by the Bank.
44	A person or a State shall not issue a bill or note for the payment of money payable to the bearer on demand and intended for circulation.

Part VII covers The Reserve Bank Service with Part VIII dealing with Miscellaneous issues.

The major amendment was enacted in 1989 (No. 129 of 1989) which repealed section 33 and sections 38 to 42 of the Act relating to the former "Note Issue Department", with the changes discontinuing the need for a separate Note Issue Department. Previously, section 34 provided that the Bank, through the Note Issue Department, may issue Australian notes....Section 35 was amended (No, 54 of 1998) to add the denomination of "one hundred dollars" to the Act. When that denomination was first issued, authority was given in terms of the provisions for the Treasurer to determine in writing, published in the *Gazette.*

The Crimes (Currency) Act 1981, (No. 122 of 1981 as amended) Part II relates to offences.

In relation to counterfeit money or counterfeit prescribed securities, it is an offence to: make or begin to make, utter, buy, sell, receive or dispose of, offer to buy, or sell, procure or dispose of such material. It is an offence to possess counterfeit money knowing it to be counterfeit - a defence to which is that the person did not make the counterfeit money, and that he did not, after the time when he first learned that the counterfeit money (or prescribed security) was counterfeit, have a reasonable opportunity to surrender it to a member of the Australian Federal Police or of the police force of a State or Territory or to any other person prescribed for the purpose of that section. Similar offences relate to possession, import or export of instruments and material for counterfeiting.

It is also unlawful for anyone without lawful authority or reasonable excuse to knowingly convey out of any premises at which the production of genuine coins or money is or was carried on, any material used in the production, designing or experimentation regarding paper money or coins.

It is also an offence to give or offer to give information to assist with the making of counterfeit money; to possess filings or clippings from genuine coins; deface, sell or possess defaced current coins or paper money; design, make, print, distribute, export or import a business card or other material capable of misleading a person into believing it to be current paper money or make or sell an article to be used in substitution for a current coin or paper money, for the purpose of operating a machine that is designed to receive current coins or current paper money.

An International Convention for the suppression of counterfeiting currency was signed by a number of countries on April 20, 1929. It now forms a Schedule attached to the Crimes (Currency) Act.

Arrangements in respect of foreign currency have been simplified over a number of years. With the exception of sanctions imposed in terms of United Nations Security Council resolutions, there are no restrictions on the movement of funds into or out of Australia. The UNSC sanctions relate to certain transactions involving Iraq, the Federal Republic of Yugoslavia (Serbia and Montenegro), Libya, the Taliban and the National Union for the Total Independence of Angola (UNITA) which are prohibited without prior approval from the Reserve Bank of Australia.

However, under the **Financial Transaction Reports Act, 1988,** if carrying \$10,000 or more (or the foreign equivalent) into or out of Australia, it must be declared to Customs on departure or arrival, likewise when shipping or mailing such amounts. The **Protection of Movable Cultural Heritage Act, 1986,** has Regulations which came into force on May 1, 1999 which prohibit the export out of Australia of certain numismatic and other items valued at \$15,000 or more which are not represented in at least two public collections in Australia by an object of equivalent quality.

Chapter 15: STATISTICS.

TOTALS OF NEW NOTES RECEIVED BY R.B.A. FROM PRINTER x 000 (Thousands)

30 June	$1	$2	$5	$10	$20	$50	$100
1965	350		-	-	-	-	-
1966	85,000	105,440	-	58,000	18,720	-	-
1967	44,650	80,960	29,920	19,000	15,280	-	-
1968	26,000	66,040	18,080	37,360	2,000	-	-
1969	80,150	107,480	9,600	42,560	14,000	-	-
1970	85,500	117,840	26,400	58,040	17,000	-	-
1971	88,350	122,960	32,000	72,560	17,000	-	-
1972	88,050	107,360	25,520	54,340	17,880	-	-
1973	73,950	84,020	20.240	36,000	17,960	-	-
1974	107,050	106,360	27,040	62,240	25,530	8,521	-
1975	84,608.5	94,008.5	27,208.5	40,408.5	30,608.5	4,920	-
1976	89,800	108,200	43,710	65,810	54,090	9,150	-
1977	90,610	110,200	41,290	51,790	43,690	5,600	-
1978	90,200	120,200	45,000	35,120	60,000	11,910	-
1979	94,600	106,600	37,800	65,800	56,190	15,510	-
1980	93,020	95,400	39,590	62,600	56,400	28,000	-
1981	130,110	91,000	28,350	35,710	61,540	7,520	-
1982	51,850	78,200	23,030	22,260	21,640	12,620	-
1983	71,050	102,800	50,430	47,200	63,970	34,580	-
1984	74,740	152,200	44,550	54,200	57,450	40,400	6,802
1985	-	164,321	78,421	80,431	82,001	40,400	19,144
1986	-	170,200	81,430	54,500	151,210	38,001	12,816
1987	-	109,310	84,780	106,270	79,790	40,800	24,940
1988	-	67,823	72,045	69,720	122,510	47,550	17,400

Years ended 30 June - actual totals of new paper notes received by Reserve Bank from printer.

Year	$5	$10	$20	$50	$100
1989	58,400,000	123,099,000	169,490,000	11,780,000	16,400,000
1990	34,440,000	36,673,000	119,745,880	67,358,320	17,903,000
1991	78,887,000	131,186,000	151,238,960	48,814,000	32,672,000
1992	92,969,000	86,040,000	134,976,000	86,186,000	28,320,200
1993	20,000	56,070,000	130,553,500	123,077,000	28,100,100
1994	-	12,900	47,938,000	184,045,000	-
1995	-	-	10,910	3,002	4,606
1996	-	-	-	-	900
1997	-	-	-	-	2,400

1995 totals of 10,910 for $20 would consist mainly of 10,000 sold in uncut sheets of 40 and 900 in Last and First Portfolios. 1996 total of 900 $100 notes used in Last and First Portfolios. 1997 total of 2,400 $100 notes sold as 75 uncut sheets of 32.

ACTUAL TOTALS OF NEW PAPER NOTES DELIVERED TO R.B.A. FOR YEARS ENDED 30 JUNE

1965	350,000	1981	354,230,000
1966	267,160,000	1982	209,600,000
1967	189,810,000	1983	370,030,000
1968	149,480,000	1984	430,342,000
1969	253,790,000	1985	464,718,000
1970	304,780,000	1986	508,157,000
1971	332,870,000	1987	445,890,000
1972	293,150,000	1988	397,048,200
1973	232,170,000	1989	379,169,000
1974	336,741,000	1990	276,120,000
1975	281,762,500	1991	442,797,960
1976	370,760,000	1992	428,491,200
1977	343,180,000	1993	337,820,600
1978	362,430,000	1994	231,995,900
1979	376,140,000	1995	18,518
1980	375,010,000	1996	900
		1997	2,400

The following totals are calculated from a summary from 1966 ending 30 June, 1984, and the sum of the totals given for all the Wednesdays in the Financial Years from 30 June, 1985 to 30 June, 1999, courtesy of the Reserve Bank of Australia.

Grand totals of new paper notes received from the Printer, as below:

$1 notes	1,549,030,240
$2 notes	2,469,874,240
$5 notes	1,151,142,240
$10 notes	1,664,272,340
$20 notes	1,840,404,490
$50 notes	865,984,422
$100 notes	204,315,206
Total	**9,745,023,178**

Figures given for 1965 to 1984 are from "Australian Decimal Banknotes" first edition (1985) as totals of notes printed by Note Printing Branch, Reserve Bank of Australia.

TOTALS OF NOTES IN CIRCULATION

From Monthly Statements, Note Issue Department, as published in the *Commonwealth of Australia Gazette* to 1972, and then as published in the *Australian Government Gazette.* December statements from 1966 to 1984 and 1987, September statements 1985, 1986. $40 = 20 pounds. Old high value notes were progressively "written off" the books if not redeemed within 40 years of issue. The June, 1985, statement showed 7 twenty pounds outstanding, but they were "written off" by September, 1985.

Year	$1	$2	$5	$10	$20	$40
23/2/66	46,161,146	83,556,384	-	43,684,671	16,560,384	38
1966	36,737,284	78,379,927	-	48,357,551	19,905,553,	37
1967	37,388,679	66,788,285	12,051,263	47,388,517	23,044,639	28
1968	39,527,268	65,332,023	14,563,410	50,633,177	26,153,853	23
1969	41,375,131	62,360,747	15,331,499	50,263,511	27,978,976	22
1970	44,901,532	64,655,061	17,717,437	57,715,469	32,795,504	13
1971	46,869,377	65,470,869	19,125,872	64,135,590	38,725,859	3
1972	49,333,437	66,736,383	20,633,922	71,214,922	45,552,845	3
1973	54,679,841	71,050,463	22,865,961	80,938,303	54,639,807	3
1974	58,455,988	72,027,015	24,344,273	78,405,997	64,629,634	3
1975	57,086,316	67,946,153	24,552,843	70,252,206	68,718,025	3
1976	61,717,576	73,208,528	26,683,792	71,657,507	83,018,059	3
1977	65,784,978	74,660,057	27,764,728	68,424,963	89,326,330	3
1978	69,432,862	76,232,366	29,137,557	66,351,555	95,696,470	-
1979	74,593,199	79,706,284	31,337,655	66,275,821	107,145,084	-
1980	78,410,853	80,716,478	32,592,537	60,524,781	107,587,806	-
1981	84,624,574	85,307,549	35,175,006	60,945,750	116,797,375	-
1982	88,231,427	88,568,596	37,316,488	60,501,059	120,126,891	-
1983	95,434,015	90,715,277	39,714,469	57,974,440	127,518,040	-
1984	46,423,608	97,896,205	42,515,591	59,191,036	131,500,506	-
1985	44,359,070	88,041,538	38,724,322	51,731,293	113,861,908	-
1986	41,882,263	87,300,201	40,717,479	52,499,576	115,835,648	-
1987	40,022,285	99,583,345	48,353,309	61,902,380	132,869,021	-
1988	38,308,559	38,877,555	45,989,816	57,647,236	124,295,090	-
1989	36 Million	27 Million	48 Million	64 Million	128 Million	
1990	43 M	38 M	47 M	69 M	114 M	
1991	43 M	37 M	50 M	68 M	102 M	
1992	42 M	36 M	52 M	59 M	92 M	
1993	42 M	35 M	59 M	59 M	91 M	
1994	21 M	35 M	63 M	63 M	90 M	
1995	20 M	25 M	66 M	61 M	92 M	
1996	19 M	24 M	67 M	58 M	93 M	
1997	19 M	24 M	70 M	60 M	92 M	
1998	19 M	24 M	72 M	62 M	90 M	
1999	0	23 M	76 M	64 M	93 M	

Year	$50	*$100	*$200	Banks $	Public $	Total $
23/2/66	-	439	203	298,070,466	683,343,858	981,414,324
1966	-	434	201	219,514,252	855,754,536	1,075,268,788
1967	-	424	200	232,380,737	933,702,297	1,166,083,034
1968	-	416	200	202,640,840	1,069,858,874	1,272,499,714
1969	-	406	185	175,046,803	1,130,000,427	1,305,047,230
1970	-	392	170	225,422,099	1,270,515,230	1,495,937,329
1971	-	378	153	281,612,940	1,407,769,135	1,689,382,075
1972	-	84	95	309,914,947	1,599,294,506	1,909,209,453
1973	2,748,874	81	90	334,783,947	2,015,975,715	2,350,759,662
1974	8,053,070	74	84	371,184,566	2,432,377,287	2,803,561,853
1975	12,870,359	38	69	366,286,450	2,669,874,617	3,036,161,067
1976	19,277,387	32	61	595,949,415	3,086,425,297	3,682,374,712
1977	24,606,195	26	60	625,046,626	3,429,982,806	4,055,029,432
1978	31,173,923	20	54	673,400,230	3,830,339,049	4,503,739,279
1979	38,820,922	14	27	600,951,334	4,536,455,498	5,137,406,832
1980	45,820,340	-	14	618,412,452	4,832,417,772	5,450,830,224
1981	56,687,722	-	2	764,785,005	5,446,123,197	6,210,908,202
1982	67,940,117	-	9	971,476,615	5,885,030,504	6,856,507,119
1983	81,467,408	-	8	1,073,160,346	6,605,753,768	7,678,914,114

*$100 = Fifty pound notes. *$200 = One hundred pound notes

Year	$50	$100	*$200	Banks $	Public $	Total $
1984	77,127,474	13,169,824	7	1,011,064,097	7,839,007,856	8,850,071,953
1985	68,225,730	17,206,339	-	812,420,978	7,528,124,268	8,340,545,268

Year	$50	$100	Banks $	Public $	Total $
1986	70,177,204	24,392,507	883,688,703	8,326,200,977	9,209,889,680
1987	81,144,994	37,151,533	1,355,983,821	10,193,778,919	11,529,762,740
1988	78,722,442	42,042,102	1,020,883,034	10,527,716,175	11,548,599,209
1989	81 Million	48 Million			12,346 Million
1990	89 M	52 M			12,981 M
1991	107 M	64 M			14,793 M
1992	114 M	67 M			15,180 M
1993	126 M	73 M			16,367 M
1994	137 M	79 M			17,577 M
1995	144 M	85 M			18,538 M
1996	159 M	84 M			19,182 M
1997	178 M	83 M			20,064 M
1998	190 M	93 M			21,651 M
1999	207 M	103 M			23,552 M

1989 to 1999, taken from statistics published in the Reserve Bank annual report and financial statements for notes on issue and value of notes on issue, as at end of June each year.

TOTALS OF PAPER DECIMAL NOTES DESTROYED for years ending 30 June.

Year	$1	$2	$5	$10	$20
1966	1,181,321	918,151	-	162,718	24,042.5
1967	44,944,221.5	67,879,320	-	14,282,536.5	1,977,553.5
1968	56,400,657.5	93,370,711	8,270,621	36,229,711	5,793,490
1969	65,865,164	101,709,281	20,960,120	45,225,962.5	9,550,766.5
1970	78,637,719	111,654,375	24,184,684	48,658,265.5	10,880,529.5
1971	85,210,540	114,061,515	26,720,166	55,080,616	13,454,437.5
1972	84,279,948	108,294,491	26,006,656	48,203,309	12,511,242.5
1973	79,473,643	94,111,815	23,390,558	42,722,041	12,316,258.5
1974	81,066,111	91,062,148	24,301,726	43,237,760.5	13,614,364
1975	80,480,354	90,884,926	26,791,199	45,698,889.5	18,185,955
1976	87,809,196	105,689,120	31,349,440	53,156,759	28,024,140.5
1977	91,991,132	106,363,454.5	34,414,240.5	50,803,897	34,667,183.5
1978	84,625,625	98,388,260.5	34,236,860	53,159,648	41,296,315
1979	92,928,277.5	102,216,563.5	36,980,377.5	54,676,870.5	46,551,286.5
1980	88,185,871	104,479,171	37,934,991	52,526,689	50,680,945.5
1981	87,193,501.5	98,826,959.5	35,777,364	46,200,659	47,739,589
1982	87,702,962	100,069,085	37,214,486	48,471,411.5	45,076,621
1983	83,076,679	93,105,738.5	36,987,081	46,292,194.5	53,927,982
1984	108,703,080	93,776,457.5	39,597,593	43,048,183	60,141,294.5
1985	18,656,881	127,930,379	53,242,090	60,962,896	81,048,591
1986	1,111,987	168,983,755	75,066,187	83,115,789	109,532,723
1987	474,450	145,130,269	67,452,740	68,292,149	96,521,699
1988	426,126	129,675,588	59,686,701	62,028,832	97,358,106
1989	367,913	76,951,874	69,791,804	74,880,121	148,343,388
1990	255,867	7,540,467	67,370,375	95,830,168	138,435,947
1991	16,907,980	1,234,902	73,208,268	95,487,002	125,083,063
1992	379,257	784,904	95,523,521	100,346,536	140,476,239
1993	675,033	631,069	67,151,672	89,552,891	117,500,333
1994	244,884	545,848	4,849,375	78,784,186	94,756,610
1995	267,395	419,994	1,037,928	7,443,307	112,880,368
1996	242,920	348,455	2,236,429	2,723,982	49,896,592
1997	218,662	334,080	1,140,858	1,685,930	5,303,880
1998	215,150	306,593	648,080	983,024	2,963,490
1999	302,115	227,061	247,391	510,490	1,401,873

.5 MEANS HALF A NOTE DESTROYED

Persons can receive half the value of half a note if the other half is lost or destroyed.

Totals of decimal paper notes destroyed - continued

Year	$50	$100	Total notes
1974	59,161		
1975	531,724		
1976	1,389,841.5		
1977	2,491,299		
1978	4,096,847		
1979	5,778,449.5		
1980	6,883,788		
1981	8,201,423		
1982	12,448,525.5		
1983	12,033,150.5		
1984	16,427,567		
1985	36,224,294	2,266,441	380,331,572
1986	38,852,254	6,183,596	482,846,290
1987	33,221,572	6,465,835	417,558,714
1988	26,855,049	5,126,300	381,156,699
1989	40,869,339	10,455,931	421,660,369
1990	40,363,714	11,385,687	361,182,224
1991	41,234,256	9,133,460	362,288,932
1992	67,042,895	12,328,526	416,881,878
1993	74,898,264	11,782,970	362,192,231
1994	63,545,305	8,392,180	251,118,388
1995	71,907,051	9,167,302	203,123,343
1996	186,248,652	32,212,209	273,909,238
1997	43,149,256	51,127,625	102,960,289
1998	11,440,196	11,955,258	28,511,790
1999	4,230,137	4,453,848	11,372,914

Totals of decimal paper notes destroyed from 1966 to June, 1984.

$1	1,468,756,003
$2	1,776,861,543
$5	505,118,163
$10	827,838,121
$20	506,413,997
$50	70,341,776
$100	-8,287

The total of the above is stated at 5,155,321,315.

To the above totals add totals from June, 1985, onwards, which are the sum of all the totals given on the Wednesdays of the Financial Years from 1 July, 1984 to 30 June, 1999.

ANNUAL SURVEYS BY AUTHOR

PERCENTAGES OF SIGNATURE COMBINATIONS IN CIRCULATION.

Annual surveys have been conducted in trading banks by the author from 1975 to determine the frequency or scarcity of various signature combinations on notes in circulation. All surveys up to 1993 were conducted in large South Australian country towns. In 1994 a combination of banks and a city security company, and from 1995, solely a security company. In most cases 2,000 notes were surveyed in each denomination and the results converted to percentages of the total checked. Reports on the various surveys were published in full in the *Australian Coin Review* each year.

Where 2,000 notes were surveyed, the following percentages mean: .05% = one note located in 2,000; .25% = one in 400; 1.25% = 25 notes or one in 80, etc. The following tables show the annual rise and fall of the various signature combinations as new notes printed with the then current signatures replaced older worn notes. In particular, the variance of percentages of current signature combinations and the previous signature combination changes quite noticeably each year.

From 1975 to 1995 inclusive, a total of $3,512,000 was checked. There were no star replacement notes found during any of the surveys, nor any significant errors, or forgeries. The last $1 survey was in 1984 and the last $2 survey in 1988 following withdrawal of those denominations in those years in favour of coins. As a result of the introduction of the NNS polymer notes, the last surveys of paper notes in the various denominations were as follows; $5 - 1992, $10 - 1993, $20 - 1995, $50 - 1995 and $100 - 1995.

Dates of surveys, totals of notes checked and total $ value checked each year.

Date of survey	$1	$2	$5	$10	$20	$50	$100	Total	Total $
May-June 1975	2,000	2,000	2,000	2,000	2,000			10,000	76,000
May 1976	2,000	2,000	2,000	2,000	2,000			10,000	76,000
2-7 June 1977	2,000	2,000	2,000	2,000	2,000	270		10,270	89,500
29-30 May 1978	2,000	2,000	2,000	2,000	2,000	500		10,500	101,000
End May 1979	2,000	2,000	2,000	2,000	2,000	2,000		12,000	176,000
Mid June 1980	2,000	2,000	2,000	2,000	2,000	1,000		11,000	126,000
9-10 June 1981	2,000	2,000	2,000	2,000	2,000	1,000		11,000	126,000
16-17 June 1982	2,000	2,000	2,000	2,000	2,000	2,000		12,000	176,000
1 June 1983	2,000	2,000	2,000	2,000	2,000	2,000		12,000	176,000
4-5 June 1984	400	2,000	2,000	2,000	2,000	2,000		10,400	174,400

Totals of various decimal notes surveyed annually - continued.(* polymer notes)

Date of survey	$1	$2	$5	$10	$20	$50	$100	Total	Total $
5-6 June 1985		2,000	2,000	2,000	2,000	2,000	–	10,000	174,000
2-4 June 1986		2,000	2,000	2,000	2,000	2,000	300	10,300	204,000
1-2 June 1987		2,000	2,000	2,000	2,000	2,000	400	10,400	214,000
2-3 June 1988		2,000	2,000	2,000	2,000	2,000	500	10,500	224,000
6-7 June1989			2,000	2,000	2,000	2,000	500	8,500	220,000
5-7 June 1990			1,000	1,000	2,000	1,000	300	5,300	135,000
(2 days)June 1991			1,000	1,500	2,000	2,000	200	6,700	180,000
1-2 June 1992			1,000	1,500	2,000	1,500	200	6,200	155,000
1-3 June 1993				1,000	1,500	1,500	200	4,200	135,000
3+6 June 1994			2,200*		3,000	2,500	1,000	8,700	295,000
1 June 1995			2,000*		1,000	2,000	1,500	6,500	280,000
Totals $	18,400	28,000	37,200	35,000	41,500	31,270	5,100	196,470	$3,512,900

In some years some denominations were not checked because there was a new note introduced and all notes of that denomination that year had the same signatures.

Only used notes were checked. Surveys continued from 1996, confined to polymer notes.

Percentages of signature combinations in circulation for $1 notes 1975 - 1984.

Signatures $1	1975	1976	1977	1978	1979	1980	1981	1982	1983
Coombs-Wilson	.05	.05							
Coombs-Randall									
Phillips-Randall	.45	.10	.15	.10	.10				
Phillips-Wheeler (Commonwealth)	15.30	1.65	.35	.20	.05		.20	.05	
Phillips-Wheeler (Australia)	84.20	98.20	7.40	1.15	.25	.15	.05	.05	
Knight-Wheeler			92.10	98.55	99.60	16.95	.95	.10	.05
Knight-Stone						82.90	98.80	99.80	71.80
Johnston-Stone									28.15

1984 - Knight-Stone 8.25%, Johnston-Stone 91.75%.

Percentages of signature combinations in circulation for $2 notes 1975 - 1988.

Signatures	**$2**	**1975**	**1976**	**1977**	**1978**	**1979**	**1980**	**1981**
Coombs-Wilson		.20	.10	.10	.10	.20		
Coombs-Randall					.05			
Phillips-Randall		1.30	.40	.25	.10	.15		
Phillips-Wheeler (C/W)		48.95	3.25	.55	.15	.10	.05	
Phillips-Wheeler (Australia)		49.55	96.25	18.60	1.00	.30	.15	.10
Knight-Wheeler (Gothic)				38.70	.70	.15		.35
Knight-Wheeler (OCR-B)				41.80	97.90	99.10	13.55	1.50
Knight-Stone							86.25	98.05

Signatures	**$2**	**1982**	**1983**	**1984**	**1985**	**1986**	**1987**	**1988**
Coombs-Wilson								
Coombs-Randall		.05	.05					
Phillips-Randall			.05	.05	.05			
Phillips-Wheeler (C/W)		.15						
Phillips-Wheeler (Australia)		.05	.10	.05			.05	.05
Knight-Wheeler (Gothic)		.05						
Knight-Wheeler (OCR-B)		.30		.20	.05	.15		.05
Knight-Stone		99.40	93.50	8.05	.75	.10	.05	.20
Johnston-Stone			6.30	91.65	99.15	29.10	1.60	.80
Johnston-Fraser						70.65	98.30	98.90

Percentages of signature combinations in circulation for $5 notes 1975-1992.

Signatures	**$5**	**1975**	**1976**	**1977**	**1978**	**1979**	**1980**	**1981**
Coombs-Randall		.30	.15	.05	.05	.05		
Phillips-Randall		1.55	.95	.50	.20	.25		
Phillips-Wheeler (C/W)		50.10	4.35	1.00	.40	.20	.05	.05
Phillips-Wheeler (Australia)		48.05	94.55	65.10	3.40	1.05	.30	.25
Knight-Wheeler (Gothic)				33.35	95.95	98.45	15.60	1.70
Knight-Wheeler (OCR-B)							76.70	12.80
Knight-Stone							7.45	85.20

Signatures	**$5**	**1982**	**1983**	**1984**	**1985**	**1986**	**1987**	**1988**
Coombs-Randall				.05				
Phillips-Wheeler (C/W)							.05	
Phillips-Wheeler (Australia)			.10	.05	.10			
Knight-Wheeler (Gothic)		.80	. 40	. 15	. 35			.10
Knight-Wheeler (OCR-B)		1.00	. 20	.05	.10		.05	
Knight-Stone		98.20	99.30	10.65	1.25	.35	.10	.10
Johnston-Stone				89.05	98.20	19.10	.55	.40
Johnston-Fraser (OCR-B)						80.55	99.25	99.40

Signatures	$5	1989	1990	1991	1992
Phillips-Randall		.10			.10
Phillips-Wheeler (Australia)		.05			
Knight-Wheeler (Gothic)		.15			
Knight-Wheeler (OCR-B)		.10	.10		
Knight-Stone		.05	.10		.10
Johnston-Stone		.10	1.00		
Johnston-Fraser (OCR-B)		40.60	77.80	22.80	1.30
Johnston-Fraser (Gothic)		58.85	21.00	1.20	.50
Fraser-Higgins				76.00	12.00
Fraser-Cole (paper)				86.00	

Percentages of signature combinations in circulation for $10 notes 1975 - 1993.

Signatures	$10	1975	1976	1977	1978	1979	1980	1981
Coombs-Wilson		1.10	.85	.65	.25	.35	.15	.10
Coombs-Randall		.50	.15	.05		.05	.05	.05
Phillips-Randall		7.75	3.60	2.10	1.20	.90	.25	.30
Phillips-Wheeler (C/W)		90.05	51.45	9.15	1.85	1.05	.40	.60
Phillips-Wheeler (Australia)		.60	43.95	53.10	5.45	1.50	.45	.30
Knight-Wheeler				34.95	91.25	96.15	89.95	20.95
Knight-Stone (Gothic)							8.75	77.70

Signatures	$10	1982	1983	1984	1985	1986	1987	1988
Coombs-Wilson		.05		.05				
Coombs-Randall				.10				
Phillips-Randall		.15	.30	.15	.05	.05		
Phillips-Wheeler (C/W)		.15	.15	.10	.05	.15		.05
Phillips-Wheeler (Australia)		.35	.10	.15	.05	.10		
Knight-Wheeler		2.35	1.45	.65	.15	.05	.10	.15
Knight-Stone (Gothic)		73.45	5.45	1.20	.20	.10	.15	.05
Knight-Stone (OCR-B)		23.50	86.40	9.85	.25	.20	.15	.20
Johnston-Stone			6.15	87.75	45.05	1.50	.55	.60
Johnston-Fraser					54.20	97.80	99.05	98.95

Signatures	$10	1989	1990	1991	1992	1993
Coombs-Randall		.05				
Phillips-Wheeler (C/W)		.10		.13		
Knight-Wheeler		.10	.20	.06		
Knight-Stone (Gothic)				.13	.10	
Knight-Stone (OCR-B)		.05	.10	.13		
Johnston-Stone		.30		.13		
Johnston-Fraser		91.15	96.1	13.20	2.13	.70
Johnston-Fraser (polymer)		8.25	3.50	4.40	1.60	.20
Fraser-Higgins				81.93	88.73	6.00
Fraser-Cole					7.40	93.00

Percentages of signature combinations in circulation for $20 notes from 1975 - 1995.

Signatures **$20**	**1975**	**1976**	**1977**	**1978**	**1979**	**1980**	**1981**
Coombs-Wilson	2.25	1.10	1.20	.55	.45	.15	.25
Coombs-Randall	.10	.10	.25	.05			
Phillips-Randall	10.05	4.10	2.15	.70	.45	.15	.25
Phillips-Wheeler (C/W)	51.45	17.65	5.10	1.30	.80	.45	.25
Phillips-Wheeler (Australia)	36.15	76.65	35.20	6.30	3.05	1.20	1.15
Knight-Wheeler		.40	56.10	91.10	95.25	60.45	15.30
Knight-Stone (Gothic)						37.60	82.80

Signatures **$20**	**1982**	**1983**	**1984**	**1985**	**1986**	**1987**	**1988**
Coombs-Wilson	.15	.10	.10	.05			
Phillips-Randall	.15	.15	.20	. 05			
Phillips-Wheeler (C/W)	.20	.15	.10				.05
Phillips-Wheeler (Australia)	.35	.25	.25	.15	.10	.10	.05
Knight-Wheeler	4.55	1.95	1.25	.45	.15	.15	.15
Knight-Stone (Gothic)	94.60	31.45	7.80	1.25	.95	.30	.35
Knight-Stone (OCR-B)	65.95	23.20	1.80	.30	.15	.35	
Johnston-Stone			67.10	70.95	4.25	1.25	.70
Johnston-Fraser (OCR-B)				25.30	94.25	98.05	98.30
Johnston-Stone (Gothic)							.05

Signatures **$20**	**1989**	**1990**	**1991**	**1992**	**1993**	**1994**	**1995**
Coombs-Wilson	.10						.10
Phillips-Randall		.05					.20
Phillips-Wheeler (C/W)			.10	.06	.06		
Phillips-Wheeler (Australia)	.05	.05		.05	.06		.10
Knight-Wheeler	.30	.10	.05	.15	.06	.06	.50
Knight-Stone (Gothic)	.30	.05	.25	.20	.13	.23	.20
Knight-Stone (OCR-B)	.30	.05		.10	.06	.10	
Johnston-Stone	.55	.25		.15	.13		
Johnston-Fraser (OCR-B)	84.30	26.30	5.60	2.45	1.06	1.26	1.90
Johnston-Fraser (Gothic)	14.10	.80	.15	.15	.13	.06	
Phillips-Fraser		27.55	3.95	.25	.06	.30	.10
Fraser-Higgins		44.75	90.00	21.00	2.66	1.33	1.40
Fraser-Cole				75.40	95.53	96.26	40.80
Fraser-Evans (paper)						.13	54.70

The calculating of percentages of signature combinations within the totals surveyed each year provides the opportunity to see the mix of signature combinations and how they constantly change as new notes with new signatures take their place. It also indicates what year a new signature combination began to circulate, increase its representation and then diminish as further new notes were introduced. The constant changing of the relativity of the current signature combination and the previous signature combination could also indicate, by their percentages, when any particular batch of notes was removed from circulation. The percentages will also show what notes were in circulation in any one year, when certain signature combinations were at their peak, and what percentage chance there was in locating a particular signature combination in a particular year.

Percentages of signature combinations in circulation for $50 notes from 1975 to 1995.

Signatures	$50	1975	1976	1977	1978	1979	1980	1981
Phillips-Wheeler		100.00	98.00	48.15	14.80	8.20	4.70	1.90
Knight-Wheeler			2.00	51.85	85.20	91.80	52.20	24.20
Knight-Stone							43.10	73.90

Signatures	$50	1982	1983	1984	1985	1986	1987	1988
Phillips-Wheeler		1.80	.90	.75	.20	.10	.15	.20
Knight-Wheeler		8.75	4.85	3.20	.65	.45	.90	.65
Knight-Stone		89.45	94.25	74.00	12.90	5.90	4.05	3.20
Johnston-Stone				22.05	86.25	92.95	23.40	11.95
Johnston-Fraser (Gothic)						.60	71.50	84.00

Signatures	$50	1989	1990	1991	1992	1993	1994	1995
Phillips-Wheeler		.25	.10	.10	.06			
Knight-Wheeler		.55	.20	.05	.26	.13	.24	.05
Knight-Stone		2.70	1.10	.75	.26	.33	.44	.30
Johnston-Stone		4.40	19.00	.95	.53	.33	.32	.50
Johnston-Fraser (Gothic)		80.20	33.30	9.60	2.33	.73	1.88	.75
Johnston-Fraser (OCR-B)		11.90		5.00	.66	.86	.68	.20
Phillips-Fraser			45.10	10.60	1.93	.26	.20	.30
Fraser-Higgins			.20	72.95	29.26	10.13	4.72	2.15
Fraser-Cole					64.66	87.20	87.48	51.00
Fraser-Evans							4.24	44.70

Percentages of signature combinations in circulation for $100 notes from 1984-1995.

Signatures	$100	1984	1985	1986	1987	1988	1989
Johnston-Stone		100.00	100.00	32.00	16.00	12.60	8.20
Johnston-Fraser				68.00	84.00	87.40	91.80

Signatures	$100	1990	1991	1992	1993	1994	1995
Johnston-Stone		5.00	3.50	4.50	1.50	2.30	2.00
Johnston-Fraser		94.67	46.00	43.50	19.00	17.80	14.27
Fraser-Higgins		.33	50.50	52.00	48.50	31.10	23.60
Fraser-Cole					31.00	48.80	60.13

Further reading: survey articles by Michael Vort-Ronald in the *Australian Coin Review;*

1975, October	*$76,000 The Odds.*
1976, July	*1976 Decimal Banknote Survey.*
1977, July	*1977 Decimal Banknote Survey.*
1978, July	*1978 Decimal Banknote Survey.*
1979, July	*1979 Decimal Banknote Survey.*
1980, September	*Commonwealth Notes Still on the Decline.*
1981, March	*Common, but not wealthy.*
1982, January	*Commonwealth notes surviving.*
1982, August	*Fewer C of A notes survive.*
1983, September	*Johnston takes bow in million dollar survey.*
1984, August	*Rapid spread of new signatures.*
1985, August	*Decimal notes - the dirty truth.*
1986, August	*Johnston-Fraser notes dominate paper money now in circulation.*
1987, August	*Johnston-Fraser notes dominant.*
1988, August	*1988 Banknote Survey.*
1989, August	*The 1988 Decimal note issues and 1989 Survey of Notes in Circulation.*
1990, December	*The 1990 Survey of Notes in Circulation.*
1991, August	*The 1991 Survey of Notes in Circulation.*
1992, August	*The Survey Or "Stick em up! I wanna check ya notes!".*
1993, October	*Nineteenth Survey of Aussie Circulating Notes.*
1994, July	*20th Survey of Notes in circulation.*
1995, September	*Banknote Survey Comes of Age.*
1996, July	*The 1996 Banknote Survey.*
1997, August	*1997 Banknote Survey.*
1998, August	*Circulating Banknotes in 1998.*
1999, July	*The Jubilee of the Banknote Survey.*

BIBLIOGRAPHY

Andrews, Gordon — *A Designer's Life,* N.S.W. University Press, 1993, now privately owned.

Ayres, Philip — *Mawson, a Life,* Miegunya Press, 1999.

Beaglehole, J.C. — *The Endeavour Journal of Joseph Banks,* Public Library of N.S.W. Trustees, Angus & Robertson, 1962.

Bickel, Lennard — *This Accursed Land,* Macmillan, 1977; *Rise Up to Life,* Angus & Robertson, 1972; *Florey, The Man Who Made Penicillin,* Sun Books, 1983.

Blakely, W.F. — *A key to the Eucalypts,* Forestry and Timber Bureau, Canberra, 1965.

Burke, Keast — *Gold and Silver, Photographs of Australian Goldfields from the Holtermann Collection,* Penguin Books, 1977.

Cronin, Leonard — Editor of *A Fantasy of Man, Henry Lawson Complete Works 1901-1922,* Warwick Jacobson, 1984.

Davis, Pedr — *Charles Kingsford Smith the World's Greatest Aviator,* Paul Hamlyn, 1977.

Ellis, M.H. — *Francis Greenway, His Life and Times,* Angus & Robertson, 1973.
John Macarthur, Angus & Robertson, 1973.

Evatt, H.V. — *Rum Rebellion,* Lloyd O'Neill P/L, Hawthorne Vic. 1971.

Fowles, Joseph — *Sydney in 1848,* Ure Smith Pty. Ltd., Sydney, 1962.

Garran, John & **White,** Leslie — *Merinos, Myths and Macarthurs,* A.N.U. Press, 1985.

Golden, F. — *Quasars, Pulsars, and Black Holes,* Charles Scribner's Sons, N.Y. 1976.

Grolier Society of Aust. — *Australian Encyclopaedia,* 3rd and 4th editions.

Herman, M. — *Early Australian Architects and their work,* 3rd ed., Angus & Robertson, 1970.

Humphreys, L.R. — *Clunies Ross Australian Visionary,* The Miegunya Press, Melbourne, 1998.

Macindoe, S.L. & **Walkden Brown,** C. — *Wheat Breeding in Australia,* third edition, 1968.

Mackaness, G. — *Sir Joseph Banks, his relations with Australia,* Angus & Robertson, 1936.

Mackersby, Ian — *Smithy,* Little Brown & Company, 1998.

Mawson, Douglas — *The Home of the Blizzard,* Rigby Limited, 1971, reprinted from 1915.

Mawson, Paquita — *Mawson of the Antarctic,* Longmans, 1964.

Maxwell, Eileen — *Written in Gold,* Gulgong Pioneer's Museum and Historical Society, Gulgong, 1975.

McGraw-Hill — *Encyclopaedia of Science and Technology,* 1977.

Note Printing Australia — *Note Printing in Australia,* (Reserve Bank of Australia) 1992.

O'Dea, Marjory — *Ian Clunies Ross. A Biography,* Hyland House, Melbourne, 1977.

Onslow, S.M. — *The Macarthurs of Camden,* Rigby, 1973.

Oxford University Press — *Ian Clunies Ross, Memoirs and Papers,* Melbourne, 1961.

Parer, David & **Parer-Cook,** Elizabeth — *Douglas Mawson, The Survivor,* Allela Books, 1983.

Peake, Harold — *Australian Accidental Banknotes,* 1994.

Price, A. Grenfell, — *The Winning of Antarctica. Mawson's BANZARE Voyages* 1929-31, based on the Mawson Papers, Angus & Robertson, 1962.

Prout, Denton — *Henry Lawson,* the Grey Dreamer.

Reserve Bank of Australia *Making Money,* 1974.

Rienets, Rex & Thea — *The Voyages of Captain Cook,* Hamlyn Publishing Group, U.K., 1968.

Roderick, Colin — *Henry Lawson: Stories for Senior Students,* Angus & Robertson, Sydney, 1962.

Ross, Ian Clunies — *Ian Clunies Ross, Memoirs and Papers,* Oxford University Press, Melbourne, 1961.

Shaw, W. Hudson & **Ruhen,** Olaf — *Lawrence Hargrave, Explorer, Inventor and Aviation Experimenter,* Cassell Australia, 1977.

Smith, Charles Kingsford *Sir Charles Kingsford Smith...The Southern Cross Story* (reprint of The Old Bus), Rigby, 1978.

Tebbutt, John — *Astronomical Memoirs,* 1908, reprinted 1986 by Hawkesbury Shire Council, Windsor, N.S.W.

Vort-Ronald, M.P. — *Australian Decimal Banknotes,* 1985, *Australian Banknotes,* 2nd ed. 1983.

Williams, Trevor I. — *Howard Florey: Penicillin and After,* Oxford University Press, 1984.

Newspapers and magazines as quoted in texts throughout this book: Advertiser, Age, Australasian Printer, Australian, Australian Coin Review, Australian Women's Weekly, Canberra Times, Currency, Coresearch, Herald, Journal of the Australian Institute of Agricultural Science, News, Pix, South Pacific Post, Sun (Melbourne and Sydney), Sunday Mail, Sunday Telegraph, Sydney Morning Herald, Weekender. R.B.A. Press Releases, Australian Government Gazettes, various Acts of parliament.

SOURCE OF ILLUSTRATIONS - Figs.

Advertiser newspaper, Adelaide.	154.
Angus & Robertson.	169.
Anonymous.	2, 195, 297, 380a, 382, 411.
Australian newspaper, Melbourne.	56.
Australian Coin Review, Dubbo.	58, 376, 465.
Australian Women's Weekly.	39, 40.
Ayres, Kevin, Canberra.	426.
Bamford, Graeme, Noranda W.A.	294, 405, 412, 434.
CSIRO, Melbourne.	302, 304.
Dawson, Phil, Adelaide.	422, 427.
Dept. of Agriculture, N.S.W., Sydney.	177.
Dept. of Agriculture, S.A., Adelaide.	170, 171.
Dixson Galleries, Sydney.	168, 196, 201.
Downies, Melbourne.	259, 290, 424.
Freehill, Mark, Narrabeen N.S.W.	235.
Fyfe, John, Northbridge N.S.W.	167, 385, 416, 421, 440, 441.
Herald, The, Melbourne.	96.
Herald & Weekly Times, Melbourne.	68, 264.
Howard Florey Research Institute, Adelaide.	298.
Jacob, Peter G., Adelaide.	323.
Larkin, Robert L.	134.
Leverington, Lloyd, the late.	61.
Mawson Institute for Antarctic Research.	319, 321, 324.
Mathieson, John, Bairnsdale, Vic.	414.
Mitchell Library, Sydney.	202, 226, 237, 240, 271.
Monetarium, Kogarah N.S.W.	366.
Morton, Grant, Adelaide.	194, 199, 377, 378.
National Library, Canberra.	120, 121, 122.
Noble Numismatics, Sydney.	153, 175, 236, 269, 301, 318, 328, 380b, 398, 408, 31, 431, 433, 442, 447.
Note Printing Australia, Craigieburn, Vic.	70, 71, 72, 74, 75, 76, 82, 83, 88,94, 95, frontispiece.
Onyet, Gil, Sydney.	1.
Peake, Harold, Buderim Qld.	261.
Pope, John, Goolwa S.A.	265, 266, 267.
Reeds Educational & Professional Publishing.	100.
Reserve Bank of Australia.	3 to 38, 42 to 55, 57, 63, 65 to 67, 69, 73, 77 to 81, 85, 86, 89, 91, 98, 113 to 119, 128 to 133, 135, 147, 148, 150, 165a, 273, 339, 375, 442, 447, 452, 453, 455, 464, 466 to 468.
Royal Society of S.A., Adelaide.	320, 321.
Shepherd, Graham.	448.
Shire of Bulla, Sunbury, Vic.	93.
Sydney Morning Herald newspaper.	41, 62, 340.
Taylor, Frank, Brisbane.	413.
Tebbutt, John Halley, Windsor N.S.W.	329, 330, 331.
Treasury, The, Canberra.	123 to 127.
Ure Smith Pty Ltd.	204.
Vort-Ronald, Michael Phillip (author).	All other illustrations and cover.
Watson, John, Melbourne.	146.

INDEX TO NOTE ILLUSTRATIONS - Pages

GENERAL INDEX TO ILLUSTRATIONS - Pages

GENERAL INDEX TO ILLUSTRATIONS continued

GENERAL INDEX

GENERAL INDEX

GENERAL INDEX

GENERAL INDEX

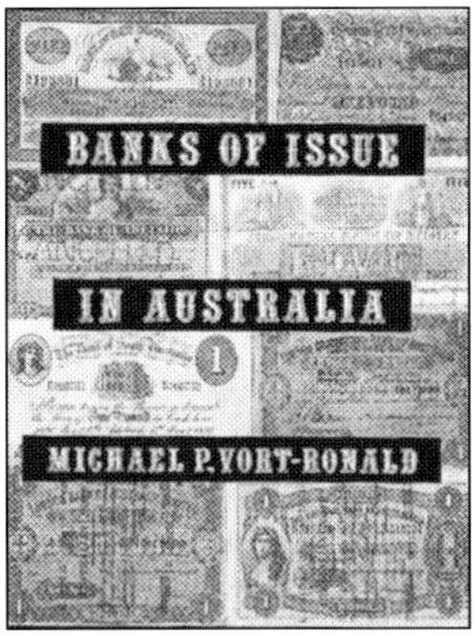

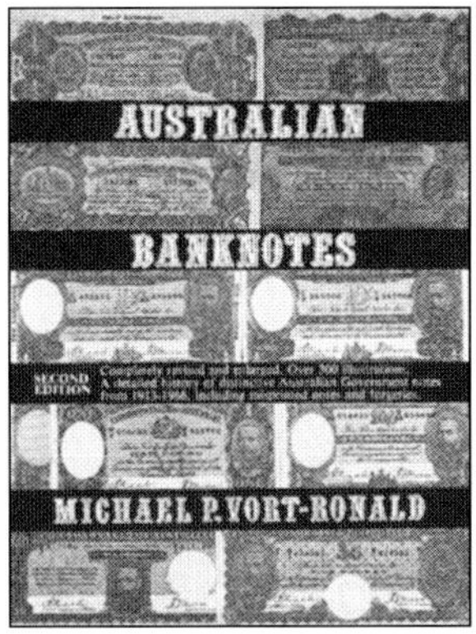

THE COMPANION VOLUMES TO THIS BOOK

BANKS OF ISSUE IN AUSTRALIA (1788-1914)

Used as the reference in Australian and Overseas auction catalogues. A detailed history and study of the note issuing banks and their notes from 1817-1910 and Australian Government Superscribed notes from 1910-1914. A brief illustrated history of currency from 1788-1817.
331 pages, 313 illustrations. Soft cover $20 Hard cover $30

AUSTRALIAN BANKNOTES (1913-1966)

An exhaustive study of the Australian Government designed and issued (pounds series). How, where, why and by whom the notes were designed and printed . Detailed history and origins of early note scenes and the people featured on the notes.
Second edition, 344 pages, 309 illustrations. Soft cover $20

Although published in 1982 and 1983 respectively, the above two volumes are the only detailed reference works of their kind on these subjects, and still represent excellent value.

OTHER PUBLICATIONS BY THE SAME AUTHOR

AUSTRALIAN DECIMAL BANKNOTE INTERLEAVES

Loose leaf pages for note albums, $1 to $100 paper, Polymer, Annually dated series, First and last prefixes, Specialist Issues. Prices vary, write, phone or fax for details.

HOSKINS OF SOUTH AUSTRALIA

The history of Andrew HOSKINS and his descendants in Australia from 1840, including the extended families of Gilbert, Dobinson and Lewis. 350 pages, 950 pictures and 2,500 people. Soft cover $20.

CHINESE EMBERS by Eva Dower

The life of the wife of a French banker in China in the 1920s told in illustrated short stories with cartoons. Fascinating book of life in China from an Australian viewpoint. 88 pages, paperback, $8.

Postage and packing at cost. Multiple book orders make postage costs per book more economical.
Michael Vort-Ronald, 3 Graves St. Kadina S.A. 5554. Ph. (08) 8821 2906, Fax (08) 8821 2901.

ABOUT THE AUTHOR

Michael P. (Mick) Vort-Ronald was born in Adelaide in 1943. As a teenager he collected minerals, stamps and coins, and was a Queen's Scout. At the age of 16 years he joined the South Australian Police Force as a Junior Constable and graduated in 1964 as a uniformed police officer. He was then stationed in Adelaide, Whyalla, Angaston, Swan Reach, Port Pirie, Whyalla (as a patrol sergeant) and Mannum.

He is still an active mineral collector and has been a member of the Adelaide Gem and Mineral Club for 35 years, and its President six times.

As a collector of Australian banknotes he began to write for the *Australian Coin Review* in 1975 and since then has been its most prolific contributor, culminating in September, 1999, with being appointed as the magazine's editor. It is now published by Hannanprint, Sydney, N.S.W. From 1976 he has co-authored and then authored the banknote half of Dion Skinner's *Renniks Australian Coin and Banknote Guides,* now published by Renniks Publications, Chippendale, N.S.W. In 1997 he authored *Collect Australian Banknotes* published in colour by Peter Steele.

His first book, *Australian Banknotes,* self-published in 1979, received the American *Banknote Reporter Award* for the best book on banknotes published worldwide in that year. That book was expanded on by *Banks of Issue in Australia* (1982), *Australian Banknotes, 2nd edition* (1983) and *Australian Decimal Banknotes* 1985, (now replaced by this book).

For his work on Australian banknotes he was elected a Fellow of the Numismatic Society of South Australia in 1985, has served three terms as its president, and is currently its secretary and treasurer. He has been president of the Northern Yorke Peninsula Coin Club (now the Yorke Peninsula Collectables Club) since 1990 and has designed five of its Cornish Festival medallions. In 1993 he received the Tasmanian Numismatic Society's A.J. Lockwood Award for his Contribution to Numismatics.

In 1988 he sold his banknote collection through Spink Auctions in Sydney and left the S.A. Police Force after 28 years service, the last nine as a sergeant, to open Australia's first and only private museum of money and banking. The Banking and Currency Museum at Kadina is housed in an old bank building (built in 1873) and has won seven Regional Tourism Awards, including best tourist attraction five times. The museum has also been featured on *Healthy, Wealthy and Wise,* and *Postcards.*

Mick has also been actively involved in four levels of local tourism for the past ten years, treasurer of the National Trust Museum at Kadina for the past five years, and is their Vice Chairman. He is also a member of the British and American Cheque collecting societies, and International Bank Note Society.

His banknote photography was used in Peter Steele's book, the 1991 and 1992 Telecom Finance calendars and a set of exclusive Telecom phone cards. In 1995 he wrote and published his family tree book *Hoskins of South Australia,* and published *Chinese Embers,* (life in China in the 1920s) by Eva Dower. He has published four editions of *Australian Decimal Banknote Interleaves,* and is a long-standing contributor to the world "Pick" banknote catalogues published in the United States.